Our Necessary Shadow

TOM BURNS

Our Necessary Shadow

The Nature and Meaning of Psychiatry

ALLEN LANE
an imprint of
PENGUIN BOOKS

ALLEN LANE

Published by the Penguin Group
Penguin Books Ltd, 80 Strand, London WC2R ORL, England
Penguin Group (USA) Inc., 375 Hudson Street, New York, New York 10014, USA
Penguin Group (Canada), 90 Eglinton Avenue East, Suite 700, Toronto, Ontario, Canada M4P 2Y3
(a division of Pearson Penguin Canada Inc.)
Penguin Ireland, 25 St Stephen's Green, Dublin 2, Ireland (a division of Penguin Books Ltd)
Penguin Group (Australia), 707 Collins Street, Melbourne, Victoria 3008, Australia
(a division of Pearson Australia Group Pty Ltd)
Penguin Books India Pvt Ltd, 11 Community Centre, Panchsheel Park, New Delhi – 110 017, India
Penguin Group (NZ), 67 Apollo Drive, Rosedale, Auckland 0632, New Zealand
(a division of Pearson New Zealand Ltd)
Penguin Books (South Africa) (Pty) Ltd, Block D, Rosebank Office Park,
181 Jan Smuts Avenue, Parktown North, Gauteng 2193, South Africa

Penguin Books Ltd, Registered Offices: 80 Strand, London WC2R ORL, England

www.penguin.com

First published 2013
001

Set in 10.5/14pt Sabon LT Std
Typeset by Jouve (UK), Milton Keynes
Printed in Great Britain by Clays Ltd, St Ives plc

A CIP catalogue record for this book is available from the British Library

ISBN: 978-1-846-14465-3

www.greenpenguin.co.uk

ALWAYS LEARNING   **PEARSON**

To Eva Burns-Lundgren: social worker, psychotherapist, wife, mother and eternal optimist

Contents

CONTENTS

Acknowledgements

This book is my take on psychiatry and how I understand it. Psychiatry is an irregular-shaped human endeavour and this book has followed its contours – I have not tried to squeeze it into a neat and pleasing symmetrical shape. The result is not a 'position statement' nor an ideological stand so I have no single guru to acknowledge. Learning to be a psychiatrist is a very personal business. You learn from your professors, your consultants, the nurses and general practitioners you work with, and, perhaps most vividly, from your patients. I have been lucky to have spent the last forty years doing a job that has really never had a dull day and where I have always had something interesting to think through in my evenings. So my thanks are diffuse but they are heartfelt. There are too many to name so I will not try.

I made a decision to keep this book free of references – it is not a textbook. However, there are three authors whose works have contributed disproportionately to shaping my thinking and particularly in shaping how I have presented it. Their books are mentioned in the text and in the reading list but I want to acknowledge their influence, which goes beyond these individual quotes and citations. Ben Shephard made sense of so many of the issues around military psychiatry that I had thought about on and off for many years. Andrew Scull's voluminous and erudite writings on the history of psychiatry have always jolted me out of my complacency. He has not always convinced me but has never short-changed me. Lastly the late Henri Ellenberger's mammoth tome *The Discovery of the Unconscious* brought to life and made sense of so much that seems bizarre and inexplicable in early psychiatry. My thanks to all three.

ACKNOWLEDGEMENTS

This book would never have happened without the expert and good-natured input of Felicity Bryan, my agent, and Helen Conford, my editor at Penguin. I am grateful to them for their encouragement and for their patience. Susan Woods-Ganz typed and retyped and deciphered my 'doctor's' handwriting with never a raised eyebrow and I hope she knows how much I have appreciated her tireless contribution. Lastly, like many authors, I owe most to my wife, Eva. She has tolerated the time devoted to writing this book and the inevitable neurotic angst it has generated. My debt is real and my thanks go to them all. The errors in this book (there will be errors) are mine and that responsibility is not shared.

Introduction: What is psychiatry and what is it for?

I wrote this book to give an understanding of what psychiatry is, what it can do and what it cannot do. Yet there is no shortage of books 'about' psychiatry. There are hundreds of books and hundreds of column-inches in newspapers published about psychiatry and mental illnesses. They include everything from cutting-edge brain sciences to self-help manuals for personal problems and emotional wellbeing. Most of these books or articles have a specific message, perhaps an axe to grind or an enthusiasm to promote. A searing criticism of psychiatry as an instrument of social control on the one hand or promising a cure for anxiety and self-doubt on the other, they generally only give enough detail about psychiatry to anchor their message. The picture of psychiatry most of us have is built from such fragments and not surprisingly it can seem confusing and rather incoherent.

Despite so much being written around psychiatry it is hard to find much on psychiatry itself. David Stafford Clark's *Psychiatry Today* was the last widely read and fully comprehensive account in the UK. Published by Penguin in 1951 it remained in print well into the 1970s. Anthony Clare's *Psychiatry in Dissent* was published in 1976 and covered several controversial issues from a psychiatrist's perspective. There has now been a whole generation without an attempt to explain the subject fully to the interested outsider.

Why should there be such a need? There is no series of books explaining all the other branches of medicine. There is no *Ortho-pedics Today* or *Dermatology in Dissent*. What is so special about psychiatry that means it needs to be explained? For good or ill, psychiatry is different. There is something about it that excites stronger feelings than other branches of medicine and attracts debate.

Faced with the sociologists' damning critiques and the utopian promises of some current neuroscientists or self-help gurus, which should you believe? Should you believe either? Is it perhaps possible to believe both? Can it really be the case that psychiatrists get things quite so wrong and if so why do we continue to let them? Why do we pay our taxes and fund a profession that is, if its critics are correct, at best irrelevant and behind the times, or at worst malign and destructive? How does it survive withering contempt such as that from one of its leading historians, the sociologist Andrew Scull:

> Reflecting the poverty of its cognitive accomplishments, its persistently dismal therapeutic capacities, and the social undesirability and disreputability of most of its clientele, psychiatry has enjoyed a perpetually marginal and unenviable position in the social division of labour – a profession always, so it seems, but a step away from a profound crisis of legitimacy.
>
> Andrew Scull, *Social Order/Mental Disorder*, 1989

Yet society does continue to support it; we have done for generations and it continues to survive. Psychiatry not only persists but flourishes and expands and does so in all developed health care systems.

I hope to clarify some of these contradictions so you can decide for yourself. To make any real sense of most of these issues needs some understanding of what psychiatry is in its entirety. Highlighting one tiny facet of it devoid of context is hopelessly misleading. A real judgement requires some familiarity with psychiatry's history and practice, the extent of its reach, and its strengths as well as its weaknesses. There is no shortcut to this: it needs a fairly detailed book. The reason for this is that psychiatry is not based on a single, tidy and coherent school of thought. This is one of the commonest criticisms of it by its detractors and it is one to which we must plead guilty as charged. It is not a tight intellectual discipline, but a complicated human endeavour. Like the rest of medicine it has been shaped by the illnesses it treats, evolving piecemeal as a practical body of knowledge and skills. Nobody sat down and designed it.

Psychiatry does not rest on a single unifying theory that shapes it and dictates the disorders it should treat or how it should treat them. We cannot predict mental illnesses and their characteristics in the way astronomers predicted the existence of the planet Neptune from New-ton's laws of gravity. There is no psychiatric equivalent of the Higg's boson, no killer-fact to confirm or refute psychiatry's legitimacy. It expands and contracts over time and in different areas depending on what confronts it. Not only are people and their needs endlessly var-ied but the illnesses themselves change over time. Illnesses such as general paralysis of the insane were commonplace in asylums a cen-tury ago but have simply vanished, or, like hysteria, have all but gone. Other conditions, such as the eating disorders, once academic rarities, have now become virtual epidemics. So psychiatry is untidy and unwieldy and if we want to understand it we have to just accept it is so. How could it be otherwise, dealing with conditions as diverse as anorexia nervosa, dementia and schizophrenia? If you were going to design it from scratch then it would probably not look like this.

The illnesses that have shaped psychiatry do, however, have a clear thread running through them. They exist *between* people. They are not contained within an organ or a body but depend on social rela-tionships, human interaction, for their very being. Mental illnesses are composed of experiences and behaviour which can only have mean-ing if they are conveyed to or observed by others. *Diagnosis* relies on a social interaction in which a meaning can be infused into observa-tion. Similarly, treatment depends on face-to-face engagement with another individual. Andrew Scull described psychiatry as 'pre-eminently a moral enterprise, involved with the application of social meanings to particular segments of everyday life'. His colleague Michael MacDonald captured it perfectly:

> Madness is . . . the most solitary of afflictions to the people who experi-ence it; but the most social of maladies to those who observe its effects.

Mental illness is something that most of us can grasp intuitively. It is easy to recognize but hard to define and gives rise to endless dis-putes at the margins. We recognize it in disturbed behaviour and strange thoughts and feelings but there is more to it than just that. Central to psychiatry's understanding of mental illness is a judgement that patients have become somehow 'different' from their usual selves and that this is not under their control. Either we experi-ence them as changed and different or they experience themselves as different. They may also be different from those around them with some odd kinds of behaviour or attitudes, but eccentricity alone is no basis for diagnosing mental illness. We can be very different from those around us for all sorts of reasons without being mentally ill, and thank heavens for that. Mental illness includes a sense of change, of 'alienation' from the normal self and a sense of lack of control over that change. This book will trace how this sense of alienation has given rise to the concept of mental illness and to the practice of psychiatry. This already complex concept is complicated further by having two separated and very different origins. These merged to form the profession we have today, with a unique, hybrid character that so frustrates those who want to pigeonhole it.

Diagnoses which imply that current behaviour is not just odd or different, but 'changed', are always going to be open to challenge. And so they are. Psychiatrists cannot confirm their diagnosis by simply holding up an X-ray and pointing out a fracture. Even if we had such tools (which sadly we do not) they would still miss this central quality of *change* and the need to locate it in some understanding of personal identity. Two people could be behaving in exactly the same way but one of them considered mentally ill and the other not. Threatening and hostile behaviour in one man may simply be how he is – a truculent and difficult character. In another who is normally quiet and diffident it may indicate a manic mood swing. So the very concepts on which psychiatry is built invite controversy.

Like the rest of medicine there is inevitably scope for mistakes and misdiagnoses. Doctors identify illnesses by recognizing patterns; they do not start from some theoretical definitions of health and sickness. Obvious cases of any illness, when all the signs and symptoms are present, cause no difficulty. But people vary, and so do illnesses. Sometimes we see all the symptoms and sometimes only some, so are very certain in some cases and less so in others. The same treatment for the same illness can sometimes cure the patient, sometimes just help and sometimes fail completely; not everyone given antibiotics for pneumonia recovers. We seem to accept this as a matter of course in general medicine but are strikingly less forgiving with psychiatry. Variations in outcome are often held up to show that psychiatric treatments are ineffective or, more radically, that the illnesses are simply bogus. These double standards contribute to persisting arguments about psychiatry, especially in controversial treatments such as electroconvulsive therapy (ECT), and I explore them in the following chapters. Psychiatry has also expanded into areas where it is unclear if it has anything useful to offer. Undoubtedly in some cases the answer is a resounding 'no'.

I worry that I may have devoted too much of this book to psychiatry's mistakes and controversies. I hope this does not come over as implying that psychiatry is a bad thing, as its sternest critics propose. I clearly do not believe this, quite the contrary. I am convinced psychiatry is a major force for good or I would not have spent my whole adult life in it. I have dwelt on the controversies for two reasons. First, because I believe they do deserve to be taken seriously; there is much of substance in what our critics say. But more importantly it is in exploring these difficult areas that we more clearly recognize what is unique and special in psychiatry. We can see how it is forced to operate in zones of ambiguity, engaging with the uncertainties of human behaviours and motivations, feelings and relationships. It is a branch of medicine and has much in common with all the other sub-specialisms but it is also very different, and different in fundamental ways. Denying these differences fools only a few. Retreating to the comfort of a rigid medical orthodoxy requires either blinkers or distorting what we do. It also results in a narrow, depersonalized and mechanical care that satisfies neither patient nor psychiatrist.

Psychiatry has made mistakes and will continue to make further mistakes. I hope, however, that a recognition of the massive good it does, and a fuller understanding of the constraints under which it has to operate, will put these failings in perspective. Most people who consult a psychiatrist benefit from the encounter; they get relief from often intolerable symptoms. That relief may not always be permanent, but it is much appreciated and for some it is life-saving. So what follows will be an exploration of the nature and meaning of psychiatry, medicine's most disputed discipline.

So why did I become a psychiatrist? Best to be frank. I had decided early on that I wanted to be a psychoanalyst. I had read my Freud and, like most adolescents, was certain I knew exactly how to sort the world out. Fate, however, took a hand. My mother suffered a serious nervous breakdown when I was fifteen. My brother and I then lived with her recurrent breakdowns for the next twenty years. As time went on these became more and more severe, and less and less comprehensible. They often required her to be admitted to hospital. She didn't receive psychoanalysis but she did have psychotherapy sessions on and off for several years. She took antidepressants and tranquillizers and on two occasions had ECT. I had been strongly prejudiced against pills and ECT but had to eat my words when I saw the enormous relief they brought her (and us). By the time I was a medical student I had become set on being a psychiatrist.

The things my mother's illness taught me are the basis of this book. I learnt that mental illnesses are among the most awful a person can suffer. I still believe this, even after working on cancer wards and acute surgery units. There is something uniquely devastating about the way that they can rob you of your sense of identity and self-worth. Secondly I learnt that psychiatric treatments really do make an enormous difference; there is nothing second-rate or trivial about their effects. When the treatments began to work the improvements in my mother were simply wonderful.

I also learnt over the years that relationships are key. The kindness of nurses, the concern and engagement of doctors, still mattered enormously even when the ECT was working its apparent magic. Even at her worst my mother knew and appreciated when she was listened to and taken seriously (and so did we). My brother and I had no illusions about this; we knew just how difficult our mother could be, how hard she could make it for staff to be nice to her. Over these years I also learnt that there is an enormous variation in psychiatric care and that the difference between the good, the mediocre and the poor really does matter. Lastly her illness taught me to recognize the limits of what we can understand, to accept a level of uncertainty and to be intolerant of dogma. Psychiatry abounds in theories and we do need theories. We need them to structure our thinking and to guide research, but they are just theories, just tools. Theories come and go; it is what works that matters.

So this book is probably more descriptive than explanatory. It does not try to give (and certainly does not succeed in giving) a simple explanation of psychiatry and mental illness with all the loose ends tied up. There is much we know about mental illnesses and their treatment, but less about the reasons for them or their ultimate causes. One thing that is clear is that they are not arbitrary; they are not like catching influenza or breaking an arm. I believe they are intimately linked to that which makes us human in the first place and they arise from our complexity as sentient creatures and our engagement with others.

The existence of mental illnesses is only possible because we are self-aware and reflective. They have always been with us. Just as mental illnesses reflect what is human and difficult about us so the drive to relieve this suffering is even more human. Psychiatry, for all its flaws, currently represents our best attempts to discharge this most human of impulses. It is not something we can just ignore or decide to leave. It is our necessary shadow.

WHAT CAN YOU EXPECT FROM THIS BOOK?

When sitting down to write this book I made three decisions that I need to explain. First, I have allowed some repetition in the chapters; hopefully not too much, but some. This is not a novel or a textbook and I do not expect it to be read religiously from first page to last. I assume you will pick it up and put it down and perhaps skip first to the bits that interest you most. Sometimes the same brief background is needed to set the context in different chapters and help make them comprehensible. It seemed easier to summarize the more important bits than to keep referring back to preceding chapters. I have tried to avoid jargon and where technical terms are unavoidable I have usually defined them briefly when I first use them. But for simplicity most of them can be found in the glossary at the end of the book.

You will decide where you want to start but I would encourage you not to skip over Chapters 2 and 3. These deal with the dual origins of psychiatry. They provide the scaffold on which so many of the subsequent developments build, and from where the inherent tensions and confusions stem. Chapter 2 describes the origins of the more medical, or organic, side of psychiatry with the classification of 'madness' and the building of asylums. Chapter 3 outlines the less well-known psychological origins of psychiatry, the development of our modern understanding of the mind and in particular the role of unconscious thought.

The second decision was not to give references to scientific papers and books. This was a more difficult decision and I should explain my reasons. Reading habits have changed, as I am very aware in myself. We now often go to the web to get extra background, to get more detail or find pictures of places or characters. You don't need me to include a picture of Carl Jung to see what he looked like: Google will provide a selection in seconds. There is also the problem of where to draw the line; it would be all too easy to end up with literally hundreds of references and what would be the point of that?

There is, however, a much more important reason for not including references. Indeed it was one of the things that got me to write this book. While reading a particularly influential and critical book about psychiatry it was the reference list that got under my skin. Let me explain. References to previously published work are included in scholarly texts to support the point being made or to direct readers to source material for further research. However, the expectation in scholarly work is that *all* the relevant source material should be cited. In science that means those references that support the author's argument but also, crucially, those that contradict it. Most scientific papers go through a peer-review process to get published. In this process the reference list is scrutinized by the reviewers as carefully as the text and tables. If we find partial or biased citing then the paper is likely to be sent back to the authors for revision to include and account for them.

I assume that reference lists are balanced and comprehensive because they have been through this peer-review process. This is not necessarily the case in books. The critique of psychiatry I mentioned above is erudite and powerful in its own right, but I found myself increasingly irritated by the citing of the papers and books that supported the author with an absence of those advancing the alternative viewpoints. I am steeped in the subject, it is my job, so I knew many of these counter-arguments and recognized how much was missing. Many readers would have assumed that the references confirmed the settled academic consensus on the topic. Partial or inconsistent citing of references risks confusing opinion with science so I do not want to do it. It is all too easy to cite a weak counter-argument and then demolish it. I have tried to make clear what is my opinion and what is firmly established and accepted. I have included a bibliography of major sources and further reading. However, if you want more information then modern technology puts the tools at your fingertips to hunt for a broader understanding.

'Only the future is certain, the past is always changing' was a repeated quip in the old Soviet bloc. So it is with science generally, including medicine. Old certainties are constantly reformulated by new data. New evidence can convert opinion to knowledge, but also convert knowledge to opinion. Increasingly accurate astronomical measurement of the movement of the planets 'proved' Newton's theory, but as they became even more accurate the very same measurement disproved Newton and confirmed Einstein. Absolute certainty is rare: there is no shortage of disagreement even about apparently obvious historical data, as I found in my research for this book. Where things seemed uncertain I have made every effort to check the facts, but this is not a work of historical scholarship. I have *not* gone off to obscure libraries to confirm and compare original sources. I have relied on a broad reading of accepted texts and authorities.

The scope and shape of this book inevitably reflect my opinions of what is important in psychiatry. I have included what is durable and important in treating patients but also several theories that are central to understanding the discipline. This is ultimately a personal judgement. I am pretty mainstream, but lean more towards the psychotherapeutic side of psychiatry than most in my profession. The emphasis of the book reflects this. There are many psychiatrists who are intensely antagonistic to Freud and psychoanalysis and will think I have given him and it far too much space. In terms of current clinical practice they are right – psychoanalysis is not a significant treatment in modern psychiatry. On the other hand it has had enormous influence on both psychiatric thinking and practice and also on our Western world view. The space given to it reflects my bias and you can judge it in that light.

I have tried to be open about where my views are minority ones (such as about addictions). I hope I have succeeded in conveying both sides in the debate and that declaring my own beliefs allows you to factor that into your conclusions. Similarly I have tried to indicate those areas where I believe there is little real doubt, where our understanding is well established, and those areas where our understanding is still quite shaky.

CAN WE REALLY KNOW WHAT IS GOING ON IN ANOTHER'S MIND?

Many people do seem to find psychiatry interesting and have strong opinions about it. This should not surprise us. Whether our preferred reading is celebrity gossip magazines or Dostoevsky we are interested in people and in what makes them tick. We want to understand their motives. What is it about him that makes him do that? Why is my boss such a stickler for detail? What does she see in her awful fiancé? Wanting to know why people are the way they are, and behave the way they do is not just nosiness. We *have* to be interested in how other people think and behave.

Biologists tell us that the success and survival of each individual animal (whether a pigeon, a baboon or a human being) depend as much on how well it copes with members of its own species as with escaping its various predators. In the race for survival our main competitors are our own kind; we compete for the same food, the same partners, the same shelter. Being able to work out what the other person is likely to do is crucial, and we often have to decide instantly. If someone has pushed in front of us in a queue should we tell them to wait their turn, or is discretion the better part of valour? We have to be able to distinguish a friendly interest from a sexual approach, frustrated irritation from impending violence, curiosity from cunning, tolerance from indifference.

These decisions are so frequent in our daily lives and they happen so quickly and so automatically that we take them for granted. In truth such intuition is a remarkable and sophisticated process. It involves an assessment of what is going on in another person's mind. We may base these decisions on fairly obvious considerations such as how intoxicated they are, or something more intangible such as an air of hostility or truculence. We may decide from their facial expression or body language, how unsteady they are on their feet, or even from their dress. All this implies understanding the mental processes of those we meet, inferring meaning from observation. If we are unable to work out what others are thinking and feeling we are at an enormous social and personal disadvantage. This is cruelly demonstrated in autism, where this ability is severely restricted or missing.

Psychiatry is firmly anchored in the belief that we can understand fairly well what is going on in another person's mind. Psychiatrists assume that by being able to get a sense of what their patients are going through and how they are responding to it, grasp their inner world if you will, we can help them. Psychiatry is concerned with the thoughts and feelings of people who are unwell, no longer their normal selves, and it calls these states 'mental illness', now more commonly 'psychiatric illness'. In doing this psychiatry is simply refining and using more intensively skills we all use every day, so why should it be controversial? All these concepts have led to bitter arguments, as we shall soon see.

There are crucial qualitative differences between mental illnesses and normal functioning: there is a line that gets crossed. However, most of the symptoms and signs – the external manifestations of mental illnesses – lie along the spectrum of normal psychology, the wide repertoire of thoughts and feelings common to us all. They are exaggerations and distortions of common, familiar experiences. We recognize them and the words we use to describe them are drawn from our own, very similar, mental processes. When we meet someone suffering from a mental illness we can see the difference in them and yet experience a deep identification with what they are going through. We can recognize clinical depression because we have experienced sadness and depression ourselves, but we still sense that it is something different.

Psychiatry touches directly on that which is most human in us, the central core of our being – our identity or, if you wish, our 'soul'. Consequently it is almost impossible to be neutral about it. Psychiatric problems have their origins in the very fundamentals of our humanity, the basic contradictions in our design. These contradictions, these 'design flaws', presumably arose during the evolution of our enormous brains to become the planet's most complex and sophisticated species. Yet despite our remarkably overdeveloped rational sense and self-awareness we human beings retain a bewildering range of strong, primitive emotions and drives. Compromises along this evolutionary journey to make us uniquely human have left their marks. Overall the endless interactions of these various contradictions make us a rich, varied and creative species. But for some of us these same qualities can combine to produce enormous suffering. It is the price we pay for our humanity.

A second reason for controversy is that psychiatry is fundamentally a hybrid. Its origins lie in two very different but equally powerful sources, each bringing its own heritage and philosophy. These two philosophies converge in the process of diagnosis.

A unique cornerstone of psychiatry is this understanding of others achieved initially by reflecting on ourselves and using this to recognize what is going on in their minds. It is from this understanding, called 'descriptive psychopathology', that we derive our diagnoses. Psychopathology is intimately linked to the symptoms and signs of mental illnesses but is not *just* symptoms and signs. When we describe the psychopathology of patients we attempt to describe what is going on in their minds and what they are experiencing, not just list the obvious symptoms that indicate it. We will return to this later, in particular when considering schizophrenia and so-called 'criterion-based diagnosis' (Chapter 11).

We clarify psychopathology during the psychiatric consultation and to do this requires obtaining an understanding of the personal meanings of what the individual describes. Such 'guided empathy' provides a recognition of the uniqueness of each individual patient and in particular the meaning of the symptoms for him or her. Without it psychiatry becomes impossible and meaningless. Yet the paradox is that psychiatry's development as a separate profession is based on a quite formal codification of this human understanding. Just at the point when it has obtained an understanding of their unique significances, it steps back to organize them into diagnoses.

This step backwards can make psychiatry seem alien and impersonal. It starts off by focusing on the unique and personal meaning of experience but then appears to abandon it. Through a process of observation and organization psychiatry has constructed a relatively rational, and increasingly scientific, approach to its classifications and treatments. This can appear detached and cold. Psychiatry has to oscillate back and forth between understanding the meaning of experiences for patients and retreating to diagnoses and treatments that ignore this *content* and personal meaning. To make a diagnosis we have to understand the content and meaning of experiences, but in treatment we focus on their *form*.

This tension between 'understanding' and 'explaining' runs like a refrain through psychiatry and its history has been shaped by their relationship. Both have been dominant at different times. One hundred years ago the German philosopher/psychiatrist Karl Jaspers described these two approaches as *verstehen* (understanding what the patient is experiencing) and *erklären* (explaining what is happening to the patient). He eventually fell out with Sigmund Freud (the founder of psychoanalysis), who he believed had blurred the distinction. Each approach has strong and dedicated adherents; over the years psychiatry has swung wildly between emphasizing understanding (psychotherapy) and explaining (neuro-psychiatry). It is not really possible for one to finally 'defeat' the other, however, as they are two faces of the same coin. This shifting emphasis shows across time and between practitioners.

The tension between them is not just some factional spat between dedicated psychotherapists and pharmacologists. It has long-standing origins in the two pillars on which psychiatry rests, one broadly aligned to psychology and the social sciences and one to biology and the natural sciences. What came to be called psychiatry at the start of the nineteenth century arose independently from two quite separate endeavours which exert their influences to this day.

The 'understanding' or psychological approach arose in the search to help individuals with a range of emotional and behavioural problems that baffled both them and those around them. These are what we commonly called neuroses, such as depression, hysteria and panic. These individuals were not 'mad', they did not lose control of themselves or contact with reality. They were sometimes able to carry on relatively normal (albeit distressed) lives in their families and communities. The 'explanatory' approach initially consisted of little more than labelling and classification. It was an attempt to get some descriptive understanding of the psychoses, what was then called 'lunacy' or 'madness'. 'The mad' were grossly disturbed individuals who had utterly lost their grip on reality. They had originally been confined in various institutions, prisons and workhouses for their care if their families could not cope. Bringing these individuals together in one institution (a 'lunatic asylum') had at least one positive consequence – it stimulated efforts to distinguish different types of lunacy. The resulting classification was the most prestigious development of nineteenth-century psychiatry, solidly manifest in the bricks and mortar of the asylums that were erected during this era.

From the very start these two approaches were well aware of each other. Asylum psychiatry drew heavily on what was happening outside its walls. For two centuries now the relationship between the two, like that of close siblings, has ranged from friendship and cooperation to fierce antagonism.

Does this history matter? I think it does. In everything that follows in this book these two perspectives will play their part. Making sense of psychiatry is often difficult. To have any chance of success we need to know a bit about both approaches and bear them in mind. Chapters 2 and 3 of this book recount these two histories in considerable detail, perhaps too much detail for the reader keen to dive into the dilemmas of modern psychiatry. However, current controversies, and especially the vehemence with which they are argued, are hopelessly baffling without some grasp of this history and how it has shaped attitudes and thinking. Take the role of genetics as just one example. The 'nature versus nurture' argument (whether your upbringing or your inheritance is responsible for your illness) has raged, literally *raged*, for a century in psychiatry. It clearly involves much more than can be answered by simply calculating a figure for heritability. It is a meeting point for two opposed psychiatric perspectives (and fiercely opposed world views) of whether man is a product of his nature or can shape his destiny. These two schools of thought draw on the same material but infuse it with starkly contrasting values and aspirations.

For most of this book it will not matter too much how it is read: Chapter 11 before Chapter 9, or straight to Chapter 8 for the antipsychiatrists if that is your interest. It would, however, help to read Chapters 2 and 3 before the rest. That way you will understand these points of reference in presenting the various arguments and be better placed to form your own opinion.

PSYCHIATRY, PSYCHOLOGY AND PSYCHOTHERAPY – WHAT ARE THE DIFFERENCES?

Some clarification of confusing terminology is probably in order. Psychiatry, psychology and psychotherapy tend to be run together in popular usage. Not surprising really. There is a lot of overlap in their meaning and in truth there is often a lot of overlap in their practice. The 'psych' refers to the mind so they all are concerned with what we think, and feel, and what we do. Their differences are, however, important.

Psychology is the *science* of human behaviour. It is often taught as an undergraduate degree (currently one of the most popular) and can even be studied at high school. Psychology had its origins in philosophy, from introspective philosophers who tried to understand the nature of the human mind by examining their own consciousness. Psychologists are experts in so-called 'normal psychology' – personality, emotions, how we think and react. Experimental psychology came into being in the late nineteenth century, finally separating itself from philosophy and biology. In experimental psychology mental processes are broken down into their simplest components, and experiments are conducted to manipulate, test and measure them. The first experimental psychology laboratory was established in Germany, in Leipzig University, in 1879. Experimental psychologists do not restrict themselves to human psychology, but also examine animal behaviour.

In the USA William James (older brother of the novelist Henry James) was the pioneer. He taught a course in experimental psychology at Harvard in 1875 and became professor of psychology in 1889. His 1890 book *Principles of Psychology* dominated the discipline for decades. The Russian Ivan Pavlov's description of the conditioned reflex in dogs gave a real boost to the scientific status of psychology. It laid the foundations for learning theory and the behaviourist school of Skinner and colleagues half a century later. Experimental psychology is an ever more sophisticated discipline which now explores all mental processes, including thinking, memory, feelings and attributions. Modern psychology has a range of well-tried instruments, including IQ and personality tests, and it increasingly uses direct measurements of brain functioning. As well as being a highly scientific academic discipline, psychology has given rise to a number of professions.

Clinical psychology applies psychological theories to assess and treat individuals with mental health problems. It is a postgraduate professional qualification requiring three to four years' full-time training. The training specializes in 'abnormal psychology' (very similar to what psychiatrists would call the signs and symptoms of mental illnesses or psychopathology) and assessing and treating mental health problems with psychological techniques. These treatments are now dominated by cognitive behaviour psychotherapies (CBT). Clinical psychology is closely related to psychiatry. *Educational psychologists* work in schools, *organizational psychologists* are engaged in industry, *occupational psychologists* help with training and employment, and *forensic psychologists* work in prisons and secure mental hospitals. Clinical psychologists often work in mental health teams.

Psychiatry is a medical specialty. Psychiatrists are doctors, just as general practitioners or surgeons are doctors. To become a psychiatrist you start as a medical student and do the same training as any doctor (including working for a year or two on medical and surgical wards). Having qualified, most doctors decide nowadays fairly early on which specialty to follow. Whatever it is, surgeon, family doctor, anaesthetist or psychiatrist, it will involve a similar structured 'postgraduate' training, of between three and six years but varying markedly between countries. In the UK postgraduate psychiatric training requires a minimum of six years but in some of the former Soviet republics it can be as short as two years. This training is mainly practical. You work in your specialty assessing and treating lots of patients under the close supervision of a senior doctor. It is common to rotate through different branches of the specialty. There are formal exams which have to be passed but most of the training is hands-on experience under supervision. Only when you have completed your specialist training and passed the required exams can you be fully responsible for your own patients and practise independently.

Psychiatry is the medical specialty responsible for the assessment, diagnosis and treatment of mental illnesses. This is a bit circular as in many countries mental illnesses (often now called, rather loosely, mental disorders) are defined as those which are diagnosed and treated by psychiatrists. Much of the thinking (and much of the language) will overlap between psychiatrists, psychologists and psychotherapists, but the psychiatrist is unique in two ways. First, he or she can prescribe medicines. Second, in most countries it is only the psychiatrist who has the legal power to decide on compulsory treatment. How this happens varies. Judges or magistrates may sign the formal papers but in practice it is only psychiatrists who can treat patients against their will.

Psychiatrists broadly share the same approach to their task as the nurses, psychologists and social workers they work with, but they bear a special responsibility for the 'medical model'. In essence the medical model is a very practical approach to treatment with a little less emphasis on theory ('if it works keep doing it, if it doesn't work stop doing it'). Psychiatrists do, of course, use theories to structure their thinking and guide what they do, but they are not restricted to any one theory. There is no '-ology' for psychiatry. For different patients (or even for the same patient at different times) they may rely on biology, pharmacology, psychology, physiology or sociology. They draw on whichever seems most helpful there and then. Psychiatry also displays its medical pedigree with its strong emphasis on personal responsibility; you, and you alone, are responsible for your decisions once you are trained. The working practices of psychiatrists are very like those of other doctors (night duty, cross cover, the balance between assessment and treatment). This medical approach is sometimes experienced as rather old-fashioned and authoritarian in the mental health teams in which most psychiatrists now work.

Psychotherapy as we now usually understand it arose from *psychoanalysis* but, in truth, it is both older and wider in its scope. The term can be applied to any structured use of the relationship between a therapist and a patient which uses discussion and talking to explore and to help relieve the patient's distress. How important understanding the causes of this distress is varies between different psychotherapies. What they all have in common is that they build on a trusting relationship and on dialogue to promote healing. The primitive psychotherapies outlined in Chapter 3 made no attempt to help the patient understand the origin of their problems, but used a powerful relationship and suggestion to bring relief. Sigmund Freud started with this approach but rapidly became aware of its limitations, subsequently introducing a greater emphasis on understanding unconscious processes. His treatment, outlined in Chapter 4, became increasingly sophisticated, drawing on free association and dream interpretation. It eventually included a detailed exploration of the therapist–patient relationship itself.

There are now many psychotherapies. Between the traditional psychodynamic therapies derived from Freud and Jung and the highly scientific behavioural and cognitive therapies lies every possible variant (art therapy, primal scream therapy, family therapy, group therapy, existential therapy). All of them demonstrate two characteristics. First, the maintenance of a safe, trusting relationship that permits risk taking and exploration, and second, the belief that the patient's experiences (past and present) really do matter.

The status of psychotherapy within mental health services and psychiatry is contested. Is it just one specific treatment option among many, or is it an essential component in all work with mental illness? Does every psychiatrist need to have psychotherapy training or skills? Or is it enough that they can recognize when it is needed and refer the patient on, as a surgeon might recommend a physiotherapist? Psychiatrists have endlessly debated this and it will become clear that I believe these skills are central.

Psychiatrists treat people with widely differing types of problems. Even before diagnosis, one of their most crucial functions is deciding whether the problem is serious or not. In many parts of the world you can refer yourself directly to a psychiatrist. In the UK and much of Europe, however, you will generally only see a psychiatrist if your family doctor thinks you need one. Still, about a third of patients I assess do not need psychiatric care. Their family doctor can treat their depression or anxiety perfectly well and my function is just to give advice. For about one in ten patients I can reassure them that they have no psychiatric disorder at all; what was troubling them was, though distressing, quite normal and will resolve itself. What sort of problems do the rest have?

WHAT ARE THE MAIN MENTAL ILLNESSES?

We used to divide psychiatric illnesses roughly into two main groups, psychoses and neuroses. Psychoses are those severe mental illnesses which used to be lumped together as 'madness', with disturbed behaviour and a loss of 'contact with reality'. Patients' symptoms are so severe and so vivid that they may even fail to recognize them as symptoms at all and may deny that they are ill. It is now unfashionable in psychiatry to use the term 'neuroses', partly because defining them is difficult and partly to distance us from psychoanalysis. However, it is still a widely used and understood term and will serve us here. People with neurotic disorders are distressed and know that there is something wrong. They are troubled by painful thoughts or feelings, most often anxiety or depression. Not all problems fit easily into these two categories. Drug and alcohol abuse, eating disorders, autism and the so-called 'personality disorders' are a significant part of psychiatric practice as we shall see but are not usefully considered as either psychoses or neuroses. In our ageing population there is also the growing problem of dementia, which is shoe-horned into the psychosis category for intellectual tidiness but really fits poorly.

Schizophrenia is the iconic mental illness. Over a century after its first description it remains the most disabling and, in many ways, controversial and complex of all the mental illnesses. It does not mean split mind or split personality, it is not Doctor Jekyll and Mister Hyde. Schizophrenia takes several forms and can display just about any symptom but most often patients hear voices, have strange and frightening ideas, and have difficulties in thinking clearly. It is relatively easy to recognize but not that easy to define. Most definitions focused on the central experiences of a loss of a secure sense of personal identity, and with this a disrupted engagement with the world around. The rest of us take this so much for granted that we hardly stop to think about it. There is a quality of 'difference' with schizophrenia patients that we sense, but we often cannot put our finger on exactly what it is, a sort of disengagement, an 'other-worldly' feel. Some early psychiatrists described it as being as if a pane of glass had been placed between them and the patient.

The voices that patients hear (called auditory hallucinations) most often talk about them. Hallucinations may also be of strange sensations in the body. Patients often develop powerful fixed beliefs (delusions) to explain these hallucinations and they frequently involve a sense of persecution (paranoid delusions). They can drive the sufferer to hide from, or even attack, their imagined persecutors. Schizophrenia patients often attach enormous significance to otherwise prosaic events or objects. Such 'ideas of reference' may lead them to believe that a radio or television news broadcast is about them. Obviously this can be very frightening.

Schizophrenia starts when people are young – usually in their twenties. A century ago its onset was about ten years younger and nobody knows why this change has occurred. Patients often withdraw from others and neglect themselves. Breakdowns are often associated with drug use, which can obscure the diagnosis because some drugs such as LSD, amphetamines and cocaine can produce brief psychotic illnesses. Although a number of patients do recover, many remain ill on and off for much of their lives and need ongoing psychiatric care. Acute breakdowns are separated by long periods when the active symptoms are absent but the patient may be demoralized, and lack energy or motivation. In acute episodes patients may need hospital admission, sometimes against their wishes.

Manic depression was the other major psychosis distinguished from schizophrenia in nineteenth-century asylums by the German psychiatrist Emil Kraepelin (Chapter 2). Manic-depressive patients, although just as ill as schizophrenia patients during their hospital admission, made better recoveries. They could often be discharged home, although they frequently relapsed and returned. There is a lot of overlap in symptoms between schizophrenia and manic depression and some psychiatrists believe they are extremes of the same disease. Manic-depressive patients may also have hallucinations and delusions, but these are overwhelmingly coloured by their depressed or elated mood.

In the 'manic' phase patients are overactive and over-confident; their mood is usually cheerful but easily tips over into irritability. Manic patients display very poor judgement – spending money they do not have, starting unwise sexual liaisons, irritating strangers. They can do terrible damage to their relationships and reputations, especially early on before the breakdown is recognized. They can bankrupt their businesses, buy houses they cannot afford and destroy old friendships by ill-tempered arguments. Hospital care is usually needed during acute mania. The depressive phase is also often very severe, sometimes with savagely critical hallucinatory voices and delusions centring on guilt and punishment and awful diseases.

Several manic-depressive patients have been very creative. Composers such as Robert Schumann and Handel (who wrote the whole of the *Messiah* in twenty-three days, reputedly handing sheets out of the window to his waiting publisher) clearly had significant mood swings. The author Sylvia Plath drew heavily on her depressive episodes in her novel, *The Bell Jar*. Many artists are reluctant to take medicine for their manic depression for fear that it will dull their creativity. Some comedians, such as the late Spike Milligan, even attribute their success to the rapid thinking and punning that is a characteristic of mania. The price paid for this creativity can be great. Milligan wrote movingly of his recurrent severe depressions and Plath took her own life tragically young.

These two very serious illnesses, schizophrenia and manic depression, still dominate psychiatric wards. They affect men and women about equally, each in about 1 per cent of the population. Psychoses are very consistent across time and culture; they occur throughout the world, from the Amazon rainforest to Manhattan. You are broadly as likely to develop one wherever you live although they do seem somewhat more frequent in city dwellers than in the countryside and they are much more common in migrants. Nobody understands why there is this variation, though we do know it is not explained by genetics or race. Several theories have been proposed but it still remains a mystery.

Manic-depressive disorder is now referred to as 'bipolar disorder'. This is not just a change of name but is a much broader diagnosis with a lower threshold. Bipolar disorder includes patients who have never suffered a manic episode (bipolar II). This expansion of the bipolar diagnosis is still controversial and will be picked up later in this book.

There are other psychoses beyond the two major ones described here. Delusional and paranoid disorders are like schizophrenia but usually start later and do not show the characteristic identity disintegration, self-neglect and deterioration. They are common in elderly people in the early stages of dementia and in those who abuse alcohol and drugs. Some are very specific. 'Morbid jealousy' is a paranoid psychosis that affects alcoholics and punch-drunk boxers. 'Paraphrenia' is encountered in elderly single women who become tormented by vivid hallucinations of electric shocks and sexual interference. 'Postpartum psychosis', which develops within days or weeks of childbirth, is a remarkably striking psychosis, so severe that the mother is usually unable to look after her baby, but it has happily become much less common.

The word neurosis has now been written out of psychiatric classifications because it was considered pejorative – 'he's so neurotic' – and because it implied psychoanalytical explanations. In common speech it still includes people who are just a bit cranky or puzzling. Within psychiatry it was (and in truth still is) restricted to specific disorders such as depressions, anxieties and phobias, rather than a sweeping judgement.

Depression is now often used as a catch-all for all neurotic psychiatric disorders, displacing older terms such as 'nervous breakdown' or 'nerves'. Its advantage is that it is so familiar and non-stigmatizing. Its disadvantage is that it is just too all-inclusive. We have all been depressed but, luckily, most of us have not 'suffered from depression'. The boundary is unclear and requires judgement. The problems in defining and diagnosing depression are a good example of how psychiatrists work. Psychiatrists see hundreds of people who 'feel depressed'. With experience we learn to recognize those whose depression will resolve on its own and those who will need treatment. Depression appears to be starting at a younger age and to be increasing in frequency. The World Health Organization predicts that by about 2020 it will be the most pervasive and disabling disease worldwide, more than cancer and more even than malaria. Depression will be responsible for more early deaths and lost years of good-quality life than any other illness.

It is no simple task to find a clear dividing line between 'clinical depression' and normal depression or sadness. Nor is it easy to impose some order on the varieties of clinical depression despite half a century of concentrated effort. Psychiatrists try to identify different types of depression because there is such variation in how it responds to treatment. The hope is that if we can define the types that respond well to treatment we can make sure we identify and treat them early. As the old diagnosis of melancholia was expanded to the broader concept of depression, attempts were made to separate 'neurotic' from 'psychotic' depression. Psychotic depression was more like melancholia, often with morbid hallucinations and delusions. A brief detour through 'typical' and 'atypical' depression led to the distinction between 'reactive' and 'endogenous' depressions. Reactive depression was thought to result from depressing and stressful events such as illness or bereavement, whereas endogenous, as the term indicates, originated spontaneously from within the patient. Research, however, showed stressful precipitants were equally common in both forms. While the explanation of the differences in causation did not hold, the symptoms of endogenous depression did predict a better response to medical treatments. These features are slowing up, broken sleep, weight loss, and a dead or empty sensation which is worst on first waking and improves as the day progresses. Nowadays depression is simply classified by severity as either major or minor. A 'melancholic type' subgroup of major depression with very endogenous symptoms does seem to respond to different treatments.

There is a wide range of treatments used in depression. These stretch from simple support and counselling through to ECT, but most patients are treated with antidepressants plus counselling or psychotherapy. A puzzling feature of depression is that the more severe it is the more effective the medical treatments appear to be. In most illnesses the more severe forms are harder to treat. Delusional depression (the most severe) responds very well to the ever-controversial ECT. Antidepressants work well in both moderate and severe depression but not so well (some believe not at all) in mild depression. The more old-fashioned antidepressants such as amitriptyline work better with melancholic depression. CBT is equal to, or even better than, antidepressants in mild depression, and about equally effective in moderate depression. However, it is of no value in severe or delusional depression. Many depressed patients recover rapidly and never look back, but unfortunately many suffer several episodes. So clearly a careful diagnosis does matter.

Anxiety disorders attract less public interest than depression but are just as widespread and, in many ways, just as disabling. We all get anxious: it is a healthy and necessary response to stress. The heightened awareness and preparedness we experience when anxious equips us to deal rapidly with an impending threat. In anxiety disorders, anxiety levels appear to rise as they do normally with stress, but they then fail to settle down when the threat is past. They remain elevated, often until the next stress comes along and the result is a constant state of arousal and tension. Not surprisingly anxiety sufferers become 'worried about worry', making it even less likely to go away. Anxiety is not only unpleasant; it is exhausting, is bad for our physical health and can stop us from thinking clearly.

Two major groups of anxiety disorder are general anxiety disorder and phobias. General anxiety disorder is just what it says – a state of over-arousal with an exaggerated startle response and an inability to relax or stop worrying. Phobias, on the other hand, are more limited and are exaggerated fears of specific things or situations. Most of us have one; mine is of heights. Simple phobias, such as of spiders, snakes, heights, start in childhood, remain constant through the years and generally only cause minor inconvenience. 'Complex' phobias such as agoraphobia or social phobia start in adult life, come and go over time and can be very severe. Agoraphobia, a fear of going out of the house into spaces crowded with strangers, can be very disabling. It is not, as often believed, a fear of open spaces; the term comes from the Greek *agora*, for market place, not *ager*, the Latin for field. It was once called the 'housebound housewife' syndrome because it started most often in women at home with young children. It has become less common, as women return earlier to work, but social phobia has become increasingly diagnosed.

Social phobia can lead individuals to avoid company, and in the extreme make them unemployable. It is prone to overuse as a diagnosis and the question of whether this is an example of the unnecessary medicalization of normal experience is picked up in Chapter 11. Anxiety responds very quickly to sedative drugs such as valium. However, the effect is very temporary and people easily become addicted, needing higher and higher doses. Behaviour therapy is effective in phobias and some of the newer antidepressants also work with anxiety disorders so sedatives are much less prescribed.

Post-traumatic stress disorder (PTSD) is an anxiety state dominated by nightmares, intrusive thoughts and flashbacks starting from a dreadful experience such as a car crash or rape. It is a complex disorder, prone to over-diagnosis and with differing approaches to treatment. It is discussed in more detail later. As with all the depressive and anxiety disorders patients may seek relief from their symptoms in alcohol and drugs.

Obsessive-compulsive disorder (OCD) is a very unusual anxiety disorder which has always fascinated psychiatrists, psychologists and psychotherapists. In OCD the patient is troubled by strange, repeated and disturbing thoughts or actions. They find that they have to think these thoughts (for example, counting specific number series, or repeating blasphemous or distasteful words in their heads) or complete highly specific actions or rituals such as touching fence posts or checking door locks. These have to be repeated a set number of times and they have to follow a rigid order. Fears of dirt or contamination are common, as is so-called 'magical' thinking ('If I don't check the door lock three times my mother will die').

OCD symptoms can be very bizarre indeed and very time-consuming. They differ from psychotic symptoms in that the patient knows only too well that they are absurd and resists them. Despite this patients can become very distressed indeed if prevented from repeating the thoughts (obsessions) or actions (compulsions). Most of us have experienced obsessional thoughts, particularly in childhood, but they fade and are easily resisted. OCD is now diagnosed much more readily than it used to be, often in association with depression. In its purer form it starts early and patients can be so embarrassed about their symptoms that they go to great lengths to disguise them, and only seek help when forced to. I once became aware of a woman with very severe OCD only because the school was concerned about her son's isolation. He was too embarrassed to take his friends home because his mother followed them around washing down every surface they touched with bleach.

Alcohol is responsible for a number of psychiatric disorders besides alcoholism itself. The body quickly becomes used to a regular intake of alcohol, needing greater quantities for the same effect. Over time alcoholics get used to drinking amounts of alcohol that would poison most of us, and the same is true for most drugs of addiction. People can get trapped in the habit as much to avoid the consequences of stopping ('the shakes', 'cold turkey') as for the intoxication.

Whether drug and alcohol abuse should be considered psychiatric illnesses is explored later. What cannot be doubted, however, is the host of psychiatric disorders they cause. Sudden alcohol withdrawal in very heavy drinkers can cause delirium tremens. This consists of terrifying hallucinations such as rats swarming across the floor or ants crawling over the skin, plus confusion, a racing pulse, high temperature and even epileptic fits. Untreated it can be fatal. Amphetamine and cocaine use can cause acute paranoid psychoses in which users believe they are being persecuted. These can lead to violence as they defend themselves from their supposed persecutor. Prolonged excessive alcohol consumption can also cause paranoid psychoses, dementia and neurological disorders. Many drugs such as cannabis, LSD and cocaine can precipitate psychosis in vulnerable individuals and their use invariably slows down recovery. Psychiatry has to get involved with drug and alcohol abuse.

Eating disorders are a scourge of our time, particularly for young women. They were not always common. Anorexia nervosa was first described in 1873 simultaneously in London and Paris, and has become increasingly common since then. Anorexia is severe self-starvation with weight loss, loss of menstrual periods, and a stubborn belief by an emaciated patient that she is too fat. It occurs typically in anxious and perfectionistic teenage girls but it can occur in men and it can start later. Many anorexics use self-induced vomiting and laxatives to control their weight. Sufferers of bulimia nervosa, first described in the 1980s, often vomit after eating to excess but, unlike anorexics, remain at normal weight or a little above. These are now a major mental health problem and with each passing decade have become more common in the developing world.

Anorexia can become chronic with a significant risk of early death. Bulimia is much more common, but less dangerous and more likely to resolve spontaneously. Effective psychotherapies have been developed for it and along with dietary advice are also used for anorexia. Because most patients are female and most psychiatrists used to be male, and because weight and shape are currently such sensitive issues for young women's identity, eating disorders have become highly politicized. Several websites present them as a legitimate life choice, advising against treatment.

Two so-called personality disorders cause major problems in psychiatry. One is antisocial personality disorder, usually diagnosed in men, the other is borderline personality disorder, usually diagnosed in young women.

Psychiatry is based on the meeting between two individuals, both of whom have their own personalities. Personality is massively important in all of psychiatry. It is an easy concept to grasp but a difficult one to define. Most of us know what personality is and we can describe the personalities of those close to us. At its most simple it is that collection of characteristics and behaviours we use to distinguish between people. For each of us it is a combination of temperament (outgoing, timid, flamboyant, careful) and character (rigid, tolerant, seductive, thorough) and it is pretty permanent. When we meet old school friends decades later and register how little they have changed, it is their personality we recognize. Personality is important to psychiatrists for several reasons. Some personality types increase the risk of mental illness, e.g. an over-anxious personality. They affect how well people can engage in treatment, and difficult or prickly personalities can hamper recovery by depriving the individual of supportive friends.

Some personality patterns are very striking and psychiatrists encounter them with great regularity; some are so extreme they cause real suffering in their own right. Psychiatrists call these personality disorders, with the status of a diagnosis themselves, albeit controversial and subject to intermittent name changes. Cruel and thoughtless individuals who show little remorse or concern for others were originally referred to as psychopaths. They were renamed sociopaths and their condition dyssocial personality disorder, but currently labelled as antisocial personality disorder. Emotionally volatile young women with intense, insecure relationships who take overdoses or cut themselves are now diagnosed with borderline personality disorder.

This is a recent diagnosis, with a confusing name – it does not 'border' on anything; the name is a quirk of psychiatric history. It has so far stuck, but is expected to be renamed something like 'emotionally unstable personality disorder'. These two, antisocial and borderline, are the only personality disorders routinely referred to psychiatrists for treatment in their own right.

People have very strong, and differing, views on the origins of personality. There is undoubtedly a substantial genetic component but that is not the whole story. Antisocial personality disorder has been associated with early childhood separation and neglect, and borderline personality disorder with early sexual abuse. Few psychiatrists believe we have effective treatments for antisocial personality disorder but some psychotherapies for borderline personality disorder show promise.

Most other personality disorders are diagnosed (if they are diagnosed at all) alongside mental illnesses. Because personality is part of an individual's fundamental identity, not a pathological change like a mental illness, and because the terms can appear very judgemental, some psychiatrists believe personality disorders should be removed from diagnostic manuals. There are important practical and ethical implications to this decision. Both borderline and antisocial personality disorders are strongly associated with risky and suicidal behaviour so psychiatrists are often called upon to intervene. However, in contrast to mental illness, there is little reason to believe that a personality disorder is likely to change, as it is, after all, the person's normal self. How justified then would it be to force treatment on such individuals? Different countries, and different psychiatrists, take very different positions.

Intellectual ability varies steadily across the general population with a small 'bump' at the lower end. This bump comprises a group of severely disabled individuals with a range of genetic disorders and brain damage. Psychiatrists are no longer generally responsible for the care of people with intellectual disabilities except when they also develop mental illnesses (which they do).

Autism is now a very troubling problem. It used to refer to a rare, easily identified and profound disorder detectable in infancy. The child is often slow to learn to speak and, more distressingly, cannot relate emotionally to others. It cannot distinguish its own identity and perspective from that of people around it (hence the characteristic confusion of pronouns, saying 'he wants a ball' instead of 'I want a ball'). The ability to understand how the world appears from another person's perspective is called having a 'theory of mind' and autistic people classically lack this ability. Autism is about three times more common in boys and seems to be becoming more frequent. Those affected are often excessively preoccupied with order and routine, and some have remarkable isolated talents such as mathematical ability or the capacity for prodigious feats of memory. However, the vast majority do not have such talents and many have significant learning disabilities.

One current theory is that autism is an extreme form of the 'male brain' with diminished emotional intelligence. Diagnostic criteria have widened considerably to 'autism spectrum disorder'. This includes the much less severe Asperger's syndrome, which fades into extreme eccentricity and emotional clumsiness. As with eating disorder some affected individuals and their self-help groups insist that it should be seen as simply an alternative lifestyle and reject the suggestion of mental disorder. Whether this reflects a societal change with more self-confident patients or is more a consequence of the ever-lowering threshold of the diagnosis (see Chapter 11) is unclear.

Suicide is sadly a constant risk in mental illness and psychiatry. People with mental illnesses are about ten times more likely to die by their own hand than the rest of the population. About a quarter of those who take their lives are being treated in mental health services. It is not true that those who talk about suicide do not do it. Nearly two thirds have been to see their GP in the preceding month and nearly half in the preceding week. They may not all have shared their suicidal thoughts and it can be difficult to know what to do. Many people in extremis during a personal crisis consider or even threaten it. The risk of suicide increases with age and is three times as common in men as women while the pattern for suicide attempts (mainly overdoses) is the mirror opposite. Suicide rates are highest in depression and alcoholism but are also high in schizophrenia and anorexia nervosa.

Our attitude towards suicide is changing rapidly. Until the 1960s it was actually illegal in the UK and sometimes patients who had attempted it woke in hospital to find a policeman by their bed. Prosecution was vanishingly rare but there were consequences for suicide such as shame for the family, refusal of burial in consecrated ground and denial of life insurance payments. A strong taboo against suicide still exists in many countries. I was taught that all people who committed suicide suffered from a mental disorder, a highly improbable proposal.

Rates of suicide vary enormously between different countries and between different groups. The French sociologist Emile Durkheim's ground-breaking text, *Le Suicide* (1897), stressed the role of social factors rather than individual ones. He attributed the higher rates in Protestant countries to lower social cohesion, which he labelled *anomie*. Catholicism, he believed, provided more sense of belongingness, although it might also be that Catholics under-report because of stigma. Evidence for social forces has grown: rates fall during wars, when people share a greater purpose, and rocket when societies disintegrate, as in the former Soviet Union. There, a staggering 70 men commit suicide in each year in every 100,000 inhabitants compared to 17 for the USA and 12 for the UK. Women seem more resilient in the face of social disintegration, perhaps being more reliant on family and children for their self-worth. The different European countries have very stable differences in suicide rates and these differences even persist when their inhabitants emigrate to the USA or Australia. Contrary to popular belief Sweden has never had the highest suicide rate, but ranks in the middle along with the UK. The high rates are in the countries of Central and Eastern Europe (and the former Soviet Union). Suicide does seem remarkably rare in some developing countries. I vividly remember visiting a large, impoverished mental hospital in Ghana and the nurses, many of whom had worked there for decades, telling me that none of them could remember a suicide.

All of this may suggest only a limited role for psychiatry in suicide but there is a role and there is some progress. Many suicides are impulsive or may be the result of what might otherwise have proved to be temporary despair. So we ask about it and take it very seriously; it can be one of the more obvious reasons for compulsory admission. Public health measures such as removing coal gas, putting warning notices or netting on high bridges and providing twenty-four-hour help lines such as the Samaritans have had positive effects. Providing people with time and space to think makes a real difference. High-risk groups such as farmers, dentists and doctors show the risks of easy access to lethal methods. Earlier identification and treatment of depression can also reduce suicide, as does careful follow-up after discharge from psychiatric units.

Suicide is, however, increasingly being recognized as a legitimate personal decision. Assisted suicide is legal in Switzerland and increasingly doctors are involved with it in the Netherlands and Belgium. It is effectively not prosecuted in the UK and the laws are expected soon to change. Most patients who choose this route suffer from incurable and distressing physical illnesses but there already have been a number with psychiatric disorders (depression and chronic fatigue syndrome). Obviously the incurability of such disorders is open to challenge, as is the patient's mental capacity when making the judgement. Most psychiatrists take a pragmatic and conservative approach to those threatening suicide and take action to prevent it. We know, however, that some of our patients will continue to want to end their lives, sometimes for understandable reasons, and a number of them will succeed.

This book focuses mainly on the psychiatric care of adults. This is because most psychiatric illnesses occur in adult life and it is in the diagnosis and treatment of this age group where most controversy and misunderstanding has arisen. Unlike general medicine, where clinics and wards are now populated by patients in their sixties and seventies, psychiatry patients are still predominantly of working age, many in their twenties and thirties. However, there are some disorders which become more common with age and this, combined with our rapidly ageing population, has produced a subspecialty of 'old-age psychiatry' or 'gero-psychiatry' (in the UK 'psychogeriatrics'). As mental faculties wane people are more prone to depressive and paranoid disorders. Psychogeriatricians pay particular attention to the effects of physical illnesses and cognitive decline.

The greatest challenge to old-age psychiatry is the growing number of people with Alzheimer's disease. Dementia care will soon absorb about 1 per cent of the world's gross income – that is, *all* income, not health care spend. Later this century it will overtake depression as the major disease burden. Although there are some drugs (the cholinesterase inhibitors) that delay decline for about a year, there is currently no cure. Psychiatrists are involved with Alzheimer's disease because it often results in difficult and disturbed behaviour.

HOW DOES PSYCHIATRY SET ABOUT TRYING TO HELP?

This is not a medical textbook so it will not describe treatments in any detail. The range of treatments in psychiatry is relatively limited compared to other branches of medicine but providing them effectively requires considerable skill and judgement. The 'medical model' in psychiatry is often mistakenly assumed to mean just pills but is much broader than that.

The medications we have are relatively few, falling into four main groups: antidepressants, antipsychotics, sedatives and mood stabilizers. All have impressive evidence for their efficacy, but none is a 'magic bullet'. None of them cures everyone with their target illness. Antidepressants improve the rate of recovery in an episode of depression from about 30 to well over 60 per cent. Antipsychotics control extreme disturbance and shorten acute psychotic episodes. They also reduce the risk of another breakdown in schizophrenia from 80 per cent within two years to about 20 per cent. Sedatives control extreme anxiety and agitation, often preventing self-harm and exhaustion. Mood stabilizers reduce the risk of breakdown in bipolar disorder but they do not eliminate it entirely.

Few patients with major mental illnesses are treated completely without medication. The choice between medicines from within each group is more often determined by individual tolerance and response rather than by specific symptom profiles. Despite the claims of the pharmaceutical companies there are only modest differences in effectiveness between the various drugs in each group. However, all of them have side effects and these vary. For some patients sedation will be an intolerable side effect, for others who are agitated it can be a welcome relief. The newer antidepressants such as Prozac have fewer side effects than the older ones such as amitriptyline and they are less dangerous in overdose. However, they do not suit everyone. Similarly the newer antipsychotics are less likely to cause muscle stiffness or restlessness but more likely to make patients gain weight and develop diabetes. Individual choices have to be discussed and decisions made. The discovery and application of several of these medicines will be taken up in following chapters.

There is now a wide range of psychotherapies, including psycho-dynamic, cognitive behaviour and cognitive analytic therapy. Therapies can involve individuals, groups or families. It will become clear from this book that I am a psychiatrist who believes psychotherapy is cen-tral to psychiatric practice, not an optional add-on. I doubt that you can successfully treat any mental illness unless you can engage with each patient's fears and concerns, their wishes and aspirations. Estab-lishing and sustaining a trusting relationship with a troubled and suspicious patient is a skill. It requires more than just being kind or being 'sensitive'. It demands training in listening, listening both to the patient and to your own responses. You have to take seriously your patient's story, and you have to be prepared, in many senses, to be a partner in the process.

Most psychiatric treatment now takes place outside hospital, by teams including several disciplines (doctors, social workers, nurses, psychologists). Medications are effective in controlling the extremes of symptoms so that admissions are now generally weeks, not months or years. Patients still have long periods when, although not acutely unwell, they remain disabled and in need of care and support. Mental illnesses are profoundly demoralizing. Those afflicted lose confidence and need someone to believe in them, and to help them find ways of coping day to day.

Social support keeps patients in treatment but it also helps them to achieve the life they want. Indeed such support probably occupies most psychiatric time and effort. Lacking a prestigious theory behind it, or a profession to champion it, social support is often over-looked in descriptions of community care. Without it, however, such care (indeed any humane care) would fail. It is simply not the case that psychiatrists only focus on symptoms and prescribing pills. Some colleagues and I videotaped a series of outpatient interviews between senior psychiatrists and their schizophrenia patients. We were staggered to observe that the overwhelming majority of the time was devoted to social issues ('How are you getting on with your sister now? Are you able to visit her?'). It was the patients who kept returning to their symptoms, which occupied less than 10 per cent of the interview.

The old asylums are fast disappearing, virtually gone. Mental illness is no longer hidden away behind high walls. Few regret their demise but this new visibility has brought tougher scrutiny of mental health care. Awful abuses used to occur within these closed institutions, but their impact was limited. Now when failures occur they do so in the full glare of public gaze and explanations are, quite rightly, demanded. Tabloid journalism whips up a frenzy of fear about dangerous mentally ill people roaming the streets. The conviction that there is an epidemic of random assaults is a constant preoccupation yet violence from the mentally ill has not increased at all. During the move from mental hospitals to community care over the last fifty years the rate of homicide by the mentally ill has remained absolutely unchanged while that by the 'healthy' population has more than doubled. Psychiatric abuse and neglect are now, rightly, held severely to account. A better-educated public is more aware of mental illness and it asks searching questions.

SO WHAT IS THE PROBLEM WITH PSYCHIATRY?

It is all too easy to assume that this criticism is a recent phenomenon and that psychiatry was held in high esteem until patients moved out from behind the asylum walls. Far from it. Psychiatry has always been controversial and it has always had its critics. The reasons for this were touched on at the start of this chapter; psychiatry concerns itself with aspects of us that we feel uneasy about and may want to ignore. Its practices are difficult to understand and can easily seem mysterious and sinister. It has also, it cannot be denied, made mistakes, sometimes very bad mistakes, and it probably continues to. Surgeons also make mistakes, yet surgery is held in very high esteem. Surgeons have the luxury of 'burying their mistakes'; the victims of psychiatry's errors live to tell the world about it. This book will make no attempt to hide psychiatry's errors.

Critics of psychiatry fall into two broad groups, taken up in more detail in Chapters 8 and 9. The first accepts the legitimacy of psychiatry and our need for it but points to its failings, both personal and institutional. It demands a better psychiatry, one with more oversight holding those who fall below proper standards to account. The second group questions psychiatry's legitimacy altogether. It is not a matter of poor practice but the very practice itself. A wide coalition of philosophers and social scientists (including several dissident psychiatrists) has questioned the fundamental validity of psychiatry. They challenge the philosophical status of 'mental illness' and view psychiatry as a thinly disguised agent of social control.

I spent three months as a medical student in 1968 in an enormous state hospital in the rural USA. It nearly killed my ambition to become a psychiatrist. It was the uniformity of it that got to me, how everyone seemed to be treated exactly the same. The sociologist Erving Goffman wrote about the damaging effect of this sameness in his stunning book *Asylums*. He concluded that this imposed uniformity was not just poor practice but a deliberate process to erode personal identity.

Practice within the large asylums often did fall very short of decent care. Asylums were initially a revolutionary improvement in the lot of the mentally ill, treating them with kindness and attention. Unfortunately many deteriorated as they grew in size, overwhelmed by chronic and incurable patients. With size came anonymity, which, combined with inadequate numbers of poorly trained staff, led to undignified and dehumanized care. Sometimes this included deliberate abuse. Excessive and brutal treatments, such as leucotomy or intensive ECT, were tried in desperate attempts to relieve intractable disorders.

It is a mistake to think that all asylums became degraded, the 'snake pits' of lurid Hollywood films. I have worked in some excellent mental hospitals. But keeping them humane was an endless and exhausting task, struggling against the grain of institutional and human inertia. Not all hospitals were up to it. Asylum staff of earlier times were confronted by intensely distressed and disturbed patients for whom they had few effective treatments. Most were motivated then, as now, by a genuine desire to help those in their care. Still, all too often practices were tolerated that never should have been and we are better off without them.

Psychiatry has also been severely (and rightly) criticized for being too willing to knuckle under to social and political pressure. Its collusion in the extermination of the mentally ill and mentally handicapped under the Nazis is a lasting stain. Similarly so the use of bogus diagnoses such as 'sluggish schizophrenia' to detain political dissidents in the former Soviet Union. Some critics draw parallels with these historical aberrations and some current psychiatric practices although they are not so extreme. They point to the detention of dangerous individuals who are not obviously mentally ill and the medication of vast numbers of agitated children living in impoverished urban environments. They accuse us of serving the interests of the government or pharmaceutical company shareholders before our patients.

There is a school of thought which argues that psychiatry, the whole of psychiatry, is simply a high-quality confidence trick. The psychiatrist Thomas Szasz argued so in his book *The Myth of Mental Illness*. The French philosopher Michel Foucault contended that the label of 'madman' was basically invented as a convenient ruse to sweep up unruly social elements and stabilize a shaky French state in the seventeenth century. Several sociologists see psychiatry as a medical disguise for the oppression of troublemakers. Feminist analyses of how psychiatry has pathologized female identity are even more scathing. Several psychiatrists have shared these concerns. The charismatic Marxist psychiatrist Franco Basaglia led the Italian reforms in the late 1970s under the banner of 'liberty is cure'.

Of these so-called anti-psychiatrists the Scottish psychiatrist and psychoanalyst R. D. (Ronnie) Laing was arguably the most charismatic and persuasive. For him the unique existential position of the psychotic individual offered a much needed and astringent insight into the mad world we all inhabit. Laing thought, as many of his followers still do, that psychiatry is not so much evil as simply blind. It is even more blind than society in general to the potential wisdom of the 'mad'. Laing's personal charisma and undoubted sincerity, his legendary ability to relate to the most disturbed patients, and his wonderful prose made him an international celebrity. He was enormously influential despite being so frustratingly inconsistent in his thinking and will be considered more in Chapter 8.

It is my position in this book that psychiatry is broadly a legitimate medical specialty. It is different in many important ways, but still best considered as part of medicine. I believe that psychiatry, since its origins just over 200 years ago, has been a real power for good and is increasingly so. Yet its progress has followed a dramatically different pattern from the rest of medicine. This is probably most clearly seen in the USA, which has the greatest concentration of psychiatrists (and by far the greatest concentration of academic psychiatrists) in the world. In the last hundred years American psychiatry has lurched wildly from a broadly biological understanding to an almost exclusively psychoanalytic one between 1940 and 1970, and now back to an unapologetically and aggressive biological discipline. The same cycle, though much less extreme, is discernible in most developed countries.

Most areas of medicine have competing theories, its researchers busy producing incremental improvement within them, but psychiatry is still plagued by fierce ideological debates and strongly opposed positions. Attempts have been made to bridge psychiatry's factionalism with overarching theories. An early example was Adolph Meyer's 'psychobiology' in the 1920s. Currently we teach a 'bio-psycho-social approach' to medical students. Just saying it out loud confirms that it is not *an* approach. It just lists the three essential, but still contrasting, intellectual frameworks which are needed to practise coherent psychiatry.

We probably have to admit that we do not yet have a robust unifying theory for psychiatry although we do have serviceable organizing principles. This is sometimes taken to imply that psychiatry is 'less advanced' than the rest of medicine, 'where medicine was a hundred years ago'. Well, yes and no. Yes, we are still using diagnoses that are essentially 'syndromal'. This means we can recognize them consistently and can provide effective treatments but can only confidently identify the underlying causes in a handful. Yet neuroscience is as sophisticated as any branch of medical research; the care and attention devoted to psychiatric diagnosis and the accumulation of evidence for treatments is equal to that in most branches of medicine. Despite this, progress is undeniably slower.

This slowness of progress may lie more in the complexity of the subject. Brave statements such as 'mental illnesses are just brain illnesses' and comparisons of a 'broken brain' to a broken leg may be well intentioned, but they fail to convince. The involvement of the brain in a disorder does not settle the matter. We think of schizophrenia as a mental illness but we do not think of Parkinson's disease as a mental illness. Yet both undoubtedly have their anatomical and physiological seat in the brain. No, mental illnesses really are more complicated; the mind is not just the brain. Our self-awareness and identity are *us*. They are not just a part of us, in the way our elbows or our liver are a part of us.

The medical language of 'having an illness' ('suffering from schizophrenia', rather than 'being a schizophrenic') helps remove some of the judgemental overtones inherent in talking about what a person *is*. However, it does not remove the brute fact that suffering from manic depression *is* different from suffering from cancer. It affects everything about how we experience ourselves, and how others experience us. Mental illnesses are also different in that they invariably affect how we experience *them*. It is possible to stand above a disorder such as cancer or arthritis while you are suffering from it; it may take enormous effort and courage but you still can make a clear dispassionate assessment of what it means for you. It is not so with mental illnesses. The 'you' that is making that assessment of your illness is already different from the 'you' without that illness.

Psychiatry has to grapple simultaneously with the 'illness' as a collection of distressing symptoms, with its impact on the patient's identity and also with the ripples spreading out from that illness and that identity. These ripples affect how we respond to the mentally ill person, and that response sets up feedback confirming the experience. Trying to ignore this resonance may be temporarily reassuring but it is a dead end. Psychiatrists and their mental health colleagues have to balance all three levels in understanding and treating their patients. Their practice will never seem as sharp and confident as a surgeon or physician who can blot out 'irrelevant' considerations and insist on one focus for consideration. Human beings are messy. Their treatment is messy and complex, and nowhere more so than in psychiatry.

This introduction has proposed that psychiatry is a hybrid. It contains at least two distinct cultures (understanding and explaining) and draws from a range of theories (psychological, biological and social). It also has to operate in a changing society with shifting demands and expectations. The ethical challenges faced by psychiatry do not diminish with each technological advance; they evolve and metamorphose. Just as we establish practices which engage patients more as partners and respect their autonomy, we find ourselves faced with the challenges of neglect and stigma. We are social beings and everything that is most important to us happens in relationships, yet our codes of medical ethics treat patients as self-contained entities in an increasingly fragmented society. The right to privacy and confidentiality trumps virtually all other rights. Helping people recover from mental illness runs utterly contrary to this. What are we to do to resolve these contradictions? There are no simple answers to these questions, but hopefully this book will give some insight into such enduring but constantly changing challenges.

Psychiatry is with us to stay for the foreseeable future. It is 'our necessary shadow' in that it deals with illnesses that are part of what we are, not things that just happen to us such as flu or a broken leg. Like a shadow it takes its form from us, but also like a shadow it is distorted and shifting. We cannot escape these problems any more than we can run away from our own shadow. We may not always like what we see of ourselves reflected in psychiatry. What we learn may be puzzling but it is real. It is *us*, and understanding it better can only make us richer and more alive. I hope the following chapters that explore psychiatry past and present will do that.

I

What to expect if you are referred to a psychiatrist

Being referred to a psychiatrist is not that unusual. It is almost certain to happen to you or someone in your family. On average every one of us will have at least one relative (aunt, cousin, nephew) with a serious mental illness. I remind medical students that about half of them will have an immediate family member with such an illness. It is not rare. Seeing a psychiatrist is no more unlikely than seeing a surgeon or a solicitor but it still seems frightening.

Because fear and stigma still surround mental illnesses people do not gossip about them on the bus or in the shop as they do with their other ailments and hospital appointments. So when we are mentally ill we think we are the only ones and do not share our worries. There are also the various stories about psychiatrists – the evil or mad doctors from novels or movies who take control of patients and manipulate them. More serious movies show us as remote and inscrutable, posing impossible questions in an ominous tone: '. . . and what can that mean for you?' Even worse we are seen nodding knowingly in response to some innocuous remark or interpretation of the dreaded ink-blot test. Who would willingly endure such an ordeal?

Fear of psychiatrists is also sustained by folk-memories of asylums and the threat of being 'locked away'. These images are often kept alive in local expressions ('You'll end up in St Margaret's if you go on like that') long after the institutions themselves have been levelled to the ground. The possibility of compulsory care casts a long shadow. How we may have felt at the time also affects our memory of that first contact with a psychiatrist. We are rarely at our best, confident or upbeat. Our emotional state, anxious, despairing, self-critical or confused, will colour the encounter and any memory of it. So, all in all, the psychiatric consultation starts with the odds stacked against it.

Luckily the reality is usually quite benign. Most people find the experience reassuring and comprehensible. For many it comes as a real relief to unburden themselves of long-standing worries and it can be surprisingly powerful. I was struck as a medical student by how patients would tell their history to us in a fairly composed manner and then dissolve into tears when repeating it to the consultant psychiatrist. There was obviously an extra, emotional dimension to the exchange. The same happened to me several years later at my assessment for a group analytical treatment I undertook in training. I was utterly unprepared for it. As I spoke about myself to my future therapist I felt hopelessly exposed and undefended. This fear and vulnerability was matched by a quite absurd wave of confidence in and idealization of him. I even felt physically tiny alongside him. I had been working as a psychiatrist for over five years and thought I understood all about the doctor–patient relationship but had clearly not even begun to grasp its intensity. It is a good lesson for a psychiatrist to learn, and to remind oneself of occasionally.

This first meeting may be cathartic and is often therapeutic in its own right. Frightening, inexplicable and embarrassing thoughts and feelings are received as familiar, even commonplace occurrences. Realizing that they are not unique, that they even have a name, can reassure. Psychiatrists have heard most things already and are unlikely to be shocked or surprised. However, we are getting somewhat ahead of ourselves.

Most diagnoses of psychiatric disorders and most treatments for them do not involve psychiatrists at all; they take place in general practice. The vast majority of episodes of depression and anxiety are identified by GPs when patients come to them, often with a range of physical symptoms (aches and pains, tiredness, poor sleep) mixed with psychological symptoms such as sadness or worry. All medical students now get basic training in psychiatry and about half the family doctors in the UK spend six months working full time in it during their specialty training. So most know quite a bit about it, and they need to.

Anywhere between a quarter and a half of all GP consultations have been estimated to be primarily psychological or psychiatric. Personally I think these figures are a bit exaggerated as they are usually based on questionnaires that measure distress. It is not surprising that people who are physically unwell are also distressed – illness is distressing – but for most this disappears as they get better. What is beyond doubt, however, is that many people attend their GPs with psychiatric problems and that their GPs identify and treat most of them. On the whole GPs are more interested in solving problems than in attaching diagnoses. I worked closely in a study of GPs' recognition of depression and saw how, while they did not always record a diagnosis of depression, they often spotted something was amiss and asked patients to come back. They wanted to check if the lowered mood persisted or if it got better naturally. In some patients they even prescribed antidepressants or referred to the practice counsellor but recorded a diagnosis of chronic pain or poor sleep rather than depression. GPs take this responsibility seriously and many go on extra training courses to improve their detection and treatment of psychiatric problems. An influential project on a small Swedish island showed such training not only increased the recognition and treatment of depression but even reduced suicides.

If GPs find that their treatment is not successful they will refer on to a psychiatrist. If they believe the problem is too severe (perhaps with a risk of suicide) or is too complex they may refer straight away. If GPs suspect a psychotic illness they will generally refer immediately; few will attempt to diagnose or treat these illnesses without the involvement of a psychiatrist. So if your GP believes you are depressed and you have not recovered with his or her treatment you will probably be referred to a psychiatrist. What happens then?

The first thing to say is that you will *not* be sent to a psychiatric hospital ward. You are most likely to be seen in an outpatient clinic either in a general hospital or in a local health centre, occasionally in the grounds of a psychiatric hospital. In countries with extensive private psychiatry, consulting rooms may be separate from any hospital and which private psychiatrist, psychologist or psychotherapist you see is entirely up to you or your GP. Private office-based provision encourages self-referral by patients but public mental health care psychiatry, such as in the UK, Italy and Scandinavia, is generally restricted to those already assessed by their family doctor. Well-developed community services can provide assessment in your home, particularly useful for the very ill, elderly or frail patients, and for anxious or reluctant individuals.

There is a healthy professional rivalry between psychiatrists, psychologists, nurses and psychotherapists with disagreement on whether all patients need to be assessed by a psychiatrist. In the past psychiatrists were the only gateway to mental health services and they would always conduct initial assessments. Thirty years ago this made obvious sense. Only those suffering from quite serious mental illnesses were referred and these usually needed a psychiatrist's input. It is only in this last generation that we have begun to seek help for a wider range of less disabling problems. For many of these the full psychiatric assessment with its years of training may be considered excessive and unnecessarily expensive. A generation ago family doctors also had far less knowledge about psychiatry so their judgements about who needed psychotherapy or who needed ECT were fairly unreliable. Things have changed. Now, in mental health services such as the UK, people may be assessed by a nurse, a psychologist or a mental health social worker. There are good arguments for and against this practice. In reviewing them I should, however, declare that I have finally settled on the belief that psychiatrists should conduct them.

Assessment purely by psychiatrists is accused of excessively skewing mental health services towards a 'medical model' which shoe-horns complex personal and psychological problems into rigid diagnoses and medicalizes human suffering. The term 'mental distress' is often used instead of mental disorder or mental illness to emphasize how the process of diagnosis disempowers individuals. It removes from them the responsibility for their problem and, more crucially, the responsibility and power to change it. There is much truth in this, as we will explore later. The argument against is that the medical diagnostic approach is best suited to identify those conditions where professional help is needed and where being a patient makes clinical and personal sense. A clear distinction helps everybody – it is as important to clarify when something is not an illness as when it is.

Assessments translate into treatments. People do what they know best and think works. Psychotherapists recommend psychotherapy, psychologists recommend psychological treatments and psychiatrists often recommend medication. Psychiatric assessments may lead to too much reliance on pills, and a common complaint is that medication is used too much and psychotherapy too little. Too much authority for psychiatrists may distort resources, with too much spent on drugs and doctors and nurses and not enough on day centres or counsellors. Personally I believe this is true; we have an excessively biological view of mental illness with not enough social and psychotherapeutic interventions.

Despite this I support psychiatric assessment as the gatekeeper to mental health care. It is important to understand that the medical model does not just mean prescribing pills, far from it. It has always been much broader, including advice, counselling, diet, exercise, etc. It does, however, prioritize diagnosis, which means coming to a decision on what best describes the condition that the patient is suffering from and deriving the treatment from that diagnosis. Diagnoses are very practical, theory is not so important, in the medical model.

Two things follow from an emphasis on diagnosis. First, the medical model is very hard-nosed and judged almost entirely on its results. If a diagnosis broadly predicts outcome it is useful, if it does not then it is of no use and is simply abandoned. Both diagnosis and treatment are firmly linked to outcomes and evolve with new knowledge. So if a form of psychotherapy based on mindfulness is shown to be a successful treatment with recurrent depression then the medical model should direct us to it. Of course we can have our individual blind spots or become over-reliant on pet theories, but in time this will usually give way to experience. Second, the conditional language of all the above – 'should protect us', 'usually', 'often' – is characteristic of medicine and should guard against excessive dogma. An early lesson driven into all students in medical school is 'never say never'. People vary and you should be open to exceptions and be prepared to be flexible. I say 'should' because doctors are a fairly over-confident group and we can be quite dogmatic. However, that is a problem with us as a profession, not with the medical model.

Getting into arguments about who – doctor, nurse, psychologist – is 'better trained' is particularly futile. It is not so much a matter of which is 'better' as which is more appropriate. What characterizes medical training is practice and repetition; we assess hundreds and hundreds of patients. Our training is more akin to that for a 'craft' skill such as the sociologist Richard Sennett described in *The Crafts-man*. What takes so long is not the volume of information that has to be mastered, though there is plenty of that. No, time and experience are needed to hone the skills required to detect the same signs and symptoms in very differing people. Sennett confirms that such skills (in carpenters, musicians, surgeons) are learnt, not inherent, and it takes about 10,000 hours of practice to become a master of just about any skilled art. The skill of the cellist beyond simply playing the notes lies in being able to adapt to a cold or echoing auditorium or to an over-enthusiastic orchestra. The skill of the psychiatrist lies in being able to diagnose the same depression through the emotional under-statement of the army officer or the turmoil of the terrified mother. Such intensive repetition has been shown to alter the very structure of the brain. Brain scans of London taxi drivers have shown that one part, the hippocampus, gets steadily bigger over time as they learn their way round the city.

So what psychiatrists bring is a greater experience of individual variation and the ability to detect illness patterns through it. They obtain and maintain this skill by doing lots of assessments. This becomes something of a circular argument – psychiatrists should do most of the assessments because they do most assessments. However, experience is what we want from a professional, even more than knowledge. When we sit in a jet about to take off we want to know that the pilot has flown and landed this sort of plane hundreds of times; we are not that bothered whether the person at the controls understands aerodynamics.

TAKING THE HISTORY

The psychiatric assessment consists almost entirely of a discussion. Specific tests are rare and there are certainly no 'trick questions'. Ini-tial assessments conducted by psychiatrists, nurses, social workers, psychologists or psychotherapists may differ somewhat, but overall the similarities are greater than the differences. Psychologists and psychotherapists will want to know more about earlier experiences and your thoughts about them while social workers are likely to ask more about wider relationships and the practical conditions of your life. Nurses and doctors alone can examine patients physically, although in practice such examinations are not common apart from with elderly patients. What follows now sets out a model psychiatric assessment. In practice parts of it may be omitted, but psychiatrists have such a structure in the back of their minds and the box on the next page shows the main headings that guide them.

The immense advantage of being drilled again and again in taking a history and examining the mental state (exploring and noting mental processes – the psychiatric equivalent of a physical examination) in psychiatric training is that you do not have to think about the structure when you are doing it. It is essentially automatic, something you can almost do in your sleep. All your attention is on the individual patient in front of you and what he or she is saying; but the structure means that you do not forget important areas or get too distracted. By the time psychiatrists are trained they should be able to follow the flow of your story with only minimal interruption and questioning and collect a full history. The framework should be a guide and a support, not a straitjacket. Taking a psychiatric history closely follows the pattern of the standard medical history but with much greater detail on personal and emotional development and relationships. Taking medical histories has evolved gradually over decades into a conversational style that mirrors fairly well how people would themselves describe their problems. So although it is structured it should not usually be experienced as clumsy or intrusive. I am not sure if it is a compliment or not when patients often recall this one-hour meeting, when a detailed and comprehensive history was taken, as 'just a chat with a psychiatrist'.

The next few pages outline the nature of this assessment – what the psychiatrist will ask after and look out for. Of course, it will vary depending on the person and the problem, but probably not that much. We can anchor the journey through the questioning by

PSYCHIATRIC HISTORY

History of present condition
- Patients' description of the problem
- Details of the problem including its severity
- Other relevant problems and symptoms
- Onset and course of problems and symptoms
- Social circumstances

Past illness
- Past medical history
- Past psychiatric history

Family history
- Parents: age (now or at death), occupation, personality, and relationship with the patient
- Similar information about siblings
- Social position; atmosphere in the home Mental disorder in other members of the (extended) family, and abuse of alcohol and drugs

Personal history
- Early development
- Childhood separations, emotional problems and illness
- Schooling and higher education
- Occupation
- Sexual relationships
- Marriage and other partnerships
- Children

Personality
- Relationships
- Leisure activities
- Prevailing mood
- Character
- Attitudes and standards
- Habits

Drugs and alcohol
Biological features

MENTAL STATE EXAMINATION

Appearance and behaviour
- General appearance
- Facial expression
- Posture
- Mobility

Speech
- Rate
- Amount
- Content

Thinking
- Preoccupations
- Obsessional and compulsive symptoms
- Delusions

Perception
- Illusions
- Hallucinations

Cognitive function
- Orientation (time, place, person)
- Attention and concentration

considering a typically depressed patient. Let us call her Alison and she comes with an excellent referral from her family doctor, who has known her for several years.

Dear Prof Burns

I would be grateful for your advice on this 46-year-old patient of mine who has been struggling with feelings of anxiety and hopelessness for several years. She has been worried about her children and her own future. This has interfered with her sleep for some time, but she now regularly wakes in the night terrified that she will die and convinced her children will be taken into foster care. Her marriage has been shaky for several years, and her husband has left her on a couple of occasions for unsuccessful short-term relationships. However, she always takes him back. He is an ineffectual and unreliable individual who drinks a bit too much but is never actively unpleasant to her. He does, however, seem uncommitted to her and to the children, obviously resenting her attention to them. She is an attentive and over-anxious mother, not surprisingly perhaps as the youngest of her three children, a nine-year-old, has severe asthma. This often requires hospitalization and treatment with steroids which is affecting his growth.

She has coped with this situation for several years now. She finds her part-time job in a supermarket a welcome distraction, but recently even this is proving difficult. She now sleeps very badly indeed and has been losing weight. She has become convinced that this indicates a cancer and is not reassured despite thorough investigation including a hospital outpatient referral. At times I have wondered if these concerns have become almost delusional, they certainly seem to dominate her life and the elder daughter tells me she thinks her mother has become 'different'. For the last six or so months she has found herself so exhausted and preoccupied that she has had to miss work on several days and the sense of utter hopelessness has become overwhelming. She denies active suicidal thoughts although sometimes she admits to wishing on going to bed that she might not wake up. I don't really think she would try anything.

She looks thin and careworn and is frequently tearful when she comes in. I have prescribed a course of antidepressants over the last two months but there has been no improvement. I have tried talking to the husband but get nowhere – he insists it is just a phase and will resolve when Jonathan's asthma improves. Alison has been reluctant to see a psychiatrist but I am at a loss to know what to do next and things are clearly going downhill.

The *presenting complaint* is how most consultations begin. The first thing to do is find out why the patient is here today. Even if the psychiatrist has a letter of referral from your family doctor he or she will almost always start by asking you to describe in your own words what the problem is. 'Your doctor's letter says you have been depressed. But everybody's depression is different. Tell me what has been the matter in your own words.' This is a crucial part of the interview – it never fails to amaze me how penetrating this first description often is. It is referred to as the 'history of the presenting complaint' – even if you are not complaining. Putting it in your own words means that not only are the important symptoms described but it gives a clear indication of what matters most for *you* and a sense of the meaning you have made of the whole thing. Our patient Alison, for instance, might be much more worried about her marriage or her job than the GP had picked up. Good psychiatrists listen carefully and allow plenty of time for this initial description.

Once you have explained what the problem is the psychiatrist will ask you all about it in detail. 'When did you first notice it? Is there anything that you think may have brought it on? Has it happened before? When was the first time you thought that you might be seriously ill and dying? Is there any particular event you can recall that sparked it off?' Knowing now what the main problem is he or she will ask you targeted, specific questions. If your problem is anxiety, for example, they may be about typical physical symptoms of anxiety (sweating, palpitations, light-headedness) and about what makes it worse and what makes it better. 'Do the worries also trouble you at work or only at home?' Understanding what helps can be very important in guiding treatment. The meanings we accord our very similar experiences differ enormously and stem from our personal histories. Understanding the history is therefore key.

A *personal and family history* is central to an assessment. A decent psychiatric assessment must aim at an understanding of the patient's experience and the meanings they give to it. I have put personal and family history together as some doctors prefer to start with family history and some with personal history. I usually begin with family as knowing where someone 'started from' helps me make sense of their personal journey, but others find this illogical. Family history is not only a family history of illnesses; indeed, in psychiatry it is not even primarily about illnesses. 'Are your parents still alive? Tell me about your family.' I always specifically ask about age, jobs, and health of parents and brothers and sisters and enquire directly about the patient's current and past relationships with them. Growing up with a loving mother who was bed-ridden with arthritis, or an angry hard-working father who drank too much, is bound to colour how one approaches life and copes with illness. Knowing about families is also vital for understanding what support there is to fall back on.

The *personal history* is just that – an overview of your life up to now. It is best introduced with a very open, general question. 'Have you always lived here?' How detailed it then needs to be will depend on circumstances and to some extent on the problem. People vary enormously in the level of detail they provide. One almost has to prise it out of some, for others it can be hard to interrupt.

Early *development and milestones* (age when you first talked or walked and so forth) can indicate disabilities but can also shed light on the family atmosphere, such as overprotection later in life. It used to be obligatory to note such features as bed-wetting and stammering but we now know these have little real significance for adult problems. On the other hand they may leave lasting effects on self-confidence.

Probably the most relevant part of this enquiry into early years is the experience of parenting. It is the emotional tone of the relation-ships that matters: specific incidents rarely matter that much other than as points of reference. Most patients volunteer this spontan-eously when we ask them about their family: 'Dad was wonderful, we were always together, he was shy but you always knew he loved you' or 'I never really got on with Dad, hardly knew him, he was so strict I was always a little frightened.' Patients often tell us about their parents' problems – Mum was 'depressed', or 'housebound with agoraphobia' or 'arthritis', Dad was an 'alcoholic' and 'gambled'. Obviously these are major issues to be taken seriously. Most psychiatrists have learnt the hard way, however, not to jump to conclusions from such details. Some people grow up resenting, even hating, their negligent parents but others may feel very close to them and, despite all, report a happy childhood. The main purpose of the history is to gain a rich understanding of our patient's present, not to draw hasty conclusions about antecedents and causes. As we shall see later in this book these experiences may be *risk factors* but it is a mistake to conclude hastily that they are the *causes* of current problems.

School sometimes presents a very contrasting perspective to home life. Usually 'Did you have any difficulties with school?' suffices. Education and work history tell us about general abilities (both intellectual and character) that can help in coping with current problems. 'How have you been able to cope with work feeling this way and dealing with Jonathan's crises?' This *educational and employment* history also helps to understand routines and pressures but also strengths and potentials.

A *relationship and marital history* is a key part of any psychiatric history. For most of us our close, intimate relationships are the strongest influence on how we feel, on our illnesses and on our recovery. A hang-over from Freud was that my generation of psychiatrists was expected to take a detailed *psychosexual* history. The fine details of someone's sex life may occasionally be important but not usually. We will simply ask whether things are OK or if there are any problems. It is a pity that this image of psychiatrists prying into our sex lives has persisted (the old joke is that a psychiatrist is a sex maniac who failed the practical exams) because it understandably causes anxiety. So be reassured that if you consult a psychiatrist you are unlikely to be probed about sex unless you raise it. What we will ask you about is your close relationships. The effects go both ways. Psychiatric disorders affect our personal relations and our personal relationships affect our disorders. The emotional landscape for someone who has never had a boyfriend or girlfriend is very different from someone who either forms such relationships easily or has endless problems with them.

This focus on historical data may obscure the purpose of the exercise, which is to get a good understanding of what is happening just now in your life. We take a history to understand the present – not to understand the past. Consequently one of the most important parts of the assessment is asking about *marital history and current relationships*. Most of us have a 'key' relationship which is more important than any other. For many adults this is their spouse or partner but it may be a parent or child. For Alison it is Jonathan's health that appears to dominate. The person we live with is usually our most supportive, but also potentially our most stressful, relationship. Understanding it forms an essential part of the psychiatric history. For many patients discussing this is particularly complicated, a mix of gratitude, resentment, love, annoyance. We do not expect it to be simple nor to be all that logical. Psychiatrists know that most human relationships are messy, and our job makes us slow to pass judgement.

A *medical and psychiatric history* is always necessary. Alison's symptoms remind us that distinguishing between mind and body is little more than a necessary fiction. There is also an enormous overlap between physical and mental health. Those with mental illnesses have more than their fair share of physical illness. People with psychoses die fifteen to twenty years earlier than the general population, and many physical illnesses give rise to psychiatric ones. Virtually all hormone diseases directly cause psychiatric disturbances and several neurological disorders such as Parkinson's disease and multiple sclerosis routinely cause depression. Severe, long-lasting or disabling illnesses also cause depression simply because they are so exhausting and demoralizing. Equally many of the powerful drugs now in use can themselves cause psychiatric problems. Steroids and some blood pressure tablets can lower mood substantially and brief psychotic episodes or confusion can be caused by steroids and some anti-malarial and anti-Parkinsonian drugs. The potential of prescribed drugs to interact with one another and affect the mental state is particularly high in elderly patients. These may have several physical conditions being treated simultaneously when they first see the psychiatrist. So a medical history is vital.

If there has been treatment for psychiatric problems in the past then the psychiatrist will want to know about it. What was the problem, was it like now, what treatment was given, did any of it help, and what were the dates? Past responses are a good, though not infallible, guide to current ones. If Alison had suffered a similar episode after the birth of one of her children and it had recovered well with a specific antidepressant then it would be worth considering that drug again.

A *drug and alcohol history* is taken for most patients nowadays. Recreational drugs and excessive alcohol consumption are no rarity, confined to delinquent subcultures. Psychiatrists have always enquired about drugs such as cannabis, LSD and ecstasy when assessing young people with psychosis. Cannabis, amphetamine and cocaine are now extensively used by settled and 'respectable' individuals up into middle age and they can have a significant impact on mental health. The same has always been true for alcohol – it is not just the obvious alcoholic or derelict who needs to be asked. A classic mistake is to fail to ask the middle-aged lawyer, doctor or priest admitted to hospital about their drinking only for them to become seriously unwell after a few days' withdrawal.

So psychiatrists will ask about alcohol and street drugs. Most of us ask if you take them, and if so how much, rather than if you have a problem with it. I would ask Alison, 'Have you tried drinking or taking anything to get to sleep?' Most people now understand 'units of alcohol' (one small glass of wine, half a pint of beer, a pub measure of spirits) and the recommended weekly safe limits of 14 units for women and 21 for men. Asking how often you drink alcohol and how many units gives a pretty clear picture. Most people underestimate their intake, either because they pour large measures or forget to count, or because they are embarrassed to admit it. Doctors used to be told to double their patient's estimate but this is probably unnecessary in these more enlightened times. Similarly with drugs it is usual just to ask if you have been taking any and then try and get a sense of how much and how often. An accurate estimate is very difficult as dose size, strength and purity vary so much. People may be reluctant to disclose drug use, worried about legal implications, but on the whole medical confidentiality is well understood on both sides. Drugs are often adulterated and the availability of 'legal highs' means that often nobody, neither patient nor psychiatrist, really can know what is being taken. In 2012 over 600 different psychoactive substances were reported to be in circulation.

THE MENTAL STATE EXAMINATION

Assessing a patient's mental state is the signature skill of a psychiatrist just as operating is for a surgeon. It is what we must be able to do better than anyone else, otherwise there is not much point to us. The first thing to say about it is that it is not like a school examination. You will not be peppered with difficult or trick questions. The psychiatrist simply makes a thorough and structured assessment of your thoughts, feelings and behaviour. Much of it is done by careful observation using questions to refine the details. Psychiatric training emphasizes learning 'descriptive psychopathology'. This involves becoming familiar with all the unusual and strange experiences and mental processes that occur in mental illnesses. For historical reasons focusing on these mental processes in great detail is referred to as a 'phenomenology' and was most highly developed in German psychiatry.

Learning to recognize these experiences is not something that can be done from books. Many of these so-called mental 'phenomena' have to be teased out in the interview, with a sensitive use of the evolving relationship. The 'bible' of phenomenology is *General Psychopathology*, published in 1913 by the young German psychiatrist, and later philosopher, Karl Jaspers. Jaspers pointed out that the only way to get a full understanding of what is going on (which often includes processes that may not be fully conscious) requires an active *empathic* engagement with patients, a very active listening. We have to pay attention not only to what patients say, but how they say it and what they do not say. We have to observe with our feelings as well as with our intellect.

Jaspers wrote that the psychiatrist had to 'operate as a whole person'. This does not mean we abandon professional objectivity but we need to draw on wider perceptions and intuitions during our consultations, not just note down answers to questions. For example, with someone who is profoundly depressed we *feel* it. When Alison enters my consulting room I feel the tension and misery. It is not just that I observe her sad face and slow, monotonous speech – there is a palpable sense of emptiness and desolation. Psychiatrists sometimes have to assess patients who say nothing at all. It is surprising how quickly you know if this silence is an inability or a refusal; an angry or paranoid silence feels quite different to a depressed one.

The phenomenological approach places more emphasis on the form of experiences than their content. This was because Jaspers and his contemporaries were so preoccupied with that most complex of diseases, schizophrenia. Schizophrenia is recognized by characteristic disorders of thinking, perception and attribution that occur together often in subtle combinations. German psychiatrists like Jaspers and Kurt Schneider described these with wonderful clarity, giving them cumbersome German names. My generation was expected to know and use these – *vorbeireden* for talking past the point, *gedankenlautwerden* for hearing your thoughts out loud, *gegenhalten* for the active resistance to movement in catatonic patients and so forth. We now use ordinary English for these phenomena but their exotic German names serve to remind us that these are not random abnormalities. They are timeless and central features of the disease.

Much of the mental state will be gathered during the history taking, both observing how the patient is and from what he or she says. The description of the mental state that follows is very structured and organized and that is generally how it is recorded. Having a predictable approach to recording helps both in looking back to see what has changed and to communicate with others (other psychiatrists, but also other team members or the family doctor). Judgements recorded under individual headings are not made in isolation but may depend on other features for their meaning. For instance, whether a delusion is more indicative of bipolar disease or schizophrenia depends crucially on its relationship to the patient's mood. In the same way slowness of thinking would most usually be attributed to depression or obsessional disorder but would not be if the patient has more global cognitive impairments such as in dementia. The balance between observation and questioning in assessing the mental state will vary and the order in which the observations are made or questions asked should follow the course of the interview. It is unhelpful (except when just starting in training) to insist on a rigid order; much better to follow the flow of the encounter.

General appearance and behaviour describes how people behave in the interview, how they are groomed and dressed and, to some extent, their facial expressions. Most patients come in, sit down, start to tell their story and answer questions. Some, however, may be too agitated to sit still, or sit wringing their hands, others will hardly move or gesture at all or totally avoid eye contact. Alison looks anguished and exhausted. Her hair is lifeless, her mouth dry and her face tense and sad at the same time. Her clothes hang on her as she has recently lost weight and she sits fidgeting on the edge of her chair, looking down at her hands constantly tearing at a tissue.

How people behave tells us a lot about how they are feeling; as do neglecting their appearance or dressing strangely. Obviously one must avoid casual stereotyping – people vary. In our multicultural society a familiarity with the different norms of different groups in terms of both dress and self-expression is essential. Self-neglect, not washing your hair, scruffy and dirty clothes, broken nails are common when people are distracted or depressed. Weight loss, obvious from ill-fitting clothes, facial expression and appearance all speak volumes. Chronic anxiety or depression can be etched on people's faces with deeply furrowed brows or dejected, downturned mouths.

Appearance and behaviour can occasionally be diagnostic in themselves, such as in the case of an elated bipolar patient who has put on excessive make-up and garishly coloured clothes, and is noisy and effusive. More often they are simply part of an emerging picture. General appearance and behaviour are very sensitive to change and can signal early improvement or deterioration. Depressed people sometimes begin taking more care of their appearance or speaking with more animation well before they report any lifting of their mood.

There is, however, no need to feel anxious about being judged and pigeonholed on the grounds of your appearance. All comparisons between psychiatrists and the general public show that experienced psychiatrists are less likely to rate behaviour as abnormal. This is not really surprising – our job exposes us continually to such a wide variety of people and behaviour.

Speech refers more to the production of speech, its speed, volume, clarity, than its content. Depressed people may speak slowly and monotonously, agitated or elated patients may speak fast and loud with lots of emphasis and detail. Sometimes it can be hard to understand what people are saying if they speak too fast or mumble quietly. Alison spoke quietly with little emphasis, often trailing off at the end of sentences. Suspicious or paranoid people may whisper to avoid being overheard. As with appearance and behaviour these have limited diagnostic significance but are sensitive indicators of change.

Mood can be almost a diagnosis in itself (depression, anxiety, mania) and is a vital part of the mental state exam in everyone. Psychiatrists need to have a wide vocabulary to describe mood – it is not enough just to say that it is depressed or elevated. There are many mood states that most of us can recognize – agitated, perplexed, suspicious, ecstatic, angry, empty, cold, affectionate, indifferent, hostile. In addition to noting the dominant mood we usually record its character. Is it responsive to external events or is it fixed? If responsive is it sensitive or blunted, is its range restricted or extreme, is it sluggish or labile, shifting unpredictably? Alison's mood is an equal mixture of depression and anxiety. She speaks readily of her cancer fears and how she is constantly tense, watching for more signs. She talks of being jumpy and snappy. She talks less of her despondency and depression but it pervades the room and subtly colours every thought.

Confronted with a mixed picture of mood most psychiatrists place more emphasis on depression. Psychiatrists also make a judgement of how appropriate the mood seems. The classic example of this is the calm acceptance, the so-called *belle indifférence*, observed when patients with dissociative disorders (what used to be called hysteria) describe apparently crippling physical complaints. Embarrassment or extreme anxiety can cause people to laugh in strange circumstances or behave oddly but it is usually easy to recognize.

Form of thought is assessed simply by listening; only in very rare situations would you be asked any specific questions. Then it is likely to be simply 'Have you experienced any problems with your thinking?', nothing more sinister. Disorders of the form of thought are most common in psychoses, especially schizophrenia. Indeed 'formal thought disorder', which means that the logic of thinking is abnormal rather than its focus or content, is rarely found in any other condition.

There are many highly characteristic examples of formal thought disorder in schizophrenia. Very disorganized thinking can make it hard to understand patients. The form of thought can also be affected in its rate and quantity, such as in 'poverty of thought in depression,' where the mind seems slowed down or empty, and in the 'flight of ideas' in mania, when thinking leaps from one idea to another, often very fast with the words tumbling over one another in what is called 'pressure of speech'.

The *content* of thought often points accurately to pathology. Preoccupation with personal failings and imminent disaster as with Alison is common in depression, as are thoughts of suicide. In psychotic illnesses thinking may be dominated by delusions or paranoid preoccupations.

Delusions are strange, fixed ideas which are alien to the person's culture. What is most striking is usually their intensity – they have an enormous emotional hold on the patient. Their delusional quality can be very obvious, especially when they are bizarre: 'I am currently changing sex and will give birth to the messiah.' Some strange ideas may be understandable given what we know of a person; for example, some new age individuals express what are (to me) very odd ideas about lines of force and destiny. But they are not delusions; they fit perfectly within that individual's belief system. Obviously in our increasingly multicultural society one needs to be careful before labelling differing views as pathological. Alison's GP was worried that her conviction that she had cancer might be a delusion. Delusions of terminal illnesses are sometimes a feature of very severe depression so it needs to be checked. 'Your GP says you are worried about having cancer – tell me about it. What makes you so sure? Is it that you feel so awful and keep losing weight or is it that you can sense it some other way?' Delusions have a very obvious insistent and rigid quality that is striking and Alison's fears seemed to have a more normal, albeit exaggerated and pessimistic, quality. Delusions of persecution or of being very different or 'chosen' are common in psychoses, and delusions about sin and worthlessness are common in depression.

Disorders of perception will for most patients be noted, like that for thought disorder, as 'none'. It was so for Alison. For psychotic disorders, however, this may be the most detailed part of the mental state as it outlines the hallucinations and delusions that can plague such patients.

Most *hallucinations* are auditory so we ask, 'Have you been hearing voices when there is nobody speaking?' If the answer is yes a series of questions will usually follow. These aim to clarify if the voices are experienced as 'real', not just your own thoughts, which has no psychiatric significance. Most of us carry out conversations in our heads. If the voices are experienced as real voices then we want to know if they are clear ('Can you distinguish what they say?'), are there several voices or just one, who are they and then what do they say? Often voices are distressing and critical or persecutory. In schizophrenia they often talk *about* patients rather than to them and may keep up a critical running commentary. Some people hallucinate strange and unpleasant bodily sensations, and others strange smells. Visual hallucinations (seeing things) are more common than often thought but they tend to be less distinct and are overshadowed by the voices. Seeing things in the absence of auditory hallucinations is rare and may point towards organic disorders such as epilepsy or what used to be broadly called hysteria.

Hallucinations are not the only disorders of perception. Misinterpreting real sounds (bird song as coded messages, running water as mumbling conversations) is referred to as an *illusion*. There are also strange experiences that hover between hallucinations and delusions and are called *passivity experiences*. In these patients experience thoughts being withdrawn from or inserted directly into their heads. Similarly, ordinary experiences can be imbued with new and profound personal significance. In such *ideas of reference* the TV newsreader is assumed to be talking about the patient, or simple observations take on a new and unshiftable meaning: 'That girl is wearing a green pullover, which means everyone knows I am homosexual.' This phenomenon of a totally new understanding arising fully formed is referred to as *delusional perception* and Jaspers and the phenomenologists gave it great significance. It is not often encountered but is unmistakable when it is.

Cognitive function refers to the patient's ability to think and remember. Most psychiatric patients are alert and fully aware of their surroundings. Indeed if patients appear confused (which to psychiatrists means not knowing where they are or what the date is and possibly not understanding who they are), our first thoughts are of a physical disorder such as drug intoxication or a head injury. In old-age psychiatry, impaired cognitive functioning and poor memory are often cardinal features of dementia and in extreme cases this can lead to disorientation and confusion. Where there are concerns about impaired memory or cognitive function then some tests may be carried out and a full neurological examination is likely. Tests are relatively simple – asking what is in the news, who is the prime minister, to remember an address for five minutes or to subtract seven repeatedly from a hundred.

Biological features may seem a strange heading in the mental state but it has to go somewhere. Changes in sleep and appetite and energy levels are important in assessing somebody's psychiatric condition and need to be recorded clearly. These are very prominent in Alison's case. Asked about her sleep she explained that she was tired all day and fell asleep as soon as the children were in bed but invariably woke several times in the night and lay brooding about the future. In the morning she woke feeling as if she had not slept at all. She worried about her weight loss but had no appetite and had to force herself to eat anything apart from tea and biscuits. Some psychiatrists record them as part of the history and some here. What matters is that they are brought together, carefully recorded and easily found.

Insight is a global assessment based on the whole consultation. Rounding up the interview the psychiatrist will usually make some judgement about what he or she thinks the problem is and what you think it is, and will attempt to make a judgement about your *insight* into the illness and the need for treatment. For the vast majority of patients you will both agree and insight is simply recorded as 'full' or 'good'. This means that they understand the need for treatment and what it entails, but sometimes the illness can distort their understanding and patients may question or reject the psychiatrist's assessment. In extreme cases they may have simply no idea that they are ill at all and hotly deny it; this is particularly common in mania.

Insight is a tricky concept. It can be caricatured as meaning simply whether or not you agree with your doctor, with the implication that the doctor is always right. Most of us recognize that there is more to it than that. People can have very different opinions on the correct treatment for a diagnosed disorder without it implying an absence of insight. I am very sceptical about many 'alternative' treatments for mental illnesses but would not conclude that someone lacks insight because they insisted on them. I might, however, draw such a conclusion if someone insisted that *all* they needed for their schizophrenia was more rest and fresh air (excellent though both of these are). Our treatments may not always be acceptable to everyone so a rejection based on a clear understanding is perfectly compatible with full insight. Insight indicates our judgement of whether patients understand our assessment and proposals, not whether they agree with them.

PHYSICAL EXAMINATION AND INVESTIGATIONS

Psychiatrists are trained doctors and it is still taught that a physical examination is an integral part of all new psychiatric assessments. That is the theory but not the practice. In truth it is rare for a psychiatrist to conduct a full physical examination unless there is some strong indication of a complicating disorder. There are physical signs associated with several psychiatric disorders such as a fast pulse and sweating in anxiety, a slow pulse and downy body hair in anorexia nervosa. However, they are of only marginal importance in making the diagnosis. It can be reassuring for the psychiatrist to take a patient's pulse and perhaps conduct a basic neurological examination but that is about it. These words will not be welcomed by some of my colleagues keen to stress the medical nature of psychiatry. Some argue that we should exclude physical causes in every case.

However, the norm is for no physical examination, especially when patients have come from family doctors, who tend to look for organic causes first. A physical examination is, however, routine on admission to hospital and is common in the frail elderly. If an underlying physical cause is suspected then a simple physical examination may confirm whether onward referral is needed or not. My own experience of identifying physical disorders in psychiatric referrals is that it is not that rare. However, my suspicion has usually been raised by the unusual pattern of the psychiatric symptoms rather than spotting an exaggerated reflex or abnormal pupils. Most senior psychiatrists, apart from those in elderly care, do physical examinations very infrequently so it might be unwise to rely on their skills beyond signposting for more specialized investigation.

The same is true of laboratory investigations: none are done routinely at an initial psychiatric assessment. A full blood screen is usual on admission but more extensive investigations such as X-rays or magnetic resonance imaging (MRI) scans contribute little other than to the bill in private practice. For a number of specific psychiatric treatments, however, laboratory investigations are required, such as regular blood tests for patients on lithium or clozapine, and electro-cardiography (ECGs) for patients on some antidepressants and antipsychotics.

In modern psychiatry it is rare for physical causes of mental problems to go undiagnosed for any length of time. I am regularly asked by parents to arrange a brain scan to exclude a brain tumour in their son or daughter who may have been ill a decade or more. Obviously a good doctor remains alert but endless investigations rarely yield anything and they can delay a realistic adaptation to the disorder. Persisting with ineffective physical treatments and failing to diagnose psychiatric illnesses in medical settings is quite another story, and probably much more common.

The failure to diagnose and treat the physical health problems of psychiatric patients is an increasingly recognized international scandal. We know that the seriously mentally ill die about fifteen to twenty years prematurely and nearly all of this is because of raised rates of physical illness, mainly heart and lung problems and diabetes. Only a small contribution is from suicide. There is divided opinion on what to do about this. Some argue that psychiatrists should become better all-round doctors and treat the whole patient. Others consider this unrealistic, and insist that general medical services should provide more proactive treatment for these patients. Depressed or confused individuals may not seek treatment promptly and need a more structured approach. Personally I favour this latter solution; having a mental illness should not exclude you from the services used by the general public.

Some flexibility and common sense is, of course, needed. When I ran a team for very psychotic patients many simply would not go to their doctor and so we had to at least coordinate their physical treatments. A couple were so scary that the district nurse would not visit; with one we ended up giving him his daily insulin injections. Not optimal, but it worked. The newer antipsychotics make patients gain weight, raising the risks of type II diabetes and obesity, so psychiatry carries extra responsibility for having prescribed the offending drugs. Advising patients on diet and healthy living obviously falls to us but it can be argued whether the more intensive management of these conditions is best managed by us.

DIAGNOSIS AND DISCUSSION

Once your psychiatrist has finished all these questions and listening to your story she will almost certainly share her thoughts with you and ask what you make of them. As she has gone through the history she has been drawing a number of conclusions, but these are inevitably provisional. She will want to know what you make of them and if they make sense to you. New perspectives can often surface at this point, as the very process of discussion can stir up memories and awaken awareness.

Nowadays it is standard practice to tell the patient what you think the diagnosis is before outlining and discussing proposed treatments. To Alison I would say, 'I think all this worry and stress has tipped you over into a depression. Both the tension and the sadness are part of this and it is an illness that you cannot expect to just shake off. It will get better but it will need treatment and that will include antidepressants.' The letter to the family doctor summarizing the assessment, which includes the history, the diagnosis and the proposed treatment, is copied to the patient. It used to be common to 'shield' patients or families from grave diagnoses and many psychiatrists avoided even recording them in frank terms. This has virtually died out in the English-speaking world. Doctors increasingly recognize that patients have a full right to know what we think and to be equal partners in the decision-making process. It is after all your health and your body. However, in many parts of the world withholding such details is still commonplace and the family may be fully informed but not the patient.

Your psychiatrist will discuss the diagnosis with you and may discuss what she calls a 'differential diagnosis'. This means the diagnosis is not absolutely clear and although one diagnosis may be the most likely, others have to be kept in mind. Severe anxiety is a common feature in depression (as with Alison) and the psychiatrist may not be entirely sure which is the driving force. In that case she may make a differential diagnosis of general anxiety disorder with a possible underlying depression. In rare instances a diagnosis may be deferred for further clarification or to allow it to become clearer with time. Treatment options will also be discussed.

We are getting better in psychiatry, and in medicine generally, at listening to patients' preferences about treatments. This is particularly so with milder disorders in which many people have a distinct preference to avoid medication. Where sensible alternatives exist we will go along with them. In part this reflects a desire to respect individual choice but it is also pragmatism. Experience has taught us that if patients really do not want a suggested treatment then they will probably not follow it. I say, 'Where sensible alternatives exist', and that is important. If a patient with severe bipolar disorder says he or she does not want medication but wants hypnosis and herbal remedies or aromatherapy and yoga then I am unlikely to support it. I believe my professional duty includes not only informing patients of the best treatment, but also in such a case as this trying to encourage them to rethink. What happens if I fail and they insist on their plans? There are different schools of thought on this.

Some insist that we should offer our opinion and then leave it entirely up to the patient to accept it or reject it. This is fine for most patients but only the most radical insist on it for all of them. In some extreme cases we can legally overrule disagreement and oblige treatment. For severe illnesses that do not warrant such drastic action most of us strive to convince or persuade the patient. When this is unsuccessful we can do one of two things. Many older psychiatrists would 'agree to disagree' and refer such patients back to their family doctor, inviting re-referral if they change their mind.

Psychiatrists, being human, may unfortunately make it obvious to the patient that they are irritated at having their advice rejected. This is unhelpful and best avoided if possible. You are unlikely to return, even if you do change your mind, to someone who showed such impatience with you. Psychiatrists who take this approach (and there is some merit in it) argue that if they do not take a firm line they are colluding in, and thus indirectly encouraging, a course of action that is bad for the patient. By playing along they are putting themselves in a dishonest position and failing in their primary professional duty to make the best, evidence-based treatment available. They may also argue that they are 'wasting time' which could be better devoted to effective treatment for other patients. I have considerable sympathy with this position. For instance, I do not continue long-term contact with individuals whose only disorder is a severe personality disorder, even if they want it and value it. I think it misleads them about what I am capable of contributing and distracts them from finding alternative solutions to their problems.

When the illness is very severe some form of compromise is needed. If patients reject the proposed treatment but I am sure they are going to need it eventually and that they may come to recognize this over time then there may be much to gain by continuing to see them. The establishment of a trusting relationship is a fundamental building block of any long-term treatment. Current treatment approaches address a wide range of human needs, including that for companionship and support, not just 'pushing pills'. Taking a neutral stand on the value of the alternative treatments (after all, it is good that people take an active role in trying to manage their illness) you can hope to keep promoting more conventional treatment. You can also try to steer patients away from treatments that may be positively harmful and also be around to spot early deterioration.

There is currently a movement in psychiatry aiming to shift this balance even further, to prioritize the patient's view of treatment and desired outcomes. This *recovery* movement stresses that the removal of symptoms should cease to dominate the treatment process and that quality of life, personal choice and self-determination should be the cardinal goals. If patients prefer to live with their symptoms but construct a different and fulfilling way of life then that is what we should support. Most psychiatrists find little that is controversial about this.

After all, we are endlessly negotiating our treatments with patients and finding compromises. How much individuals are prepared to sacrifice to rid themselves of symptoms varies enormously in psychiatry as it does in medicine generally.

Sometimes intensive treatment to fully control symptoms may cause levels of side effects that are simply not worth it. With the older antipsychotics the trade-off between abolishing hallucinations and delusions and the side effects of stiffness and tremor was a balance worked out with each patient. Few considered completely abolishing the voices worth it if the patient ended up rigid and immobile. Cancer doctors have exactly the same discussions. Whether patients will accept the most aggressive chemotherapy depends often on just how important extending life by an extra few months is. At a practical level we have already seen that psychiatrists who do not take their patients' own wishes into consideration will achieve poor results. It pays to listen, even for the most medical-model psychiatrist.

The recovery agenda is quite diffuse and it is difficult to form a clear opinion about it. Two aspects are resisted by many psychiatrists (including this one). We are criticized for being too pessimistic about mental illnesses. There is undoubtedly some truth in this. We spend most of our working lives with those patients who do not recover fully or quickly; the more fortunate ones disappear from our clinics and get on with their lives. So it is good to be reminded that, in general, people do better than we might otherwise conclude. The recovery approach, with its emphasis on support and optimism, can seem to encourage us to be over-optimistic and mislead patients and families while most professionals consider our primary obligation is to be honest. We should weigh up the evidence as well as we can and share our conclusions with our patients so that they can make well-informed choices for themselves. It is often our fate to be the bearers of bad news. However, as medicine is not an exact science it does not stop us being hopeful and emphasizing this. In psychiatry offering support and hope are important parts of the therapeutic relationship. Personally I think this is not incompatible with honesty, but where the two do conflict then truth should prevail.

The second point of disagreement is over how much psychiatrists should 'push' their view of the correct treatment. We want patients to have the outcome they desire and lead the life they choose – we are not masters of their fate. Our limited contribution is to help them manage their illness and, sadly, we cannot always achieve even that. If we can help patients control their illness we believe they will generally be better placed to manage their lives and achieve fulfilment. So if my patient says he or she does not want the treatment I think will help, or sometimes any treatment, but wants my active support in pursuing an alternative route I am unlikely to agree for the reasons we have touched on. In practice this is far from black and white, but it is a pretty clear distinction in principle. It is an important choice and one where the recovery movement, in my opinion, seems not to have got the balance right.

What happens after this first assessment varies enormously. You may be referred back to your family doctor and have no further contact with psychiatry. In most instances, however, the psychiatrist will agree a course of treatment with you and meet you at intervals (usually between once a week and once a month) to monitor your recovery and adjust the treatment. He or she may refer you to a colleague for more specific treatment such as psychotherapy or for more intensive help and support. Social workers, nurses, occupational therapists, drug or alcohol workers, rehabilitation therapists may also become involved. Each of these is likely to ask you about your problems, perhaps not so comprehensively as in the first assessment, but often with more detail about their specialist areas.

HOSPITAL ADMISSIONS

Psychiatric treatments are people-based; they do not depend on complex equipment or facilities such as operating theatres or dialysis machines. Admission to psychiatric hospital is generally only used if people are so unwell that they need round-the-clock nursing, or if we are worried that they will not take treatment or may harm themselves. Crisis admissions, such as when people are suicidal or where we are not sure what is going on and need closer observation to decide, are often just for a few days. Most admissions for psychoses or severe depression are for a number of weeks, often a month or two, although this varies markedly between different countries.

The first few days are usually spent clarifying the situation and discussing treatments with both the nurses and doctors. Only a fraction of wards, usually one in each hospital in the UK, are 'locked' these days in the sense of being restricted. Doors are locked in most psychiatric wards in the same way they are at home: they are not left open for anyone to wander in and out. However, except in the special circumstances of compulsory care you are at liberty to come and go although the staff need to be kept informed. You will keep your own clothes and be up and about during the day either in your room or in the day rooms, or will perhaps spend time in forms of occupational therapy. You will eat your meals in the ward dining room or cafeteria. Staff will also probably have no uniforms (no nursing uniforms, no white coats for doctors), although this is still the habit in some parts of Europe. This can be confusing until you get to know people. Usually you will have a 'primary' nurse who has a special responsibility for you, meets regularly with you and helps you find your way round. Reviews of how you are doing may involve the whole team, a bit like a traditional hospital ward round. This can be rather forbidding but increasingly reviews are conducted more individually. Psychiatric units usually have liberal visiting hours and families and friends can spend long periods with you and take you out for walks or a coffee when things begin to settle. Going home for trial overnight stays is common to reassure you and the staff that improvements are durable.

In many countries acute inpatient care is 'generic'; that is, all adult admissions go to the same ward. In others there are different wards (in some German cities even different hospitals) for less ill and more ill patients. Sometimes there is specialization by diagnosis or a designated 'observation' ward for all new admissions. There are invariably different wards for children and adolescents and for the elderly and there can be other highly specialized wards. There is also a broad range of different structures (day centres, accommodation, hostels) to support people on discharge but they are so varied it would be impossible to try and summarize.

Overall visiting a psychiatrist is remarkably like visiting any other doctor. Of course it is anxiety-provoking, but you will find that psychiatrists are quite human and there really are no dark arts. The tools at their disposal are very simple, talking and listening. There is nothing to be gained by tricking you or catching you out – it is your experience and your wishes that they want to understand. I may be a bit biased, but I think psychiatrists as a group tend to be warmer, more approachable and more understanding than most doctors. We are generally less formal and less forbidding. We know how difficult life can be and are unlikely to be critical. We have seen most things and we know how hard people try to solve their problems before they come to us. We are unlikely to be shocked or moralistic and will almost certainly have come across in others what you are going through. We should be able to help you make some sense of it and obtain relief. It really is not something to be avoided.

HOW DID PSYCHIATRIC CARE EVOLVE TO THIS?

Because psychiatrists are doctors we talk about patients and illnesses and we work in hospitals and wards and outpatient clinics. So it is easy to think of psychiatry as just one more subspecialty of medicine. We readily assume that psychiatry separated out from general medicine in the same way that, for instance, cardiology or oncology have. They happened because the growth of the knowledge base made it impossible for one doctor to master it all. But it is not so. Psychiatry is like the other medical specialties but also unlike them in some quite fundamental ways.

Psychiatry was already established when it joined with medicine, it did not evolve from it. Understanding something of this history is the subject of the first section of this book and is essential for grasping how psychiatry is practised. Perhaps more importantly, knowing the history helps to make sense of the varied dilemmas and contradictions that psychiatry constantly throws up. These are the subject of the second part of this book.

PART ONE

How modern psychiatry developed

2

The origins of institutional psychiatry

Madness and mental disorder have been mankind's steady companions. We have puzzled over them and written about them since records began. However, the history of 'psychiatry' is not the same as the history of madness and mental disorder. Psychiatry is relatively young, just over 200 years old, and it has been controversial for most of those two centuries. Are psychiatric disorders (until recently called 'mental illnesses' and before that 'lunacy') illnesses like pneumonia or arthritis? Or are they just a part of an individual's unique identity? Indeed do mental illnesses 'really' exist? And if they are not like physical illnesses why do we call them illnesses? What purpose (scientific, political or personal) is served by such a terminology? Why can we force people to have treatment against their will for mental illnesses but not for physical illnesses? Such philosophical questions engage serious thinkers in heated debates in a way that does not seem to happen in dermatology or neurology or any of the other medical specialties. There is clearly something that has always been different about psychiatry.

'Psychiatry' was first coined as the name for my profession in 1808 by Dr Johann Christian Reil in Halle, in what is now Germany. Reil was very particular about the term and formed it from the two Greek words, *psyche* (soul or mind) and *iatros* (doctor). His aim was to drive home the *rational* nature of mental illness and wrest it away from philosophers and theologians. However, his insistence on 'doctor' did not imply a narrow biological or biomedical approach, far from it.

Reil's term conferred an identity on a profession which was already established and one that was rapidly expanding. Its status was confirmed by the 1840s with the establishment of several professional associations. In the UK in 1841 the Association of Medical Superintendents was founded, becoming the Royal Medical Psychological Society in 1865 and finally the Royal College of Psychiatrists in 1971. In the USA in 1844 thirteen asylum superintendents formed the Association of Medical Superintendents of American Institutions for the Insane (AMSAII) and this became the American Psychiatric Association in 1921. The German Society for Psychiatry, Psychotherapy and Nervous Diseases (DGPPN) was founded in 1842 and the first French *Journal of Psychiatry* was founded in 1843 to report the papers of its Medical-Psychological Society. So psychiatry had really come of age.

The birth of psychiatry is generally attributed to the introduction of an approach called 'moral treatment' at the end of the eighteenth century. This was ushered in with two almost simultaneous historical events. In Paris, in 1795, Philippe Pinel struck off the lunatics' chains in the Bicêtre and Salpêtrière, and in 1796 the Tukes, a Quaker family, opened the York Retreat. Both marked a decisive turning point in society's attitude towards the mentally ill. The Tukes introduced a radically different approach, which they called 'moral treatment', and which is clearly recognizable in that practised today. To grasp the importance of these momentous events we need to understand how madness was previously understood and managed.

'Madness', what we now think of essentially as psychosis, was clearly described in antiquity. Their behaviour characterized by outbreaks of disorganized and irrational speech and activity, 'mad' individuals appeared to be in the grip of violent moods or driven by inexplicable internal forces (visions, voices, Furies) which those around neither experienced nor understood. Alternatively they may have become withdrawn and distracted, neglecting themselves and their obligations. In either case the mad person seemed no longer of this world. Sometimes these episodes were self-limiting and lucky individuals were 'restored to reason' over time. Often they drifted away from their families, wandering alone, lost in a world of their own, dependent on the charity of strangers.

In these states people appear to lose contact with external reality, preoccupied with their internal voices and bizarre ideas, unlike in the group of generally less severe 'neuroses'. Neuroses only moved from physicians and neurologists to the care of psychiatrists much later, in the second half of the nineteenth century.

Hippocrates (c.460–357 BC) left convincing descriptions of both epilepsy and of some chronic behaviour disturbances which we now easily recognize as psychoses. He insisted that epilepsy was a normal illness, not a divine disorder, and he advocated a pragmatic approach to it. He located consciousness in the brain and even described operations to open the skull to release pressure on the brain from bleeding following injuries (*Treatise on Wounds in the Head*).

Hippocrates based medical theory on four humours, which had been written on in various forms since ancient Egypt. He associated each humour with natural elements, bodily organs, qualities and temperaments. His ideas were taken up and firmly established by the physician Galen (AD c.131–201) in Rome, in his book *On the Temperaments*. Enhanced in Islamic medicine by Avicenna (980–1037), their influence persisted, off and on, well into the nineteenth century.

The humoral approach sought to explain disorders of both body and mind in terms of imbalances between four constituent elements. The first humour, *blood*, was associated with air and the liver; it was warm and moist and contributed to a 'sanguine' temperament (courageous, hopeful and amorous). *Yellow bile* was associated with fire and the gall bladder; it was warm and dry and contributed to a 'choleric' temperament (easily angered, bad-tempered). *Black bile* was associated with earth and the spleen; it was cold and dry and contributed to a 'melancholic' temperament (despondent, sleepless and irritable). Lastly *phlegm* was associated with water and the brain/lungs; it was cold and moist and contributed to a 'phlegmatic' temperament (calm, unemotional). Treatments such as blood-letting, purges and enemas were developed to remove excess humours and redress their balance.

Humoral theories retained their hold in general medicine but in Europe from the Middle Ages through to the end of the eighteenth century mental disorders came under the authority of the church. Madness was considered a moral or spiritual affliction; the coarse and

---

The humours and temperaments

Blood
air and liver   warm and moist
sanguine temperament   courageous, hopeful, amorous

Yellow bile
fire and gall bladder   warm and dry
choleric temperament   easily angered, bad tempered

Black bile
earth and spleen   cold and dry
melancholic temperament   despondent, sleepless, irritable

Phlegm
water and the brain/lungs   cold and moist
phlegmatic temperament   calm, unemotional

---

disturbed behaviour of the mad showed their estrangement from grace. While many physicians still held to a humoral understanding of madness most patients were managed by well-meaning individuals and clergy with no specific training for the task. More often they were simply contained for everyone's safety. Having 'lost their reason' the mad were broadly equated with brute creatures and treated accordingly. It was assumed you could not reason with such people so they were managed either by neglect or by savage punishment and physical restraint.

Public and intellectual interest in the mad grew markedly in the seventeenth century, with increasing attention to their behaviour and containment. The controversial French philosopher Michel Foucault wrote that Europe experienced a wave of incarceration in the mid seventeenth century which he called 'the great confinement'. Two enormous *hôpitaux généraux* were opened in 1657 in Paris (the Bicêtre for men and the Salpêtrière for women). These really were enormous. The Salpêtrière housed over 10,000 inmates just before the French Revolution. They were not hospitals as we understand them but institutions that gathered together and housed all the undesirable elements of the poor of Paris. These included vagrants, prostitutes, alcoholics, petty criminals as well as epileptics and a really quite small number of the mentally ill. Foucault's book *Madness and Civilization* (1961), though long and difficult to read, remains highly influential. His thesis was that while *madness* had undoubtedly always existed, the specific identity of being a 'madman' was a new and artificial construct. Foucault believed that the constitutionally unstable French royal court needed such labels to legitimize it in locking up unruly and threatening subjects. The mentally ill were simply swept up with the rest.

The American historian David Rothman sees echoes of this in the nineteenth-century USA. In his book *The Discovery of the Asylum* (1971) he attributes their rapid expansion to the strain on the USA's social fabric from successive waves of immigration. Foucault's case is now considered rather exaggerated but there was undoubtedly a rapid growth in madhouses across Europe in the late seventeenth and eighteenth centuries. His message that the identity of 'madman' deprived individuals of a voice (it neutralized what their madness had to say of society) was taken up by the anti-psychiatrists (Chapter 8).

Most early madhouses were small establishments where members of wealthy families were secluded at their own expense. They had few, if any, aspirations to treatment or cure. Their purpose was to protect the patient from harm and the family from embarrassment. There was no qualification required to run a madhouse, although some doctors and clergy did become involved. The mentally ill were viewed as having 'lost their reason' and the reputation of practitioners depended on their ability to discipline and control them. Shackles and brutal physical punishment, including beating and whipping, were commonplace. Such treatment was considered a necessary part of management, not, as we would now assume, just a desperate last resort.

Bedlam in London was the first madhouse exclusively for pauper lunatics. Founded as a priory in 1247 it became a hospital in 1330 and admitted its first mentally ill patients in 1403. Bedlam exhibited its inmates as a popular entertainment in the eighteenth century at one penny a visit. In some years as many as 100,000 did visit, so there could be no ignorance about its practices or too much squeamishness about them. Visitors went for the ghoulish frisson but they did not feel morally compromised. The regime was recognized as horrific but not thought of as cruel. On the contrary, it was considered necessary to dampen the patients' rages, which would otherwise become uncontrollable.

King George III of England suffered several bouts of severe mental illness. Francis Willis, who treated him in 1788, demanded that he should have the same authority over the King as over any commoner, and that he be chained, whipped and threatened. He boasted of the power of his threatening gaze ('the eye') to subdue patients. He believed that a king, used to getting his own way, would need an even more forceful regime. Many of the medical cures available in the mad-houses at the time were equally awful (purging, bleeding, cold douches) but they were incidental to their main purpose – the containment and subjugation of their inmates' fury.

'Moral treatment' brings the birth of modern psychiatry. Two independent events brought about the end of the brutality of the eighteenth century for a radically more humane approach. Swept along in the reforms of the French Revolution the physician Philippe Pinel took charge of the Salpêtrière in Paris and publicly, in 1795, symbolically struck off the chains from the inmates. While there is some dispute about the exact dates and just how responsible Pinel himself was, this was a momentous and historic event. Despite his medical training, and his insistence that doctors should be in charge of the insane, Pinel came to consider the success of the new moral treatment so evident that he questioned whether there was any place for a medical or disease-based approach. He wrote: 'it gives great weight to the supposition, that, in a majority of instances, there is no organic lesion of the brain nor of the cranium'. Moral treatment was developed and established its reputation across the Channel, in England.

The driving force for reform came not from medical men but from social reformers, in particular Nonconformist religious groups such as Quakers and Unitarians. The Quakers in York founded a small establishment for the humane care of their lunatics. The York Retreat was established in 1796 by William Tuke (1732–1822), initially for thirty residents. The Tukes had been convinced by Pinel and his pupil Esquirol that a calm atmosphere, kindness and a regular routine were the most powerful forces in restoring harmony and wellbeing to the mentally ill. This 'moral therapy', or 'moral treatment' as it was soon called, was remarkably successful. 'Moral' had a different meaning in the seventeenth and eighteenth centuries, closer to what we would call 'social'. 'Moral treatment' comprised a regime of predictable social routines and relationships, infused with useful activity. It was not a set of ethical principles or religious edicts.

The Tukes were able to do away with harsh treatments altogether ('Neither chains nor corporal punishment are tolerated, on any pretext, in this establishment') and most of their early patients were discharged recovered. Kind and considerate personal relationships were the basis of the treatment. They acted to engage the patients' natural 'desire for esteem' ('The comfort of the patient is therefore considered of the highest importance in a curative point of view'). The Tukes believed that the potential for recovery lay in the patient, and that the purpose of their regime was to support and foster it. Regular work was encouraged ('Of all the attitudes by which patients may be induced to restrain themselves, regular employment is perhaps the most generally efficacious').

The York Retreat soon became internationally famous and doubled in size. It received visitors from all over Europe and the USA and was the model for the first four 'corporate asylums' on the US East Coast (so called because they were funded by public subscriptions). The Bloomingdale Asylum in New York, which opened in 1815, and the Friends Asylum in Frankford, Pennsylvania, in 1817 were strongly influenced by the Tukes. They emphasized moral treatment and deliberately insisted on having a non-medical superintendent. The McLean Hospital in Boston, which opened in 1818, followed their practices but made the historic, and possibly fateful, decision of choosing to have a physician in charge.

The spread of moral treatment in the USA stalled with the opening of the Hartford Retreat in Connecticut in 1824. While modelled physically on the York Retreat, it was medically led and emphasized medical interventions (predominantly opium and morphine for calming patients). Its vigour and successes led to a transformation in the other corporate asylums and it became the new model for the rapid expansion of the state hospital programme in the USA.

WHAT BROUGHT ABOUT THIS CHANGE?

The momentous change in practice ushered in by moral therapy seems so obvious and humane to us now that the question is not so much why it happened, but why did it not happen earlier? The harsh treatment of the mentally ill induced revulsion in many circles. Hogarth's prints of Bedlam and Goya's painting of a madhouse are clearly not dispassionate observations; in England there was widespread outrage about the treatment of King George III, a popular and sympathetic figure. Andrew Scull, a leading historian of psychiatry, acknowledges the importance of the humanitarian Quaker tradition, but places their action in a much broader social movement. Fundamental changes were sweeping through society, affecting its attitude towards all marginalized groups. Reforms affected not just insanity but also the upbringing of children and the running of prisons and schools. Their high-water mark was in the Slave Trade Act 1807, leading to its eventual abolition in 1833. The same group of influential public figures was involved in all these reform movements.

Scull sees the rise of industrialization and capitalism as the driving force. These obliged a fundamental re-evaluation of man's agency in society. Men could now shape their lives, most obviously their environment and their working conditions, rather than simply follow an established order. Men (people) were capable of change. Indeed they *had* to change. Their lives were no longer determined by the cycle of sowing and harvesting or their ordained place in a feudal or divinely ordered society. They could respond to new, man-made imperatives and they had choices. Industrial workers also required more sophisticated training. To become reliable they had to internalize the same motivations (money) as their employer, and they had to acquire the necessary flexibility to earn it. Punishment and force were simply not effective: skilled workers could always find a more congenial employer.

These changes were widespread. The philosopher John Locke had written of the need of education to develop children's 'sense of emulation and shame' rather than simply beating obedience into them, which echoes the Tukes' observations.

It is the recognition that man's nature is to some extent malleable that is so revolutionary. Previously man's reason was a unitary given in a fixed universe. Reason was what distinguished him from brute creation, the external marker of his soul. It was what raised him above lower creatures in the 'great chain of being'. If you had reason you were human, you had a soul; if not, you were an animal, a brute. Slaves and the mentally ill were thought not to have reason and so forfeited any call on our common humanity. They could and, it went, they should be treated accordingly.

Scull argues that recognizing that people could train and improve their reasoning shattered this simplistic view that reason was an unchanging given. Children, criminals, slaves, the mentally ill, the new thinking ran, may lack some of our finer qualities but they are not totally bereft of reasoning. They have a soul and can respond to kindness and encouragement. This insight made the brutal treatment of these individuals seem not only inefficient but morally repugnant and indefensible. Scull's interpretation is highly persuasive and helps us understand why society was so receptive to this thinking. It does not, in any way, diminish the importance of what Pinel and the Tukes contributed. Throughout psychiatry's history we will see how powerful and charismatic figures (Pinel, Kraepelin, Freud, W. H. R. Rivers, R. D. Laing) embody a growing awareness but whose force of character contributed to radical changes in our thinking.

THE ASYLUM ERA

These new ideas about mental illness were converted into bricks and mortar. The nineteenth century witnessed an unparalleled investment in the building of asylums for the insane. In the UK this expansion occurred in four waves, following the County Asylum Acts of 1808 and 1828, the Lunatics Act of 1845 and the Lunacy Act of 1890. The Poor Law Amendment Act of 1834 prohibited parishes from providing support to its impoverished members in their own homes; they could only receive aid in institutions such as the workhouse or asylum.

The enormous reach of this building programme has to be seen in the context of its time to be properly appreciated. A 'county rate', essentially a local tax, was established to build and maintain the asylums and to ensure quarterly inspection. They were to be located in an '. . . airy and healthy situation but able to afford the probability of medical assistance'. They provided board, lodging and care without charge when no such guarantee was available for the physically ill. They were built away from the pestilential squalor of Victorian city slums with separate male and female wings and included day rooms and gardens. The 'convalescent' patients were separated from the 'incurable'. Between 1811 and 1842 sixteen such county asylums were built in England.

An equivalent movement in the USA saw the establishment of the four 'corporate' asylums on the East Coast between 1815 and 1824, setting the stage for the state hospital building programme. Worcester County Hospital, Massachusetts, and Utica Hospital, New York, were early, influential models. The USA movement was encouraged by the highly optimistic, somewhat exaggerated claims of the corporate asylum superintendents. These men talked up their results to generate income but also to encourage investment in the state hospitals. 'The expense incurred in making a proper provision for this class of paupers is a very profitable investment' (Pennsylvania, 1845). State hospitals were also needed so that the corporate asylums would not be overrun with unprofitable pauper patients whose recovery was less predictable. Dorothea Dix (1802–87) was the USA's leading advocate for investment in mental health care. She had enormous influence and really was remarkably optimistic – 'All experience shows that insanity reasonably treated is as certainly curable as a cold or a fever.'

Early asylums have been criticized for serving patients' needs less than they served society's need for control. These criticisms usually assume that asylums swept up the mentally disordered from society and hid them from view. In truth most of the mentally disordered had already been swept up in one way or another. Most were in workhouses or prisons, where they spectacularly failed to fit in: 'sending pauper lunatics to workhouses and prisons is . . . highly dangerous and inconvenient' (1808 County Asylums Act). Rather than a massive confinement this may be one of the first examples of 'transinstitutional-ization' (moving individuals from one form of incarceration to another), still a major concern in our era of community care (Chapter 7).

Asylums were originally fairly domestic establishments housing 50–80 patients each but rapidly expanded as the building programme took off. There were 1,046 patients in English country asylums in 1827, 7,000 by 1850, 74,000 by 1900 and 140,000 by 1930. The census peaked at 155,700 in 1955. The first sixteen British asylums contained about a hundred patients each but by the 1840s they averaged 300. Hanwell, the largest and most prominent, was home to over 800 patients. By the 1870s the average population of an asylum was 540 and by 1900 had reached 960. In the USA the building programme, which started later, was even more energetic, producing over 300 institutions in less than a century. In 1840 there were only eighteen asylums but by 1880 there were 139. Initially the US Association of Asylum Superintendents only approved hospitals to a maximum of 250 beds but by 1875 the average USA asylum had a population of 432 and about a third housed between 500 and 1,300. By 1948, 261 state hospitals alone accommodated 539,000 patients, which gives an average of over 2,000 each.

This expansion was driven partly by population growth but more by changes in the definition of who needed care. The dwindling of effective social and family support in mobile urban populations, and the accumulation of chronic and untreatable cases added to the increase. Morale suffered. Many asylums lost their therapeutic ambitions and became effectively 'warehouses' for the chronically insane. Investment in maintenance fell with deterioration in the fabric of the buildings (particularly during the two world wars). Improvements in care between the wars with the admission of many voluntary patients (Chapter 5) also contributed to overcrowding.

One of the most striking features of the asylum-building programme is its characteristic architecture. The Tukes took the design of their building very seriously: they believed it could help their patients to feel good about themselves. Early asylums were built on a grand scale befitting their high moral purpose. The Tukes also used asylum structure to organize care, separating settled from disturbed patients. This not only provided a more suitable environment in which to recover but was soon recognized as a potent tool to shape behaviour. By being more compliant patients could hope to move to the more comfortable areas; similarly those in these convalescent areas knew that disruption would return them to the disturbed units. This thinking clearly demonstrates the momentous change that had taken place. It is now taken for granted that the mentally ill, even the very disturbed, can distinguish these differences and make decisions for themselves. The tiny York Retreat was essentially domestic in spirit. It resembled in many ways a large country house shared between staff and patients, with the same distinct upstairs–downstairs social divisions customary at that time.

The architecture of asylums soon became a subject of careful thought. Luther Bell, quoted by Dorothea Dix in 1850, expounded: 'An asylum or more properly a hospital for the insane ... [is] an architectural contrivance to meet its specific end. It is emphatically an instrument of treatment.' George Paget topped this in 1866, calling them 'the most blessed manifestation of true civilisation the world can present'. Two major styles developed to replace the domestic York Retreat. The first was a corridor design and then, as asylums grew even larger, the pavilion or villa design.

Corridor design asylums were initially built around the superintendent's residence but expanded to become enormous edifices. Characteristically they stretched out as two impressive symmetrical wings (one male and one female) from a central reception hall. The façade of Colney Hatch Lunatic Asylum, opened in north London in 1851, was a third of a mile long. Domes, turrets and towers were very much favoured, and in later examples the combined water tower and furnace chimney became a distinctive feature.

In the USA this design was called the 'Kirkbride Plan' after the superintendent of the Philadelphia State Hospital. USA asylums were much bigger, often the biggest buildings in their neighbourhoods. The New Jersey State Asylum, opened in 1876, had the largest continuous foundation of any building in America until the Pentagon seventy years later. State hospitals were prestigious projects and rural communities competed to attract them. Their construction, and then their staffing, brought employment and prosperity. Invariably the major employer in their local communities, they were often the *only* employer. The cost of running asylums was staggering, usually between 20 and 25 per cent of the total revenues of an American state or a British county. They were often the most significant single item of expenditure.

Asylums were so similar that they could have all been by the same architect. As a junior doctor I found it spooky how easy it was to find my way round when I moved between such hospitals. Walking into the main entrance hall of a new hospital I seemed to know instinctively which way to turn to find the dining hall or the male admission ward. A disadvantage of this design was the need for long, echoing corridors. Friern Barnet Hospital in London had one unbroken corridor half a mile long and Colney Hatch Hospital had six miles of corridors in total. As hospitals became overcrowded the corridors were often used as day rooms.

With increasing size the corridor structure became impractical. By the turn of the twentieth century the largest asylums were built as a series of pavilions or villas, reflecting then current thinking on the classification of patients. As with the corridor hospitals, acute patients were housed near the front and more chronic or disturbed individuals progressed step-wise towards the back and periphery. Here they were increasingly neglected in what came to be called 'back wards'. Many corridor asylums were repeatedly expanded with additional buildings and lost their coherence and symmetry, ending up like untidy rabbit warrens.

This steady increase in size of asylums planted the seed of their eventual destruction (Chapter 7). Decent psychiatric care, indeed any decent care, is a personal and individual process and increasingly difficult in impersonal 'factory-like' institutions. In the USA, especially, scale got completely out of control. The photographer Christopher Payne has collected a beautiful, evocative record of these buildings (*Asylum: Inside the Closed World of State Mental Hospitals*) that conveys their huge size. Many state hospitals contained several thousand patients. Milledgeville in Georgia had over 10,000 and Pilgrim State Hospital, New York, holds the sorry record with over 13,000.

Whether such asylums' façades looked grand and impressive or gloomy and foreboding depended on your mood and on the weather.

Inside, by the end of the twentieth century, they were invariably oppressive and gloomy. They were, however, very well built and have proved enormously difficult to adapt. Inappropriate for mental health care in the second half of the twentieth century, most have been sold off and converted to apartments or knocked down.

CURE OR CONTROL?

As asylums increased in size they acquired many more severely ill patients who became long-stay and it became increasingly difficult to maintain the early ambitions. Although there was no return to active punishment with beating or the use of chains, straitjackets and belts were routine. In the 1840s a 'non-restraint' movement committed to treating patients without such mechanical restraints arose in England. This became one of the defining features of the British system then, and remains so today. It was controversial from the beginning and the first motion passed by the USA Superintendents' Association in 1844 was 'It is the unanimous sense of this convention that the attempt to abandon entirely the use of all means of personal restraint is not sanctioned by the true interests of the insane.'

The non-restraint movement is attributed to John Conolly, superintendent of the Hanwell Asylum in west London from 1839 to 1845. Conolly learnt it from Robert Gardner Hill in the Lincoln Asylum in 1838 but it was Conolly's charismatic advocacy that spread the policy. Conolly was a strange character with an unsuccessful career as a general practitioner, including a brief, disastrous, spell as a professor of medicine, before being appointed medical superintendent at Hanwell in 1839 on his second attempt. Throughout his life he was remarkably inconsistent in belief and practice, changing his opinions as his circumstances dictated. His one major publication (*An Inquiry Concerning the Indications of Insanity*, 1830) was a scathing attack on the asylum movement:

> ... confinement is the very reverse of beneficial. It fixes and renders permanent what might have passed away and ripens eccentricity or temporary excitement or depression, into actual insanity.

46

Who has the strength . . . to resist the horrible influences of the place? A place in which a thousand fantasies, that are swept aside almost as soon as formed in the healthy atmosphere of our diversified society, would assume shapes more distinct: a place in which the intellectual operations could not but become, from mere want of exercise, more and more inert; and the domination of wayward feelings more and more powerful.

Hanwell was at that time the largest asylum in England and had a very high profile because of its position in London, still the world's most populous and richest city. The asylum was also in a state of near chaos because of administrative in-fighting. Conolly was an immediate success. He was supportive of his staff and within a year had essentially done away with restraints, resulting in a calmer and more harmonious institution. He went further, liberalizing the regime with social activities and greater freedom for patients. His practice was publicized in the medical journal *The Lancet* and he became the protégé of the great social reformer Anthony Ashley-Cooper (later Lord Shaftesbury). Lord Shaftesbury was to become the driving force in UK asylum reform and legislation. By 1844 Conolly was a national figure, receiving various awards and visited by alienists from around the world. Conolly's later life was as full of paradox as his earlier life, and far from distinguished. However, his influence has been enduring. Physical restraints are still in widespread use in Europe, the USA and the developing world, but their absence in any form remains a distinctive feature of British mental health care and systems developed from it, such as in Australia and New Zealand.

The early Asylum Acts obliged local authorities to provide for the care of the mentally ill. As the asylum movement gathered momentum and the threshold for admission fell, public concerns settled on fears of unjust incarceration. There had long been such concerns about private madhouses, that families would seize wealth by getting relatives declared insane. There were fears that asylums could also be exploitative and repressive.

John Thomas Perceval was the son of Britain's only assassinated Prime Minister, Spencer Perceval, shot through the heart in the lobby of the House of Commons in 1812 by a mentally ill man. John himself spent three years in private asylums and was no admirer. He wrote in 1845: 'The glory of the modern system is repression by mildness and coaxing, and by solitary confinement.' He was one of the founders of the exotically named 'Alleged Lunatics' Friends' Society'. This aimed to prevent or challenge unjustified certification and it attracted wide public and parliamentary support. Georgina Weldon ('a spirited, attractive, wealthy and well-connected woman') filled London's Covent Garden Opera House in 1883 with a rally challenging her committals and won her case in the courts. Growing public suspicion of psychiatry resulted in the 1890 Lunacy Act. This restricted admissions with so many bureaucratic safeguards that early intervention and treatment became almost impossible for the next half-century. This ambivalence about asylums (strong public support for them as a humanitarian endeavour but deep suspicion about those who run them) remains characteristic of psychiatry to this day. The tricky challenge of balancing therapeutic ambitions with civil liberties is further explored in Chapters 7 and 10.

WHY DID DOCTORS TAKE OVER?

Moral treatment and the asylum movement have shaped this chapter because they were the essential precursors to modern psychiatry. They identified the mentally ill as a specific group deserving special attention and brought them together for care. As a result detailed knowledge of the nature of disorders was acquired and theories about the underlying processes were developed. The USA and particularly the UK (an early centralized nation state with unified practice and legislation) have served our purposes so far as pioneers in the field of asylum building. However, the development of psychiatry as a profession, and its intellectual flowering, takes us to mainland Europe, in particular to France and the German-speaking states.

Asylum psychiatry gained the status of a legitimate medical specialty in the second half of the nineteenth century. It achieved this by careful descriptions of disorders and efforts to group them into consistent diagnoses. These diagnoses were then used to develop and test treatments. Inevitably most early effort went into description and classification. Theoretical elaboration was fairly minimal and treatments few and generally ineffective. Most psychiatrists considered that some vague disturbance of the brain or nervous system was responsible for mental disorders. Heredity was the commonest explanation and 'degeneration' the mechanism in the absence of obvious infection or injury. Psychiatrists were trained essentially as neurologists, and joint training with neurology persists still in much of central Europe.

Initially France and the German states were on a par but the Germans soon came to dominate. This may be a consequence of the competitive relationships between the independent German princely states. Each had its own capital, its own opera house, orchestra and university, which have survived the establishment of a unified German nation in 1871. The roll call of German-speaking psychiatrists is truly breathtaking – Griesinger, Morel, Alzheimer, Kraepelin, Bleuler, Freud, Jung. It justifies its claim to be the birthplace of both scientific and clinical psychiatry. Leading German psychiatrists increasingly worked and taught in university clinics while their UK and US counterparts were still based in asylums. Berlin appointed the first professor of psychiatry (Griesinger) in 1864 and by 1882 there were six German professors. In the USA the drive to link psychiatry to medical schools started in the 1890s and the first professors were appointed just before the First World War. Adolph Meyer was professor of psychiatry in Cornell from 1904 to 1909 before moving to the Johns Hopkins Medical School in Baltimore. Harvard established a chair in 1912. Edinburgh established a chair of psychiatry in 1918 but England came very late to the game and appointed its first two in 1946, one in Leeds and one at the Maudsley Hospital, London.

In centralized France things happened in Paris or, with the exception of Nancy, hardly at all. In Paris the great neurologist Jean-Martin Charcot (1825–93) commanded an international reputation with his work on hysteria. French research into dissociation and the unconscious is probably its greatest contribution to nineteenth-century psychiatry (Chapter 3). Since that time France, despite its distinguished history, has become surprisingly isolationist. It has recently only had a limited impact apart from the discovery of the first antipsychotic drug, chlorpromazine, in 1952 (Chapter 7).

Emil Kraepelin (1856–1926) is often called the father of modern psychiatry. His great contribution was to describe the course of the major psychoses and to differentiate schizophrenia (then called 'dementia praecox') from manic-depressive disorder. The importance of this rather crude classification, which is frequently challenged but never abandoned, should not be underestimated. Careful classification is an essential first step to finding effective treatments. It also allowed psychiatrists to distinguish what we would now consider 'true' mental illnesses from the wide range of physical disorders such as intoxications, dementias and syphilis which accounted for a substantial proportion of asylum inmates. These two major disorders were referred to as 'functional psychoses' because no obvious anatomical disease could be found, so consequently they were thought to be disorders of brain 'function'. They formed the bulk of the asylum population (and still do). If these two illnesses did not exist I doubt if psychiatry would exist.

Kraepelin distinguished between the two psychoses by how they developed over time rather than by their symptoms. The symptoms were highly variable and could be found in individuals with either disorder. Individuals with dementia praecox came into hospital early, often very disturbed with a range of bizarre delusions (false beliefs) and hallucinations (voices and visions) and over time developed a marked withdrawal from normal interaction. While these symptoms fluctuated over time, patients hardly ever fully recovered. Kraepelin's view was that schizophrenia, as it came to be called, usually followed an episodic or chronic downward course. Those with manic depression, on the other hand, had a different pattern to their illness. They might be just as desperately ill and disturbed on admission, but generally recovered fully. They were usually discharged, even if often readmitted.

Kraepelin made his observations while working in the asylum in Dorpat in what is now Estonia. He had had to take the job, abandoning his university research position, because he had recently married and he needed the money (the same circumstances shaped the career of his illustrious peer Sigmund Freud). Kraepelin was not fluent in his patients' language, so as he was unable to make careful examinations of their symptoms, he took to recording in detail the changes in their behaviour over time and thus made his epoch-defining discovery. He returned to professorial posts in Heidelberg (1891–1903) and Munich (1903–20) and he became a towering figure. A tireless evangelist for the temperance movement, he was a puritanical and forbidding individual. His textbook *Lehrbuch der Psychiatrie* (1893) remained in print for decades, going through eight editions.

Kraepelin's view of schizophrenia is now considered overly pessimistic. To some extent this was the result of working exclusively with very severely ill inpatients. He had no direct experience of those schizophrenia patients whose illnesses resolved without hospital admission; nor did he fully register those who got better and left. He would anyway, having made his mind up, have excluded them from his diagnosis on the grounds of their recovery.

Eugen Bleuler (1857–1939) first coined the term schizophrenia in 1911. He introduced a more balanced, less gloomy, estimate of its prognosis. Bleuler worked in the Burghölzli Hospital in Zurich, the Swiss canton of his birth. Unlike Kraepelin he was a very approachable individual and spent a lot of time talking with his patients (his sister was a patient in the hospital, possibly suffering with schizophrenia). His description of schizophrenia was based on his attempt to understand his patients' experiences and he listened carefully to what they said. He believed schizophrenia was a breakdown in the individual's sense of personal identity and integration with the outer world. It was this disruption rather than hallucinations or delusions that mattered most. It was characterized by what subsequently came to be called 'Bleuler's four As', *autism* (withdrawal), *ambivalence* (lack of motivation), *affect* (mood disturbances) and *association* (disordered thought with bizarre associations between words).

Hallucinations and delusions have since become key to the diagnosis of schizophrenia but Bleuler considered them only secondary elaborations. They were attempts by patients to understand, and explain to themselves and others, the more fundamental disturbances of their shattered sense of identity and functioning. This was the true core of the illness. Bleuler believed that a significant proportion of schizophrenia patients did recover, and some fully.

Neither Kraepelin nor Bleuler settled psychiatry's classificatory disputes but they did lay the foundations for the investigation of major mental illnesses that continues today. Whether their broad categories serve us better than the increasingly fine-grained divisions that characterize twenty-first-century psychiatry remains a live issue. While distinguishing between these disorders remains controversial it is dwarfed by the controversy of defining the boundary between these acknowledged mental illnesses and normal human variation. These issues will be further explored in Chapter 11.

Asylums persisted through the first half of the twentieth century, through two world wars, until changes in psychiatric practice and changes in society and its values rendered them anachronistic and irrelevant. They peaked in the 1950s with over 150,000 patients in the UK and over 550,000 in the USA. Asylums then began their inexorable decline with psychiatry's move into the community (Chapter 7).

Both wars had important impacts on psychiatry and the asylums (picked up in Chapter 6) and they disturbed comfortable orthodoxies. Between the wars asylums were not static. Indeed they experienced a mini-revolution with the introduction of new and dramatically effective specific interventions. New treatments generated a confidence and enthusiasm that were responsible for a radical and permanent change in psychiatry's view of itself and the wider world's opinion of it. The torpor of the asylum was energized and staff had things to do. A more active, optimistic atmosphere was generated with closer relationships with the general hospital. They began to erode the extreme isolation of the asylums.

The return of peace after the Second World War spelt the beginning of the end for the asylum. Not surprisingly after 150 years of building and investment its demise was not sudden but has taken several decades. Advances in treatment played a part in the demise but they are far from the whole of the story. Changes in social attitudes, improved communication, welfare provision and education all contributed.

Within ten years of the Second World War the seemingly inexorable rise in the number of psychiatric inpatients reversed, falling to less than a third of what they were. We have witnessed the closure or the radical transformation of nearly all these vast edifices that once dotted our landscape and which dominated my profession. Despite their undoubted magnificence and the part they played in the origins of humane psychiatric care, there are few who now seriously regret their passing.

3

The discovery of the unconscious

The impact of the Enlightenment on mental health care was not restricted to the introduction of more humane and rational care in asylums. The end of the eighteenth century also saw the defeat of centuries of belief in demonic possession as a cause of mental illnesses. Prayer and exorcism had been the widely accepted methods for treating mental disturbances across Europe. Exorcisms were often brutal affairs sometimes involving beatings, and still persist in some isolated and superstitious societies. They can involve physical punishment, or administering drugs to make the patient violently sick or delirious. The rationale behind this approach was (and is) to make the patient's body and mind too uncomfortable for the devil assumed to possess them and thus to 'drive it out'.

In the late eighteenth century reliance on prayer and exorcism gave way to a series of treatments based on suggestion and hypnosis. From what now seem like bizarre and superstitious beginnings the foundations of modern depth psychology and psychotherapy were laid. These have had far-reaching consequences for the treatment of neurotic illnesses and also for our understanding of ourselves. It started with one of the most remarkable men in the history of psychiatry, if not of the whole of medicine, Franz Anton Mesmer.

Whenever we say that something is 'mesmerizing' or that someone 'mesmerizes' us we recall the German physician Mesmer. Between his humble origins in Swabia in what is now Germany in 1734 and his death in nearby Meersburg in 1815 he was to marry a wealthy noblewoman, become an international celebrity, introduce a revolutionary treatment and be branded a charlatan. He became the highest-paid doctor of his time, but was hounded out of Paris to die in obscurity two decades later. Mesmer rose to fame by challenging the work of Johann Joseph Gassner, a Munich priest with a towering reputation as a healer and exorcist. Gassner was renowned for distinguishing normal from paranormal disorders, most of which we would now recognize as emotional or 'hysterical' conditions.

The two most common forms of such disorders were 'the vapours' in women (fainting and fits) and 'hypochondriasis' in men (depression and irritability). Wide-ranging symptoms such as paralyses, seizures, blindness or periods of inexplicable behaviour caused enormous distress and suffering, often in relatively young patients. Gassner used a well-established exorcism process with three stages. First he called forth the symptoms to connect with the devil, then gained control of the devil, before finally casting it out.

Mesmer had moved to Vienna in 1768 after his marriage. He became convinced that he could treat such disturbances by what he called 'animal magnetism'. He successfully treated a Fräulein Osterlin in 1774 by getting her to swallow an iron-rich drink with magnets attached to her body. She reported experiencing 'currents', which Mesmer attributed to animal magnetism. He considered himself richly endowed with this power and he thought of it as a 'fluid'. Mesmer elaborated a theory about his cures which was based on the use of magnets plus his own personal influence. This involved redistributing his patients' magnetic fluids, leading to a crisis followed by a cure. We now easily recognize the process of hypnosis and suggestion in the detailed descriptions of his practice, which came to be called 'Mesmerism'.

Mesmer was called to Munich in 1775 to give evidence on Gassner's methods and emerged the clear victor in a public test of their approaches. While both theories may sound equally implausible to us now, there was a critical difference in their interpretations of the seizure that was central to both techniques. Gassner viewed the seizure (or 'crisis') as diagnostic. It was evidence of demonic possession and provided the justification for his efforts to drive the devil out. Mesmer, on the other hand, thought that the crisis was itself the treatment, that it relieved the disorder. Henri Ellenberger (who wrote the authoritative, but lengthy, text on this period, *The Discovery of the Unconscious*, 1970) considers this confrontation between Gassner and Mesmer as decisive for the future development of dynamic psychiatry. Mesmer represented the rational, sceptical thinking of the Enlightenment age with an emphasis on enquiry and empiricism. Although Mesmer's theory and practices seem frankly ludicrous to us today, they were revolutionary in that they relied on no 'higher power'. His was a normal, not a paranormal or divine, process. His victory was a blow against an established theological order and the received wisdom. Gassner rapidly faded into obscurity while Mesmer rocketed to fame (albeit with some setbacks).

The first of these setbacks was a high-profile failure to cure a prominent and well-connected blind musician, Maria-Theresia Paradis. Mesmer was humiliated and in 1778 fled to Paris, where after a brief period, possibly of depression, he re-established himself. By 1782 he was back at the peak of his success and fortune, an eighteenth-century medical celebrity. He had now abandoned the use of magnets altogether and relied on his own natural 'animal magnetism'. He had so many wealthy patients he could not treat them all individually and developed a bizarre group treatment for up to twenty at a time. Each patient held an iron rod reaching from a central urn called a *baquet* to the parts of their bodies thought to be afflicted. Assistants helped with the crises and the atmosphere was enhanced with eerie music from a 'glass harmonica' (graduated glass bowls rubbed with a wet finger). He was nothing if not a showman.

With individual patients Mesmer sat opposite them, fixing them with his gaze and making 'passes' with his hands along their bodies and pressing their abdomen and hands. This generated strange experiences and sometimes convulsions. Sessions were often very protracted and his presence was experienced as enormously charismatic. Mesmer believed that the currents he generated in his patients overcame obstacles and blockages to the normal flow of magnetic fluids. He believed this flow was necessary for health.

Mesmer's methods seem like so much hocus-pocus today but they were a radical break with a superstitious past. His approach relied on supporting the body's natural healing processes. Animal magnetism was no supernatural phenomenon: it was a perfectly normal quality, though not equally distributed. Some people, such as Mesmer himself, had more than did others. No higher powers were invoked. If we substitute current concepts such as 'tension', 'stress' or 'libido' for his 'magnetic fluid' then it does not seem so strange or offputting. A highly dramatic treatment to unblock trapped energy providing relief by catharsis makes perfect sense to modern thinking. Mesmer was very aware that a strong relationship of trust (which he called *rapport*) was an essential part of his treatment. His patients had to have faith in him and they had to have faith in the treatment for it to work.

The dramatic nature of the treatment, the obvious impact of Mesmer's charisma and the suggestibility of his patients all led to repeated accusations that he was a charlatan. In 1784 the clamour became such that Louis XVI convened a Royal Commission (including the American ambassador to Paris, Benjamin Franklin) into Mesmer's methods. They concluded that there was no magnetic fluid but they did acknowledge that he achieved cures ('probably by imagination'). Scandals continued to beset him, culminating in a furore when his earlier nemesis, Maria-Theresia Paradis (still blind), came to perform in Paris. He fled the scene in dismay and gradually faded from the stage.

Hypnosis was gaining ground beyond Mesmer, away from the glitterati of Vienna and Paris. In rural France the Marquis de Puységur (1751–1825) was working with 'the new magnetism' during the 1780s. Although he always considered himself a faithful disciple of Mesmer, de Puységur's practice and thinking evolved rapidly. He repeatedly hypnotized one of his family employees, the 'easily magnetized' 23-year-old Victor Race, and induced a special state that he called a 'perfect crisis'. In this Victor was calm and appeared awake, lucid and responsive, what we would now call a hypnotic trance. On awaking from it he had no memory of what had taken place and de Puységur called this state 'artificial somnambulism'. During it his patient often displayed remarkable understanding of his personal difficulties, insights denied to him in his normal waking state. Victor could be induced to do things in his waking state following instructions during the trance (what we now call 'post-hypnotic suggestion'). While in a trance Victor Race described an intractable, distressing problem in his relationship with his sister and de Puységur gave him suggestions on what to do about it. Victor acted on these suggestions when awake although unaware of having received them. Relations with his sister did, indeed, improve.

De Puységur attracted many patients but, unlike Mesmer, he worked with ordinary, often uneducated, people rather than the wealthy. He rapidly became aware of the dependency that repeated trances could cause and he was concerned from the beginning about the erotic risks. Like Mesmer he experimented with group treatments, though his more modest patients sat round an elm tree linked with ropes to the branches. Unlike Mesmer he avoided self-publicity and showmanship and rejected all talk of fluids. He insisted that Mesmerism relied entirely on the *desire of the patient* to enter the trance and the *belief of the therapist* that he had the power to induce it. He understood that this was an *interpersonal therapy* based on suggestibility. His practice and theory are really quite in tune with ideas we use today. Strip it of its strange language and elegant eighteenth-century aristocratic French trappings and it would easily find its place among current alternative therapies.

De Puységur's fame and practice spread widely throughout France and beyond. His society to train magnetizers and provide free treatment had grown to over 200 members in 1789, when it was abruptly shattered by the French Revolution. As an aristocrat de Puységur was imprisoned for two years but subsequently freed to return to his experiments and writing. He was considered the true father of Mesmerism in nineteenth-century France.

Jean-Martin Charcot's use of hypnosis in the treatment of hysteria in Paris in the 1880s is such a celebrated episode in psychiatry that it is easy to overlook Mesmer's and de Puységur's work. We should not dismiss it as simply an exotic interlude or primitive precursor to modern psychiatry. Theirs was the essential foundation, the break with the past. Theirs was the paradigm shift equivalent to Pinel's and Tuke's moral treatment for the mad. Like Pinel and Tuke the magnetizers demonstrated that the capacity for recovery lay within the mentally disordered individuals themselves. Like them, Mesmer and de Puységur rejected supernatural explanations and emphasized natural processes.

The magnetizers had, however, done more than just move from a religious or supernatural understanding to one built on experience. They had established that we have ideas and memories of which we are not conscious. Indeed, that there are different states of consciousness. Victor Race had no memory of events during his 'magnetic sleep' when he was awakened and yet fully recalled them when next in a trance. There were things he was aware of only in his trance, such as the problems caused by his conflict with his sister. He could even be made to act on these by post-hypnotic suggestion still without conscious understanding of why he was doing so.

The radical nature of these findings and their implications are all too easy for us to overlook in the twenty-first century. An indivisible consciousness was the dominant philosophical touchstone for man's identity at that time. Descartes's 'Cogito ergo sum' ('I think therefore I am') says as much about the 'I' as it does about the thinking. If conscious thought is the essence of being a human how could 'humanness' exist in any form without conscious thought? Even more confusing, how could the same person be simultaneously conscious and not conscious? The early foundations for Charcot's and Janet's celebrated work in Paris at the end of the nineteenth century, and even for Freud's psychoanalysis, had been laid.

In the next half-century hypnosis continued to be practised and investigated mainly in France and the German-speaking states. In Britain and America it met considerable resistance. Despite this it was a British physician, James Baird, in 1843 in Manchester, who first called it 'hypnosis' because of what he saw as its similarity to sleep (*hypnos* in Greek). Baird popularized the technique of focusing steadily on a single light source such as a candle. In the 1840s there were even British reports of surgical procedures performed under hypnosis (over 300 in India), but with the introduction of anaesthesia that particular interest faded.

In the German states a national commission on hypnosis was convened in 1812 and professorial chairs in Mesmerism were established in 1816. This enthusiasm was intimately bound up with the then current German Romanticism, a preoccupation with a 'World Soul' and a belief that there was something much richer and more mysterious behind life's material façade. Hypnosis became more a branch of experimental metaphysics than a therapy. In America hypnosis was rapidly hijacked by the spiritualist movement centred on rural New York in the 1840s, and arrived in Europe in the 1850s. The spiritualist movement's association with fakery and fraud effectively discredited hypnotism for the next couple of decades. Successful medical practitioners either turned from it or kept their activities quiet. In France, at Nancy, Hippolyte Bernheim (1840–1910) took up a professorial chair in 1871 and, learning of hypnosis from an old family doctor, developed the technique.

All this was to change when hypnosis and suggestion were systematically applied to the problem of hysteria in Paris from the 1870s. Mid-nineteenth-century Germany and France had experienced an increasing professionalization of psychiatry as it moved into academic and university settings. Established researchers in neurology and hysteria began to explore and refine the hypnotists' practices. A fertile overlap arose between epilepsy, hysteria, automatism and hypnosis. Psychiatric defences advanced on the grounds of automatism in a series of lurid French murder trials stimulated feverish public interest.

But first a brief note on terminology. Hysteria is a central concept in much of early psychiatry, and particularly in the origins and development of psychoanalysis. It is hard to review this history without using the word. It is, however, a term that originates in a discredited view of women as inferior and over-emotional. *Hystros* is the Greek for the womb. Hysterical disorders were originally thought to be emotional disorders caused by the frustrated womb migrating through the body. It is associated with a range of derogatory stereotypes of femininity to do with emotional fragility and lability and with sexual frustration and dependency.

Initially it was believed that only women could develop hysterical disorders. Anorexia nervosa, for example, was not called anorexia hysterica when first described in 1873 because it had already been noted in a man. Hysteria's exclusive association with women was gradually abandoned towards the end of the nineteenth century. Two 'hysterical' mechanisms were identified. These are dissociation and conversion and they both remain important in psychiatry today. Even if we no longer use the term we cannot, even now, simply jettison the idea. However, its pejorative overtones do persist and I apologize for having to use it so often in this book. It has no gender or moral implications for me.

One dramatic manifestation of dissociation is the apparent existence of several distinct personalities in the same person. We tend to think of multiple personality disorder as a new phenomenon, one that swept across North America in the 1980s and 1990s. Along with recovered memory syndrome it generated bitter controversy within the profession, reigniting a furious debate about childhood sexual abuse, thought to be the cause of much of it.

Multiple personality disorder is, however, not new; nor is the psychiatric fascination with it. There seems to have been an epidemic of it in France and, to a lesser extent, Germany in the mid nineteenth century. This has been chronicled by the Canadian philosopher Ian Hacking in his books *Rewriting the Soul* and *Mad Travelers*. Albert Dadas was the first mad traveller, or *fugueur*, to be diagnosed as such. A fugue state in psychiatry describes an altered state of consciousness in which, often for considerable periods, people appear to be oblivious to their normal identity. Albert was a Bordeaux gas worker with a strange compulsion to travel widely, getting as far as Moscow, Algeria and Constantinople. During these journeys he appeared unaware of why he travelled or who he was until he inexplicably 'awoke'. Publication of his case sparked a small epidemic of *fugueurs* throughout France, Germany, Italy and Russia. Hacking explores how specific psychiatric disorders come into being, flourish and then, quite inexplicably, die away. Intense philosophical interest in the cases was inevitable because consciousness was considered the fundamental basis of identity. Philosophers at that time appeared to consider that a dual personality was a possibility, but struggled with the concept of multiple personalities.

A theory of multiple personalities was one way of trying to understand, or at least recast, hypnotic phenomena. Hypnotists spoke of somnambulistic states when individuals had access to a whole set of experiences (and even histories) denied them in their normal waking state. These had obvious similarities with 'ambulatory automatisms' where individuals, upon waking from periods of another 'identity', had no recall or explanation for these episodes. These fugue states could be induced by hypnosis but also happened spontaneously. There were several celebrated cases where individuals lived settled lives in convincing identities for months or even years. Some even started new families, apparently unaware that they had left their original families and jobs behind. Recovery was sometimes precipitated by their discovery or spontaneously arriving back in their old neighbourhood. Interest in the existence of more than one state of consciousness was already well established through studies of dreams and hypnosis and intensified by the writings of philosophers such as Leibniz.

Automatism was more than just an intellectual curiosity. It pre-occupied both the public and the courts, where it had been used by the defence in several dramatic murder cases. In France these defences were generally advanced for crimes of passion in the middle classes. The two schools of hypnosis in France at the time (Bernheim in Nancy and Charcot in Paris) disagreed about whether people could be induced to commit crimes under hypnosis. Automatisms and sleep-walking are now just a footnote in forensic practice, but 150 years ago they helped drive the engine of research into mental illnesses.

An understanding developed that an individual could have two per-sonalities. He, or more often she, was usually unconscious of one of them (the secondary one) unless it was strengthened in some obscure manner and 'broke through'. This belief in two states of consciousness ('dipsychism') was easier to accept as all of us have experience of it in our transition from waking consciousness to dreaming states during sleep. This was later refined and consolidated by Pierre Janet into his idea of an 'unconscious'. Others were encouraged by the philosopher Leibniz's concept of 'monads'. He proposed that the conscious per-sonality floats above a multitude of personality fragments, so it was possible to have several personalities. This 'polypsychism' was thought to be a more pathological state which only arose when the secondary personality fragmented.

Several celebrated cases of multiple personalities were reported from the 1790s onwards, including one in 1801 by Erasmus Darwin (Charles Darwin's physician grandfather). Mary Reynolds in Pennsyl-vania was described in 1815 as having alternating independent and quite dissimilar personalities over a period of thirty years. A complex classification of multiple personality disorders was even developed, mainly based on whether different personalities had recall for each other. Dual personality was more common than multiple personali-ties, which were thought to develop only after hypnosis. The second personality was likely to be less inhibited (particularly sexually) and to be aware of the dominant personality and able to speak about it.

From the vantage point of the twenty-first century it is hard to avoid concluding that the 'second personality' was a welcome opportunity to live out forbidden and repressed desires and wishes.

All this came to a climax in the work of the celebrated French neurologist Jean-Martin Charcot (1825–93). Charcot had already established a towering reputation as a neurologist when he took charge of the epilepsy wards at the Salpêtrière in 1870. With an established reputation and a wealthy wife Charcot mixed with the powerful, cultured elite. With so many women in his wards whose seizures appeared strongly linked to emotional issues he became interested in distinguishing epilepsy from hysteria.

Hysteria had been first named as a psychological disorder by Briquet in 1859. He had challenged the then current understanding that it was entirely restricted to women and caused by sexual frustration. He described hysteria as associated with emotions, sorrows, and often with poor education and with a degree of naïvety. It was an area of enormous medical interest at this time because of disorders following train crashes. Early railways were notoriously dangerous and there was an epidemic of legal claims arising from the frequent accidents on them. There were prolonged court-room disagreements about whether such post-traumatic disorders required a physical basis or could be entirely psychological.

Charcot held a broadly traditional view of hysteria. He believed that it was organic in origin, often related to dysfunction in the ovaries and womb in women, but he did believe it could afflict men also. In his famous public demonstrations he would induce hysterical fits by pressing hard on the patient's abdomen 'over her ovaries'. He began to treat hysterical patients with hypnosis from 1878 onwards. Charcot rehabilitated both hypnosis and hysteria in academic medicine with his defence of it to the Paris Academy in 1882. Unlike the rival Nancy school, Charcot believed that only hysterics could be hypnotized. He used hypnosis in his demonstrations to bring on hysterical fits and then to abort them. These public demonstrations on Friday mornings had become an institution in Paris attended by the social and medical elite and many foreign visitors. Sigmund Freud spent five months with Charcot in Paris (1885) but had only limited contact with him. He was more inspired by Charcot's eminence and glamour (he 'had the air of a worldly priest from whom one expects a ready wit and an appreciation of good living') and probably learnt more about public relations than psychological processes.

Charcot collected around him the most famous and ambitious of French psychiatrists and neurologists and he was clearly oblivious to the jealousies and rivalries that he generated. The painting *Une leçon clinique à la Salpêtrière* by André Brouillet (1887), shows him demonstrating a hysterical fit to the assembled dignitaries. Freud kept a print of the painting on the wall of his consulting room in Vienna. The woman shown is Charcot's most famous patient (some would say his muse), Marie Wittman, referred to as Blanche. It is clear that, deliberately or unwittingly, his patients learnt what he wanted and provided it. It is even suggested that his assistants schooled them to ensure it. There is no suggestion, however, that Charcot was anything other than naïve, there was never any suggestion of fakery.

Charcot raised the status of psychological mechanisms and the unconscious in the understanding and treatment of mental illnesses. However, his sudden death in 1893 was followed by a violent repudiation of his doctrines. His work was essentially airbrushed from Salpêtrière history. Many of his prize patients recovered. Blanche subsequently worked as a close personal assistant to Marie Curie in her researches into radium and died severely crippled in 1913. A powerful, aloof and prickly individual, she never married and refused to talk about her experiences with Charcot.

The link between severe mental disturbance and psychological mechanisms had, however, been firmly established and could not be forgotten. Pierre Janet (1859–1947), although a very different personality, continued Charcot's work. Janet was no showman but a shy, formal individual who had suffered a breakdown in adolescence and became depressive in later life. He was a brilliant student from a distinguished intellectual family and first trained as a philosopher. While working in Le Havre, he used hypnosis to treat Lucie, a young woman with recurrent bouts of terror. During this treatment he discerned a 'second personality' (Adrienne), who disclosed early trauma from the age of seven. Janet helped Lucie recover using suggestion and catharsis and based his 1889 MD thesis, *L'Automatisme psychologique*, on it.

Janet sought to avoid controversy and he downplayed the therapeutic potential of his hypnotic treatments. Partially this reflects his personality, but it may also be that he sensed the jealousies and rivalries swirling round Charcot. He moved beyond the revelation of traumatic memories followed by emotional catharsis to promote relief. He increasingly used suggestion to reframe experiences under hypnosis. In stark contrast to Freud, Janet was quite prepared to use hypnotic suggestion to manipulate his patients' memories. He was not committed to uncovering 'the truth' but to constructing 'a truth' that would bring healing. In this reframing he would actively mislead his patients, suggesting more benign experiences to displace traumatic memories. His aim was to free them from their conflicts and preoccupations with troublesome memories.

Janet's repeated claims in the latter half of his life to have 'discovered' the fundamentals of psychoanalysis before Freud have considerable substance. His 1889 thesis outlined how neurotic symptoms arose from repressed and dissociated memories and was published six years before Freud and Breuer's *Studies in Hysteria*. He used a form of free association which he called 'automatic talking' and he insisted that memories were never lost.

In his 1893 book *Psychological Analysis* he described memories, in the form of 'fixed ideas', as both the causes and the consequences of mental illnesses. His treatments took months with slow, steady reshaping of these traumatic memories. Such treatments required careful management of the strong dependent relationship that developed and from which the patient eventually had to be weaned. The catharsis of revealing the subconscious 'fixed idea' was not sufficient in itself for a cure – a process of reframing or synthesis was needed. In his later writing he moved beyond hysteria to a wider group of patients. He proposed a 'narrowing of consciousness' as the fundamental process in neurotic illnesses. Janet was also acutely aware of how neurotic illnesses could ensnare those around the patient, upsetting family members and drawing them into a web of suffering.

Janet had seen how Charcot's detractors had criticized him for his naïve showmanship and so took great pains to avoid the same error. He restricted himself to academic and clinical presentations – no public demonstrations. Most tellingly he insisted that patients should always be examined in private first and that a very detailed personal history be taken to identify any possible dissimulation. Janet agreed with the Nancy school that hypnosis was not restricted to hysterics. He went further than Charcot and proposed that hysteria was not only accessible and treatable by hypnosis, but that its origins were psychological, while Charcot always considered the causes organic.

In the awful period of revisionism after Charcot's death Janet kept his head down and continued to work undisturbed in the Salpêtrière until 1900. In subsequent years his work became increasingly philosophical, complex and speculative. He remained embittered and critical of Freud's eminence right to the end, claiming that his ideas had been plagiarized. Janet's work has received belated recognition since the 1980s with the renewed interest in multiple personality disorder and dissociation.

By the end of the nineteenth century the reality of an unconscious mind had been accepted by most professionals working in the field. The contribution of this work to the birth of psychoanalysis is clear and will be continued in the next chapter. Two less positive legacies remain. The first is the beginning of a complex, and often discreditable, relationship between psychiatry and women. Ellenberger comments on the powerful erotic forces existing between the early pioneers of hypnosis and psychotherapy and their patients. Apart, perhaps, from de Puységur's work with Victor Race the focus of all their work and writing was with young and often charismatic, emotional and highly attractive women. Some of the more alert practitioners (Janet, de Puységur) recognized the 'risk' involved in the therapeutic relationship but others (Mesmer, Charcot) appeared utterly oblivious.

Psychiatry (and not just psychotherapy, all psychiatry) is still regularly and rightly challenged for its attitudes towards women. Women still form the majority of outpatients and we have been correctly criticized for our easy acceptance of stereotyped gender-based assumptions and treatments. Improved diagnostic practices have failed to reduce this asymmetry; women still comprise the vast majority of those diagnosed with depression and some personality disorders. Historically most psychiatrists have been men, which has helped fuel the criticism that it is a social tool to 'pathologize' and devalue the female experience (Chapter 9). As we enter the twenty-first century women constitute over 50 per cent of medical graduates and this feminization of the profession is even more pronounced in psychiatry. Hopefully psychiatry's reputation and practice in gender issues will soon improve.

The second negative legacy is the taint of bad faith, the accusation of charlatanism. The use of suggestion, with its overtones of dominance and 'brain-washing' or 'mind-control', has always appealed to the fraudster and charlatan. Combine this with the subjective nature of many diagnoses and you have fertile ground for exploitation. Distressed people can be manipulated into believing they have disorders for which there is an available (and usually highly profitable) treatment. Psychiatry has, like all branches of medicine, had its share of frankly dishonest practitioners. The very protracted nature of later psychoanalysis combined with uncertainty over the indications for treatment and the criteria for recovery have kept this whiff of fraud, or at the very least exploitation, alive.

These concerns are important and require ongoing vigilance, but they should not obscure the remarkable progress that was made. We have always been confronted by strange, inexplicable states and behaviours in our fellow men. The eighteenth/nineteenth-century 'discovery' of the unconscious was a decisive break with a superstitious past. Some still argue today that the unconscious is a mystifying and obscure construction. However, the revolutionary importance of these decades was that its explanation no longer required any supernatural or divine intervention. Even if it is mysterious and obscure it is a 'normal' phenomenon, amenable to inquiry and testing.

Current neuroscience research provides endless confirmation that much of our rational mental processing occurs unconsciously (and very quickly). Our healthy functioning depends on not having to be constantly aware of all the judgements we make in day-to-day decisions. While psychiatrists and psychoanalysts have focused on the role of the unconscious in mental illness we are increasingly aware of its central role in normal mental life. Even if you have your doubts about its existence it remains a structure, a theory, with which to understand these most strange, and yet most human, experiences. Firmly based on rational, perhaps even scientific, thinking it makes possible the development and testing of treatments. As with the asylum's moral treatment it emphasized that there remains much healthy functioning in very disordered individuals and that treatments should engage with these 'normal' processes and work to strengthen them.

Even a fairly superficial reading of nineteenth-century publications confirms that there was no shortage of theories about mental processes. Once liberated from the restrictions of religious dogma, fascination with and speculation on the workings of the human mind and soul abounded. Compared with many of his contemporaries' wilder theories, which included spherical angels and a variety of subpersonalities, Mesmer seems almost dull. Dissociation and the unconscious mind were not isolated 'discoveries'. They are just the more durable and serviceable concepts from among the legion of such ideas that flourished during the 'mind-mythology' dominating French and German thinking of the time. They have survived because they were, and are, insightful and useful. An understanding of mankind that accepts and pays due respect to the unconscious has served us, and the mentally ill, very well since then.

4

The rise and fall of psychoanalysis

For many people psychoanalysis is synonymous with psychiatry. Asked to describe a psychiatrist it is likely to be an elderly man with a grey beard, holding a notebook, sitting at the end of a couch. As like as not he will have a Viennese accent and start the interview with 'Say whatever comes into your head' or 'Tell me about your childhood . . .' This image is derived from the school of psychoanalysis developed by Sigmund Freud, one of the world's most influential psychiatrists. He founded the most extensive and influential school of psychotherapy and his ideas have reached well beyond psychiatry. They have influenced philosophy, history, the arts and literary criticism, not to mention our understanding of normal human functioning and behaviour, in short ourselves. However, Freud's ideas did not appear from nowhere. He did not invent psychotherapy, nor is psychoanalysis the only type of psychotherapy. But he is the towering figure so it is right we should start with him.

Freud's contributions have had an enduring, international impact, but he was very much a man of his time and place. His Jewish origins, the culture of late-nineteenth-century Vienna and his personality all infuse his work. He was born in 1856 in Freiberg in what is now the Czech Republic and moved to Vienna when he was five. He was the youngest child of Jacob, a Jewish wool merchant, and Amalia, Jacob's much younger third wife. Amalia doted on Freud, calling him her 'golden Sigi' throughout her life. Freud was clearly gifted from an early age and was always top of his class in a demanding education system that concentrated on languages and classics.

His early years were passed in a period of professional and cultural expansion for Viennese Jews, especially for assimilated Jews such as the Freuds. 1852 had seen the Jewish emancipation, followed by full political rights in 1867, the ghettos had been abolished and there was remarkably little anti-Semitism. However, in 1873 a cholera outbreak and stock market crash led to social unrest with an upsurge in anti-Semitism. Anti-Semitism undoubtedly limited Freud's professional prospects and relationships and he was driven into exile when the Nazis came to power. However, his upbringing as a secular Jew was within a remarkably liberal and tolerant Vienna.

Freud took an inordinate time, eight years, to finish his medical studies. This was not because he kept failing exams, far from it. He spent one year studying comparative anatomy before settling into research in Professor Ernst von Brücke's prestigious physiology laboratory. Brücke was a fierce and rigid Prussian with an international reputation. It was during this time that Freud met Josef Breuer, also a liberal Jew, and a highly successful doctor renowned for his warmth and generosity. Freud was to make his first major contribution to psychiatry with Breuer. Military service in 1879–80 finally shook him out of his self-indulgence and he knuckled down and graduated.

Freud intended to continue with a research career in Brücke's laboratory leading to a university post, but fate took a hand. He fell in love. In 1882 he met Martha Bernays and they rapidly decided to marry, entering into a prolonged and very proper engagement. Marriage was not compatible with a research career which paid a pittance for long hours of selfless dedication. Freud took a post in the Vienna General Hospital working as a clinician, albeit still with considerable academic success. He became an expert on some neurological conditions and researched the uses of cocaine. Cocaine's anaesthetic properties were subsequently developed by two rivals for eye-surgery, and later its stimulant properties were employed as a treatment for morphine addiction. Freud became increasingly interested in the range of hysterical disorders that he kept encountering in the hospital.

In 1885 Freud travelled on a five-month scholarship to Paris to visit Charcot. While there he did not work that hard or have much contact with the great man, but enjoyed the cultural opportunities. He came back invigorated and convinced of the need to present ideas well for them to have impact (Charcot was a master communicator). His move into private practice has usually been attributed to anti-Semitism, but there were other factors. He needed money to provide for his wife and new family, and his work on cocaine and his personal use of it had somewhat damaged his reputation.

In 1886 Freud presented a paper on male hysteria to the Imperial Society of Physicians in Vienna. The critical reception of his paper is generally considered a defining moment for him. Freud was, and remained, deeply hurt, by the experience, believing he was frozen out. He attributed the reception in part to the radical content of the paper (hysteria was generally considered an exclusively female disorder), but mainly to what he perceived as anti-Semitism in his listeners.

It is true that the reception was cool. However, it is a distortion to see it purely as the 'isolated genius rejected by a pedestrian profession'. Hysteria in males was not unheard of; indeed (see Chapter 3) there was lively professional interest in it because of the epidemic of 'railway spine'. Railway spine was the term for back injuries resulting from the very frequent railway accidents of the time. Like 'whiplash' injuries in road traffic accidents today the distinction of physical and emotional responses was of great import because of the compensation involved. The central question was the existence or not of a 'traumatic hysteria'. There were national differences on this issue with France's Charcot strongly in favour of the trauma theory but most Austrians against. Freud may have underestimated his Viennese colleagues' familiarity with the subject. This would not be the last time he failed to recognize legitimate contrary opinions.

The radical nature of Freud's work is in strong contrast to the bourgeois regularity and solidity of his personal life. After marrying in 1886 he moved to Berggasse 19 in Vienna, where he eventually occupied two elegant conjoined apartments taking up a whole floor. He lived there until driven into exile by the Nazis in 1938. His wife's unmarried sister Minna moved in with them and the two women ran his life like clockwork. He worked in his consulting room all morning, stopping at 1 p.m. for lunch. He then varied the afternoon with going for a walk or, more often, writing. His six children, Mathilde, (Jean-)Martin, Oliver, Ernst, Sophie and Anna, were born between 1887 and 1895. Soon after Anna's birth he announced that he would cease sexual relationships. He appears to have remained celibate, although rumours of a liaison with Minna have continued to circulate. He always took great care over his appearance and is said to have maintained three suits that he simply rotated. Hardly any picture exists of him other than dressed in a three-piece tweed suit.

Freud was very much a family man attached to his children, especially to his youngest daughter, Anna, who became his closest confidante in later life. He undertook an analysis of her, something that would now be considered outrageous, and she became a distinguished child analyst in her own right. Anna Freud never married but remained her father's tireless champion and nursed him in his last illness. A diminutive figure, she established the Centre for Child Psychoanalysis in London and remained active right up to her death in 1982.

It was the publication of *Studies in Hysteria* in 1895 with his colleague and mentor Josef Breuer that launched Freud's career and which brought him to prominence. They had both been working for some years using hypnosis and suggestion to treat neurotic disorders. These were dominated by the more dramatic 'hysterical' disorders, which consisted of a range of strange and otherwise inexplicable symptoms and behaviour which seemed to be emotional in origin. Generally the hypnosis treatment worked by 'catharsis', which means that the patient experienced a release of dammed-up emotions when recalling powerful memories. This outpouring, rather than any exploration of the memories, was thought to be the cure.

In their joint book Breuer and Freud described five case histories. Four were Freud's and one was Breuer's, the most famous being Anna O. She is now known to be Bertha Pappenheim (1859–1936). From a wealthy Jewish family, she suffered a very serious illness associated with her father's death in April 1881. This consisted of hallucinations of a black snake, an inability to speak other than in English, paralysis of her arm, and periods of enormous distress and anguish requiring several months in hospital.

Breuer used hypnosis to uncover a profound conflict. The dream of the snake occurred during an exhausted sleep when she was nursing her dying father. In the dream it was obvious that the snake was going to kill her father but she found herself paralysed and unable to stop it. Under hypnosis Breuer identified that Anna O. loved her father deeply but felt trapped in nursing him. She hoped that his approaching death would come soon, giving him release but also allowing her to get on with her own life. This was the conflict expressed in her dramatic symptoms. When confronted with this insight, and an outpouring of emotion, cure followed. There was, however, nothing new about catharsis under hypnosis. What was ground-breaking about Breuer's and Freud's approach was the identification of the underlying emotional conflict (ambivalence about her father's survival) and the unravelling of its distorted symbolism. The fateful step had been taken from simply using hypnosis, or suggestion, to remove the symptoms to using it to *understand* the cause of the hysteria and effect the cure.

There is controversy over what happened with Anna O. Ernst Jones, Freud's first biographer, insists that Breuer's treatment was only partially successful and that Freud completed her cure. She did, undoubtedly, have further periods of serious illness but eventually made a full recovery. She went on to become a prominent figure in her own right establishing orphanages, and a German stamp was issued in her honour in 1954. Freud and Breuer argued about their relative contributions to the book and Freud's emphasis on sexuality, and their relationship soured. Pierre Janet (Chapter 3) was also incensed by what he considered, probably justifiably, their failure to acknowledge his earlier work on the unconscious (*Psychological Automatism*, published in 1889), a grievance he nursed to his death in 1947.

It was this focus on *understanding* the unconscious that was so revolutionary in *Studies in Hysteria*. It also shifted the emphasis from hypnosis and suggestion to the more equal and fundamentally more respectful technique of free association. This consisted of encouraging patients to say whatever came into their minds, no matter how inconsequential or embarrassing it seemed. Freud used the patterns in these free associations to unravel unconscious preoccupations. He also introduced the practice of the patient lying on a couch and the analyst sitting just out of vision. The purpose of the 'analytical couch' was to help patients relax, loosening control of their thoughts (he was dealing with a tightly controlled, self-disciplined clientele). Insisting on the importance of the *content* of the unconscious and the use of free association to lead him through it were the foundations for all of Freud's subsequent work.

Freud was not the first to recognize the unconscious. He was not even the first to identify it as the source of neurosis, nor to work directly with it to relieve symptoms. Janet and several of his predecessors have a stronger claim on these achievements. What was unique about Freud is that he took the content of the unconscious seriously and that he treated it with such respect. While Janet was quite prepared to distort unconscious material deliberately for his patient's benefit, Freud was utterly committed to the unvarnished truth. He wanted to understand the unconscious material, and for the patient to understand it, no matter how uncomfortable it was. Freud saw understanding and honest confrontation as the cure. His ideas on the unconscious and on the structure of the mind evolved continuously over his long career, but this commitment to an honest respect for the unconscious remained true. In his later years he sometimes cautioned his colleagues against too much eagerness to cure patients in case it interfered with their search for the truth.

Freud taught us to pay attention to the irrational and bizarre in our thoughts and feelings, not to ignore or deny them. This is not to say that he was some sort of early hippy who wanted us to 'let it all hang out'. Far from it: he was a highly disciplined, frankly puritanical individual. He said of psychoanalysis that its aim was to help the patient 'to be able to work and to love', its goal was to 'turn neurotic misery into everyday unhappiness'. He never promised happiness, or 'fulfilment' or 'integration' – he was far too down to earth and realistic about people. He respected duty and self-denial; what he did not respect was self-deception.

Freudian analysis and Freudian analysts are often seen as exemplars of rigidity and orthodoxy with their fixed rules for therapy and confident pronouncements. Freud himself, however, was constantly changing his ideas throughout his career. It is possible as always with sufficient hindsight to portray this as a steady, majestic progression. The reality was that Freud's professional life was full of dramatic conflicts and reversals, intuitive leaps and radical shifts in emphasis. He liked to consider himself and to present himself as a dispassionate scientist embarked on the painstaking elucidation of mental processes. He believed these would one day be reducible to biological, indeed biochemical, laws, as did his inspirational teacher Ernst von

Brücke. Few around him at the time, or since, have viewed him as such. His legacy is that of a charismatic individual with a vigorous imagination and penetrating intellect, capable of astounding insightful leaps. He brought together intense experiences with remarkable patients and a vast scholarship in literature, mythology and history as much as from medicine or psychology.

It would be hopeless to try and summarize Freud's thinking comprehensively; it runs to over fifty volumes of collected works and four million words. We shall restrict ourselves to a number of key ideas and changes that shaped his legacy of psychoanalysis.

1896 was a year of turmoil and personal crisis for Freud, filled with psychosomatic ills and fears of death. His father died. He was tormented and unhappy, turning increasingly to the self-analysis that he had been conducting intermittently for some years. During this period he made a dramatic U-turn on a central feature of his emerging theory. He had believed until then that the early sexual seductions his hysterical patients reported (often by their fathers) were the traumas that had caused their problems. He had been treating them with hypnosis, achieving relief by catharsis but with only partial success. He now became increasingly convinced that these memories were not memories of real events, but cloaked a desire for intimacy.

This reversal generates bitter controversy to this day. Many feminists, and indeed some psychoanalysts, charge Freud with cowardice and dishonesty. Did he back off, fearing society's outraged response to his previous conclusion that his patients had been sexually abused within their families? Was it just too hot? Or was it too threatening to confront such incestuous desires in himself? The extent of early sexual abuse has surfaced again as a major controversy in modern psychiatry. It inevitably remains a matter of judgement and opinion: there is no way to test it objectively. Its role in the genesis of self-harm and eating disorders and in borderline and multiple personality disorder in young women is particularly vexed (Chapter 12).

The Interpretation of Dreams (1900) is considered by many to be Freud's greatest work. Freud was clearly fascinated by dreams and called them 'the royal road to the unconscious'. He decoded the logical leaps and symbolism in them just as he did in free associations. He concluded that dreams were wish fulfilments that were inhibited and distorted by a mental 'censor'. This 'latent' purpose (wish fulfilment) was disguised in a series of processes such as condensation, displacement, symbolization and dramatization before it emerged as the 'manifest' content of the dream. It is the manifest content which we remember on waking and which always includes residues of the day's experiences. Dream analysis worked backwards from the manifest to the latent content. The book was literary, provocative and quirky and not at all badly received; it went quickly through several editions and translations. It raised Freud's status and his self-esteem.

Freud also believed that everyday errors and slips of the tongue betrayed our genuine wishes. Just as he believed that nothing was forgotten by chance he believed that errors were not really errors but what he called 'parapraxes'. When people reveal their true thoughts in such errors we call them 'Freudian slips'. Interpretation of dreams, free association and the analysis of parapraxes became the three pillars of Freud's depth psychology. All three are based on a belief in 'repression', meaning that ideas which are disturbing or unacceptable to the individual are kept out of conscious awareness. They do not disappear, however, but find expression in distorted and often symbolic forms.

It was Freud's revised view that his patients had not been seduced as infants, but had fantasized it, which brought him real notoriety. This was because, to explain it, he proposed 'infantile sexuality', the presence of powerful instinctual drives right from birth. The most powerful drive was for intimacy and he labelled it 'the libido'. These ideas were eventually published in *Three Essays on Sexual Theory* (1905). In English the libido is understood as overwhelmingly sexual, which may somewhat misrepresent Freud's understanding of this life force. However, he certainly conceived the libido as sensual, gratified primarily by physical contact. Freud's vivid sexual imagery probably confuses as much as clarifies his thinking but he was always prone to such dramatic, exaggerated language.

Freud described a three-phase development of the libido. It started with early 'oral' gratification, then 'anal' and lastly 'genital' preoccupation. These three stages, and particularly Freud's descriptions of the consequence of fixation at them, are now part of everyday language.

We use 'oral' to describe emotionally insecure and needy individuals and 'anal' to describe rigid, obsessional individuals. The genital phase was also called the 'Oedipal stage' after the mythical Greek figure. Oedipus killed his father, the king, and unknowingly married his own mother. Freud believed that this stage was characterized by longing, fear and rivalry. He believed that failure to successfully resolve it so that the child could 'share' his mother with his father or vice versa resulted in unsatisfactory over-sexualized adult relationships. We now regularly use 'Oedipal' to refer to situations where sex and family relations seem mixed up or when there is a striking age difference in romantic relationships.

'Little Hans' was a central case history in *Three Essays on Sexual Theory*. Freud only met this four-year-old son of a psychoanalytic colleague once and analysed him through his dreams relayed by his father. Little Hans was phobic about horses and Freud interpreted this as an Oedipal fear of his father's penis. This type of tortuous interpretation, combined with his exotic language, does Freud's theories no favours. However, most parents recognize such patterns in their children, with the intense need for closeness followed by battles over control in two- to three-year-olds and then the puzzling rivalries that arise soon after. The failed Oedipal triangle is all too recognizable in some neurotic adults who strive for an unrealistic, idealized and exclusive intimacy. Longing for this ideal they repeatedly forfeit the chance of more attainable, albeit imperfect, adult relationships.

Freud added a third component to his map of the mind in his book *The Ego and the Id* (1923). Initially he labelled the unconscious as the id (literally the 'It') and the conscious mind as the ego (the 'I'). Rather confusingly he thought some ego function was unconscious. He characterized the id as the primitive mind and the ego as the civilizing distillation of experience and education. Where, however, did the savage self-criticism and persecution evident in many of his depressed and obsessional patients come from? Surely such brutal and primitive thoughts could not arise in a civilizing ego? His solution was a 'super-ego' which had its origins in both ego and id. The conscious element was an internalized parental figure derived from the resolution of the Oedipus complex. The energy, however, came from the id, thereby explaining its destructive potential. We often now use the term super-ego to mean conscience, but Freud had a more technical understanding, believing the conscience was fully conscious and subject to rational challenge. The super-ego was, however, like the id not fully conscious and consequently did not soften with maturity and experience.

As Freud's analyses lengthened to several years (the initial ones often took only weeks or months) he concentrated more and more on the process of the treatment itself. Patients erected strong defence mechanisms to prevent his, and their own, access to their painful unconscious conflicts. His descriptions of these defence mechanisms are now figures of common speech – 'denial', 'repression', 'projection'. Freud recognized that these psychological defence mechanisms were themselves a significant part of the problem and he began to focus on analysing and interpreting them.

One 'defence' that troubled him greatly was when patients formed a strong emotional attachment to him, often declaring they had fallen in love with him. The puritanical Freud believed this was an attempt to avoid the analytical process and to face the unpalatable truths it threatened to reveal. He called it 'transference' because he believed it transferred emotions from other important, earlier relationships onto the analyst. Over time he came to believe that, far from being an impediment, transference was an essential part of the analytical process. Interpretation of the transference to understand the patient's present feelings about the analyst as a key to earlier conflicts became routine. Transference emotions revealed the patient's real concerns and wishes. Freud also developed strong feelings about his patients and he called these 'counter-transference'. Convinced that he had iron control over his 'own' feelings, he interpreted counter-transference as strongly defended wishes in the patient. Initially the two terms were restricted to abnormal and irrational feelings, but are now used for all the emotions between therapist and patient.

Freud was never shy of applying his ideas outside psychiatry. In later years he became increasingly interested in anthropology and cultural issues. He also became increasingly pessimistic, depressed by the carnage of the First World War. The titles of his books indicate his range and ambition – *Totem and Taboo* (1913), *Group Psychology and the Ego* (1918), *Civilization and Its Discontents* (1930), *Moses and Monotheism* (1938). Essays on Michelangelo and Leonardo da Vinci confirm his fascination with the arts and their continuing fascination with him.

By the start of the twentieth century Freud was an established, successful figure in Vienna. He had been proposed as a 'professor extraordinarius' in 1897 and eventually appointed in 1902, though not made a full professor until 1920. In 1902 he started the Wednesday Evening Club at his apartment. This gathering to present patients and discuss theoretical developments became the Wednesday Psychological Society, and eventually, in 1908, the Viennese Psychological Society. In many ways it was this establishment of a society or movement (some would say a cult), as much as its ideas or its treatment, that has ensured the success of psychoanalysis. By 1910 the psychoanalytical movement was firmly established with a steady membership and its own journal (the *Jahrbuch*).

Freud appears to have been mythologized from very early in his career. His movement attracted brilliant individuals with strong personalities who idealized him as their inspirational leader. This led inevitably to rivalries and tensions, dramatic rows and schisms. Alfred Adler, discussed below, had been an active disciple and a regular member of the Wednesday meetings from 1902. In 1911 he split from the group because it rejected his theoretical developments. Likewise with another member, Wilhelm Stekel, in 1912 and most notoriously and most painfully with Carl Gustav Jung in 1913. Jung had travelled with Freud on his Clark lecture tour in the USA in 1909 and had established and led the Swiss Psychoanalytical Association with Eugen Bleuler from 1909 to 1913. He had the strongest bond with Freud, and was clearly the favoured son and anointed successor until their catastrophic and irreversible falling out. Freud was becoming increasingly autocratic and intolerant of dissent.

Initially Freud was relatively relaxed about who could be an analyst. However, as splits proliferated and disturbing reports of all sorts of practice, so-called 'wild analysis', grew he changed his mind. Following Jung's proposal, he began to insist that to enter the association you had to be analysed yourself. This effectively changed a loose, intellectual network of men of ideas into a guild or a restricted profession. The movement was now promoted with an established theory, a defined treatment method and a substantial training requirement. The training analysis was also an initiation rite which created a strong group identification. Some would insist it robs members of any real intellectual independence.

Freud was a very proper individual who had always sought respectability and recognition. His work remained outside the medical orthodoxy of the time and he was disappointed not to be made a full professor until 1920. The figure of an isolated and embattled genius confronting prejudice and complacency permeates early reports and biographies. Certainly Freud did feel persecuted. While this picture is not entirely balanced – some of the problem was Freud's extreme sensitivity and intolerance of dissent – it has served the movement well.

ADLER, JUNG AND THE OTHER ANALYSTS

Alfred Adler (1870–1937) broke with Freud to found his Institute of Individual Psychology in 1911. He had been a faithful disciple since 1902, but a very different sort of man to Freud. Although also an assimilated Jew he was the second son from a large family with a remote mother. He suffered from rickets as a child and felt he always had to compete for attention, both within his family and later in society. Adler was also very politically engaged. Though brought up in the Vienna suburbs he was a Hungarian citizen and became an active socialist during his student years. He married a radical intellectual Russian student, Reissa, who remained a committed socialist throughout their turbulent marriage.

Even before he joined Freud's circle Adler was interested in the impact of society on diseases, both physical and mental. His first publication, *A Health Book for the Tailor Trade*, stressed the impact of poor working conditions. He retained a life-long commitment to trade unions and radical educational initiatives, and the role of doctors as educators. Unlike Freud he was not a good writer, nor a tall, commanding figure. His democratic leanings and rather disorganized personal style also limited his influence. His socialism made him even more unpopular than his Jewish and Hungarian origins. He converted to Protestantism in 1904 and became an Austrian citizen in 1911, and despite serving in the army in 1916 promotion was blocked for him, so in 1934 he moved to the USA ('the only future for Individual Psychology . . .').

Adler outlined his 'individual psychology' in *Understanding Human Nature* (1927), centred on the vision of an individual striving to achieve his personal goals. The therapist's task was to help clarify these goals and how to reach them with the patient. His therapy was essentially 'here-and-now', using early experiences and memories only to provide a frame of reference. Adler's approach was pragmatic and educational. Sessions were between once and three times a week and therapy never lasted more than a year (psychoanalysis by this time was four to five sessions a week and sometimes lasted several years). Adlerian therapists, like Jungian therapists, sat face to face with their patients.

Therapy progressed through three stages: diagnosis, agreeing on the goals, working towards the goals. Adler often started with 'If you didn't have this ailment, what would you do?' He was flexible about boundaries and would often meet family members and he considered that family, work and community activity were all essential to mental health. Marxist influence is obvious: he believed in an inescapable conflict between the individual's strivings and society's constraints.

Adler's lasting contribution is the 'inferiority complex'. He developed a theory of 'organ inferiority' while still attending the Wednesday seminars and initially associated it with feelings of sexual inferiority. Unlike Freud, he believed these conflicts arose directly from an aggressive drive, not from a blocked libido. A sense of inferiority could lead to various neurotic mechanisms such as compensation and denial. The inferiority complex was a mixture of real inferiority (organ inferiority) and experienced inferiority, often neurotic in nature.

This process of becoming over-sensitive to minor, but real, limitations and developing 'complexes' about them has an immediate appeal. Which of us cannot see it in ourselves? Over-compensation for a sense of inferiority makes such simple common sense. The ruthlessness of drive demonstrated by a Hitler or a Napoleon is all too easily attributed to their short stature and unimpressive physical presence.

Adler's legacy is far less than Freud's or Jung's, but it is not negligible. His approach was strikingly interpersonal, genuinely 'person-centred' long before such terms were thought of. It avoided the dogmatic universality of mental mechanisms that characterized other schools. His thinking was influential in the USA, where several of the so-called 'Neo-Freudians' adopted many of his concepts and, even more, his practices. Adler's focus on the here-and-now and working with the patient's own agenda are echoed in most modern schools of counselling. Individual psychology also spread psychological sophistication beyond the consulting room to influence day hospitals, educational theory and social activism.

Alfred Adler rejected Freud's increasingly esoteric and speculative theories to take a more pragmatic, a simpler, more rational approach to treatment. Carl Gustav Jung was the diametric opposite. He split with Freud to pursue an even more mystical and spiritual path. He eventually abandoned any pretence to the scientific respectability that Freud so earnestly sought. The break between Jung and Freud remained intensely painful to both men, public and unresolved for the rest of their lives.

Jung was born in 1875 in Basel, the son of a kind but boring pastor. His grandfather had been a legendary figure (also called Carl Gustav, 1794–1864), rector of the Basel medical school, a playwright and rumoured to be an illegitimate son of Goethe. Carl Gustav was not particularly close to his dull father or his reportedly distant mother. He was a shy child and a dreamy adolescent but in his mid-teens he appeared to 'wake up', experiencing a religious crisis to become an atheist. His medical training in Basel (1895–9) was hampered by financial difficulties (his father died in 1896) and by his poor maths but he qualified without delays. He escaped his background in 1900 to begin work as a psychiatrist with Eugen Bleuler in the Burghölzli Hospital in Zurich.

Jung completed his MD in 1902 with a case history of spiritualism in his cousin (he had been actively involved in parapsychology as a student). He went to work with Janet in Paris before returning to continue a successful career at the Burghölzli. In 1903 he married the heiress Emma Rauchenbach, which made him independently wealthy, a source of subsequent friction with his colleagues. By 1905 he was head of the outpatient department, appointed as 'private docent' (a status just below professor, painfully slow in coming to Freud) and was teaching a highly regarded course on hypnosis and psychotherapy. In 1906 he published a major text on word association and in 1907 visited Freud for the first time in Vienna, where they formed an immediate and powerful bond.

Jung's relationship with his chief, Bleuler, had begun to deteriorate. This may have been accelerated by Jung's financial independence (the Burghölzli was, indeed still is, a very deferential institution) but there were also real divergences of opinion. Bleuler, who was soon to gain international fame for his work on schizophrenia, was also very interested in word association. Both he and Jung were using it in exploratory psychotherapies in psychoses but differed about technique and indications. In 1908 Jung left to establish a private practice in his luxurious villa in Küssnacht on the shores of Lake Zurich. From 1909 to 1913 Jung was the Swiss lead for psychoanalysis. He spent much of his time and energy in Vienna as a prominent member of the Wednesday group and, later, editor of their journal, the *Jahrbuch*. He accompanied Freud to the USA in 1909 on the prestigious Clark lectures. He was the closest to Freud of the inner circle, their intense relationship more father/son than teacher/student. Although clearly seen as Freud's successor, Jung did not agree about everything. He rejected the Oedipus complex entirely and argued that it was a mistake to characterize the libido in Freud's highly sexual manner. Jung considered it more usefully understood simply as energy. He also emphasized the importance of the here-and-now over early childhood experiences in neuroses.

Several weighty books and many academic careers have been based on the 1913 Freud/Jung split and the letters that chronicle it. Theories abound about whether the cause was ideas, personalities or even unacknowledged homoerotic tensions. Suffice to say that, as with many intense relationships, when the break came it was with savage bitterness and mutual recrimination. When they first met in 1906 Freud was fifty years old, well established but not entirely satisfied with how he was regarded. Jung, his first non-Jewish disciple, was thirty-one, a six-foot-two rising star, self-confident and wealthy.

The warmth and intensity of the relationship are clear in the early letters. Freud to Jung, 21 April 1907: 'It's splendid of you to ask so many questions . . . I am coming to regard our exchange of ideas as a necessity, at least on Sundays . . .' Jung to Freud, 4 June 1907: 'The remark in your last letter that we can "enjoy our riches" is admirable. I rejoice every day in your riches and live from the crumbs that fall from the rich man's table . . .' Contrast this with five years later; Jung to Freud, 18 December 1912: 'your technique of treating your pupils is a blunder . . . Produc[ing] either slavish sons or impudent puppies . . . If ever you should rid yourself your complexes and stop playing the father to your sons . . . and took a good look at your own [weaknesses] for a change then I will mend my ways . . .' Freud to Jung, 3 January 1913: 'Accordingly I propose that we abandon our personal relations entirely. I shall lose nothing by it, for my only emotional tie to you has long been a thin thread – the lingering effect of past disappointments . . .' Clearly no way back. Neither party ever really forgave the other. Jung did not break just with Freud but also with Zurich University, from the psychoanalytical society and as editor of the *Jahrbuch*. He now devoted himself to his own theories and his private patients.

In his work with psychotic patients in the Burghölzli Jung had become preoccupied with recurring figures in their hallucinations which he called 'archetypes'. He proposed that these were not the result of distortion and repression, as most analysts would, but arose from some form of collective, human subconscious. He actively encouraged their expression. In 1913 he describes having heard a female voice and having become aware of a shadowy female presence in himself. He called it the 'anima'. He also reported visual hallucinations, including a 'mandala' – a circle divided into four highly decorated segments that represented the unconscious self. It is clear that during this period (1913–19) Jung was in great personal turmoil and probably unbalanced. Whether he actually became briefly psychotic or not is endlessly disputed. My own view is that he did.

Jung emerged from this turbulent period with a radically different approach to understanding neuroses, human development and human potential. His theories increasingly diverged from Western Enlightenment rationalism, drawing heavily on mysticism and Eastern philosophies. They took on spiritual, almost religious, forms. He believed that coming to terms with mortality and our place in the cosmos was central to most disorders of later life, in contrast to Freud, who had absolutely nothing to say on this matter. Many of his key ideas have entered common use, particularly influential in artistic and cultural circles. His ideas have become, if anything, more influential over time in our increasingly secular societies where existential doubts and a search for meaning are less answered by established religion.

Jung popularized the concept of personality types in his book *Psychological Types*, published in 1920. He proposed four mental functions, two of them rational (thinking and feeling) and two of them irrational (sensation and intuition). These gave rise to eight personality types, the most prominent being *introvert* and *extrovert*. Jung's name is now most commonly associated with the *collective unconscious* and *archetypes*. Jung argued that mankind's myths and religions (as well as the experiences of psychotic patients) reveal a familiar range of figures who are common to us all. These shape our experiences and understanding of the world, and not vice versa. Such figures populate our cultures and religions in different identities but are easily recognizable.

Jung also used such symbolic figures to describe aspects of the mind. Thus the necessary, but often denied, feminine side of men is the 'anima' (conversely 'animus' for women). The 'shadow' consists of all those unacceptable and unacknowledged aspects of ourselves which grow steadily stronger as they are denied. Our 'persona' is the face we present to the world and the 'imago' is our idealized image (such as a parent). Jung's psychotherapy aimed to integrate these unconscious processes, not interpret them away. His goal was harmony between conscious and unconscious processes, not a shift in the balance of their power.

Perhaps the most fundamental innovation in analytical psychology was Jung's belief that we have to transcend our ego. Freud wanted to strengthen the ego, our dull and reliable adult identity. Jung's psychotherapy had ambitions beyond removing neurosis and aimed to promote 'individuation'. Individuation involved using the ego to integrate both conscious and unconscious aspects of oneself to achieve greater spiritual potential.

Jungian analysis involves face-to-face sessions, usually one or two a week for up to three years. Dream analysis is central but does not assume Freud's distortion between latent and manifest content, and is used to access symbolic and archetypal material directly. Most of the focus is in the present, actively striving to counter distortions and re-educate attitudes. There is no Freudian encouragement to regress to a child-like dependency.

Individual stages have been suggested for the structure of a Jungian analysis. It starts with bringing into awareness the reality of the patient's situation. Then troubling secrets such as hidden trauma or guilt are sought. The third phase, similar to traditional analysis, explores these secrets – what do they mean, why are they so painful? The main body of the therapy promotes individuation by assimilating unconscious and non-rational aspects of identity. Lastly there is an emphasis on re-education, seeking alternative perspectives to old problems.

Jung emphasized what he called the 'synthetic-hermeneutic' character of his work. It was not so much about understanding (analysis) as bringing together and harmonizing (synthesis) and of learning (hermeneutic) to be different. Jung viewed the therapist much more as a teacher leading patients forward whereas Freud was more of a technician, helping patients to find out about themselves so as to decide what to do about it. Jung argued that one 'can only lead as far as you have gone' and, consequently, he was the first to insist on training analysis.

The rise of the Nazis and anti-Semitism in the 1930s dispersed psychoanalysis worldwide. A significant proportion of Europe's analysts were Jewish. Even for those who were not, Hitler's view of it as a 'Jewish science' and the prevailing anti-intellectual climate made practising it difficult and dangerous. Those who could moved abroad to the UK, the USA and South America. In the UK Melanie Klein had a profound impact on the psychoanalytical institute. With the UK's limited tradition of private psychotherapy, well-trained German psychiatrists and psychoanalysts proved an invigorating transfusion for mental health services and medical schools. They revised and rewrote textbooks and soon headed several departments.

In the USA and South America, particularly Argentina, psychoanalysts flourished and their numbers rose astronomically. There are still more psychoanalysts in Buenos Aries than any other city in the world.

They formed rigid societies which usually insisted on medical training for entry. Psychoanalysis seems more at home with the American philosophy of individuality and striving for self-improvement. It soon became the accepted treatment for neurotic disorders and completely dominated university departments and their training programmes until well into the 1970s.

By the start of the Second World War psychoanalysis was an international movement. Most developed countries had their own institutes and psychoanalysis was increasingly a part of mainstream psychiatric training. In Europe it remained a junior partner in universities and medical schools, often in an uneasy relationship with a dominant biological model. While the heads of departments and research units were occupied with classifying diseases and searching for biological explanations, their juniors wanted psychoanalytic training. They wanted the training to understand and treat their patients better, but also to equip themselves for private practice.

In the USA psychoanalysis began to take over psychiatric departments entirely. These departments were most often located in general hospitals with a focus on neurotic and psychosomatic disorders. European departments were more closely linked to mental hospitals and concerned with psychotic disorders. By the 1950s most prestigious US departmental heads were analysts and a training analysis was an obligatory part of residency.

PSYCHOANALYSIS BEYOND NEUROSES

As psychoanalysis consolidated its hold over psychiatry in the USA, its theory was expanded to cover the whole spectrum of psychiatric disorders, not just neuroses. Freud had advised strongly against this. He believed psychotic patients and severe melancholics lacked sufficient ego strength to engage properly in analysis. This had not stopped him speculating about the processes involved, with perhaps some of his most disappointing writing.

Freud developed an explanation of paranoid (persecutory) delusions in the celebrated case of the tormented Judge Schreber by attributing them to denied homosexual longings. Schreber had written a memoir of his nervous breakdown. He had become deluded in middle age that he was turning into a woman and that God had sent men to torture him. Freud's explanation involved a bizarre and tortuous construction based on repeated reversals of unacceptable thoughts ('I hate him – no, I can't hate him so I must love him – no I can't love him so he must love me – no he can't love me so he must hate me'). He used essentially the same mechanism for the 'disorder' of homosexuality. Similarly he tried to explain severe depression (with its self-critical delusions and suicidal attempts) as an inwardly directed aggressive drive. He argued that the well-recognized fall in wartime suicide rates was due to this aggressive drive being directed outwards against the enemy. These forays beyond neurosis were not Freud's finest hour.

Freud's injunctions against using his methods in the treatment of such severe disorders show his clinical sense (even if he would not resist speculating about them). In later years he became more realistic about the therapeutic limitations of his treatments and emphasized his work as a 'scientific' exploration of the mind. His followers were less cautious. Often psychoanalytical explanations were just that, explanations. As a medical student in the late 1960s I spent some months in an enormous state mental hospital in the USA with over 3,000 patients, almost all admitted against their will. Nearly every new patient received a diagnosis of paranoid schizophrenia and part of my job was to clarify the antecedents of their 'poor ego development' and the 'interpersonal conflicts' underlying their delusions and hallucinations. None of this would be considered necessary (or even acceptable) back in the UK. Despite this detailed work-up all of the patients received the same, absolutely standard biological treatments as they would have had in Europe.

This was not the case in all hospitals. Many prestigious clinics and hospitals claimed to successfully treat very severe disorders using psychoanalysis. These included disorders such as schizophrenia, alcoholism, anorexia nervosa and obsessive-compulsive disorders. The most famous of these was Chestnut Lodge in Maryland, where patients often stayed for years receiving intensive analysis for schizophrenia. It was here that Frieda Fromm-Reichmann coined the term 'schizophrenogenic mother' to describe a mother whose cold, hostile behaviour essentially 'caused' her child's schizophrenia. She did this without ever meeting the parents (prohibited in orthodox analysis). Joanne Greenberg (writing as Hannah Green) captured the patient's view of this intensive psychoanalytical treatment in her book *I Never Promised You a Rose Garden* (1964). The issue of such misguided practice is taken up again in Chapter 8.

Psychoanalysis is an intellectually vigorous movement, perennially full of splits, arguments and new ideas. It is not possible here to catalogue all its changes since the Second World War other than to mention some key figures and developments – the interested reader will find countless books on the subject. North and South America have generally been more orthodox with enormous and powerful psychoanalytical institutes, exerting a strong hold on their membership. The American psychoanalytical movement insisted early on a restriction to medically qualified members, which has never been the case in Europe. Perhaps the more routine place of psychoanalytical training in the USA, where it was once essential for promotion or to establish a successful private practice, maintained this orthodoxy. In most of European psychiatry, psychoanalysis was more an intellectual curiosity than a routine part of training. Consequently it has attracted its fair share of bohemians and iconoclasts.

In the UK Melanie Klein proposed powerful unconscious forces at a much earlier stage of development than did Freud. She argued that even newborn babies recognized their mother as a unique individual. During the first year the baby might interpret discomforts such as hunger or cold as punishment or persecution, which she called the 'paranoid/schizoid position'. The baby's sense of loss when the mother was absent was later experienced as sadness, called the 'depressive position'. Kleinian analysis has been very influential in both child and adult psychotherapy but has a rather unforgiving, confrontational tone. Her ideas contrasted starkly with the developments of 'ego-psychology' in the USA, which increasingly stressed the value of focusing on the patients' defence mechanisms, their character structure and the social context. These engaged more with the rounded adult functioning of the patient whereas Klein dived deep into primitive forces in the unconscious.

Even more remarkable were the developments in France, where Jacques Lacan's theories have come to dominate and be exported to much of Italy and South America. Lacan was a member of the post-war Existential group of philosophers and writers in Paris along with Jean-Paul Sartre, Simone de Beauvoir and Albert Camus. His theories are expressed in highly intellectual forms, too opaque for many of us to understand. Indeed some have even suggested that his later writings are a sophisticated joke on his readers. In a dramatic deviation from classical analysis he encouraged the therapist to abandon the session if the patient was not making progress. A Lacanian patient might get a session of anything from five to fifty minutes, depending on the therapist's assessment of how well it was going (though payment would still be for the hour).

There is an important cultural difference here. English-speakers, whether UK or USA, tend to be impatient and suspicious of complexity and intellectualism. They will only tolerate theory if the results justify it. The French, like most continental Europeans, admire intellectual sophistication for its own sake. For them Lacan's complexity is a virtue and they maintain a traditional Gallic contempt for the tiresome Anglo-Saxon emphasis on evidence and results ('*Bien*, it may work in practice, but does it work in theory?').

The high status of psychoanalysis and psychoanalysts meant that their advice and input were increasingly sought outside the clinical setting. Psychoanalysts and psychiatrists were active in the Second World War much more extensively than in the First (Chapter 6). They were not only called on to treat casualties but to advise on issues such as the selection of recruits and on their training. Their insights into relationships became valued in large institutions such as the military and businesses.

Educationalists and the criminal justice system also adopted analytical principles. Elite schools for the children of bohemian or intellectual parents based themselves squarely on Freudian ideas of personal expression and development. At the other extreme schools and institutions for wayward and disturbed children fostered personal development with attention to unconscious conflicts rather than simply instilling discipline by punishment as they had done previously. Rehabilitation services for drug and alcohol treatment and some prison units substituted an approach based more on uncovering unresolved conflicts, and fostering self-respect in place of didactic education and harsh discipline. Parenting theories and self-help books increasingly favoured an emotional and intuitive approach to child rearing, often couched in explicitly analytical explanations of the child's needs.

The literary and artistic world rapidly took to analysis and has remained fascinated by it. Literary criticism and art theory have at times been entirely dominated by psychoanalysis, with whole university departments devoted to it. Currently seminars and lecture series in psychoanalysis are more likely to be found in the humanities departments of universities and advertised in cultural journals than in medical or health care settings. In short, by the 1970s psychoanalytical ideas were everywhere.

How psychoanalytical ideas are applied has also been subject to experimentation and variation. Many analysts abandoned the couch to sit either directly or obliquely facing their patients. Explicitly time-limited therapies were developed such as interpersonal psychotherapy (IPT) or cognitive analytic therapy (CAT). These draw on psychoanalytical theory but have a shortened and structured practice. Analysts have increasingly accepted patients for one or two sessions a week. While this is driven mainly by financial and practical constraints it is genuinely accepted that good results can be achieved in this way. In the UK John Bowlby's attachment theory, derived from investigations into the mental health of abandoned children after the Second World War, has become increasingly influential. This explains disorders in terms of poor or insecure bonding with the mother and is based on real experiences rather than fantasies.

Psychoanalytical approaches were applied within the increasingly popular group therapies. Group analysis involves interpretation of unconscious processes using 'group transference' as the key technique. Group analysis modelled itself on traditional individual practice with a blank-screen therapist and regular contact over several years. Psychoanalytical day centres and day hospitals became popular, and there were even inpatient units run on explicitly psychoanalytical approaches. The Cassel Hospital in London differed from Chestnut Lodge in that the analytical treatment was delivered in the living situation, all of which was open to interpretation, and not just in the timetabled psychoanalytical sessions. The reality of both patient and therapist personalities could not be avoided so unconscious material merged with conscious work. The Cassel was the first so-called 'therapeutic community' but this term soon became applied to day hospitals and inpatient units, such as the Henderson Hospital established by Maxwell Jones in 1948, where analytical principles were displaced by social learning approaches.

These developments moved quite a long way from psychoanalytical practice, but their practitioners still identified themselves with psychoanalysis. The staff in therapeutic communities and day hospitals often had no formal psychoanalytical training but psychoanalysts usually still supervised the units. Individual sessions with patients using analytical principles were often considered the highlight of the week by both sides and many staff went on to train as analysts. These new practices were often thought of by outsiders as 'diluted' forms of analysis, a pragmatic solution to resource constraints, rather than the innovations that they surely were.

THE TIDE BEGINS TO TURN

The 1970s were psychoanalysis's high-water mark, its zenith. While not immediately obvious at the time, the tide had turned and powerful forces were converging to bring the era to its close. The splits and schisms that have always characterized psychoanalysis began to be played out very publicly. A more educated and literate public took notice of what previously would have been dismissed as arcane and esoteric squabbles. Books began to appear that not only disputed theory but questioned Freud's probity. It was proposed that he had had a long-term affair with his sister-in-law, Minna Bernays; that he had been instrumental in driving a colleague called Tausk to suicide; and even that he had plotted his colleague Fleiss's murder. Morton Schatzman's *Soul Murder* (1974) implied that Freud deliberately ignored clear evidence of savage early abuse of Judge Paul Schreber. The glamorous and maverick analyst Jeffrey Masson caused a worldwide stir with his claim that Freud was deliberately and consciously dishonest when he abandoned his seduction thesis to develop his theory of the

Oedipus complex. Masson, who was director of the Freud Archives at the time (1981), argued that Freud blamed the victim because he feared the social and professional consequences of honestly blaming the abusive parent. Masson's falling out with the establishment resulted in court cases for astronomical sums and became an international cause célèbre argued out in the broadsheet newspapers. His 1984 book *The Assault on Truth: Freud's Suppression of the Seduction Theory* provided ammunition to feminist thinkers and critics of analysis.

The very success of the psychoanalytic movement held the seeds of its decline. Excessive claims by its proponents and cavalier applications by enthusiasts began to undermine confidence. Unsupportable claims for successes with psychotic illnesses and disorders such as autism had been made. Long-term and dangerous disorders such as anorexia nervosa and addictions proved resistant to even prolonged psychoanalysis. Careful examination repeatedly showed very poor results. Families (and patients) began to speak out critically as the taboos around mental illnesses began to fade. Mainstream psychiatrists began to complain that analytical approaches stressing introspection could be harmful in psychotic illnesses where a patient's hold on reality might be very tenuous. Where established habits are part of disorders, such as with eating disorders, addictions or obsessive-compulsive disorders, shifting the focus away from the problem on to 'deeper' issues could slow down recovery and was justifiably criticized.

The blurring of the professional identity of psychoanalysis led to further problems. The simplistic, and sometimes rather insulting, use of psychoanalytical concepts outside clinical settings began to irritate. Foolish comments such as guided missiles being 'phallic symbols', or interpreting alternative political or religious views as 'defence mechanisms' discredited the whole endeavour. Analytical 'explanations' of exploitative relationships such as domestic violence or child abuse and of differing sexual orientations were increasingly out of step with society's more open approach to understanding personal relationships. By interpreting behaviour or explaining it away in terms of psychological processes they were seen to devalue the moral issues of personal responsibility or undeniable biological differences. They made psychoanalysis sound dogmatic, dated and narrow-minded. The use of analytical concepts within personal and professional relationships, which had once seemed novel and liberating, now risked seeming cheap and evasive. Few things are as irritating as being told that you are 'in denial' or 'projecting' when you simply disagree with someone.

The lack of a clear, consistent professional identity also permitted indiscretions within the profession. High-profile episodes of sexual misbehaviour by analysts and psychotherapists were dealt with in far too casual a manner. The erotic potential of the psychotherapeutic situation had been recognized right from the eighteenth century hypnotists. The extreme dependency of the patient, the treatment's intense focus on personal and intimate issues, its privacy and the necessary removal of customary moral prohibitions to allow consideration of taboo issues, all reduce the inhibitions on improper behaviour. Psychoanalysts and psychotherapists logically ought to have much stricter rules and procedures to guard against transgression than medicine generally. In practice the opposite seems to have been the case – they have been far too slow to police their members and punish offenders. In some notorious cases analysts have even refused to apologize, insisting that their sexual misdemeanor helped the patient. It is hard to imagine anything more calculated to demonstrate how out of touch a profession can be, or to undermine it in the public eye.

Probably the most important factor in psychoanalysis's decline was not any inherent flaws in its practice but the rise of increasingly effective alternative treatments. Effective antipsychotics and antidepressants were introduced in the 1950s and their use was widespread by the mid-1960s. Many patients who had been struggling in protracted psychoanalysis responded rapidly to these drugs.

Psychotherapy had also been changing and not just in refinements of psychoanalytical practice. A whole range of new therapies was now available – client-centred counselling, gestalt therapy, problem-based therapy, transactional analysis and more. Novel types of therapies arose, such as encounter groups, interpersonal groups, family therapies, couples therapy, drama therapy. Some of these have faded while others have flourished. However, they are not just developments of psychoanalysis: they draw on a range of new ideas.

The therapy which has challenged psychoanalysis most has been cognitive behaviour therapy (CBT). CBT was developed in the 1960s by an American psychiatrist and psychoanalyst, Aaron Beck, to deal with patients who did not seem to respond to his traditional analysis. While most patients valued emotional expression and understanding, others gained little from it and sought mastery of their symptoms. Beck worked with this group and realized that stuck and pathological thoughts, in particular intrusive thoughts and dysfunctional assumptions, troubled them more than did conflicted emotions. He developed a therapeutic style to identify, challenge and modify these thoughts. His approach used a 'Socratic dialogue' where the therapist challenges the patient to follow through logically the implications of his or her (the patient's) thinking. Socrates believed that the truth was in us and his job as a teacher was to keep asking questions, not give answers. There is also an emphasis on testing the conclusions drawn from such mistaken assumptions, trying them out in practice, referred to as 'collaborative empiricism'.

What was so fateful for psychoanalysis was that CBT is short (about twenty sessions), that it is practical (easily trained and described) and that the relationship is more equal and transparent (avoiding mystique and idealization). It fits the tenor of our times. CBT also scored over psychoanalysis by submitting itself to systematic research. The 1970s and 1980s saw the rise of evidence-based medicine (EBM). EBM has revolutionized practice across medicine generally by insisting that treatments should be subjected to rigorous evaluation of their effects. It is quite an industry in its own right and has developed powerful techniques for consolidating evidence to draw conclusions and provide guidance. The relative merits of different treatments are now reliably and routinely compared. Several respected treatments have been shown to be ineffective, or even dangerous, such as insulin coma treatment (Chapter 9), and abandoned.

CBT practitioners have enthusiastically embraced EBM and provided strong evidence for their treatments. Sadly psychoanalysts have stubbornly resisted this approach. They have failed to provide structured scientific evidence of their outcomes and paid the price.

Public health care services and insurance companies increasingly refuse to support treatments which lack an evidence base. Consequently CBT is increasingly available for the range of disorders that psychoanalysts would previously have sought to treat. Psychoanalytical treatments are hardly available any longer in the public sector in the USA or UK.

Reading the above, or going to psychiatry lectures in medical schools, you might believe that psychoanalysis was dead and gone; that its practitioners were now unemployed and looking for other work. Nothing could be farther from the truth. Analysts have no problem filling their appointment books. Analysis is alive and well, particularly in the non-English speaking world. Most analysts spend a significant proportion of their time seeing people once or twice a week rather than daily, but analytical therapy and therapy training are still over-subscribed. How to explain this paradox when there is so little real evidence for its benefit?

It is clear that both patients and therapists like analysis. It speaks to a world view that both parties understand. It embodies a respect for the individual, and their personal narrative (their unique history and experiences), that both value. Analytical therapy has very little drop-out or difficulty with motivation whereas keeping patients engaged in non-analytical therapies such as CBT can be very difficult. In the UK up to half of patients fail to complete even short courses of CBT treatment. There is also good reason to believe that non-analytical therapists often drift into incorporating analytical practices into their treatments. They, and their patients, also report their therapies are 'hard work' in a way that analysts and their patients rarely do. So currently analysis looks set to survive. This despite the absence of evidence, and despite its appearing out of touch with the current *Zeitgeist*. It will be fascinating to see how it rises to the challenge of evidence-based medicine. What will it retain and what will it abandon in the process?

Even if psychoanalysis were to disappear tomorrow we would all be better off for its existence and continue to benefit from its legacy. Psychiatry has been irreversibly changed by it, by a recognition of the importance of unconscious and half-obscured thoughts. Even those psychiatrists most opposed to its grand theories rely on its insights from day to day in their practice. It has left us a rounder view of people and a more tolerant, forgiving society. Its central lessons have become part of the fabric of our thinking so that, even as we criticize and reject its excesses, we unthinkingly apply so many of its insights. Anyone who has been on the receiving end of psychiatry has something to thank Freud for.

5

The first medical model
(between the wars)

Asylums fared badly during both world wars; no attention was paid to either their routine maintenance or their long-term residents. Many were abruptly uprooted and squeezed into other asylums to clear buildings for wounded soldiers. What energy was left for psychiatry was channelled into the war effort. New treatments were developed for new problems, particularly in dealing with traumatized soldiers, which is explored in the following chapter. These episodes were sorry times for asylum patients, with high rates of death from neglect. Even worse, psychiatry's own holocaust took place in Nazi Germany during the Second World War (Chapter 9). Yet this blighted half-century did witness really remarkable changes in the twenty years between the wars. Some consider it the most innovative two decades in psychiatry's history. The very terminology used conveys the revolution; it starts with 'lunatics' 'certified' to 'asylums' and ends with 'patients' 'treated' in 'mental hospitals'. If we think of modern psychiatry as the triumph of the medical model these twenty years were its first appearance.

Asylums after the First World War contained an enormous range of individuals with a haphazard mix of disorders and disabilities. The dominant group were the psychoses such as schizophrenia, manic-depressive disorder and chronic melancholia that we still see in our admission wards. But they also housed countless other patients suffering from organic disorders such as senile dementias and severe epilepsy and a range of individuals with various learning disabilities and autism. Alcohol-related disorders (dementias, delirium and psychoses) accounted for over 10 per cent of admissions in many asylums at the end of the nineteenth century. Less familiar to us now was the population of patients with end-stage syphilis affecting the brain (so-called 'general paralysis of the insane', or GPI). In some regions, dietary deficiencies, long since eradicated, caused disorders such as cretinism from iodine deficiency in the Alps and pellagra in the southern USA, Spain and northern Italy.

With so many conditions having obvious physical causes it should not surprise us that psychiatrists sought such underlying disorders and tried specific medical remedies. Most of these, of course, were dead-ends and some of them, such as surgical treatment for 'focal sepsis' described in Chapter 9, were far-fetched and quite outrageous. We should hesitate, however, before condemning. Given the persistence and degree of suffering of these illnesses, with an absence of any effective treatments, it is understandable that doctors tried speculative and even 'heroic' (the usual medical euphemism for 'foolhardy') treatments. Four of those introduced in the inter-war period have had profound and long-lasting effects and will be considered here. Two, the brain operation leucotomy and modified insulin coma treatment for schizophrenia, have been abandoned. The other two, malaria treatment for GPI and electroconvulsive therapy (ECT) for depression, were enormously successful. ECT remains a highly effective (if controversial) treatment to this day.

TREATING PSYCHOSIS WITH MALARIA

The first breakthrough was malaria treatment for GPI. This disorder is virtually unknown to us now but it cast a terrible shadow over late-nineteenth-century Europe. It is a very late consequence of syphilis, a sexually transmitted infection. Syphilis has been around a long time and is still with us, but it had become much more common in the nineteenth century; why is not entirely clear. The Napoleonic wars have been blamed as it certainly did follow armies, but there are alternative explanations such as the growth of cities and population mobility or changes in sexual habits. By the end of the century GPI accounted for over 10 per cent of the total asylum population, affecting a third to half of male patients in private asylums.

GPI develops when syphilis infects the nervous system and usually only shows itself ten to twenty years after the initial infection, which itself may have been only a trivial, long-forgotten rash. It particularly struck middle-class men because of their custom at that time of delaying marriage and frequenting prostitutes. Most syphilis infections were self-limiting or responded to various local treatments such as with mercury. Only a small proportion progressed to GPI but for the few that did the consequences were truly dreadful. Several Victorian novels and plays, such as Ibsen's *Ghosts*, portrayed the hovering terror of this silent, incurable and, at that time, humiliating and shameful disease.

Once GPI started the signs were unmistakable. Minor problems with speech and gait were soon followed by a mixture of delusions and hallucinations and then a remorseless decline, through fits and dementia, to an early death. Delusions of grandeur were common and gave rise to the caricature of the mental patient standing with his hand tucked into his waistcoat, convinced he was Napoleon. Grandiose patients could, and regularly did, bankrupt their families and destroy reputations by outlandish and reckless behaviour. As the victims were often well-settled pillars of society with successful careers and dependent families it is no wonder GPI was so feared.

The German philosopher Friedrich Nietzsche was a world figure at the height of his fame when, aged forty-five, he was struck down with GPI caused by syphilis he had probably contracted as a twenty-year-old. Completely out of the blue in 1889 in a street in Turin the police found him clinging to a horse's neck, disoriented and incoherent, and took him to a clinic in Jena. His decline to death over the next eleven years in various asylums included dementia, strokes and delusions. It must have seemed a terrifying and humiliating end to a towering intellectual career.

Julius Wagner von Jauregg (1857–1940), usually referred to as 'Wagner-Jauregg', was a contemporary of Freud's. They trained together in Vienna medical school and had an early rivalrous relationship. Wagner-Jauregg had no time for psychoanalysis; he focused on the biological causes and cures of mental illnesses. He distinguished himself early with iodine treatment for cretinism before moving to a professorship in Vienna in 1883. There he noted the improvement in the psychosis of one of his patients after a severe infection. He experimented for several years with inducing fevers in patients to see if they improved. He mainly used tuberculin, then available as the vaccine for TB, with no success but at considerable risk of infection.

His breakthrough came when he used malaria infections. A soldier, returned from Macedonia with shell shock in 1917, was also suffering from malaria. He injected the infected blood from this patient into one of his other patients with advanced neurosyphilis, including regular epileptic fits. The patient had a series of nine bouts of malaria fever, spiking high temperatures, during which the fits ceased. Afterwards the malaria was successfully treated with quinine and it became clear that the patient's psychiatric disorder was vastly improved. It continued to improve to the point that he was effectively cured and could be discharged. Within a year Wagner-Jauregg reported nine successful cures.

This was an astounding result. It is hard for us living in the twenty-first century with its constant stream of 'miracle medical advance' stories in the daily press to fully grasp just how astounding. Here was the first real and permanent cure of a major mental illness. Malaria fever cures worked in over half of GPI cases, returning patients to normal or near-normal lives. They soon became widely practised throughout Europe and to a lesser extent in the USA. The malaria cure was not straightforward. It was a difficult and expensive treatment with significant risks: patients could die. However, its impact, both on the otherwise doomed patients and also on the therapeutic morale of psychiatry, cannot be overstated. For his discovery Wagner-Jauregg became the first psychiatrist to be awarded the Nobel Prize for medicine in 1927. The treatment was tried across the range of mental illnesses but only worked with GPI. With the availability of effective antibiotics such as penicillin after the Second World War it became a thing of the past, but it had started a revolution in psychiatry.

TREATING PSYCHOSIS WITH SLEEP AND INSULIN

Insulin 'shock', or insulin coma treatment, occupies a unique position in the history of psychiatry on two quite separate counts. When Manfred Sakel introduced it in 1934 in Vienna it was the first specific treatment claimed to cure schizophrenia. The brains of patients with schizophrenia showed no signs of abnormal development or damage from infection or trauma. Consequently a cure of such a so-called 'functional' psychosis would have more profound and far-reaching implications for the broader practice of psychiatry than Wagner-Jauregg's malaria treatment. Insulin coma's second claim to fame is that it is the first psychiatric treatment (and possibly the first of any medical treatment) to be abandoned because it was proved scientific-ally to be ineffective by a randomized controlled trial. However, before the fascinating story of why it was abandoned, what of its origins in the range of 'sleep treatments' then being tried?

Sedatives had long been used in psychiatry to calm agitated patients. Morphine was in wide use for this in asylums from the early part of the nineteenth century as it was in society generally. Tincture of opium or 'laudanum' was used both for pain relief and for sleep. The first artificial sedative, chloral hydrate, usually just called 'chloral', was introduced in the 1860s. Like any effective sedative before and since, chloral soon became a drug of abuse with widespread addiction. It was the original 'knock-out drop' used to prepare a 'Mickey Finn' beloved of Chicago gangsters and was implicated in countless deaths, including several murders. Several prominent artistic figures were addicted to it and the Pre-Raphaelite painter Dante Gabriele Rossetti probably died from an overdose. However, these drugs, along with the cheaper and more toxic bromine, were used for short-term relief of tension or insomnia, not to cure mental illnesses.

Bromine, as its salt, potassium bromide, was in regular use from the mid nineteenth century as an anti-epileptic and sedative. Soldiers in the the First World War were convinced that bromine was put in their tea to reduce their sexual drive. It was the staple medication to ease abstinence symptoms in withdrawing morphine and opium addicts, who were kept drowsy for several days while the opiates left their sys-tem. In 1897 a Scottish doctor, Neil McLeod, working in Shanghai, travelled to Tokyo to bring back a middle-aged married English-woman who had become acutely disturbed. She was psychotic, probably suffering with mania. How could he get her back to Shang-hai (several days on a steamship) in her current state? He decided to sedate her with bromine and keep her drowsy for the whole trip. His aim was simply to make the journey less fraught and in this he was successful. However, when they arrived back in Shanghai his patient had completely recovered.

Two years later his patient relapsed and he decided to try his 'bromide sleep' on her again. Within three weeks she was recovered, convincing him that the 'bromide sleep' might cure psychotic illnesses. He treated a further eight patients with various diagnoses although at least one suffered from mania. His sleeps lasted five to nine days and patients were toileted and fed milk every few hours. McLeod's sleep treatment received some recognition and was used by a number of his colleagues. However, as it relied on bromide it was fairly toxic and not always successful and it soon faded.

In 1903 a German chemist, Emil Fischer, developed a barbiturate as a safe sedative. Sold as Veronal the drug was an immediate hit. It was palatable (unlike chloral, which tastes awful and causes bad breath) and highly effective at doses well below those that carried risks. It restored sleep in both normal and depressed individuals and calmed agitated patients. Up to the start of the First World War many new barbiturates were developed, some very short-acting and others long-acting. Although expensive, barbiturates were soon in widespread use in asylums, especially private ones.

It was inevitable that barbiturates would be tried to induce a 'sleep cure'. They were probably first tried in Italy in 1915 but their breakthrough came in 1920, promoted by Jakob Klaesi working at the Burghölzli Hospital in Zurich. Klaesi used barbiturates to induce a prolonged sleep (or 'narcosis' as he termed it) for five to six days. His initial intention was to prepare patients for psychotherapy by relaxing them and overcoming their defence mechanisms. Klaesi soon modified his ambitions, convinced that the prolonged narcosis itself was an effective treatment for schizophrenia. He published a series of twenty-six patients treated this way with nearly a third showing considerable improvement. Three patients died during the treatments and Klaesi tried to discount the risk by suggesting they had pre-existing medical conditions. However, the risks were clearly there for his colleagues to see. In time safer barbiturates were developed and prolonged narcosis spread widely. It was used for most disorders, particularly those where patients were anxious and agitated, and was considered one of the most effective interventions available in the early 1930s. Prolonged narcosis for schizophrenia became eclipsed by the development of Sakel's insulin 'shock' treatment. However, its use persisted for several decades for severe anxiety disorders, in a modified form with lighter sedation. I saw it used right into the mid-1970s in highly anxious, self-harming individuals.

The discovery of insulin in 1922 led to it being tried in almost every medical condition. In psychiatry it was tried with various disorders without success before Manfred Sakel (1900–1957), who was a Viennese psychiatrist working in Berlin, used it in 1927 to calm morphine addicts during withdrawal while also stimulating their appetites. Comas and epileptic seizures were infrequent and unwelcome side effects of the treatment. In 1930, however, Sakel recognized that the comas themselves had a calming effect on his patients.

Being Jewish, Sakel had to return to Vienna in 1933 and there he began to experiment with insulin coma as a treatment for schizophrenia. In 1934 he published a series of fifty patients treated during their first episode. He claimed full recovery in 70 per cent and partial recovery in a further 20 per cent, with one death and a handful who failed to respond. At a time when few recoveries were expected in schizophrenia these results seemed truly miraculous. Insulin coma therapy spread rapidly. It was in use by the end of 1934 in parts of mainland Europe, but made its biggest impact in the UK and USA. By 1937 it was a standard treatment, much favoured in Anglophone psychiatry (over thirty UK hospitals had 'insulin wards' in 1938), and over the next twenty years most progressive hospitals opened their dedicated insulin coma ward.

Insulin coma wards became high-prestige centres in asylums, with a concentration of highly skilled nurses and doctors. The treatment remained dangerous (fits and deaths from coma were ever-present risks) and required careful monitoring and intensive care. The doses of insulin were gradually increased so that patients drifted off first to sleep and then into deep unconsciousness. They were kept in that condition by regular injections. They were generally roused every twenty or thirty minutes with some sugar solution but in some settings this period was extended up to a couple of hours. Patients were kept sedated for up to two months, undergoing fifty to sixty comas. Modified insulin coma treatment consisting of lighter sedation for a couple of days to two weeks was introduced for neurotic and anxiety-based disorders. Its use, like the use of barbiturate sleep therapies, continued in some centres into the 1970s.

Doubts began to set in. Others failed to confirm Sakel's 80 per cent recovery rate, finding it nearer to 50 per cent. This was still above the spontaneous recovery rate expected in the first-episode patients selected for treatment. Insulin shock treatment, as it was called in the USA, was very labour-intensive and thus very expensive – particularly so compared to the pitiful sums spent on custodial care. In the UK public services it was subject to very careful scrutiny and doubts about its benefits began to surface. In 1953 a psychiatrist, Harold Bourne, published an article entitled 'The Insulin Myth' in the medical journal *The Lancet*. Bourne argued that there was no conceivable therapeutic mechanism for insulin in schizophrenia. He attributed the outcomes to the selection of good-prognosis patients and the impact of all the attention and optimism on them. It had long been known that expectations affect recovery in most medical conditions. If people believe they are being cured it is called the 'placebo effect'. The 'Hawthorne effect' is an improvement in response to increased attention and fuss and has been well documented by industrial psychologists.

Bourne's article led to a randomized controlled trial (RCT) of insulin coma treatment. RCTs had recently been introduced into medicine as the gold-standard test of whether a treatment works. They involve randomly allocating patients to alternative treatments and then measuring an agreed outcome after a predetermined time has elapsed. By not allowing either the doctor or the patient to choose the treatment or when to assess outcome the bias resulting from the natural optimism that most of us feel about new treatments should be reduced or removed. Any difference in outcome between the two groups can then be confidently attributed to the differences in the treatments themselves. Usually the newer treatment is called the 'experimental' and the standard treatment the 'control' as it controls for the normal rate of recovery.

A small trial in London randomizing schizophrenia patients either to insulin coma or to barbiturate-induced coma (already known to be ineffective in schizophrenia) found no difference whatsoever in the outcomes. The apparently wonderful earlier outcomes are now thought to be due to unintentional selection of patients most likely to recover and the optimistic attitudes of the staff caring for them. This 1957 trial by Ackner and colleagues in *The Lancet* sounded the death knell for insulin coma treatment. Another RCT in the USA by Max Fink in 1958 comparing insulin coma treatment and the newly introduced antipsychotic chlorpromazine effectively finished the job. These two trials signalled an important step forward for psychiatry and for medicine as a more scientific, evidence-based profession.

TREATING PSYCHOSIS WITH ELECTRICITY

Electroconvulsive therapy (ECT) was first used in 1938 in Rome by the Italian psychiatrist Ugo Cerletti (1877–1963). It was initially tried as a cure for schizophrenia but quickly recognized to be much more effective in depression. It rapidly spread worldwide to become the standard treatment for severe depression and some very severe cases of schizophrenia. For severe depression it still remains the most effective treatment, although the need for it has diminished considerably and controversy continues to surround it. ECT did not emerge from nothing. Electricity had been tried with mental illnesses for centuries and epileptic seizures for quite some time.

It is worth pausing to ask oneself why human beings have epileptic seizures. We know that put under sufficient stress (e.g. anxiety, fever, dehydration, exhaustion, intoxication) people with no obvious neurological damage can have a seizure. We share this capacity with many animals and, like them, we often show profound changes of mood and behaviour directly after a seizure. These changes, and the sometimes 'other-worldly' quality of the aura that can precede fits, led the ancients to attribute religious or special powers to those who suffered from epilepsy. Julius Caesar famously suffered from what was then called 'the falling sickness'. Biologists have suggested that epileptic seizures may have an evolutionary purpose in protecting the brain from overwhelming stress. Analogies are made with the need to discharge overloaded circuits as in a computer. The theory is a bit thin but what is certain is that epileptic seizures are a natural occurrence in the normal brain as well as a symptom of underlying disease.

Repeated fits can lead to brain damage and behavioural changes. As a consequence many asylums had wards specifically for epileptic patients, particularly those with disorganized or violent behaviour after their fits. Distinguishing patients with 'organic' from those with hysterical fits in these wards was one of the stimuli for dynamic psychotherapy (Chapter 3). So psychiatrists were quite familiar with epilepsy and were responsible for its management, as they are still in the developing world. It was out of research into epilepsy that electroconvulsive therapy developed.

Ladislaus von Meduna (1896–1964) was a Budapest psychiatrist who was researching histology (the study of cells and tissues) in mental illnesses. Meduna examined through a microscope the brain cells in epilepsy and schizophrenia, to see if he could detect any differences to explain their causes. His interest in this was quite logical as it was widely believed that epilepsy and schizophrenia rarely occurred together in the same patient. There might be some biological feature that 'protected' one from the other. Meduna observed in his autopsies that the brains of patients who had suffered from epilepsy had an excess of one type of cell (a 'glial' cell) whereas those who had suffered from schizophrenia had fewer such cells. He wondered if epileptic fits could stimulate the growth of glial cells in the brain. He decided to try inducing epileptic fits in patients with schizophrenia to see if it helped them recover.

There was already a precedent for inducing fits using camphor. Camphor is an aromatic oil familiar to us for its penetrating smell in mothballs and cough medicines. Originally derived from the laurel tree, in Asia, it was first produced chemically in 1900. Long before this, in 1785, a physician called Oliver reported successfully treating a melancholic patient by fits brought on by swallowing high doses of camphor. His description clearly shows what a thoroughly unpleasant process it was. Meduna, recently tranferred to a large psychiatric hospital just outside Budapest, decided to use intramuscular injections of camphor to induce the fits. This successfully produced fits in about a third of the patients but took up to an hour to work. That hour was highly unpleasant with mounting anxiety and dread.

Meduna's first trials were encouraging; three patients made a positive response and he went on to treat and publish a series of twenty-six patients. Ten of these made very good recoveries after two to three treatments a week for three or four weeks (six to twelve fits). His very first patient was a 33-year-old man who had been in hospital over four years and mute for the preceding year. After six fits in two weeks he was recovered, lucid and talking; he even absconded from the hospital briefly to visit his family at home. These were indeed dramatic outcomes.

Meduna was lucky in his work as several of his first patients suffered from the catatonic form of schizophrenia, which, for reasons that are poorly understood, is extraordinarily rare now in the developed world. Its main features are disorders of movement, most often stupor where the patient lies rigid, although conscious, for weeks and sometimes months. ECT is still used in catatonia but infrequently now in other cases of schizophrenia. Meduna had changed from camphor to its soluble form, metrazol, which was marketed as Cardiazol. This could be injected intravenously and so produced the fit almost immediately and very reliably. It also avoided that terrible period of mounting anxiety preceding camphor seizures which had made patients so reluctant to have them. His treatment was rapidly adopted internationally and continued to be used widely until the mid-1940s. It was then that the much easier, safer and more effective ECT replaced it. By this time Meduna, like so many of his Jewish colleagues, had been driven out of Europe to settle in the USA.

The success of Meduna's treatment focused attention on the therapeutic benefits of epileptic seizures. Ugo Cerletti (1877–1963), professor of psychiatry in Rome, began to explore the possibility of producing fits using an electric current. The use of electricity in medicine has a very long pedigree – right back to the use of electric eels by Hippocrates and Galen to provide pain relief. In 1792 a surgeon in London, John Birch, claimed a successful treatment of a patient with a long-standing melancholy by administering six small shocks to his skull. It is not recorded if he had fits but he returned to work and remained well for seven years. Cerletti and his assistant, Lucio Bini, had spent several years testing different effects of electric shocks on animals, initially dogs, then pigs. They had observed pigs being stunned with electric shocks before slaughter in Rome's abattoirs. Bini was the more technical, refining the minimum level of current needed to produce the fit, and together they carefully tested its safety. In their experiments with pigs they discovered that the best method was to place the electrodes on the temples and they confirmed that the voltage needed to cause a fit was much lower than that which caused death.

In 1938 they were sufficiently confident to try it with a human patient. The patient chosen was a 39-year-old engineer from Milan who had been brought in by the police from the railway station, where he had been found wandering, confused and dishevelled, clearly suffering from well-established psychosis. Cerletti and Bini tried three times to induce the fit, stepping up the voltage. When the fit eventually occurred it was a full *grand mal* fit with the classical rigidity followed by shaking movements, unconsciousness and rapid pulse, and his breathing stopped. This was a high-risk experiment, but to everyone's relief after just under a minute the patient began to breathe again and soon recovered consciousness. He received a further ten treatments over the next two weeks and was discharged home to Milan within a month and returned to work. While not entirely a cure this was a remarkable recovery, as effective as with Cariazol but easier and more reliable.

Despite the disruption caused by the outbreak of the war the use of ECT spread rapidly and by the mid-1940s had all but totally displaced Cardiazol. It was in use by 1939 in both the UK and USA, where it was vigorously propagated by the charismatic and tireless psychiatrist Max Fink. ECT was 'modified' by the use of short-acting anaesthetics (usually barbiturates) virtually from the beginning so patients are not awake when it is given. ECT has generally been more widely used in Europe than in the USA. While it was widely used in state hospitals and asylums it was little used in American university clinics or private practice because of the dominance of psychoanalysis.

Even with anaesthetics, which made the treatment less distressing, there were persisting risks of stress fractures in the spine because of the strength of the fit. The drug curare, originally extracted from the poison darts used in the Amazon, briefly paralyses muscle contraction.

This was introduced in 1940 to 'modify' the fit, reducing or abolishing the contractions. Succinylcholine, an even safer muscle relaxant, was introduced in 1942 and soon replaced curare. Now when ECT is given the patient is asleep and the 'fit' is usually restricted to a twitching of facial muscles and fingers and some arching of the back. It is far removed from the full fit of the earlier treatments.

ECT is still sometimes given to conscious patients in the developing world, where the risks of an anaesthetic are significant. It has not been administered 'unmodified' in the developed world for decades. The portrayal of unmodified ECT in a conscious patient in the 1975 film *One Flew Over the Cuckoo's Nest* was really quite mischievous. ECT is still occasionally used in schizophrenia, especially in the catatonic form and in resistant and very severe cases, but its main effect was rapidly recognized to be on mood. It is now used as a treatment for severe depression and occasionally for mania that will not settle. ECT is a scary treatment that still divides opinion and, despite its undoubted effectiveness, remains violently controversial (Chapter 9).

TREATING PSYCHOSIS WITH SURGERY

Surgery on the brain for conditions like cancer or strokes is called 'brain surgery' and highly respected and socially accepted ('it doesn't take a brain surgeon to know . . .'). However, when used for psychiatric disorders it is called 'psychosurgery' and the usual response lies between surprise and horror. Certainly psychosurgery did end up as a horror story and this is picked up in Chapter 9. It never had the same influence on psychiatry as the other treatments we have just reviewed but it did have some impact. It is not entirely a historical curiosity but is still in use in specialist centres in highly specific circumstances. It is usually called lobotomy (or 'frontal lobotomy') in the USA and leucotomy (or 'pre-frontal leucotomy') in the UK. Both terms refer to the same procedure. 'Lobotomy' and 'lobotomized' have become such pejorative terms that leucotomy will be used here.

The frontal lobes of the human brain are enormously developed compared to other animals and are probably our species' most striking characteristic. For a long time their purpose was unclear. Neurologists mapped the brain, often by noting what functions were lost when people had strokes. Soon we knew which parts of the brain were responsible for vision or taste, and could map the regions responsible for sensation or movement in remarkable detail. For sensation and movement this detail is so great that we can distinguish the fingers from the thumb and calculate how much brain matter is devoted to sensation in the lips or the fingertips. However, there remained large parts of the brain which seemed to cause no major consequences when they were damaged, so-called 'silent areas'. The frontal lobes are such areas. They are where we process fine judgements, the site of our higher functioning and much of what characterizes our unique personalities. Devoted to processing acquired experience they are highly 'plastic', which means that they can adapt over time to damage and are constantly modified.

The story usually told at this point is that of Phineas Gage, a 25-year-old railway construction foreman in Vermont, USA. In 1848 he was laying dynamite charges when a premature explosion drove his tamping iron through his skull. The tamping iron was over an inch thick and pointed. It entered just under his left eye and came out through the top of his head. The remarkable thing was that he was back on his feet and talking within minutes. Miraculously his wound did not bleed or develop an infection. Although he was physically unaffected his behaviour changed. He was reported as becoming 'coarsened' and began to be impulsive, unreliable and profane in his language. It is likely that these stories became exaggerated over time but it is undeniable that much of his frontal lobes were destroyed and that his personality did appear to change despite his amazing recovery. His experience suggested how the frontal lobes were implicated in personality, social adaptation and finer judgements.

Several early attempts at psychosurgery took place at the end of the nineteenth century. These included operations for epilepsy, GPI and even alcoholism. In a Swiss asylum in 1888 Gottlieb Burkhardt tried removing parts of the brain of six patients with schizophrenia. The results were not good. One patient died, one improved, two were unchanged and two became calmer. None of these experiments flourished and all were soon forgotten.

The introduction of leucotomies in 1935 was due to the remarkable

Portuguese neurologist Egas Moniz (1874–1955). Moniz was already a towering figure even before these operations. He had been one of the three founders of the Central Republican Party which spearheaded the Portuguese revolution in 1910. He was a member of parliament from 1903 to 1917 before becoming ambassador to Spain and then foreign minister, retiring from politics in 1920. Despite all this he continued his academic medical practice, becoming a professor in the University of Lisbon in 1911. In 1927 he developed cerebral angiography (a technique to visualize the blood vessels in and around the brain), for which he was twice nominated for the Nobel Prize. He was a man with immense self-confidence.

In 1935 he attended a neurology conference in London where he heard a description of the changes in chimpanzee behaviour after the destruction of their frontal lobes. Chimpanzees are notoriously quarrelsome but these two became calm and relatively affectionate after the operations. Moniz wondered if the same could be achieved in humans.

Moniz worked with a local surgeon to test his theory by interrupting the fibres running from the most frontal part of the brain, the pre-frontal cortex. Initially he did this by boring holes and destroying the fibres with injections of alcohol but soon shifted to using a fine knife. The patients chosen had a wide range of diagnoses, not only psychoses, but all had prominent symptoms of anxiety and depression. They operated on twenty patients and claimed a good recovery in one third, moderate recovery in another third and no change in the remaining third. They reported no deaths or epileptic seizures.

Leucotomy spread as a treatment for intractable schizophrenia or tormenting anxiety. Its excessive overuse by Freeman and Watts in the USA during and after the war (Chapter 9) brought it into disrepute and led to its abandonment apart from in very tightly defined circumstances. Moniz's life continued to be eventful. He was shot by a disaffected patient and confined to a wheelchair from 1939 but received the Nobel Prize for medicine in 1949 for his introduction of leucotomies. Despite all this he continued his private practice right up to his death in 1955 at the age of eighty.

THE WIDER IMPACT

It is tempting to consider the major impact of this era entirely in terms of the conceptual advances it generated, and generate advances it certainly did. We should not, however, overlook the relief to countless suffering individuals, which has been immense. Luckily, few reading this book will have seen or experienced the depths of depression for which ECT is so effective. Seeing the relief that ECT can bring is the reason why psychiatrists continue to prescribe it in the face of endless criticism and, indeed, some abuse. Before ECT the average admission to a British mental hospital for depression (melancholia) lasted about two years. Up to a fifth of such patients died during that admission – and these figures are from good hospitals with high-quality nursing and careful records. Only the most difficult cases of depression now languish in hospital for months; most never even come into hospital. We have no experience of GPI and can only struggle to understand just how terrifying it was, with its inexorable decline and the fear that it could be silently incubating. Perhaps the HIV/AIDS epidemic in the 1980s is our generation's closest comparison.

These treatments really did revolutionize psychiatry. I have called this chapter 'the first medical model' to emphasize their highly specific, quite explicitly physical explanations and applications. Yet much, if not most, of their impact and legacy has been on professional attitudes. They raised standards of practice for staff, both doctors and nurses. They now had specific roles and activities that went well beyond just observing and protecting, and their interventions were associated with real and visible improvements in their patients. These roles reaffirmed their professional identities and their mood and self-respect improved with a newfound optimism and focus. The changes were probably given an added vigour by an influx of new staff seeking employment in the great depression. Many of these would never have thought of being 'asylum attendants', as they were then routinely called, but were forced to look for alternatives as they lost their jobs. In many large asylums staff had previously come from several generations of the same families, often living in hospital houses – not a recipe for innovation. Many of the new staff arrived without any of the trad-itional pessimism and were keen to try out these new approaches.

Another consequence of these changes was increased contact with general hospital medicine. Because the new treatments were quite tricky and even dangerous, patients frequently had to be transferred to general wards, sometimes as a matter of urgency. Pneumonia and inhalation of vomit by comatose patients were ever-present risks, complications of malaria fevers could be life-threatening. There might be a shortage of sufficiently skilled nursing staff to continue a treat-ment in the asylum so the patient had to be transferred to a general ward. A revelation from this was that even very chronic and very ill patients could cooperate with their treatments in the general hospitals and did so.

That patients would cooperate in the general hospital was not just one revelation but two. First, in the unstimulating environment of the asylum, staff had simply been unaware of just how capable many of their patients had become. Many had made partial recoveries, which went unnoticed in large, poorly staffed asylums. The challenge of complex treatments provided the opportunity to observe it. Second, patients cooperated voluntarily. They did so despite not being com-pelled to do so by law. All asylum patients at that time (apart from in some advanced institutions in Switzerland and Germany) were 'certi-fied'; that is, they were involuntarily detained with their rights to refuse treatments removed. This certification, however, only applied within the asylum walls: any treatment outside would be as a free individual. It was a real eye-opener for staff that patients despite very serious mental illnesses would voluntarily cooperate with treatment.

This upheaval in care was associated with growing changes in soci-ety's view of mental illness. The experiences of psychiatrists and neurologists treating shell shock in the First World War (picked up in the next chapter) had challenged old ideas. Healthy men, indeed brave men, could become very ill because of stress; serious disorders could recover, and effective treatment could take place outside hospitals. Mental illness was both respectable and curable.

Nothing demonstrates these changes more clearly than the changes in the UK law. The 1930 Mental Treatment Act replaced the highly repressive 1890 Lunacy Act. It allowed for voluntary admissions and for the rapid reclassification of patients from involuntary to voluntary if they improved. It also introduced a fundamental change in language. 'Lunatic' was replaced by 'mental patient', 'asylum' by 'mental hospital', 'asylum attendant' by 'mental nurse' and 'certified' by 'detained'. These were massive and irreversible changes. Changes in recent mental health legislation are picked up in Chapters 7 and 12 but these are small beer compared to that which occurred between the wars. Mental illness and personal choice were seen to be not necessarily incompatible. The 1930 Act, and its equivalents in other jurisdictions, recognized the possibility of recovery for the mentally ill and made seeking early treatment and relief possible. Psychiatry had moved from being a relatively fatalistic profession, engaged in protecting patients and hoping they would recover, to a purposeful one with effective treatments that relieved harrowing distress. It has never been the same since.

6

The impact of war

Shell shock is what springs to my mind when anyone mentions psychiatry and war. I think of the terrible casualties and horrors of trench warfare, and the doomed young poets Wilfred Owen and Siegfried Sassoon. Sassoon's treatment by the charismatic psychiatrist William Rivers at Craiglockhart Hospital in Scotland was immortalized in Pat Barker's trilogy of novels, *Regeneration*. For a younger generation the immediate associations are as likely to be Vietnam veterans and post-traumatic stress disorder (PTSD) or even Gulf War syndrome. Wars test men to the extreme. They have always generated new disorders which capture the imagination, and they stimulate new understanding of human behaviour and mental breakdown.

This chapter is called 'The impact of war' and not military psychiatry because the impact of war on psychiatry goes well beyond the immediate treatment of military casualties. The consequences of shell shock spread far beyond the armed forces and persisted well after the First World War. Similarly PTSD was first described in Vietnam veterans but revolutionized how the whole spectrum of mental illnesses is currently classified; it changed how we now define and explain all our psychiatric disorders. Each war throws up broadly similar challenges, and yet the lessons appear to have to be learnt anew each time. Remarkably different conclusions were often drawn by opposing combatants in the same theatre of conflict.

The American Civil War brought a host of innovations – from repeating rifles to standardized clothes sizes. The US physician Jacob Mendes Da Costa (1833–1900) gave his name to a syndrome of severe chest pain observed in soldiers during that war. Incapacitating chest pain had been noted earlier in solders but attributed to their heavy knapsacks. Da Costa studied it systematically in 300 soldiers and described it in detail and recognized that 'soldier's heart' was an expression of anxiety. 'Da Costa's syndrome' remained a routine diagnosis well into the twentieth century for anxiety-based chest pain and palpitations in individuals with healthy hearts.

Silas Weir Mitchell (1829–1914) was in charge of casualties in Philadelphia and from this he developed the 'Weir Mitchell Rest Cure'. This dominated the treatment of hysteria and neurasthenia in the latter part of the nineteenth century, consisting of isolation, bed rest and massage. It became the stock in trade of the spa towns of middle Europe – as remote as can be imagined from the horrors of civil war field hospitals.

Neurasthenia itself was also first defined by a naval surgeon in the Civil War, George Beard (1839–83). He blamed exhaustion of the nervous system for a cluster of symptoms of headaches, dizziness, fatigue, and fainting with anxiety and depression. This, he argued, resulted from chronic stress. Neurasthenia was the first of a long list of psychological disorders to be claimed as 'diseases of civilization'. At first it was diagnosed so much in Americans that Europeans referred to it rather disparagingly as 'Americanitis'.

THE FIRST WORLD WAR
AND SHELL SHOCK

Charles Myers during the First World War was the first doctor to use 'shell shock' as a medical diagnosis in *The Lancet* in 1915. Myers (1873–1946) was a complex, academic and sensitive man. He was medically qualified and had accompanied W. H. R. Rivers (of whom more later) on an anthropological expedition to the Torres Straits and Sarawak in 1898. He had been appointed the first lecturer in experimental psychology in Cambridge University in 1909 but in 1915 found himself in France working as an army doctor in Le Touquet's splendid casino. This had been hastily converted into the 'Duchess of Westminster' clearing hospital to deal with British casualties. Here he made his first diagnosis of shell shock after examining and treating a private soldier with a hysterical blindness. 'Shell shock' was a term already in common use among soldiers, but Myers was the first to give it status in the medical literature.

Shell shock covers an astonishingly wide range of disabling symptoms. Of these the most conspicuous were severe tremors ('the shakes') and unsteadiness of gait, often with bizarre uncontrollable movements. Hysterical symptoms such as paralyses, blindness and inability to speak were also common. Many patients suffered from amnesias and could remember nothing of the events leading up to their breakdown. Some patients displayed a remarkable emotional state called *belle indifférence*, a disconcerting, bland acceptance of their symptoms, which had long been recognized as characteristic of hysteria. However, most were terrified and aroused, troubled by nightmares and unable to rest, eat or sleep.

Doctors of that era were much more familiar with hysterical disorders than we are now. Once it was established that the problem was psychological rather than physical the basic diagnosis was not that controversial. However, the boundary between hysterical or neurotic disorders on the one hand and 'malingering' on the other is a fraught one in a combat zone. The possibility that a soldier may be exaggerating or even putting on his symptoms to get out of the firing line is something that every military doctor must be prepared to consider.

The possible association of hysterical disorders with sudden violent injuries was not a new phenomenon and had been long debated in Paris and Vienna (Chapters 2 and 3). In the first years of the First World War the controversy was about its mechanism. Was the newly named shell shock a purely psychological injury, or was it the result of minor brain injuries from close exposure to explosions? Initially the physical explanation held sway but it yielded to a more psychological interpretation as the evidence mounted. These two explanations are not necessarily mutually exclusive. Shell shock was for some time classified as shell shock (W) for soldiers who were 'wounded' by close exposure to enemy fire, and shell shock (S) for soldiers who were just 'sick'. Shell shock (W) soldiers were initially rewarded with pensions, unlike shell shock (S) soldiers.

Shell shock's psychological origins were suggested by several observations. First the rates varied massively between units, much higher in those with poor discipline and prolonged stress. This stress was more from waiting about rather than in direct exposure to enemy fire. Indeed there was no clear association at all between rates of shell shock and levels of enemy fire or concussion. Lastly there was an almost complete absence of shell shock in prisoners of war on either side, irrespective of how much combat they had seen.

Shell shock was understood as a response to the unbearable tension between the soldier's desire to do his duty and fight, and the fundamental biological urge to get away and save his life. A 1942 psychiatry textbook expressed this succinctly as 'the conflict between his desire for self-preservation and his sense of duty'. Trench warfare in 1914–18 was unquestionably one of the most terrifying of military experiences. It went on for months, often without relief. Long periods of waiting exposed to constant bombardment were interrupted with murderous advances 'over the top' often moving the lines forward only a few yards. Against unpredictable artillery fire there was simply nothing you could do. There was neither the opportunity for fight nor for flight, the natural responses to threat. The incoming shell either 'had your number on it' or it did not.

The scale of losses in engagements is barely conceivable today. The first day of the Somme Offensive alone cost 57,000 casualties and it continued from July to November 1916 with an estimated million deaths. All this to advance six miles into German-held territory. The thirteen battles fought at Passchendaele the following year cost 140,000 Allied deaths and countless casualties for a five-mile advance that was lost less than six months later. Ben Shephard argues in his outstanding book *A War of Nerves: Soldiers and Psychiatrists in the Twentieth Century* (2001) that the slaughter was so high because retreat could only be contemplated after very high casualties. It is hardly surprising that the futility in such engagements sapped morale and discipline, and drove so many over the edge.

All the combatants in the First World War were faced with high rates of nervous breakdown and desertion. Few soldiers could have been adequately prepared for the horrors they were to confront. Maintaining the fighting machine became the top priority and savage discipline was enforced to achieve it. The British sentenced 3,080 troops for cowardice or desertion and executed 307, the French sentenced 2,000 and executed 700. In contrast the Germans only sentenced 150 and executed 48. In the German army it appeared that troops who could not fight were promptly deployed to non-combatant roles rather than evacuated from the front. The disgrace of these Allied executions *pour encourager les autres* is compounded by many of the victims being clearly mentally ill. Most had shell shock but some undoubtedly suffered psychotic illnesses.

The problem of desertion was soon overshadowed by the tide of shell-shocked troops, particularly after the 1916 Somme Offensive. Treatment rapidly shifted its emphasis to management as near the battlefront as possible with a rapid return to active duty. It would be very easy to be cynical about this decision, and to conclude that the needs of the fighting machine had triumphed over concerns for the soldiers' wellbeing. It was not that simple. It had become increasingly clear that a rapid return to fighting was generally in the soldiers' own best interests (providing they survived). Doctors genuinely believed that the army's needs and the soldiers' welfare coincided.

The chance of recovery from shell shock fell steeply the longer a soldier was away from his comrades, and the further he was evacuated from the fighting. It was not just return to active duty that became increasingly remote – the chance of return to any normal life fell off rapidly the longer the condition persisted. Three years after the war ended, in 1921, there were still 14,771 discharged soldiers in active treatment for their psychiatric illnesses. When the Second World War was declared 18,000 men were still on pensions for psychological disorders from the First World War.

Freud had already noted how a neurotic illness became chronic if it became a part of the individual's identity and especially if it shaped how those around him responded. He called this reinforcement by others 'secondary gain' to distinguish it from the neurotic 'primary gain', which he believed to be the avoidance of repressed thoughts or impulses. We see again and again the power of secondary gain to trap people in illnesses. For a few it may tip over into conscious malingering, but not for many. For the majority secondary gain is simply one more obstacle to recovery. Receiving a war pension during the 1920s when there was widespread unemployment inevitably slowed recovery. There was also the very real fear that getting better might be taken as a sign by others that there had never been a 'real illness', that the patient was a coward and had been faking it all along. Many patients recovered soon after the Armistice.

In Germany war pensions were simply abolished in 1926 and most recipients soon recovered. The French had never awarded them. The USA established the Veterans' Bureau (later to become the Veterans' Administration, 'the VA') in 1921. Over a third of admissions to VA hospitals were for psychiatric disorders. The USA has always been more generous to its military veterans ever since the Civil War, and the VA has grown to become an enormous institution.

Proximity, immediacy, expectancy (PIE) became the watchwords of military treatment. Treating soldiers as soon as possible ('immediacy'), and without removing them from the battle arena ('proximity') were central. Speed was vital to prevent the symptoms solidifying so that the soldier came to think of himself as having a serious, potentially long-term 'illness', rather than an understandable 'reaction' to a terrifying and overwhelming situation. The services had to be as close to the fighting as possible to reduce delay in treatment. Forward stations, already established for the wounded, now became the sites for treating shell-shocked soldiers. Proximity had a second advantage: it kept everybody (patients, doctors, orderlies) focused on an imminent return to the fighting, 'expectancy'.

Myers had argued for psychological treatment close to the fighting from the start. Over time a similar 'tripartite' structure developed across the Allied services for psychological casualties. Different terms were used in different forces and the structure was most clearly described by the Americans. Its first response was a psychiatric service at divisional level for immediate 'first aid' of the shocked troops. Those who failed to respond within days would be moved back to the 'advanced neurological hospital' (Charles Myers's 'forward stations') some miles away. Here more complex treatments usually lasted a number of weeks. Finally those who simply could not be rehabilitated to return to fighting were evacuated to the 'base hospital' and possibly (though only as a last resort) back home, where treatment might take months.

There were essentially three strands in the treatment of shell shock and they varied significantly over time and between the combatant nations. Political and cultural factors played a major role in the

shifting profile of what was in, and what was out. The following sum-
mary is, of necessity, an over-simplification. A common theme
throughout was the desire to abandon the term 'shell shock' altogether.
It was viewed as an all-too-easy escape route from the battleground to
a pension back home. It was also thought to 'mystify' the experience
with ominous overtones that inhibited recovery. Many officers and
doctors tried unsuccessfully to replace it with simpler terms such as
'emotional strain'. The French and Germans had no similar unifying
term for shell shock, although they had equally ill patients, and they
developed their own treatments.

Psychotherapy was the first and most widespread treatment for
shell shock in the forward stations. You should not, however, think
this meant anything like psychoanalysis. Psychotherapy here means
that treatment was based mainly on talking and included some
attempt to understand and explain the suffering. It drew heavily on
the doctor's force of character. Treatment was usually brief and very
active. Hypnosis, persuasion, encouragement and suggestion were the
tools; the soldier was reassured that he would soon recover and that
this was temporary. It was especially emphasized that he was fundamentally unchanged as a person and would soon be back with his
comrades and be his normal self again.

The entry of the Americans into the war in 1917 brought with it a
large number of medical staff well versed in hypnosis and simple psychotherapy to treat their soldiers. Their very able medical officer,
Thomas Salmon, emphasized screening (of which more later) and
rapid access to eclectic, that is to say practical and un-dogmatic,
psychotherapy.

Rest (sometimes with sedatives) and food were also key factors in
the treatment of shell shock. The Germans were less likely to use psychotherapy but instead withdrew their affected soldiers a short
distance from the firing line for some days or weeks. During these
brief periods they made sure that they had rest, food and plenty of
non-threatening, but tiring and meaningful, work. In this way their
self-esteem was not destroyed, and the expectation of being invalided
out was not raised.

The sophisticated psychotherapy provided for severe cases sent
home has captured the public imagination and remains our iconic

image of shell shock. The horror of it is brought home by grainy black-and-white pictures of tormented, terrified eyes staring from emaciated figures, hunched or shaking. To this is added the romantic story of Britain's gilded youth, the poets Siegfried Sassoon and Wilfred Owen, exploring their anxieties and exposing their souls to the charismatic (and equally tormented) psychiatrist William Rivers. All this in the gothic splendour of Craiglockhart Hospital has ensured a stream of novels. The psychotherapies pursued in these units, albeit atypical and restricted to a few privileged patients, conferred an enduring legacy on psychiatry.

Before discussing them, however, it may be useful to say something about the celebrities involved. W. H. R. Rivers (1864–1922) was a psychologically minded psychiatrist who had also earned himself a considerable reputation for his anthropological work on kinship. He led the Torres Straits and Sarawak expedition in 1898 which included Charles Myers. He was a stiff, rather aloof, individual who had grown up handicapped by a serious stammer. He remained unmarried and novelists and biographers have made much of a perceived homoerotic tension between him and his famous patient Sassoon. He was clearly humane and open in his psychotherapy and unhappy about sending his patients back to the Western Front.

The two war poets treated at Craiglockhart were very different to each other. Sassoon (1886–1967) was an upper-class officer, already well known and decorated for conspicuous bravery in the trenches. His men called him 'Mad Jack' and he had been awarded the Military Cross and even nominated for Britain's highest order for bravery, the Victoria Cross. However, in 1917 he published a searing criticism of the war ('Finished With War: A Soldier's Declaration') and this pacifist message from such a renowned and dashing soldier was a considerable embarrassment for the government. His transfer to Craiglockhart for treatment may have been more for political convenience than medical need. It remains unclear exactly what he suffered from. Wilfred Owen (1893–1918), however, did suffer from typical shell shock. He was from humble English/Welsh origins and is now widely considered the greatest of the First World War poets ('Anthem for Doomed Youth', 'Dulce et Decorum Est'). He hero-worshipped Sassoon, who helped him develop his poetry while at Craiglockhart. It is unclear whether he was homosexual (unlike Sassoon, who became much more open about it after the war). Owen recovered and returned to the trenches just in time to be killed one week before the Armistice.

Rivers based his treatment on Freudian ideas of unconscious forces and conflicts. Psychotherapy of shell shock seemed to confirm Freud's views about the nature of the unconscious, of resistance and of the value of suggestion and catharsis. However, his theories of sexual conflict were not helpful and were soon abandoned. Rivers and most of his colleagues saw the origins of the disorder in the drive for self-preservation and its conflict with duty and patriotism. They encouraged the soldiers to confront rather than suppress their traumatic memories. They acknowledged that fear and weakness were natural and inevitable, and encouraged the men to own up to their emotions, express them and to try and understand them. It was a long way from the stiff-upper-lip tradition of the officer corps.

Although psychotherapy was probably the commonest approach used in the Allied forces, physical approaches figured more in the medical literature, particularly in the psychiatrically more sophisticated German and French services. Using physical treatments does not mean you have to believe in a physical origin for the disorder. It was simply an alternative approach to treating what was by then widely recognized as a psychological problem. Nor were physical treatments the only ones used in these services. Suggestion, support and hypnosis were also widely used and the Germans and French had their own towering figures in their application. However, their physical treatments dominated the professional discourse. Many had a strikingly brutal quality, which undoubtedly damaged psychiatry's reputation in both France and Germany.

The most notorious of these was the electrical treatment developed by Dr Fritz Kaufmann (1875–1941). He introduced his so-called 'surprise cure' in Mannheim in 1916. Kaufmann's cure started with the imposition of strict discipline and suggestion followed by a series of very painful electric shocks lasting two to five minutes. He aimed for full remission within *a day*. Kaufmann believed that as an overwhelming shock had caused the disorder then another shock should right the system. His treatments are reported to have resulted in over twenty

THE IMPACT OF WAR

deaths and several suicides. Rumours of his approach leaked out and many soldiers refused treatment and some mutinied. Kaufmann himself relented in 1917 but the distaste and reputation lingered. Wagner-Jauregg (Chapter 5) instituted the same approaches with electrical treatment for military casualties in Vienna. In France the treatment was called *torpillage* (torpedoing). It became a source of outrage and the resistance to it drew attention to the severe disciplinary problems then current in the French forces.

In the aftermath of the war military psychiatrists were severely criticized in Germany and Austria for their brutal treatments and there were a number of public enquiries. Such treatments, although not as prominent, were tried in England and France though not subject to any enquiries. What is so damaging about these treatments was that even if they worked their mode of action was so clearly more as a punishment. They were hardly treatments as we would understand the term, despite the explanations proposed for them. You sense that these doctors did not really believe their patients. They thought they were shirkers who should be unmasked.

Shell shock was not a popular idea with governments or the military establishment. As early as 1916 documents record a strong lobby to outlaw the use of the term. Even Charles Myers, who introduced it professionally, argued that it was not just unhelpful but had become positively damaging. Psychiatrists thought it unhelpful because it consolidated an otherwise fluid emotional state into a fixed 'illness'. The military found it threatening because it challenged the maintenance of discipline and undermined the commanding officer's authority. The authority to send shell-shocked soldiers back to a base hospital was removed from doctors and transferred to the commanding officer. He even had to issue a special certificate (form AF343). More troublingly, shell shock threatened the government with an escalating pensions bill and the prospect of thousands of men excluded permanently from the work force.

Despite the best efforts of all these groups we still talk a hundred years later of shell shock and 'being shell-shocked'. And this with our having little experience of armed conflict. Shell shock is a psychiatric concept that has always 'punched above its weight'. More than just a catchy phrase to summarize feeling emotionally overwhelmed, it started a process of destigmatizing mental illnesses. This was a mental disorder which attracted sympathy and conferred respect and even honour on its sufferer. There was no taint of bad blood or degeneration about brave men who had been scarred by truly horrendous experiences. Good, courageous people could also have nervous breakdowns.

Psychiatrists had, on balance, proved their worth in the First World War. As the Second World War approached, the need to prepare for psychological casualties was anticipated. Military psychiatry in the Second World War is also judged a success story. There were important innovations to improve the soldier's immediate welfare, the level of chronic invalidity was much less than after the First World War, and lasting improvements in clinical practice were developed.

THE SECOND WORLD WAR AND NEW PHARMACOLOGICAL TREATMENTS

The armies of 1939 were different from those of 1914. Troops were physically healthier and better educated. They were more psychologically aware and understood more about their emotions. So their breakdowns, when they occurred, were different. Hysterical disorders have steadily diminished in industrialized societies as we have become more psychologically sophisticated. Soldiers, just like the general population, now suffered from anxiety states and depression rather than shakes and paralyses. The war itself was also different. It was more mobile and was concentrated more in individual battles rather than the grinding attrition of the trenches. *Battle trauma* and *battle fatigue* replaced shell shock. The psychological origins of these disorders were never in any real doubt.

The lessons of 'PIE' had been taken to heart. There was now considerable psychiatric manpower and it was deployed close to the fighting. The emphasis was on support and reassurance, rest and peer pressure and all with an expectation of a rapid return to active duty. *Exhaustion* and *battle fatigue* were the deliberately downbeat terms used. It was recognized that every man has his breaking point, so limits on the duration of active service were introduced. In the USA this

THE IMPACT OF WAR

was just over 200 days, and in Britain 400 days but with regular scheduled rest periods. This was an important innovation and protected many men. However, it could undermine group morale, as became evident in the Vietnam War.

The revolutionary innovation in front-line psychiatry in the Second World War was the use of drugs. Roy Grinker from Chicago introduced 'narco-synthesis' and William Sargent from London used 'amytal-abreactions'. Both used injections of the new, safe and quick-acting barbiturates to discharge emotion. These allowed soldiers to relive their experiences and, through catharsis, to overcome their trauma. Recoveries could be dramatic, almost miraculous and virtually instantaneous. The abreacted memories were often vivid and harrowing. However, the actual details of the memory mattered less than the discharge of emotion, the apparently traumatic incident had sometimes never occurred. Despite this the violent expression of overwhelming emotion and the calm that immediately followed it were healing. Amytal and Pentothal abreactions remained in use long after the war for acute disorders and for 'unlocking' stuck ones. Their value has been questioned and results from more traditional psychotherapy and rest may have been equally good. However, the champions of abreactions were powerful, charismatic figures and their treatments had an enormous impact on the profession. Big personalities have always had a disproportionate effect on the course of psychiatric advances.

RELATIONSHIPS AND COPING

Improvements were not limited to acute treatment but also occurred in the base hospitals. Those returning suffered from the whole range of psychiatric problems. The treatment of the neurotic disorders, predominantly anxiety and chest pain (Da Costa's syndrome, or soldier's heart, was now renamed disordered action of the heart, or DAH), gave rise to radical new thinking and developments. These laid the foundations of social psychiatry and much of the post-war community care, described in the following chapter.

The military is an extremely disciplined, hierarchical organization with a wide class divide between officers and men. In the First World War, for instance, British officers could only be appointed from public (i.e. private) schools. Army doctors were not only better educated than most of their patients but they had a higher military rank, spoke with a different accent and came from a very different social background. In psychiatry, where trust and openness are essential, this is a problem. These conflicts were played out in a remarkable manner in the Northfield Military Hospital in Birmingham. The solution found has changed not just psychiatric hospitals but also prisons, educational establishments and drug rehabilitation services. It came to be called the 'therapeutic community'.

In a nutshell, the psychiatrists in Northfield were faced with an animosity towards the officer class (them), high numbers of patients, and a treatment regime that seemed to work against itself. Northfield had 200 places for 'psychiatric treatment' and 600 places for 'rehabilitation' or 'training'. Rehabilitation consisted of the reintroduction of army discipline and uniforms, along with structured work and activity to restore self-confidence and routine. The soldiers had every reason to sabotage their progress, which otherwise inevitably led to their returning to war. Remaining ill offered the prospect of discharge to civilian life. Something had to change.

Two eminent psychoanalytically trained psychiatrists (John Rickman and Wilfred Bion) were drafted in. Bion (1897–1979) was a forceful character who never compromised on anything throughout a distinguished career. He had been awarded the DSO and the Légion d'Honneur for conspicuous bravery as a tank commander in 1918. He approached the Northfield challenge in the same spirit as he had approached the enemy. An over-ambitious and disastrous start resulted in virtual anarchy in the training wing (the 'First Northfield Experiment'). The hospital had to be shut down and reopened 'under new management'. Michael Foulkes, an expatriate German analyst, continued to run therapy groups in the treatment unit. The rehabilitation unit run by Harold Bridger, who was not a psychiatrist, became much more active. It placed a greater emphasis on social interaction and engagement in the practical running of the hospital.

Tom Main (1911–90) arrived in 1945 and took over leadership of the whole hospital. He brought together Foulkes's group therapy and the more social activities developed by Bridger into a coherent 'living–learning' environment. The hospital was suffused with an atmosphere of exploration and enquiry and characterized by an egalitarian ethos quite remarkable for the era. Main's revolutionary contribution was to insist that the hospital routines were not just the framework for treatment but *were* the treatment. In a 1946 article, 'The Hospital as a Therapeutic Institution', he called this approach a 'therapeutic community'. After the war Maxwell Jones (1907–90) further developed the 'living–learning' approach of the therapeutic community into a model of care widely applicable not only in psychiatric units but in a variety of institutions – schools, prisons, drug units and more.

Screening out unsuitable soldiers had been tried in a rather timid fashion in the First World War, mainly in the USA. Having comrades who are likely to break down, or are simply unable to understand or carry out orders, is highly dangerous in combat. It is not just that it carries risks for the vulnerable individuals themselves: soldiers under fire need to be able to rely on each other, their very lives depend on it. Most armies rejected those with really obvious physical or mental limitations. A US screening programme in the First World War introduced the idea of systematic assessment but was hopelessly lenient, rejecting only 1 per cent. General 'Black Jack' Pershing, the US Commander in France, complained that he had 'at least 3000 soldiers manifestly unfit' for service. He insisted on a tightened screening, and some basic intelligence testing was introduced.

In the Second World War the procedures were much more professional. After an initial false start the programme in the USA organized careful screening and a coherent classification of the psychiatric disorders encountered. In both the USA and the UK the newly evolving discipline of clinical psychology received a boost from this screening programme, standardizing and administering tests.

The striking success of the Germans in their officer selection drove the point home. The German army had been severely restricted in size since the end of the First World War so it could only afford to recruit the best. Its elite officer corps was selected using a panel which included over 200 psychiatrists. Convinced that it was indiscipline at home that lost them the First World War, the Germans took a hard line with casualties and treated psychological problems as essentially a disciplinary issue. This rigid, harsh discipline was observed, however, to be associated with high morale and low casualties. Because of their highly able officers they could run a decentralized army based on trust and local initiative. Selection was clearly worth the investment.

The British selection process was clearly hopeless. Officer cadets had a gentlemanly interview with some senior officers, rather like applying to an Oxford college. Some tests currently used in dynamic psychiatry and psychology were eventually incorporated. One was the thematic apperception test (TAT), in which you described what you saw in ambiguous pictures, and another was the word association test, where you were asked to say the first word that came into your head in response to one from the interviewer. Both of these tests have now faded from the stage but a new technique, 'the leaderless group task', was developed by Wilfred Bion. This has become a staple in selection processes. Essentially it involves giving a group of applicants a joint task to work on and observing how they go about it. It rapidly becomes clear who has initiative, who can engage the others' cooperation, who can think creatively, all qualities essential in an officer. Many of us who have been subjected to a 'leaderless group task' may not be quite that grateful to army psychiatrists for it.

Psychiatrists are experienced in understanding mentally ill patients but they can get it dramatically wrong speculating about normal actions. Planning in Britain for the approaching Second World War was wildly off-target. Aerial warfare was a new and terrifying development with the prospect of civilian targets being bombed. How would civilians stand up to it? There was very real concern about an outbreak of mass panic. Estimates of three to four *million* cases of acute panic and hysteria were predicted for the first six months. London was anticipated to be most affected as it would be subjected to the heaviest and most sustained bombing. Indeed it *was* subjected to such bombing – especially the poorer and densely populated East End. The Blitz (as it came to be called) lasted from September 1940 to May 1941. It started with seventy-six consecutive nights of air raids in the capital and killed over 40,000 civilians, over 20,000 in London, and damaged or destroyed over a million houses. Horrendous though these figures are they are much lower than the 600,000 deaths predicted. In the event mass panic did not occur. There were episodes of dismay and stunned confusion, particularly in cities subject to sudden and overwhelming bombing such as Coventry, Hull and Birmingham. On the whole the population managed remarkably well. Indeed the 'spirit of the Blitz' has become a by-word for a cheerful pulling together.

Why was this response to prolonged exposure to explosions and the threat of random death so different from the experience of the trenches? It certainly was not because people felt protected. Air raid shelter provision was meagre. The iconic scenes of families sleeping in Underground train stations are misleading. Only eighty tube stations were opened and probably fewer than 200,000 people (about 5 per cent of London's population) ever used them. The habit of 'trekking' (which the government tried vigorously to suppress) may give some clues. Many families went into parks and into the nearby countryside and slept the night there, 'trekking' back to work and school the next day. This reduced their exposure to the fear from falling bombs. The difference from the soldiers in the First World War was that civilians had some minimal control over their fate or, more importantly, at least believed they had. Whether they 'trekked' or simply decided to stick it out at home or to go to the air raid shelter, they had some *choice* in the matter. The unique horror of trench warfare was that there was simply nothing at all you could do; you had no choice but to sit out the bombardments.

All in all psychiatry came out of the Second World War with its reputation enhanced (apart from Nazi Germany; Chapter 9). Psychologically minded and humane psychiatrists had risen to positions of considerable national prominence. They had generally overcome the military establishment's scepticism of them as 'trick cyclists' or 'head-shrinkers'. There was an enormous increase in their numbers – particularly in the USA, where they doubled from 2,423 in 1940 to 5,856 in 1950. Important and influential books had been published, such as *Men Under Stress*, by Roy R. Grinker and John P. Spiegel (1945), and *The Traumatic Neuroses of War*, by Abram Kardiner (1941). The advances in social treatments and improved understanding of institutional relationships, epitomized by the therapeutic community, have shaped practice throughout the succeeding half-century.

The response to psychological casualties in this war was much more successful than in its predecessor. There were nothing like the same rates of chronic disability or pensions. In part this was due to psychiatric treatment but it was also due to the very different conditions to which the soldiers returned. The Tommy coming home from the First World War was quite likely to find himself unemployed and unsupported. After the Second World War, soldiers returned to full employment. In Britain he was met by the establishment of the welfare state and 'homes fit for heroes'. In the USA he was met with the generous GI Bill with its educational subsidies to take him through college. Military psychiatry in the Second World War had confirmed the place of psychological processes in both the causation and the treatment of mental disorders. Through this it had significantly humanized psychiatry. It had also taught us to recognize the powerful influence of the group on our wellbeing and recovery. This formed the springboard for the social and community psychiatry revolution to follow. No small achievement.

VIETNAM REFRAMES PSYCHIATRIC DIAGNOSIS

US military psychiatrists entered the Vietnam War with the lessons learnt in the Second World War hardened by their experience in the Korean War (1950–53). Proximity, Immediacy and Expectation remained their watchwords, with the slogan that the army's interests and the soldiers' interests were the same. The USA had been involved in Vietnam and deployed 'military advisors' there since before the colonial power, France, left in 1954. Its military campaign, however, only began in earnest in the early 1960s. It radicalized a generation throughout the world, traumatized America and changed psychiatry for ever. With the ready access to immediate TV newsreels, the horror and injustice of war was brought into homes nightly. It gave rise to a stronger anti-war movement than any war before it or probably since. For all the soul-searching, the number of US fatalities was remarkably low at 58,159 by the time the Americans withdrew in 1973. Compare this with the 57,000 casualties on the *first day* of the Somme. What, however, of the psychological casualties?

Initially these were few until the Tet Offensive in 1968. Soon after that things began to deteriorate, and to deteriorate dramatically. The Vietnam War shared some characteristics with trench warfare. It was generally marked not by pitched battles but by drawn-out conflict with an unseen and unpredictable enemy. After problems with screening in the Second World War, the Americans had abandoned it in Vietnam and there were high levels of enlisted men who really struggled with basic military tasks. Two psychiatric phenomena have become indelibly linked to the Vietnam War and the 'Vietnam vet'. The first was their extensive drug use, the second was PTSD.

Soldiers have always used drugs, whatever intoxicant is to hand. Fighting is terrifying so anything that dulls the fear or gives a sense of energy and invincibility is welcomed. The word 'assassin' derives from the hashish used by a group of Shia fighters to impart courage in resisting Crusaders. Air force pilots in the Second World War kept going with liberal supplies of amphetamines, and vast quantities of alcohol have been consumed by armies throughout the ages. Only now, in our high-tech professional armies, are alcohol and drugs restricted for combatants.

In Vietnam drug and alcohol use spiralled out of control. It resulted from, and in turn contributed to, a rapidly deteriorating disciplinary situation in the late 1960s. Many of the enlisted men came from neighbourhoods where drug use was endemic and would return to them on demobilization. By 1970 over a third of enlisted men were heavy users of either heroin, marijuana or alcohol; in 1971 more soldiers were evacuated for drug abuse than for wounds. Heavy drug use also contributed to the atrocities that so shamed the US campaign.

Both this drug problem and the rates of battle stress may have been unwittingly increased by the decision to give all troops rigidly fixed, individual tours of duty of precisely one year. Traditionally fighting units such as regiments went overseas together, fought together and returned home together. Building on observations of the upper limits of a soldier's endurance, the practice in Vietnam became to replace each individual casualty, or soldier withdrawn at the end of his tour of duty, with a fresh recruit. The crucial protective esprit de corps that sustains most fighting men was lost. Neither group support nor effective peer-pressure, normally the military's most potent forces, was now available to manage stresses.

Soldiers returning with established drug problems also found themselves confronted by a disaffected society that rejected them rather than honouring them. Their continued drug use after demobilization may have been, in part, a defence against this hostility but also undoubtedly inflamed it. The image of the angry, wired-up and unemployable Vietnam vet, drifting in an out of VA hospitals, sinking ever further into drug and alcohol abuse, became the public image for an unpopular war. It is easy to exaggerate the contribution of the war. Drug and alcohol abuse are common; they are particularly common in young, single, poorly educated men with limited employment skills. Vietnam and Gulf War veterans in both the USA and the UK do not necessarily have higher rates of mental disorder than their peers in the general population. After Vietnam they were, however, a highly visible, very damaged and tragic group of young men. Psychiatry had to respond.

The Vietnam War gave us a new disorder. PTSD not only generated a new diagnosis, but kick-started a complete redesign of diagnostic classification in psychiatry and a radically different way of making those diagnoses. PTSD may have changed our approach to mental illness irrevocably and this will be taken up again in Chapter 11. Several forces conspired in this revolution, forces in society at large and forces within psychiatry, and their relative contributions are hard to apportion. This was a time of real change in psychiatry, particularly in the USA, where it had been severely embarrassed and was on the defensive.

Psychiatry in the USA had been under enormous pressure from the newly vocal Gay Rights Movement to declassify homosexuality as a psychiatric disorder. The traditional hegemony of psychoanalytical thinking which had dominated US teaching and practice had also begun to yield to a more scientific, biological psychiatry heavily reliant on drugs. Outside psychiatry the psychological problems of the Vietnam vets became a focal point in the anti-war movement. A highly political psychoanalyst, Chaim Shatan, described a 'post-Vietnam syndrome' in 1974. This was thought to descend on the veteran about a year after return to civilian life, when the initial demobilization euphoria had worn off. It was characterized by dismay, despair, anxiety and instability. Post-Vietnam syndrome started to overlap thinking then current about stress response syndromes in Holocaust survivors.

Mardi Horowitz published his book *Stress Response Syndromes* in 1976 and, along with Shatan, advanced the idea that any trauma could cause psychological problems if it were severe enough. It was not restricted to battle trauma. Post-Vietnam syndrome became absorbed into this more general category of psychological disorders resulting from terrifying experiences. Post-traumatic stress disorder was born. PTSD became a prototype diagnosis for the new psychiatric *Diagnostic Statistical Manual, DSM-III*, produced by the American Psychiatric Association in 1980. *DSM-III* made a decisive break from older, more theoretical and descriptive formulations. It stressed the overwhelming importance of easily definable and reliable diagnoses based on a limited number of simple criteria.

The box on the next page lists the criteria for diagnosing PTSD updated from *DSM-III* to *DSM-IV* and demonstrates this crisp, structured approach. It rapidly became the default diagnosis for Vietnam vets irrespective of whether or not they were also abusing drugs or alcohol. By 1990 (seventeen years after the last US troops left Vietnam), 480,000 vets were in treatment for PTSD, including many who had never seen active service. The attraction of PTSD as a diagnosis is that it confers an honourable explanation for the patient's current situation. It states unequivocally that the war experience *caused* this problem and establishes eligibility for free health care in the VA. We have already seen in two previous international conflicts how two-edged this can be and the risks involved in following this path. We will explore again in Chapter 11 the consequences of such simplistic diagnostic formulations in psychiatry.

PTSD remains a controversial diagnosis. Its supporters point to the volume of high-quality, sophisticated research that it has generated, research that often links psychological and biological processes. Its critics argue that it over-simplifies the process and ignores all-important social dimensions and practices that protect against trauma and promote healing. Military psychiatry in the Vietnam War has, undoubtedly, impacted far beyond the army. In helping to deliver

Diagnostic criteria for 309.81 Post Traumatic Stress Disorder

A. The person has been exposed to a traumatic event in which both of the following were present:
   1) the person experienced, witnessed, or was confronted with an event or events that involved actual or threatened death or serious injury, or a threat to the physical integrity of self or others
   2) the person's response involved intense fear, helplessness, or horror

B. The traumatic event is persistently re experienced in one (or more) of the following ways:
   1) recurrent and intrusive distressing recollections of the event, including images, thoughts, or perceptions
   2) recurrent distressing dreams of the event
   3) acting or feeling as if the traumatic event were recurring (includes a sense of reliving the experience, illusions, hallucinations and dissociative flashback episodes, including those that occur on awakening or when intoxicated)
   4) intense psychological distress at exposure to internal or external cues that symbolize or resemble an aspect of the traumatic event
   5) physiological reactivity on exposure to internal or external cues that symbolize or resemble an aspect of the traumatic event

C. Persistent avoidance of stimuli associated with the trauma and numbing of general responsiveness (not present before the trauma), as indicated by three (or more) of the following:
   1) efforts to avoid thoughts, feelings, or conversations associated with the trauma
   2) efforts to avoid activities, places, or people that arouse recollections of the trauma
   3) inability to recall an important aspect of the trauma
   4) markedly diminished interest or participation in significant activities
   5) feeling of detachment or estrangement from others
   6) restricted range of affect (e.g. unable to have loving feelings)
   7) sense of a foreshortened future (e.g. does not expect to have a career, marriage, children, or a normal life span)

D. Persistent symptoms of increased arousal (not present before the trauma), as indicated by two (or more) of the following:
   1) difficulty falling or staying asleep
   2) irritability or outbursts of anger
   3) difficulty concentrating
   4) hyper vigilance
   5) exaggerated startle response

E. Duration of the disturbance (symptoms in Criteria B, C, and D) is more than 1 month

F. The disturbance causes clinically significant distress or impairment in social, occupational, or other important areas of functioning

Specify if:
Acute: if duration of symptoms is less than 3 months
Chronic: if duration of symptoms is 3 months or more

Specify if:
With Delayed Onset: if onset of symptoms is as least 6 months after the stressor

American Psychiatric Association, *Diagnostic and Statistical Manual of Mental Disorders (DSM-IV)*

DSM-III and 'criterion-based diagnosis' it has ushered in one of the most profound changes in psychiatric practice. Hard though it is to imagine that something as dry and dusty as a classificatory manual would have far-reaching effects on thinking and practice, it undoubtedly has.

It is probable that *DSM-III* would eventually have happened even without the Vietnam War and PTSD. It might, however, have developed more slowly and with more reflection; PTSD and military psychiatrists certainly set the pace.

Military psychiatry in all three major conflicts has enriched and strengthened our understanding of psychological illness as responses to stress and as consequences of psychological events. This is so much a feature of how we now think about mental illness that we hardly pause to consider it, or recognize how relatively new it is. We now take for granted that the human mind can suffer psychological (mental) injuries from psychological (mental) traumas just as the body suffers physical injuries. PTSD, like shell shock before it, has entered our international consciousness and irrevocably changed psychiatric diagnosis and thinking. There is no going back.

7

Out of the asylum – the origins
of community care

The asylum movement, which started with such great hopes in the early nineteenth century, peaked and started its decline in the middle of the twentieth century. In 1955 there was a staggering total of 560,000 patients in USA public mental hospitals and over 150,000 in British ones, nearly one person in every 200. By the turn of the century the figures were down to well below a third of this and these figures understate the reversal. In Britain deinstitutionalization (as this process is called) had started by 1955, accelerating slightly through the 1980s to arrive at fewer than 27,000 at the time of writing. In the USA deinstitutionalization really took off with the Medicaid and Medicare Bills of 1965. The fall to 71,619 patients in the USA by 1994 is an effective reduction of over 90 per cent when you consider the USA population grew over that period from 164 million to 260 million.

The initial impact of early deinstitutionalization was to reduce the appalling overcrowding in mental hospitals. Patient numbers fell during the first decade but the institutions themselves were basically unchanged. Neither wards nor hospitals were closed; nor were staff laid off. Instead of two or three harassed nurses managing a ward of forty patients that same ward became home for twenty. Care became more humane, but consequently much more expensive. From the 1980s hospitals began visibly contracting, first by shutting wards, and then they started closing altogether. The vast majority of mental hospitals in the developed Western countries are now gone; those left rarely contain more than a tenth of their original number. Their sites are now often campuses containing new smaller purpose-built acute units and units for elderly patients.

This chapter describes the move out of the asylum and the rise of community mental health care. Deinstitutionalization has been an international movement, but not a uniform one. It varies enormously between countries both in its extent and in the approaches adopted. It has been embraced most whole-heartedly in English-speaking nations and in Italy. The pace has been patchy and slower in mainland Europe generally and quite minimal in some countries. One or two countries such as Japan have actually increased the number of mental hospital beds. It is sobering, however, to realize that in the early years of the twenty-first century, mental hospital care is still the only available service in much of new Europe. Admission to asylums remains the only alternative besides the family in much of the developing world.

The discovery of antipsychotic and antidepressant drugs in the 1950s is the usual explanation advanced for deinstitutionalization, but this is an over-simplification. The drugs were indeed critically important but they were never the whole story. Changes were afoot before they were discovered and, even when they were introduced, their uptake and impact varied remarkably.

The forces for change came from both within the profession and from outside it. Their relative importance is unclear, and we lack the necessary distance for a settled historical view. In summarizing it I have drawn on my experience working in psychiatry through this period and what I have read. I advise caution. It can be impossible to be sure whether any individual development was a cause of deinstitutionalization or a consequence of it, or (quite possibly) whether both were the result of some other underlying process.

Three actors in the drama are indisputable, whatever priority we give them. The first was, of course, the new drugs. The second was new understanding of the damaging effects of asylums. The third was the radical and wide-ranging change in social provision and attitudes following the Second World War. Before charting the demise of the mental hospitals and the newer services that replaced them, let us pause to consider what they were like at their height.

Their enormous size, more than anything else, spelt their extinction. The first mental hospitals described in Chapter 2 were conceived on a domestic scale to care for a few dozen patients. Most residents, both staff and patients, would know each other. Their social relationships, while quite formal, mirrored those on the outside. The rapid growth of asylums in the nineteenth century transformed them into immense, anonymous establishments, often with harsh, even brutal, regimes. All states in the USA had at least one ('state hospitals'), as did all counties in the UK ('county asylums'). Built some distance from the towns they served they were conspicuous by their looming joint water towers and chimneys.

Immense here really does mean immense. In the UK most mental hospitals in the 1950s housed between 1,000 and 2,000 patients. In the USA the average was more, usually 2,000–4,000, but with some truly gargantuan institutions. The Georgia State Hospital in Milledgeville was home to over 10,000 patients and Pilgrim Hospital in Long Island, New York, was the largest ever. Built in 1931 with its own railway station, fire station, post office and farm, it peaked in 1954 with a complement of 13,875 souls. These hospitals were often the main employer in their local communities, sometimes the only one. In the 1930s the patients and staff in the six mental hospitals centred round the market town of Epsom, south of London, outnumbered its other inhabitants.

To change such institutions was a truly ambitious proposition. The British health minister, Enoch Powell, captured this in his famous 1961 'water tower speech':

> This is a colossal undertaking, not so much in the new physical provision which it involves, as in the sheer inertia of mind and matter which it requires to be overcome. There they stand, isolated, majestic, imperious, brooded over by the gigantic water-tower and chimney combined, rising unmistakable and daunting out of the countryside – the asylums which our forefathers built with such immense solidity to express the notions of their day. Do not for a moment underestimate their powers of resistance to our assault.

THE DRUG REVOLUTION

Of the three forces that mounted this assault we will start with the drugs. They did not come first but their role is clearest and most familiar. Psychiatry was changed out of all recognition in the 1950s by the introduction of antipsychotic drugs and antidepressants. Both groups of drugs (like so much in medicine) were stumbled upon while looking for something else.

The first antipsychotic was chlorpromazine, marketed as Largactil in the UK and Thorazine in the USA. It was discovered by a French naval anaesthetist in Vietnam who was using it to lower body temperature during surgery. He reported that his patients were much calmer though not drowsy for several days after their operations. In St Anne's Hospital, Paris, Doctors Delay and Deneke decided to test it on forty schizophrenia inpatients in 1952. The results were so dramatic that they abandoned the study after only ten patients. Over the next four years chlorpromazine spread internationally, becoming the first-line treatment for acute psychosis. The impact was overwhelming. 'Chlorpromazine tore through the civilized world like a whirlwind and engulfed the whole treatment of psychiatric disorders' (*British Medical Journal*, 1954). It calmed and humanized wards. Staff could communicate with patients when previously they were fully occupied in controlling and protecting them. Patients were less disturbed and recovered more quickly, able to be discharged home to their families. By the 1960s it was clear that antipsychotics not only controlled acute breakdowns but reduced relapses in schizophrenia if taken regularly for long periods.

Over twenty alternative antipsychotics have since been developed, mostly variants of chlorpromazine. The first alternative, haloperidol, is a 'high potency' antipsychotic with a significantly different chemical structure, and was introduced in 1958 in Belgium. Although chlorpromazine and its derivatives are not primarily sedatives they do cause drowsiness and lethargy and have other troubling side effects such as stiffness and tremor. During the 1990s a group of newer so-called 'second generation' or 'atypical' antipsychotics was introduced. These newer antipsychotics were initially thought to be much more effective but we now know they are about equally effective as the older ones. They have different side effects. They cause much less stiffness and tremor, and usually less lethargy, but they cause weight gain and a raised risk of diabetes. One, clozapine, appears markedly more effective and is recommended for patients with very severe illnesses. It needs regular blood tests and can make patients very drowsy so, despite its undoubted benefits, many patients reject it or cannot tolerate it.

No antipsychotics are entirely free of side effects. Individual patients may respond better to one drug than another and differ in their tolerance of different side effects. Consequently treatment often involves a degree of trial and error matching the drug to the patient. In the late 1960s a technique was developed to dissolve antipsychotic drugs in oil so that they could be injected into muscle and slowly released over a number of weeks. 'Modecate' was the first of these preparations, introduced in 1968. This meant that symptoms could be controlled without the patient having to remember to take tablets every day. These long-acting injections, so-called 'depot' antipsychotics, are used in long-term maintenance treatment. They have become a mainstay of relapse prevention in schizophrenia, particularly for patients who are chaotic and forget tablets or those who are not convinced that they need them.

The benefits of antipsychotics are undeniable. They are the first-line treatment of schizophrenia but are also widely used to control agitation and hallucinations in bipolar disorder, other psychoses and in dementia. Before their introduction first admissions for acute schizophrenia averaged about two years, but now last only about six to twelve weeks. If patients with schizophrenia take regular maintenance antipsychotics only about one in five will have a breakdown needing readmission to hospital within two years. If they do not take maintenance antipsychotics four out of the five will be readmitted over the same period. So the drugs' undeniable side effects have to be weighed against real benefits.

Antidepressant drugs followed fast on the heels of the antipsychotics. Prior to the 1950s morphine derivatives and sedatives were used to blunt anxiety and tension in depressed patients but there was nothing other than ECT to lift the actual depression. The drugs isoniazid and iproniazid were discovered by pure chance simultaneously in the USA and France to elevate mood when they were being tested to treat tuberculosis in the early 1950s. A Cincinnati psychiatrist, Max Lurie, coined the term 'antidepressant' in 1952 after a successful trial with isoniazid.

Antidepressant prescribing really accelerated with the introduction of 'tricyclic antidepressants' (so called because their chemical structure comprises three carbon rings). The first, imipramine, was produced in Switzerland and had been tested on schizophrenia patients, who became more active and alert with them. In 1955 it was tried successfully with depressed patients and introduced commercially in 1958. Imipramine was soon followed by a wide range of other tricyclic antidepressants. Another group, the 'mono-amine oxidase inhibitor' (MAOI) antidepressants (Parnate, Marplan, Nardil) was first identified in the early 1950s and their use complemented the tricyclics. This group of antidepressants interacts dangerously with some foods and they are potentially habit-forming so generally reserved for resistant depression. By the start of the 1980s USA physicians were writing over 10 million prescriptions a year for antidepressants and the upward trend seems unstoppable.

THE MOVE TO CLOSURE: 'DEINSTITUTIONALIZATION'

Closing mental hospitals is simply not possible until there is an adequate alternative system of support for severely disabled individuals. Most long-term patients had no family or income. The hospital provided them not only care for their mental illness but also food and clothing, shelter and company. In the period up to the Second World War most European states were developing social welfare systems for those unable to care for themselves. Most were based on forms of national insurance administered through local authorities.

The end of the war brought a renewed commitment to establishing these comprehensive social and health care services. Most of the combatant states had made pledges to their fighting men to ensure the equivalent of 'a home fit for heroes'. Forms of universal comprehensive health care were established along with a range of retirement pensions, social security and welfare payments. In most states all individuals were guaranteed basic accommodation and enough money to survive on even if they were permanently unable to work. With these practical provisions sorted out the only thing stopping discharge from mental hospitals should be persisting symptoms or disturbed behaviour. If these were under control then there was no longer any clinical need to stay in hospital.

Of course it is not quite that simple. This blunt dichotomy between needing inpatient care and managing independently obscures a wide range of needs and disabilities. Severity is a highly subjective judgement and things can change rapidly in either direction. What levels of odd behaviour or eccentricity or what degree of disability is tolerable also varies between societies, and in different parts of the same society. What goes unmarked in a busy, culturally diverse London district might raise eyebrows or even attract police attention in a prosperous village. The types of patients discharged also varied. In the 1960s and early 1970s they were generally fully recovered individuals who had, in truth, often been quite self-sufficient in hospital for considerable periods. Not surprisingly they settled easily into quiet, independent existences. As time passed the patients who were discharged had more severe residual disabilities, and still needed support and shelter. There was, after the war, a positive attitude to providing such support; an optimistic and inclusive world view dominated.

Asylums and mental hospitals were originally conceived as benign institutions. They served to shelter and protect patients while they recovered and, where possible, they strove actively to promote that recovery. The persisting disabilities observed in patients, such as their apathy, withdrawal, and deteriorated personal habits and self-care were seen by the staff as proof of their need for ongoing care. True, there had always been some misgivings about the effects of asylums. John Conolly, quoted from 1830 in Chapter 2, was perceptive but not influential:

> confinement is the very reverse of beneficial. It fixes and renders permanent what might have passed away and ripens eccentricity or temporary excitement or depression, into actual insanity. . . . Who has the strength . . . to resist the horrible influences of the place? . . . a place in which the intellectual operations could not but become, from mere want of exercise, more and more inert.

The asylum in the post-war period was now being reappraised. Critical reports of scandalous and brutal treatment had begun to surface. In the USA a series of shocking exposés was published, many originating from conscientious objectors who had been sent to work in state hospitals. A *Life* magazine article in 1946 had page after page of harrowing photographs of neglected and dejected patients in one such hospital. Many were naked or tethered, all were dirty and aimless, crowded together in squalid and dilapidated wards. Mary Jane Ward's novel *The Snake Pit* dramatized these conditions; it became a bestseller and was made into a successful and influential Hollywood film in 1948. Across Europe and the USA investigations into episodes of abuse in individual mental hospitals shook public confidence in such institutions.

At the same time psychiatrists and social scientists were revisiting and reviewing the accepted wisdom about disabilities and long-term mental illness. A British psychiatrist, Russell Barton, published a book entitled *Institutional Neurosis* in 1959. In it he proposed that the so-called 'schizophrenia defect state', on which Kraepelin had placed so much diagnostic emphasis, was as much a consequence of the hospital environment as of the illness. The deadening effect of living in such institutions with their rules and regulations and monotonous routine removed all personal responsibility and choice over long periods. It was this, he argued, that caused the apathy and self-neglect. Two years later the Canadian sociologist Erving Goffman brought out his blockbuster *Asylums: Essays on the Social Situation of Mental Patients and Other Inmates*. This contained four essays on the reality of life in a mental hospital based on a year (1955/6) that Goffman had spent effectively 'under cover' in the enormous St Elizabeth's Hospital in Washington DC.

Goffman's message was even more radical than Russell Barton's. He concluded that 'total institutions' (such as mental hospitals, but he also included others, like prisons and the army) *deliberately* eroded their members' identity and sapped their initiative. They did this to maintain discipline and to make the management of the organization easier. He called this process *institutionalization* and believed that it was achieved by an active 'disculturation'. Goffman's book struck a chord in the anti-authoritarian 1960s and was rapidly adopted by students and intellectuals. It gave impetus to the 'anti-psychiatry' movement (Chapter 8), which was the final nail in the coffin of the mental hospital.

Professional enthusiasm to move patients out from mental hospitals materialized in the 1960s from this new thinking. It acquired the rather ugly epithet 'deinstitutionalization'. Quite soon governments realized that closing mental hospitals might save them money and backed it with vigour. In the USA the speed of closure soon outstripped any reasonable provision of rehabilitation or accommodation support, producing a very visible scandal of homeless mentally ill individuals. This rush to close mental hospitals brought together two very different groups, liberal mental health workers motivated by a desire for better lives for their patients and politicians seeking to reduce public spending. It was dubbed 'an unholy alliance of therapeutic progressives and fiscal conservatives'. Not surprisingly such a massive change in practice has had its share of successes and failures. There have been various approaches. The two most researched and written about are those followed in the UK and USA on the one hand and the radically different path taken in Italy on the other.

In the USA and UK the approach to deinstitutionalization was essentially one of 'reprovision'. The first step was to identify those patients whose recovery had been overlooked in the hospitals and who were ready for discharge. It used to be relatively easy for such patients to get lost in large asylums. Nurses were preoccupied with the more disturbed patients and left the quieter ones to themselves, or even appreciated their help in running the ward. Now places were found for them to live outside the hospital, often with minimal support. Once this first wave had been discharged the task started in earnest to prepare those who still had persisting problems for a life outside. Appropriate accommodation and support had to be found and provided. Disability and symptom levels in those being discharged steadily increased as the pace of the closures accelerated.

Ambitious rehabilitation programmes were established in some hospitals. In north London the TAPS (Team for the Assessment of Psychiatric Services) project was established in 1985 in two enormous mental hospitals and carefully followed the progress of all discharged patients for several years. Their findings were in stark contrast to the public's increasingly critical view of the process. Only a handful of patients were readmitted other than for brief crises, none became homeless and very few were lost to follow-up or ended up in prison. Most were housed in small hostels of between ten and twenty residents and none regretted their discharge or wanted to return to hospital. The financial costs were initially much lower than hospital care but as iller patients were resettled their community care costs were more than standard hospital costs, in some cases very much more. Good community care is not necessarily a cheap option.

Obviously TAPS was a highly motivated and well-resourced team but it was not unique. The resettlement of long-stay patients has generally gone better than anticipated across Europe, although the USA has seen a more varied picture. The more liberal states mirrored the European experience but some of the more populous ones such as New York and California allowed quite shocking and shameful practice. With no coherent health and social care system or guaranteed rights to accommodation, enormous, privately run 'board and care' homes took many discharged patients. These can have a hundred or more residents with negligible privacy, no security of tenure, and only rudimentary medical input and oversight. Many are threatening and violent places.

The plight of the discharged mentally ill in the USA is compounded by its more libertarian approach to compulsory care. The USA is very sensitive to any infringement of individual rights and the threshold for compulsory treatment in mental illness is very high. Generally compulsion can only be used in situations posing an immediate serious risk so rehabilitation and stabilization of very ill patients lacking insight is highly problematic. More worrying still is the enormous number of them who have simply ended up in prison, 'transinstitutionalized' rather than deinstitutionalized. Los Angeles County Jail has the largest mental health facility in California, with more psychotic inmates than in any hospital in the state. The reprovision for more elderly long-stay patients has probably gone better than generally acknowledged in both Europe and much of the USA, although it is clearly patchy.

WHAT IS THE ALTERNATIVE
TO THE ASYLUM?

What has not been so successful is the long-term care for a new generation of patients who *would previously have become* long-stay.
These so-called 'new long-stay' patients spend repeated periods in
hospital but between admissions are enormously difficult to support
in the community. Unlike the previous generation, perhaps precisely because they have escaped the effects of institutionalization,
they are often fiercely independent and resist the help offered. Their
illnesses are also often made much worse by heavy drug and alcohol
abuse, though this is often not that different from their healthy neigh-
bours. As a result they are highly visible, both distressed and
distressing, especially in large cities. They may become homeless and
live undignified and squalid lives on the streets, like the 'bag lady'
drifting with all her possessions and scavenged trash. Contrary to
popular belief, most are known to both health and social services but
vigorously reject regularly offered help. This can only be forced upon
them when they are very ill indeed. Mental health services no longer
struggle with the rehabilitation and resettlement of long-stay mental
hospital patients; there are very few such left. Their current problem
is the long-term care of those with severe illnesses who vigorously
resist hospital care.

The Paris student riots of 1968 and the upheaval that followed
them had a more far-reaching impact on continental Europe than is
often recognized in the UK and USA. Universities and professions
were shaken to their core and the challenge to accepted authority
was profound. In Italy a charismatic psychiatrist, Franco Basaglia
(1924–80), led a veritable revolution reforming Italy's neglected
and inadequate mental hospitals. A Gramscian Marxist, Basaglia
focused on the corrosive effects of the power imbalance in the
psychiatrist–patient relationship. His movement was called *Psichi-
atria Democratica* and its slogan was 'liberty is cure'.

Basaglia was energetic, eloquent and influential. It also helped
that his wife was an Italian senator. Consequently the 1978 Italian

mental health reform, Law 180, was a truly radical affair; mental hospitals were effectively outlawed. From the date the law was enacted no new patients could be compulsorily admitted to a mental hospital, none. From then on new patients could only be admitted compulsorily to small diagnostic wards in general hospitals each with a maximum of fifteen beds, and then only for seven days at a time. Mental hospitals could readmit known patients but were obliged to formally close, even to them, within three years. They often did this by redesignating some of their wards as free-standing residential units. Perhaps not quite the complete revolution envisaged, but still an enormous change with a more equal and participatory atmosphere. The Italians closed the 'front door' to the institution.

The success or otherwise of the Italian reforms generates endless debate within the psychiatric professions. They were only executed comprehensively in the rich and educated north and hardly heeded in the south (Italians seem remarkably relaxed about legislation). The quality of their best is outstanding, their approach to community care and their engagement of psychotic patients in society exemplary. The reforms were, however, built upon the traditional Mediterranean family in a stable society with few migrants. Since then Italy has become more secular, with smaller families, and acquired a significant drug problem and more social mobility. The Law 180 reforms are increasingly under pressure as Italian society approximates more and more to that found across Europe.

Provision of public mental health care outside mental hospitals started long before anyone thought that they were ever going to be closed. Various isolated schemes from boarding out to agricultural colonies had existed but few became generalized or survived. Psychiatric outpatient clinics were established in the USA and across much of Europe in the 1930s. In the 1920s outpatient services were provided from 'dispensaries' in the Soviet Union along with the establishment of social security pensions for disabled individuals. The first psychiatric day hospital was opened there in 1930 and several were subsequently developed alongside the dispensaries, often with training centres and workshops. In Amsterdam a social psychiatrist, J. G. Querido, introduced a travelling outreach service to identify and support patients. However, the origins of what we now understand as modern community care lie in the 1960s.

The Kennedy family in the USA was strongly committed to the welfare of the mentally ill and those with learning disabilities. President John F. Kennedy came from a large family which had its share of difficulties. His younger sister, Rose, had a lobotomy in 1941, though whether this was for her mild learning disability or a mental illness is unclear. Whichever it was, John F. Kennedy was alive to the needs of those with mental health problems. During his short presidency he pushed through a most ambitious bill legislating for community mental health centres (CMHCs).

With hindsight, CMHCs were probably *too* ambitious. They had fourteen individual targets, which ranged from education and prevention of behaviour disorders, through treating substance abuse to the care of the long-term mentally ill in the community. They were explicitly multidisciplinary in their practice and employed social workers, nurses and psychologists as well as psychiatrists. They were initially well funded and optimistic but rapidly ran into trouble.

CMHCs were essentially resources for patients to attend; staff did not actively seek them out. Consequently the most seriously ill, those with psychotic illnesses and limited motivation or insight, were poorly served. Staff came to focus on the more rewarding counselling and psychotherapy for individuals with relatively minor problems. This drift from serving the severely mentally ill, which had been recognized from the outset as *the* most important of the fourteen goals, was worsened by difficulties recruiting psychiatrists. The early 1970s were, internationally, a high point for anti-psychiatry with its strong anti-medical model rhetoric (Chapter 8). CMHCs often consigned their psychiatrists to low-status roles, restricted mainly to signing prescriptions. Not surprisingly psychiatrists found this 'pill-pushing' unfulfilling and sought work elsewhere. Over time the CMHCs were criticized for this obvious neglect, and lost their appeal, funding and influence. By the end of the 1970s the USA began to evolve some services for the severely mentally ill similar to those which had developed in Europe.

SECTOR PSYCHIATRY AND THE MULTIDISCIPLINARY TEAM

Sectorized psychiatry developed simultaneously in France and the UK in the 1960s. *Le secteur* embodied a sophisticated, sociological approach to mental health that had long been influential in French psychiatry. Half a century earlier Emile Durkheim, the father of modern sociology, had emphasized the importance of relationships and neighbourhood for an individual's sense of self. The French moved to localize services around a specific area and its population, the *secteur*. This consisted mainly of a crisis service based in local general hospitals rather than remote mental hospitals. Some *secteurs* developed into more comprehensive services with continuity of care and outreach. For a variety of reasons, the *secteur* system has faded and, despite some very impressive individual services, it failed to become fully established.

Sectorization of mental health care in the UK was a far less intellectual process, but in the end a more durable one. The 1950s NHS was very impoverished. There was no psychotherapy tradition, and no significant alternative private sector, and the NHS lacks the fee-for-service and financial incentives that might foster professional protectionism. British psychiatrists encouraged flexibility in professional roles and responsibilities to cope with staff shortages. In 1953 two nurses decided to provide the aftercare of psychotic patients discharged from their south London mental hospital. They visited their patients regularly in their homes, monitored their care and provided support. The success of their work led to the evolution of a new profession, the 'community psychiatric nurse', or CPN. The CPN was to become the backbone of the British sectorized system and its multidisciplinary teams.

Sectorization in the UK was also fuelled by the 1959 Mental Health Act. This Act required that any hospital admitting involuntary patients must *itself* provide them with follow-up after discharge. It also legislated to make local social services and social workers integral to psychiatric care. This included obliging local social services to provide accommodation and support for long-term patients. Social workers were also designated as the final decision makers in whether a patient was to be compulsorily admitted. Doctors made the diagnosis, assessed severity and indicated the need for treatment, but it was social workers who had the final say. They decided whether hospitalization was the only possible option or whether there might be a less restrictive alternative; they decided whether the potential health benefits justified the removal of liberty. This is clearly rather an uncomfortable relationship and it was meant to be. Its purpose was to make sure that compulsory detention was not undertaken lightly, or for the convenience of professionals or families. The case had to be argued out and the social worker had to ensure that the patient's best interests were served.

Making this difficult relationship work required cooperation and the development of trust between those involved. Hospitals had already decided that they should restrict the catchment area from which they took their patients. This was for purely practical reasons if they were going to provide outpatient follow-up. Rather than take patients from all over London, for example, each mental hospital would limit itself to one or two boroughs, where it could then place its outpatient department. The need to work closely with individual social workers, both for compulsory admissions and for housing and support, made it more sensible to divide these catchment areas even further. By the early 1970s virtually the whole of the UK was divided into sectors of about 50,000 inhabitants, each served by a single mental health team (Community Mental Health Team, or CMHT). The CMHT worked closely with the local social services and often with an agreed list of family doctors. In effect both family doctors and potential patients would know the name of their individual local psychiatrist.

As mental hospitals contracted throughout the 1970s, CMHTs had to expand beyond just doctors and nurses. Patients with profound and complex needs were now common outside hospital; no one individual, no matter how well trained, had the skills to meet all these needs. CMHTs became larger, often with ten to fifteen members. These included several CPNs and social workers, and, increasingly, clinical psychologists and occupational therapists.

The development of this form of generic 'sector' CMHT is most clearly found in the UK but the basic pattern is widely distributed. In most of Europe the CMHT is not responsible for the care of its patients while in hospital, whereas until recently it always was in the UK. In countries with well-developed private practice CMHTs focused on only very severely ill and psychosis patients, but in Scandinavia and the UK they would deal with all adult psychiatric disorders. Over the last thirty years parallel teams have evolved for patients over the age of sixty-five years in most countries to deal better with the special needs of mental illness combined with physical frailty and dementia. CMHTs usually only dealt with patients over the age of either sixteen or eighteen years and children and adolescents were cared for by separate services.

While CMHTs seem to have been successful and durable they are not without their problems. Mental health services have a tradition of informality and sharing responsibilities and tasks is common. While this can lead to mutual respect and a strong team spirit there is also plenty of scope for misunderstanding, professional rivalry and conflict. Doctors have traditionally led the teams but this is increasingly challenged and their much higher salaries can lead to resentment when tasks are shared. Any lack of clarity over responsibility is a particular concern when caring for very severely ill and potentially risky patients.

After forty years of evolution by trial and error, CMHTs have recently experienced a period of intensive research and specialization. In the USA a study from Madison, Wisconsin, in 1980 reported on a highly resourced multidisciplinary team. Its members visited patients in their homes and resulted in massively reduced hospital admission rates. This approach, Assertive Community Treatment (ACT) was taken up internationally. In truth it is not that different in practice or results from generic sector CMHTs. However, the research study spearheaded a drive to divide the functions of the CMHT, with a more explicit description of the staffing and processes. ACT also helped establish internationally the importance of home-based care in severe mental illness.

Specialized CMHTs are now common and the most usual ones are these ACT teams plus first-episode psychosis teams and crisis teams. ACT teams provide intensive support (usually at least once a week) to severe-psychosis patients and have very small caseloads of about ten to fifteen patients per full-time staff member. First-episode psychosis teams aim to concentrate maximal resources at the start of a psychotic illness. In particular they provide intensive social and psychological support to protect education and family relationships, so often early casualties in these disorders. Once lost these bonds are enormously difficult to repair so the approach makes obvious sense. Crisis teams aim to provide short-term intensive care when patients are particularly unstable. The aim is to help patients function without disruptive hospital admissions and perhaps help them to learn alternative ways of dealing with their problems. Such team specialization brings increased focus and improved professional skills but also, inevitably, brings with it a loss of continuity of care and the flexibility characteristic of the generic CMHT. Whether the benefits of this increased specialization outweigh the loss of continuity of care is a hotly debated issue. My own belief is that for most patients continuity of care – being treated by doctors and nurses who know what you are like when you are ill and what you are like when you are well – is much more important. However, this balance will inevitably change as treatments become more complex and sophisticated.

Several super-specialized mental health care teams take patients referred on from CMHTs. The commonest are forensic mental health teams, which deal with the mentally ill who commit crimes or who pose significant risks of violence when ill. Originally providing just secure inpatient care, forensic services now increasingly provide community care. The approach is very similar to intensive CMHT services but with particular attention to risk. Specialized teams for eating disorders are now routine as these have become so common in developed countries and they require a highly specific and care-intensive approach. Various ultra-specialized community services cater for groups such as deaf patients, patients with combined mental illness and learning disability, etc., but few countries provide them comprehensively.

Having started with such idealism and optimism, community care is now mired in controversy. Reduced stigma and greater visibility have raised public awareness of mental illness and with this have come increased expectations and demands. Two issues dominate the current debate. The first is the very visible spectre of homeless and manifestly disturbed individuals living on the streets, neglected and vulnerable. The second is a fear of violence from the mentally ill. There is good evidence that violence from the mentally ill, and most obviously the rare but shocking cases where someone mentally ill kills a stranger, has not risen at all in the last forty years during the period of deinstitutionalization. Homicide by the mentally ill has remained remarkably stable. While each such death (approximately fifty a year in the UK) is a tragedy, only a handful occur outside the family. This figure also includes homicides by individuals not suffering from core mental illnesses but also those diagnosed only with personality disorders or drug and alcohol abuse. Its consistency is remarkable, particularly so as rates of assault and murder by the non-mentally ill have more than doubled during this time. Sadly such facts have no impact on the persisting public belief that deinstitutionalization has unleashed an epidemic of violence.

There is not that much that psychiatrists can do about this misperception of risk. It is not restricted to crimes committed by the mentally ill – crime has fallen steadily for a couple of decades yet we remain convinced it is rising. We have become risk-averse societies and psychiatry has responded to this with efforts to increase the intensity of supervision and treatment of patients in the community. A disappointing result of an increased emphasis on risk has been some deterioration in the therapeutic relationship between staff and patients. Patients correctly sense this erosion of trust and the shift in balance from care to control and staff resent it but feel unable to do much about it. A second consequence has been the extension of compulsory care. Compulsory treatment was initially restricted to patients detained in hospital but is now permitted for outpatients in many countries.

In the USA, Australia, New Zealand, England and now several other countries in Europe it is possible to insist that patients living in their own homes take regular medicine or face compulsory return to hospital. This is a radical change in our professional powers with their long-established and relatively uncontroversial provision for compulsory hospital care. Resistance to it has been considerable and some of the ethical questions it raises are further considered in Chapter 12. To most of us there is something rather disturbing, indeed something quite scary, about psychiatrists being able to force treatment. How much more scary then that this could happen in our own homes. The experience so far is that these powers have been used consistently and apparently sensibly. They have not been applied too widely but have been restricted mainly to isolated, self-neglecting psychotic patients nearly all of whom have previously been detained in hospital. There is no convincing evidence that they make a difference but most doctors and nurses who have used them are confident they do.

Managing compulsory treatment in the community involves a tricky balance. The aim is to help the patient experience the real personal independence that can only come from a sustained period of remaining well. Hopefully, as a consequence, they may choose to continue with treatment voluntarily. For this aim to have any chance of success the patient will need careful monitoring, yet such monitoring inevitably compromises the very experience of independence that the treatment aims for.

In the early, heady days of the move into the community it was thought that hospitals would soon be swept away. Such expectations are now long gone. Few doubt that comprehensive psychiatric services need both hospitals and community services. The earlier distribution of activity and resources, with 80 per cent going to the hospital and 20 per cent to the community is now reversed, with up to 80 per cent going into the community and 20 per cent to the hospital. All psychiatric care is now 'community psychiatric care': what was the exception has become the norm. Whether achieved by the steady plodding of the Anglo-Saxons or with the dash and glamour of the Italian reforms, mental hospitals have yielded their place at the centre of psychiatric care. Few mourn their passing.

Only as the mental hospital exited the stage did we fully realize the breadth and depth of the support it had provided to patients. This extended well beyond just treatment and containment to include companionship, structure and some personal safety. There is a dawning recognition that the same may also be true for the profession of psychiatry itself. Now we no longer have these enormous hospitals we realize what they meant for us in terms of our self-image, professional identity and status. Now they are gone we can appreciate the opportunities they had provided for mutual support and education in what is often an emotionally demanding vocation. The slower pace of practice they encouraged allowed for more reflection, the necessary time for a more detailed examination of complex problems. Time also to develop and respect relationships and to appreciate the place of the illness in each patient's personal narrative rather than a technological focus on fragmented episodes of care. Their very solidity and inertia provided some protection against anxiety and the day-to-day preoccupation with risk and efficiency that can dehumanize our work.

It is a mark of how far we have moved on that I can allow myself these self-indulgent, nostalgic and rose-tinted musings. Mental hospitals were grim places; for all the imperfections of community care we are well rid of them. The move into the community with all the public scrutiny it attracts is our strongest assurance against the abuse and poor practice that have disfigured periods of our history. It returns our attention to the whole individual, the patient as person, firmly placed at the centre of what we do. It has given patients back their voice. It has taught us that it is not so much *where* the care takes place but the content and quality of that care that matter. Psychiatry is not about bricks and mortar but about trusting relationships and respectful treatments. Community care constantly reminds us of this.

PART TWO

The questions psychiatry asks about us and the questions we ask of it

8

Is mental illness real?
Psychiatry's legitimacy

Is there really any justification for psychiatry existing at all? Is it just a terrible mistake, an elaborate hoax? Or indeed is it a malevolent abuse of power? There are many who think so. Their criticism is not just that psychiatry makes awful mistakes or fails to meet its own standards; these are taken up in the next chapter. They question whether psychiatry has any place at all in a civilized society, whether it has any coherence as a profession or any philosophical justification. Suspicions about psychiatry's legitimacy have been voiced right from the beginning. Mesmer's flamboyant showmanship did nothing to help and some of the treatments for shell shock were perceived as thinly disguised and distasteful punishment. The intended benevolence of the 'medical model' has always generated an unease and has tested our faith somewhat, right from the origins of the asylums ('The Alleged Lunatics' Friends' Society', Chapter 2). There is little indication that this scepticism is fading, even as our understanding of human behaviour and of the workings of the brain are scientifically explored in this era of triumphal neuroscience.

This questioning is not just stubbornness or intellectual posturing. There are good reasons to feel uneasy about psychiatry. No matter how many times experts repeat the mantra that 'mental illnesses are brain diseases', most of us distinguish between the mind and the brain. Our brain (like our heart or our liver) is a *part of us*, but our mind, our consciousness, *is us*. Our mind is who and what we are. We are vividly aware of our mind, our consciousness, every waking minute, and many sleeping ones too. Our brain, however, is unknown to us. It is silent unless something goes seriously wrong with it; even then we are not aware of our brain itself but only of its effects on us. The brain has no sensory or pain receptors. Even when damaged we cannot 'feel' it as we would feel an inflamed liver or bladder (headaches arise in the blood-vessels and lining around the brain). Modern brain-imaging techniques such as *f*MRI (functional magnetic resonance imaging) do allow us to visualize brain activity (Chapter 13) as various bits 'light up' when we speak or feel pain. But we still understand it as what is going on in the brain 'while we speak', 'while we feel pain'; we don't think it *is* speech or pain.

This distinction between consciousness and brain activity is often called 'mind–body dualism' and routinely blamed on the French philosopher René Descartes (1596–1650). Sometimes to rub it in it is referred to dismissively as 'Cartesian dualism'. Descartes certainly did try to understand how the mind and the body interact. He is famous for his dictum 'Cogito ergo sum' ('I think therefore I am') and for his metaphor of the mind as the ghost in the machine. He even went as far as to suggest that the pineal gland (a tiny, pea-sized nodule at the base of the brain) might be where mind and body met. Why such a sympathetic figure as Descartes should take the entire blame for dualism is hard to understand. Perhaps it is the price for putting it so memorably: everybody remembers 'Cogito ergo sum.' Philosophers, particularly the empiricist philosophers contemporary to him but also most of those in the following centuries, have struggled to try and explain the relationship of consciousness to the physical world. They still do and with no more obvious success.

Psychiatrists are generally very impatient with 'dualism', which we see as trying to distance mental processes from physical processes. We point to the frequency of physical symptoms in mental illnesses (pain and tiredness) and mental symptoms in physical illnesses (depression, anxiety, hallucinations). This overlap is so routine as to go unquestioned. One of the reasons for under-diagnosis of psychiatric problems in general practice is that psychological symptoms are part and parcel of most physical illness. In the developing world doctors may not even make the distinction. In an Indian clinic I have watched a psychiatrist take a history from a depressed woman who volunteered not a single psychological symptom, just aches, pains and tiredness. He prescribed antidepressants for her pains and lethargy without any attempt to 'reframe' them as depression. Four weeks later she was much better.

Repeating that a functioning brain is essential for mental life does not, unfortunately, get us very far. We all know that, and really always have. Most of us think of the mind as being essentially non-material but still able to initiate physical actions (we speak and move in response to our thoughts). How this gap is bridged is unclear. There is a philosophical mystery here and this psychiatrist, for one, admits that he is baffled by it.

The philosophical and conceptual critiques of psychiatry are addressed later in the section on 'anti-psychiatry'. This could be dismissed as historical, fairly recherché stuff with its heyday in the 1960s and 1970s. However, the conflicts that fuel it have been fought out in furious public arguments for decades, most intractably in the dispute over nature versus nurture. Are our lives broadly determined for us (fate, biology, luck, constitution) or are we and our families the authors of our own destinies? Can we rise above the circumstances of our birth and shape society in our own image, or are we 'doomed from the womb'? All political and social movements since the Enlightenment have engaged with this question in one form or another. None of us is untouched by it. The argument, however, acquires an extra edge within psychiatry, producing bitter oppositions. How much of our fate really is in our, and our parents', hands? How much of the tragedy of mental illness is just that – a tragic illness arising from human biology and constitution – and how much of it is caused by how we and our parents behave and have behaved?

Nature–nurture discussions are widespread in medicine and are generally accompanied by little in the way of drama or fireworks. The interaction of constitution and lifestyle in the origins of most diseases is simply taken for granted. Diet and genes both contribute to breast cancer or diabetes, exercise and family history both affect our risk for a heart attack. The disagreements, when they occur, are about the *relative contribution* of the various factors. That both are involved is a non-issue. Their relative contributions are constantly modified by research findings and can change abruptly with new data.

When I was a medical student peptic ulcers were very common; few Friday nights on call passed without a perforated ulcer. At that time it was believed that people with a 'driven' personality, those who worked and worried too much, produced too much gastric acid, which eventually burnt a hole in their stomach. In 1982 two doctors in Perth, Western Australia, discovered a bacterium, Helicobacter pylori, that lived in the stomach. Previously it was 'known' that the acidity in the stomach made it impossible for bacteria to survive. In 1984 one of the doctors, Barry Marshall, swallowed a dose of the bacteria to test the idea. The bacteria survived and multiplied, he developed awful gastritis and his wife promptly made him take antibiotics. In 2005 he and his collaborator, the pathologist Robin Warren, received the Nobel Prize for medicine. Long before the prize, however, and with only minimal fuss, the treatment of gastric ulcers had completely changed from bed rest, a bland diet and often protracted psychotherapy, to a simple course of antibiotics. There was no philosophical controversy, no acrimonious debate. Nurture (stress) had yielded to nature (germs) with hardly a fight.

We easily accept the interplay of nature and nurture in the physical sphere, whether physique, disease or sports prowess, but the mood changes when it comes to 'mental' attributes. Whether it is IQ, criminality, over-eating, alcoholism, gambling or mental illness (in short anywhere choice and free will could be involved) we polarize. Few are neutral and opinions can be fiercely held and argued. Obviously this cannot be just an issue of the availability of information or access to the necessary facts. The weight we give nature and nurture determines, and is determined by, our own personal values. It reflects our fundamental attitudes to free will and individual responsibility. Anyone with the most rudimentary knowledge knows that most criminals are much more likely to have had a deprived upbringing and a poorer education, and to have grown up in fragmented families with less affection and security. Yet despite the same information our responses to their behaviour range from 'poor devil, he never had a chance' to 'nobody ever said life was fair, lots of people have to overcome adversity, he knew what he was doing'.

An endorsement of nurture has usually been more common among liberal, left-wing and politically progressive individuals, people who instinctively question the status quo. The variation in human abilities and achievements is attributed most to unequal opportunities, often with the optimistic belief that all will achieve equally if treated fairly. Nature's dominance is generally advanced by more conservative individuals who believe the natural order reflects the variation in our inherent abilities. Politically they are more likely to encourage us to accept the reality of inequality. They support social structures which recognize and adapt to our innate differences rather than strive to remove them.

A world view formed upon rigid, inborn differences in rank and status characterized the old monarchies of Europe. Emigrants to the USA rejected these to establish a society dedicated to the proposition that 'anyone can become president'. This has remained linked to a libertarian reluctance to interfere with the self-determination of others, even when they are manifestly failing. These fundamental differences in political and social perspective between the USA and Europe are played out in psychiatry. They became a significant factor in the debate about nature–nurture as a cause of schizophrenia outlined below and underpin major differences in health care ideology overall and mental health care in particular.

We know that our choices are constrained by circumstances, including our upbringing. Yet we cannot function without the presumption of free will. Our *need* to believe in free will may explain the strength of our attachment to nurture and personal agency even when the facts speak loudly against them. It explains why families blame themselves so readily for things quite outside their control such as the occurrence of mental illness. We consider the family and our upbringing as the crucible of our identity. Humans devote enormous time and energy to rearing their children; family life revolves around them for decades, schools and universities are established to educate them. All aim in some form to 'mould character'. All of this investment simultaneously expresses and confirms our belief that adult behaviour and character are formed by these earlier interactions and relationships.

Even many of those sceptical of the role of nurture recognize that a belief in it is a biological necessity. Evolutionary biologists suggest that our behaviour may shape our thinking rather than vice versa. Because human children are dependent for so long on their parents it makes evolutionary sense for the parents to believe in their unique contribution to that upbringing. At its most cynical the parental bond is an essential mechanism to ensure the parent devotes so much time and energy, even at a risk to its own survival, to its offspring.

Following the same logic falling in love is proposed as a 'necessary emotional and cognitive structure' to sustain our prolonged mating practices and keep fathers involved in childcare. Few of us would accept quite such a bleak view of human nature. However, the biological imperative that it illustrates does drive home why we are so committed to our relationships and why we consistently err on the side of valuing nurture. Psychologists call this automatic assumption that our actions determine outcomes an 'attribution bias'.

It is a frequent and humbling experience for psychiatrists to hear family members who have endured intolerable and distressing consequences of their relative's illness with love and patience blame themselves and question what they did wrong. It feels doubly cruel. Yet blaming oneself can reduce our sense of helplessness. If I did it wrong then perhaps I can do it right next time and then things will be better. The same mindset is often encountered in victims. Rape victims frequently accuse themselves of being 'careless' or 'provocative' despite the utterly unpredictable and brutal behaviour of the rapist. It feels in one way less frightening than accepting that there was *nothing* one could have done, and by implication nothing one can do in the future to avoid it. Even a capricious and vengeful god that one can pray to may seem less frightening than a purely random universe. All in all we have a strong bias as a species towards attributing outcomes to our actions.

I have elaborated so much on the forces at play in the nature versus nurture consideration because the furious intensity of the debate about it in psychiatry is otherwise quite incomprehensible. It is a debate that has often been utterly disproportionate to the question: passionate, at times vitriolic, and frequently highly personalized.

Schizophrenia has always been known to run in families; nobody contests that. However, over psychiatry's 200-year history the pendulum has swung widely between attributing it to nature or to nurture. In the late nineteenth century, when schizophrenia was first described as a separate disease, it was considered unequivocally a genetically determined biological disorder. The statistics in favour of inheritance have fluctuated modestly but have always been sobering. Having a parent or a sibling with the disorder increases the chance of developing it about tenfold. The identical twin of a patient has about a 50 per cent chance of developing schizophrenia (against a population risk of about 1 per cent) and a non-identical twin about 10 per cent (the same as for any sibling).

What might have seemed an open-and-shut case of genetic transmission in any physical disorder such as diabetes or heart disease was hotly contested for schizophrenia as the twentieth century progressed. Schizophrenia manifests itself in disturbances of behaviour and thinking so it is no surprise that clues have been sought in upbringing and family behaviour, especially as the families of many schizophrenia patients were observed to behave rather oddly. Two types of odd family functioning were identified as 'causes' of schizophrenia. Both are now scientifically entirely discredited but they retain a powerful hold on popular imagination so we will consider them here.

THE 'SCHIZOPHRENOGENIC MOTHER' AND THE 'DOUBLE BIND'

Not surprisingly it is the mother who gets the blame, and generally it is the mother who blames herself. Frieda Fromm-Reichmann (1889–1957) developed this particularly damaging construct in 1948 while psychoanalysing wealthy hospitalized schizophrenia patients. Fromm-Reichmann concluded that her patients had become schizophrenic because of their cold and emotionally hostile mothers. She described these mothers as 'rejecting, impervious to the feelings of others, with a rigid moralism concerning sex and a fear of intimacy'. Fromm-Reichmann, tiny and brilliant, a refugee from Nazi Germany like so many of her US psychoanalytic colleagues, appears to have been an extremely talented psychotherapist. Her formulation of the schizophrenogenic mother, however, was reputedly based on the analysis of only eleven schizophrenia patients and without ever meeting the mothers in question. Not meeting family members was common with orthodox psychoanalysts at that time to avoid contamination of their understanding of their patients' inner world. She believed that this early experience undermined her patients' confidence and 'drove' them back into an inner world that felt safer. Trapped in their worries and preoccupations they failed to engage securely with the world around them, a central feature of schizophrenia.

Fromm-Reichmann was not an isolated or evil maverick. Such ideas were common at the time and they were developed further by, among others, the Yale professor and psychoanalyst Theodore Lidz (1910–2001). Lidz was more systematic: he studied seventeen families with a member suffering from schizophrenia and seventeen without one. He also studied the whole family, not just the patient. Lidz basically sub-scribed to the 'schizophrenogenic mother' idea but he formulated the problem in two patterns of dysfunctional parental relationships, which he called 'schism' and 'skew'. He claimed to detect these pat-terns in families which otherwise appeared calm and well-functioning on the surface – 'as we studied these seemingly harmonious families it became apparent ...' In skew, domestic peace was obtained only if one of the partners yielded totally to the bizarre and eccentric ideas of the more disturbed one (as in a *folie à deux*). In schism, there was 'a chronic failure to achieve complementarity', which led to a persisting, stressful tension in the relationship. An awareness of this vulnerability in the parental relationship bound the desperate child to the parents in an effort to hold them together. This crippling, but unacknow-ledged, bond paralysed the anxious child, stopping it from maturing and achieving its own independence.

Both these writers considered that a defective emotional upbringing with inadequate nurturance caused schizophrenia. The child did not receive enough love and security to surmount the developmental chal-lenges to establish an independent identity. Early analysts often spoke of schizophrenia patients being stuck in a 'pre-Oedipal' phase; they had not been able to differentiate from their parents by challenging their dependency. Similar ideas are expressed in Melanie Klein's 'paranoid-schizoid' position, when the child is unable to recognize and cope with the ambiguity of real parents. However, Klein described it as a developmental stage, not a cause of psychosis.

Schizophrenia is distinguished more by its disorders of thinking and behaving than of emotions. The *double-bind* theory attempts to explain this by the acquisition of faulty logic and communication pat-terns. Gregory Bateson (1904–80) was a British anthropologist, once married to the more famous American anthropologist Margaret

Mead. He was settled in Palo Alto, California, and described the double-bind in an article, 'Towards a Theory of Schizophrenia', in 1956. Bateson had been interested in feedback in communication in his earlier anthropological work. He had also been influenced by Bertrand Russell and A. N. Whitehead's book, *Principia Mathematica*, with its exploration of the theory of numbers. One of Russell and Whitehead's postulates was that a number used to indicate a specific series of numbers cannot itself be a member of that series; it has a quite different logical status.

Bateson and his colleagues drew a comparison between numbers and communications. As communication consisted of series of statements, there could be specific statements which designated these series and gave them their context in the same way one number could designate a number sequence. He called these special statements 'meta communications' and proposed that, like Russell and Whitehead's numbers, they could not logically be part of the series of communications they designated. Meta communications were most often non-verbal and they set the *context* for understanding the verbal utterances. A double bind existed when there was an unequivocal contradiction between the spoken message (communication) and the non-spoken message (meta-communication). Thus a mother (always the mother) expresses her affection for her child in words, 'Come and give mummy a hug', but simultaneously indicates anger or resentment in her body language or tone, thereby generating confusion in the child.

Of course, Bateson was not so naïve as to suggest that simple ambiguity or dishonesty caused illness; these are far too commonplace. For a double bind three further conditions are needed. First there must be a family taboo, often unspoken but still powerful, on acknowledging the contradiction; second the 'victim' cannot simply leave the arena; and third there must be an emotionally significant consequence in the choice of their response. Such a triad is not rare in families, particularly in emotionally close or anxious ones.

The double bind is certainly ingenious and we all recognize it. It has entered our vocabulary, albeit in its simplified form. Like the schizophrenogenic mother it has not withstood scientific scrutiny and is much easier to test than the Fromm-Reichmann proposal. Recorded speech samples from schizophrenia families and normal families have been examined by raters 'blind' to which was which. They have consistently failed to find differences, even when the raters were disciples of the theory. The schizophrenogenic mother theory is harder to disprove (simply re-read Lidz's pronouncements and you can see why). However, direct observation of families and, more importantly, the evidence from adoption studies explored below make it an entirely implausible hypothesis. Despite their refutations these theories exert a powerful hold on the popular imagination and even more so with afflicted families. Psychiatrists have to be familiar with them even if we now know they are nonsense.

IS SCHIZOPHRENIA INHERITED?

The nature–nurture war was predominantly waged as a conflict between genetics and parenting although wider experiences such as trauma are now commonly included in nurture. The genetics models used at the time were generally simple, so-called 'Mendelian' genetics, named after the father of genetics, the Russian monk Gregor Mendel (1822–84). Mendel was the first to demonstrate inheritance patterns, identifying dominant and recessive genes in garden peas. In Mendelian inheritance, characteristics are either passed on or not passed on dependent on the presence or absence of a single gene. The results are either one quarter or one half of offspring demonstrating the traits. Examples are blue or brown eye colour or blood groups. This is not the case for most mental illnesses. Indeed it is not the case for most illnesses overall, with important exceptions such as sickle-cell anaemia, haemophilia and cystic fibrosis. Most genetically transmitted illnesses have much lower rates in the offspring. The modern genetic case for schizophrenia and other mental illnesses is not built on single-gene patterns but assumes that several genes are involved, each one having only a small effect. Genes act more as cumulative risk factors than as simple on/off switches and their action may sometimes require additional environmental influences and experiences such as cannabis use or early trauma to have an effect.

For a couple of decades geneticists and analysts traded alternative interpretations of the same figures. That schizophrenia runs in families can support either theory. The absence of simple Mendelian patterns made the nurture argument quite persuasive. Twin studies were used by both sides. That identical twins had greater risks than non-identical strongly indicated the influence of genes but could also represent their similar experiences growing up. Parents of identical twins often strive to be scrupulous in treating them the same. More tellingly, if genes were the explanation, why did half the identical twins of schizophrenia patients not develop the disorder?

These nature–nurture wars took place long before the technology to identify individual genes. The final blow to an exclusively 'nurture'-based explanation of the cause of schizophrenia came from studies of children adopted away at birth from mothers with the illness. In 1966 a paper reported on forty-seven Danish adults separated decades previously from their schizophrenic mothers within three days of birth. Five had developed schizophrenia. This is 10 per cent, the same risk regularly found in schizophrenic families. Further elegant studies were carried out in Denmark, which has excellent nationwide databases, tracing the biological families of thirty-three adults with schizophrenia who had been adopted as children. They found high rates of mental disorder and schizophrenia in the biological families but not in their adoptive families. Upbringing may have *some* effect, but genes clearly exerted a stronger effect. Schizophrenia is now generally accepted to have a 'heritability' of 80 per cent. Nature is the dominant, but certainly not the exclusive, influence, and these rates still mean that most people developing schizophrenia will *not* have a parent with the disease.

Why did this controversy last so long and consume so much energy and passion? After all it has no obvious impact on treatment or health policy. Only the exceptionally rich received psychotherapy for schizophrenia; most received the same institutional care and antipsychotics after they were discovered. There is, of course, the issue of professional pride (never to be underestimated) plus the momentum of intellectual commitment and accumulated arguments. But clearly there was more. We have noted that the nature–nurture issue acts as a lightning rod for more fundamental social and personal attitudes. An even more profound issue was hovering in the wings during this debate.

THE RISE OF
ANTI-PSYCHIATRY

Running through all this nature-nurture controversy is a sense that the issue is not just about the mechanism of transfer of mental illness but *whether mental illnesses themselves are real or not*. The genetic hypothesis appears to carry the implication that schizophrenia is unequivocally a 'real' illness with everything that follows from that. Its proponents were usually confident advocates of the medical model. The family upbringing hypotheses implied, on the other hand, that in some sense it might be something less definite, more a difficulty in relationships, an intellectual construction. Indeed with some careful reconsideration and perhaps some minor changes in language, it might simply disappear altogether. In short that it *is not a real illness*. The nurture proponents may not have said this outright (after all many were psychiatrists earning their living from treating mental illnesses) but there is a lurking sense that this was what they really believed.

In the 1960s this concern stepped from the wings and took centre-stage. The 'anti-psychiatrists' launched what was surely the most coherent and sustained assault on psychiatry's legitimacy we have witnessed to date. For the following two or three decades it was no longer fine detail about diagnostic criteria or a criticism of poor prac-tice. No, now it was an all-out war questioning whether psychiatry was a real discipline at all or if it was a sham, an imposture with highly questionable motives. The more radical questioned the very existence of mental illnesses, claiming that psychiatric diagnoses were cynical tools to denigrate and manipulate untidy or uncomfortable members of society.

Things have moved on since the time of the anti-psychiatrists. However, the sheer power and eloquence of their arguments have altered the language and context of the debate, leaving a lasting leg-acy both within the profession and in our wider understanding of the human condition. No understanding of psychiatry would be complete without acknowledging these broadsides. Psychiatrists who ignore their messages and insist there is no issue, that mental illness and psychiatry are absolutely the same as any other branch of modern medicine, will convince nobody but themselves. The anti-psychiatrists articulated some timeless truths within their often overblown rhetoric.

The anti-psychiatry books of the early 1960s were not the product of a coordinated movement, anything but. The main proponents may have been responding to the current *Zeitgeist*, but each was highly individualistic, preoccupied with his (and they were all 'he') own conclusions. Nor is there any clear progression, no sense that they built upon each other's ideas. The order in which I present them reflects what I think makes sense. Foucault was the one who looked back to history and who in some ways made the most sweeping criticism, so he can be our starting point.

Michel Foucault (1926–84) was the typical French intellectual. The scope of his work is extensive and defies pigeonholing. He is most famous for *Madness and Civilization*, the abridged English translation of his doctoral thesis, published to acclaim in 1961. Foucault argued that although madness has always existed, *madmen* had not. They were an artificial product of the seventeenth and eighteenth centuries. He links the creation of the specific identity of the madman to the 'Great Confinement' (Chapter 2). This he describes as sweeping across Europe in the seventeenth century, but most markedly in France. There it was a response to the growing instability of the French monarchy and later to the rational impulse of the Enlightenment. In the drive to strengthen the state, unruly and threatening individuals were rounded up and incarcerated. Specific classes of people had to be identified to justify and organize this process, the madman was just one along with anarchists, drunkards, vagrants, prostitutes, etc.

Foucault was an inveterate rebel. He considered it his artistic and intellectual duty to constantly test society's boundaries and taste. He seems to have opposed almost every establishment position he stumbled upon. His writing is rich and discursive but also dense and imprecise. Foucault approaches complex issues by adding extra layers of detail and examples rather than stripping them down for clarity in the style of Anglophone philosophers. It can be frustrating to try and grasp his nuances. However, his central message is blunt: the label of madman was a violent and denigrating act which served the state's needs, not the 'madman's'. This is not an isolated or outrageous view.

The Nobel Laureate Amartya Sen challenges the use of a single identity to define someone, arguing for context-dependent identities. We can have several: I am a man, a psychiatrist, British, a father, a brother, etc. All are legitimate identities, but none uniquely defines me. Indeed for Sen choosing your identity, rather than having it imposed upon you, is an essential human right. Foucault would probably have agreed.

Foucault has been criticized for exaggerating the extent of the Great Confinement. He himself has criticized the romanticizing of madness that has been attributed to him. He was an openly gay man when it was not easy to be so, and one who had been treated for depression early in his life. It is perhaps not surprising that he was sensitive to the power of labels. He believed that psychiatric diagnoses were fundamentally an exercise in raw institutional power rather than a humane medical procedure. This view, in one form or another, is common to all the anti-psychiatrists.

Erving Goffman would not have called himself an anti-psychiatrist, but simply a sociologist. But then none of those described here would have applied the term to themselves. Arguably the most famous of them, R. D. Laing, protested loudly against the term, which was first coined by his colleague, the South African psychiatrist David Cooper in 1967. Goffman also differed from the typical anti-psychiatrist in that his message is based on evidence, on data he gathered, not from theories and reformulations. Goffman concluded from his research that psychiatry, and in particular mental hospitals, were malevolent institutions. They were instruments of control and subjugation rather than cure and emancipation.

His first book, *The Presentation of Self in Everyday Life* (1959), established his reputation in sociology but it was his second book, *Asylums: Essays on the Social Situation of Mental Patients and Other Inmates* (1961), that echoed round the psychiatric world. This was based on a year he spent effectively 'under cover' in St Elizabeth's Mental Hospital in Washington DC. Like Foucault, Goffman was unconvinced of the fixity of individual identity. He described how the mental hospital acted to consolidate selected aspects of an individual's behaviour into a firm, but malleable, identity. Hospital routines and practices gradually socialized them into their role of mental patient, emphasizing their passivity. This fitted them to the smooth and efficient running of the hospital. He called this process 'institutionalization'.

Much of the detail of Goffman's book focused on the nature of the power structure and the rituals of the hospital. It was not the doctors and administrators who really ran the show, although they thought they did. Goffman demonstrated that real power, particularly the shaping of identity and transfer of culture, was exercised by individuals low down the formal hierarchy – nursing aides, cleaners and other patients. These were the individuals who spent the most time with patients and thus had the opportunity for influence. The real culture was based predominantly on moral judgements of 'good and bad behaviour' rather than illness and health. It related to patients' motives rather than to their symptoms or diagnoses. Goffman described convincingly and eloquently the rigid hierarchies in the hospital and the strict routines, or as he saw them 'rituals', which functioned actively to erode identity. These were particularly intensive directly after admission.

I vividly remember as a medical student in the late 1960s working in a large, locked mental hospital in the rural USA with over 3,000 patients. All new admissions, irrespective of diagnosis, were put through exactly the same procedures for the first two weeks. This involved bathing, delousing, having their clothes taken from them and then, some days later, returned cleaned. A long series of medical examinations, including X-rays and electroencephalogram (EEG), psychological tests, close observation, and an exhaustive medical and personal history, then followed. Absolutely nothing varied, nothing at all, unless the patient was so disturbed that immediate sedation and seclusion were needed. Goffman saw these routines as both symbols and instruments of the institution's authority. They were initiation rights into a new identity. It was the clarity with which he described this wielding of power to shape, some would say crush, patients' individual identities by institutionalization that gave the book its impact.

What was new and really shocking in Goffman's book was that he insisted that this was all *deliberate*. It was not just an unfortunate side effect of a large, impersonal or poorly staffed institution as earlier writers such as Russell Barton believed. Goffman was convinced that 'total institutions' such as mental hospitals (or prisons or the army or monasteries) consciously strove to induct their new members into a role, into an identity, that fitted the institution's own goals, before their own needs. Its particular power came from the pervasiveness of its influence. You not only 'worked' there, you slept there, ate there, and made your friends there. Each interaction reinforced the other. There was no opportunity for the odd reminder of another, earlier more authentic identity (remember Conolly's chilling description 130 years earlier in Chapter 2). Goffman was probably the most influential of all the anti-psychiatrists with his portrayal of the humane medical model of psychiatry as at best a naïve aspiration, and at worst just a reassuring fig leaf over a naked exercise of power. His message was taken up even by the psychiatric establishment and permanently altered practice and policies for mental hospitals.

In the same year as Goffman published *Asylums* Thomas Szasz published *The Myth of Mental Illness*. Szasz, who died in 2012, was born in Hungary in 1920 and came to the USA when he was eighteen years old, studied medicine and psychiatry, and trained in psychoanalysis. From 1962 he held a position in the Department of Psychiatry in the State University of New York. Szasz has fundamentally one message. He believes psychiatric disorders are not real illnesses and that psychiatry, and virtually everything else (sex, drugs, suicide, etc.) are entirely personal matters. They are for the individual to decide on. The state, medicine, the legal profession, in short any would-be do gooder, should simply keep out of it unless specifically invited in by the person concerned.

His most persisting battle with psychiatry was his crusade against involuntary treatment. He was opposed to it in *all* circumstances. As a psychiatrist and psychotherapist, mainly experienced in private practice, he insists that he and the patient have to *choose* to work together. If somebody is mentally ill and refuses treatment then that is fine by him; it is their decision. If they commit a crime while psychotic then they should be tried like anyone else. If found guilty they may be imprisoned, but they still retain the right to refuse treatment. Mental illness is no excuse for criminal behaviour. Unlike Goffman or Laing you don't read Szasz for lucid prose or rich insights. He had his one message and he has continued to drive it home in book after book for fifty years.

There are many civil libertarians who oppose compulsory psychiatric treatment. Many argue that detention is only justified to prevent risk to others, or if the person clearly lacks capacity to make decisions, as in dementia. Such individuals are not generally considered 'anti-psychiatrists'. What gets Szasz classified as one (which predictably, he strongly resents and repeatedly denies) is his view that mental illnesses are only metaphors or myths. He believes they are simply not 'real illnesses'. I will try and do Szasz's views justice but you will quickly note that I find him deliberately simplistic and (even more irritating) slippery and prone to shift his ground in mid-argument. You may want to read him yourself.

Szasz argues that mental illnesses are not real illnesses on two grounds. The first is that a 'real illness' needs a known and demonstrable physical cause, an anatomical fault that can be shown in an autopsy or a clear physiological abnormality that can be measured, such as high blood sugar. There are many problems with this apparently straightforward proposal. Medical progress is continually improving our understanding of the biological basis of illnesses, both physical and mental. Absolutely certain biological explanations that we believed we knew can later be refuted and replaced with a completely new one (for example, the gastric ulcer story). Was it a 'real' illness when we 'knew' the wrong mechanism? Few doctors would insist that one *cannot* make a diagnosis in the absence of a clear physical cause, nor that finding a cause is sufficient to predict the illness. Doctors diagnosed heart failure ('dropsy') and treated it successfully for centuries with foxglove, the plant from which we obtained digitalis, without understanding the underlying pathology or the mechanism of action of either the heart failure or the foxglove. Similarly, nobody denies that chronic fatigue syndrome is an illness; the continuing controversy about whether it is mental or physical just demonstrates that we do not know what causes it. What would Szasz say of Huntington's disease? This devastating illness has been clearly described since the mid-1800s and regularly diagnosed despite nobody knowing what caused it. Its genetic cause (a gene mutation) was eventually clarified in 1993. Was it not an illness before, but it is now?

There is also no certainty that finding 'a cause' will fully clarify our understanding of a disease. The same bacterium in the lungs of one person can cause pneumonia, in another bronchitis and in a third nothing at all. It will all depend on their age, immune status, general resilience, etc. Just to complicate matters several other agents, not just bacteria but viruses, funguses and even inanimate irritants, can cause either of these illnesses. Is this one disease or two, or many? Both diseases were also well known and regularly diagnosed long before our germ theory of infection was developed. What would Szasz have made of the accumulating evidence of relative over- and under-activity of neurotransmitters in various psychiatric disorders? Do they constitute a 'biological cause' or are they simply a manifestation of the disorders? In this particular dilemma he would not have been alone; I am equally unsure.

The second argument is from analogy. Szasz simply ridiculed the criteria for psychiatric diagnoses and implied that their only basis is 'unusualness'; for example, 'If I talk to God I am praying, if God talks to me I am schizophrenic.' This is a fairly cheap caricature of psychiatric diagnosis. We do not make a diagnosis simply because an individual has a strange idea or describes a strange experience. Diagnoses are based on recognizing patterns of disturbance which are confirmed over time to be associated with particular outcomes, not spotting the odd eccentricity. No psychiatric diagnosis – *none* – can be confidently made on the basis of a single symptom or sign. The diagnosis of a mental illness, as repeatedly stressed in this book, reflects a judgement, albeit often imperfect, that individuals have become different from their 'normal' selves in some fairly recognizable way. It is not that they are different from *us*, or that they are socially deviant, but that they are different from what we and they usually understand as their normal selves. There is simply no idea, no matter how outlandish, that invariably proves mental illness. Over four million Americans are reported to believe that they have been abducted by aliens, which strikes me as fairly odd, but I do not conclude they are mentally ill. Szasz was, of course, right to point out that psychiatry has been abused by the use of such simplistic labelling in totalitarian states – in the former Soviet Union, for example. Eccentric and dissident individuals had been incarcerated. This is a *misuse* of psychiatry, not evidence against its fundamental legitimacy.

A particularly irritating feature of Szasz's style (for this reader anyway) is that he often built an argument on one disorder, often a relatively mild one such as hysteria or anxiety, and then applied it to the treatment decisions made in much more severe disorders such as psychosis. Arguments about the legitimacy of coercion need to be anchored in the disorders where it is used, and where the consequences of its use or non-use can be honestly and meaningfully considered.

Szasz remained very active right up until his death. He had become an influential figure for the Scientology movement, which takes an implacable stand against all psychiatry. Scientologists insist that there are better alternative ways to recover from emotional problems. Some of their methods have attracted their own controversy and several of their ideas would test the bounds of credibility more than any psychiatric theory. Scientologists still picket most psychiatric conferences with banners baldly proclaiming 'Psychiatry Kills'.

R. D. (Ronnie) Laing (1927–89) was probably the most eloquent and charismatic of all the anti-psychiatrists. He became an international celebrity after the publication of *The Divided Self: An Existential Study of Sanity and Madness* in 1960. The book became a campus bible for most of that decade and much of the next. Laing's prose is lucid and gripping. He rejected psychiatric diagnoses but had a remarkable facility for engaging with profoundly disturbed, psychotic individuals and understanding their experiences.

In *The Divided Self* he proposed that the individuals we call psychotic were engaged in a desperate struggle to make sense of their lives and experience. Their uncertainty about their identity communicates itself to us, echoing our own uncertainties. We find this unsettling and need to deal with its threat to what Laing called our own sense of *ontological security* (our confidence in a stable persisting identity). We do this, he argued, by distancing ourselves, attacking and neutralizing their message through diagnosis and treatment. Laing believed that understanding the psychotic condition required a technique he called *existential phenomenology*. In contrast to identifying the signs and symptoms of the disorder to form a sense of the patient's experience (the classical phenomenology of psychiatry) we needed to understand the features of the patient's struggle for identity (their existential process). To do this we have to engage fully in the process, often a scary and disorienting experience. Laing argued that objectifying patients in the process of diagnosis was incompatible with simultaneously recognizing the most important quality of any person – their personal agency, that we all make our own world.

Laing enriched his argument with vivid and moving descriptions of his patients. You are left in no doubt of his respect for their struggle and their achievement. The picture of psychosis that emerges is of a tormented, but brave and authentic individual confronting the core dilemmas of being human. These are the very same dilemmas for us all that most of us studiously avoid thinking about. It is a heroic and respectful view of the patient, perhaps an over-romantic one. It is certainly one that is critical of society's response, casting it as impoverished and ungenerous.

Laing was an improbable counter-culture hero. From a working-class Glasgow background he had trained in medicine and then worked for two years as an army psychiatrist. After a brief spell as a consultant in a large mental hospital he went on to train as a psycho-analyst at the very proper Tavistock Clinic in London. However, his personal life belied this staid progression. His parents were eccentric and his own relationships chaotic. He had ten children with four women. He drank heavily throughout his life and was a man who clearly delighted in being unpredictable and mischievous. As a speaker he was usually charismatic and inspirational but could be utterly incomprehensible and, at times, just plain drunk.

Laing was a restless and impulsive individual. He had a brilliant and creative mind which never stood still. His ideas constantly evolved and the focus of his thinking moved on. There were two further, quite distinct, stages in Laing's understanding of psychosis after *The Divided Self*. In 1964 he published *Sanity, Madness and the Family: Families of Schizophrenics* with Aaron Esterson. In *Sanity, Madness and the Family* Laing and Esterson cast schizophrenia as a consequence of the emotional violence of the nuclear family, focusing especially on its inhibited and repressive features. Bateson's double bind figures prominently. The book, surprisingly, avoids being moralizing in tone or apportioning blame, and it struck a chord in the rebellious sixties. It was made into an influential film (*Family Life*, 1971) whose rather simplified message spread Laing's influence beyond his previous student and intellectual readership.

Laing was unlikely to remain satisfied for long with such 'mechanical' causal explanations. His life was becoming increasingly turbulent. He was experimenting heavily with psychedelic drugs and becoming fascinated by the practices of natural healers and shamans. His third 'phase' moved into a more transcendent, psychedelic understanding of psychosis. In *The Politics of Experience and the Bird of Paradise* (1967) he cast the psychotic experience as a creative journey. Just as a shaman enters a trance to communicate with the spirit world and bring back solutions, the psychotic could access new insights and emerge a stronger, wiser individual with an expanded consciousness.

It is hard now to appreciate just how powerful and pervasive a social phenomenon the anti-psychiatry movement was. The 1960s and 1970s were a period of intense political, intellectual and social unrest. There were demonstrations against the Vietnam War; students rioted on the streets of European capitals; and universities were rocked by occupations. Change was demanded and expected. Almost any of the UK anti-psychiatry group (Laing, Cooper, Esterson, Burke) could fill a lecture hall in any university in Europe and all appeared regularly on television. Laing so galvanized the student body with a lecture in Tokyo in 1969 that they went out and burnt down the university administration building directly afterwards.

The last ten years of Laing's life were less productive. He was chronically short of cash and drinking altogether too much, but he continued to work with patients and to teach. For such a radical counter-culture individual his death was remarkably bourgeois. He suffered a heart attack, while playing tennis on the French Riviera at the age of sixty-two.

A visit to any bookshop will quickly confirm that texts critical of psychiatry are not in short supply. Indeed it is one of the reasons for this book – to try and explain why psychiatry survives despite this tsunami of criticism. However, there is a difference with such books as Richard Bentall's *Doctoring the Mind: Why Psychiatric Treatments Fail,* or *Madness Explained: Psychosis and Human Nature,* or Joanna Moncrieff's *The Myth of the Chemical Cure* or Peter Breggin's *Toxic Psychiatry* or *Brain Disabling Treatments in Psychiatry* (the list is almost endless). In many ways these books would be more at home in Chapter 9 or Chapter 11 of this book. While the authors are fundamentally opposed to current psychiatric practice, and like their predecessors insist that they are not anti-psychiatrists, their criticisms draw on evidence of psychiatry's failures and excesses and its overall ineffectiveness.

The *traditional* anti-psychiatrists (how they would hate being called that) were philosophically opposed to psychiatry in any of its forms. This new group are, as it were, *evidence-based anti-psychiatrists*. They may share a deep suspicion of the fundamental legitimacy of psychiatry and psychiatric diagnoses; most undoubtedly do. However, their arguments are generally that psychiatry is too full of itself, or is corrupted by pharmaceutical companies, or that it makes endless mistakes. It is the *damage* done by psychiatry and psychiatrists that they warn against. If psychiatrists are false prophets it is because they fail to deliver what they promise; it is not their mistaken metaphysics. It is their *incompetence* rather than their *omnipotence* that is the issue.

Anti-psychiatry was not all bad news for psychiatry, far from it. Recruitment to psychiatry has never been as good as in the 1970s. Whatever else it is, psychiatry is a profession that celebrates the mind and engages the curiosity of patient and doctor, or psychologist or nurse or social worker. Its excitement lies in relationships and intellectual complexity. So it is no surprise that such thoughtful and provocative writers energized a generation of medical students and health care workers. Anti-psychiatrists' ideas and concepts also live on in the vocabulary of the 'user' and 'survivor' movements.

Nor should we underestimate how many of their ideas, originally resisted, have been absorbed into psychiatry and now shape its everyday practice. Few psychiatrists today are blind to the power imbalance in the therapeutic relationship. Goffman's ideas have found a full and extensive expression in the development of rehabilitation psychiatry with its attention to personal agency and meaningful activity. The evils of institutionalization were recognized and 150 years of asylum building reversed. The vast mental hospitals have gone, a truly staggering achievement. 'Personalized care' and 'person-centred practice' may sometimes seem like tired slogans but they are now the real platform for all mental health services, whether in the community or on the ward. Implementation may be imperfect but it would be hard to find a clinician who disagrees with their aims. Similarly an increasingly liberal set of mental health laws (particularly in the USA) owes much to the anti-psychiatrists.

Perhaps the purest example of anti-psychiatry's triumph was in the Italian *Psichiatrica Democratica* reform in Italy. Foucault's and Goffman's ideas resonated with Franco Basaglia's Gramscian Marxism. He focused his reforms on liberating patients from psychiatry's and society's excluding oppression, what Gramsci called 'hegemony'. After radically reforming the deteriorated mental hospitals in Gorizia and Trieste in northern Italy, Basaglia marshalled a powerful political and humanitarian reforming zeal in 1978 to initiate Law 180, which effectively outlawed mental hospitals. The central message of the anti-psychiatrists, that you cannot deal humanely and effectively with psychotic individuals without taking their experiences seriously, and entering into their world at least in part, remains as true today as when Laing wrote about it fifty years ago.

9

Is psychiatry trustworthy?
Psychiatry's sins and abuses

There are altogether too many skeletons in psychiatry's closet so it is really no surprise that people are suspicious. More and more of us recognize the need for psychiatric treatment and more and more get real benefit from it, but the steady stream of criticism continues. Our increasingly liberal and educated society both clamours for psychiatry but finds its paternalistic overtones unacceptable, or at the very least uncomfortable. A culture that prizes the inalienable rights of the individual is bound to struggle with a profession that can, and regularly does, override those rights. With our emphasis on self-determination and personal choice and our increasing rejection of deference, a profession that reinterprets and categorizes our experiences risks being rejected as arrogant or condescending, even if it brings considerable relief.

It is ironic that such attacks remain unabated when psychiatry's treatments are safer, more effective and basically more scientific than ever before. Of course psychiatry has never been free from criticism (recall 'The Alleged Lunatics' Friends' Society') and probably never will be. In its very nature it is open to errors and, indeed, to abuse. It comprises a potent mix of dependent and relatively powerless patients, public fear and stigma, isolation and secrecy. Add to this the unpredictability of many of the disorders, the interpersonal nature of the diagnoses and the unique power of compulsory treatment.

The risks *are* undoubtedly much less now. Psychiatry is in the open, out from behind the walls of the asylum. It operates in a society not just more interested in mental health but willing to talk honestly about it. Scrutiny, both within the profession and in society, has been strengthened by a worldwide commitment to evidence-based medicine.

Judgements are made increasingly on facts and figures and on what research shows, rather than on the pronouncements of authority figures. This open and questioning approach is our strongest protection against a repetition of the aberrations and disasters that have unquestionably disfigured parts of psychiatry's history.

There is a temptation to dismiss these past errors as irrelevant to modern psychiatry, to put them behind us and concentrate on where we are now. In many ways this makes good sense. They often seem dated, and things are very different now with better treatments, more oversight, less fear. Things do, of course, still go wrong but they are usually quickly spotted and remedial action taken. However, there are good reasons to examine these mistakes. First we cannot just decide to forget the past: it is part of us and it will continue to nag at us unless confronted. An air of complacency would hang over us. Like our patients, psychiatry also needs to face and understand its history if it is to avoid making the same mistakes again and to fully understand itself. We saw in Chapter 6 how military psychiatry had to relearn many lessons forgotten from previous conflicts. We could avoid such soul-searching and insist that these episodes only reflected a very minor part of psychiatry's overall contribution, and this is undoubtedly so. We could also reassure ourselves that even when these awful things were happening, most of psychiatry consisted of decent, well-meaning staff doing their best for their patients in the face of uncertainty and ignorance. Indeed we do need to remind ourselves of this; errors and abuses were, and are, very much the exceptions. Yet confronting these uncomfortable, even shaming, episodes in our history can yield a richer understanding of what psychiatry is and what it aims to achieve.

For me the most important reason to examine past mistakes is that they illuminate the uncertain and shifting territory in which psychiatry operates and bring into sharp focus the unavoidable dilemmas that arise from this. This territory is one in which psychiatry *must* operate if it is to serve its patients well. Ambition and the quest for improvement carry real risks as well as promising cures. Even sticking to what is familiar and established is not without risk – our history demonstrates how context, attitudes, even political ideologies can obscure our judgement. This is not restricted to psychiatry: other branches of medicine have committed serious errors and found themselves down ethical cul-de-sacs. But we are more vulnerable to it. A discipline where diagnoses require social attribution for their salience must remain alert to the risk of getting it wrong, as we will explore in greater depth in Chapters 11 and 12. Just as psychiatry with its focus on the problems we humans encounter can explain much of what it is to be fully human (our necessary shadow) so psychiatry's errors may give us a similar, fuller insight into its nature.

Psychiatry's mistakes can be placed into three broad categories. The first comprises the excesses of isolated and misguided enthusiasts. These affect fewer patients and are usually very localized but are still shocking. Such enthusiasts are usually well intentioned but their ideas can be deeply mistaken, and in some cases frankly hare-brained. The problem is that zealots respond to failure not with self-doubt and a reappraisal, but by trying even harder. They rarely conclude that their treatment was simply wrong. They display a mixture of desperation and omnipotence; convinced they really do have the right idea, they think it only needs just one more push to make it work. The all-powerful psychiatrist whose technical brilliance outstrips his moral judgement is the evil figure of novels and films. In truth it is more often psychiatry's relative powerlessness that is its tragedy.

The second type involves psychiatry's political naivety or weakness, allowing itself to become part of the machinery of oppressive regimes. Its lowest point was undoubtedly in the Nazis' extermination of hundreds of thousands of mentally ill patients. Similarly, declaring political dissidents in the Soviet Union to be mentally ill has left an enduring distrust in Central and Eastern Europe. The third is the troubled history of psychiatry's relationship with women. This is less a story of isolated abuses (though those have existed) but the pervasive legacy of an asymmetrical and often bigoted relationship. The discriminatory and unfair treatment of women in the past is not limited to psychiatry but there are features peculiar to this relationship that have left deep scars and continuing controversy.

We have already seen that discovery of the most effective treatments in psychiatry involved a degree of chance. Psychiatry lacks a strong, overarching scientific model, so it has been a fertile ground for exotic theories. Several treatments arose from quite bizarre intellectual twists and turns. The most frequent and forceful criticisms of psychiatry concern the use of electroconvulsive therapy (ECT) and psychosurgery, so these treatments will be dealt with at some length. Both continue to have a place in modern psychiatry. ECT has a significant one and leucotomy (known as 'lobotomy' in the USA) a specialized and very, very minor one. Their discoveries were described in Chapter 5.

WHAT IS SO WRONG WITH ECT?

ECT remains one of the most effective treatments for severe depression, often working when antidepressants fail. This is particularly so in elderly patients suffering from severe depressions, with delusions of worthlessness or guilt. ECT remains highly controversial, partly because of its effects on memory but probably more because of its overuse in the decades before antidepressants. It is undoubtedly a frightening and off-putting treatment. All of us recoil at the thought of an electric current through our brain and an induced epileptic fit. However, it is worth pausing and reminding ourselves that many treatments in medicine and surgery are much more intrusive and painful. Somehow they do not evoke the same fear or condemnation.

In the 1940s and 1950s ECT acquired a malign aura of a punishment in many mental hospitals. Its main use was to relieve agitated depression and disturbed arousal in psychotic patients, but it was undoubtedly also used to control anger and hostility. Doctors and nurses used the language of 'therapy' but patients saw it as punishment and the threat of it hung over some wards. In Milos Forman's cult 1975 film *One Flew Over the Cuckoo's Nest* the troublesome anti-hero receives unmodified ECT to quell his defiant behaviour. Showing it without anaesthetic or muscle relaxant underlined its violence, although 'unmodified' ECT had not been used since before the Second World War. So strong are the feelings that ECT generates that it remains essentially outlawed in several countries. This highly effective treatment has been damaged by early overuse and denial of its effects on memory. Just how did psychiatry fall into this trap?

Probably the main reason is that ECT is so dramatically effective when it works. Those who so strongly condemn it may never have seen its effects. A tormented, agitated elderly woman, restlessly pacing and blaming herself for delusional past 'evil' behaviour, may be relieved and calmed almost immediately. After just a couple of treatments she may be able to sit still and to eat and drink. Often within a week or two the delusions have receded and she can talk to her family again and begin to look forward to getting home. Similarly an exhausted manic patient who has not slept for days, hardly has time to eat or drink because of his arousal and fights every offer of a sedative or tranquillizer can be calmed often with just one or two treatments. When it works it is wonderful to see.

Most psychiatrists can easily name patients that they are absolutely sure would have died without ECT. In my case there are four or five faces that immediately spring to mind: very different people, ranging from their mid-twenties to over eighty years old, often firmly committed to taking their own life or intent on starvation. For over a decade after organizing a course of compulsory ECT I regularly saw one ex-patient, who had been successfully starving herself to death in deluded self-punishment, out in the evenings walking her little terrier near my house. The crudity of ECT does little for psychiatry's self-image. However, it seems arrogant in the extreme to deny a highly effective treatment in such an awful illness because it offends our aesthetic or philosophical sensitivities.

It is easy, given the chorus of criticism, to overlook the view of ECT held by the people who have had it. Asked soon after treatment, about 70 per cent of patients report that it worked well despite many noting memory problems. Asked specific questions such as 'Did the treatment help you?', 'Would you have it again if you fell ill?' and 'Would you advise a friend or relative, ill in the same way as you have been, to have it?' ECT gets higher approval rates than either antidepressants or antipsychotics.

So ECT undoubtedly works – but at what cost? Patients are often confused for an hour or so after the treatment and have limited recall of the hours leading up to it. More troubling is the loss of discrete memories, often of significant events or even people's names. Psychiatrists were slow to recognize this, mainly because overall mental functioning improves so much after ECT. Complaints of poor memory were interpreted as consequences of the patient's increased self-awareness as the depression lifted. Discrete memory loss is also difficult to pick up using standard tests of memory processing, which routinely indicate improvement in ECT patients. However, such memory loss has now been firmly established as a side effect of ECT to be weighed against its potential advantages.

ECT administration has been modified to reduce memory problems. Since the 1960s the current is usually passed only over the 'non-dominant' hemisphere, for most of us the right side. This avoids the speech centres, causing less interference with verbal memory. Control of the current has also been improved to deliver the minimum strength that will induce a seizure (it is the seizure, not the electrical current, which lifts the depression). There have been a few controlled trials of ECT, although these are not easy to conduct. Half the depressed patients receive normal ECT and half receive 'sham ECT' with anaesthetic and the electrodes applied but no current passed. All but one trial showed a clear superiority for the real ECT. So ECT is not an error in itself, but it has undoubtedly been misused: how?

Early enthusiasts for ECT gave it to all their depressed patients, including those suffering from relatively mild disorders. With any new medical treatment it takes time to establish the threshold for its effectiveness. That ECT worked with severe 'psychotic' depression led to its use with less severe 'neurotic' depression but the results were not good. Many patients who received ECT when I started psychiatry in the early 1970s would now be treated with antidepressants and psychotherapy. Overuse receded as it became clear that it did not work well with less severe depression and as alternative effective treatments became more widespread. During the 1960s very intensive ECT, so called 'regressive ECT', was tried. Attempts to speed up ECT's effects by giving it more frequently than twice a week were unsuccessful. In one well-reported trial ECT was given daily or occasionally twice a day but abandoned after just eighteen patients.

Ewen Cameron is associated with intensive ECT and is one of psychiatry's genuinely sinister figures. A Scottish-born psychiatrist, he worked in Canada and the USA, a protégé of the USA's leading psychiatrist, Adolph Meyer. He was trained in elite centres in both Europe and the USA and was enormously energetic and influential. He gave evidence at the Nuremberg War Crimes Trial and went on to become the president of both the American Psychiatric Association and the World Psychiatric Association. He conducted extensive trials of the most intensive ECT, which involved several treatments a day. Cameron believed that this would clear the mind of recent preoccupations and maladaptive patterns of thinking and behaviour. The resulting confusion would lead to a 'depatterning'. Once the grip of pathological thinking had been released patients could 'relearn' how to manage their lives. Cameron persisted despite patients becoming confused and even incontinent.

Why Cameron persisted when others rapidly abandoned this approach eventually became clear in the 1970s. He had been part-funded by the CIA in its notorious and secret 'MKULTRA' mind control research programme. This included various clandestine projects for manipulating mental processes, including sensory deprivation and testing drugs such as LSD on unsuspecting subjects. Cameron's view was that the brain was like a computer and could be reprogrammed when the old software was wiped. This appealed to the CIA's Cold War ambition to alter the behaviour of hostile individuals and even nation states.

Early reports of intensive or 'regressive' ECT trials make grim reading but it was rapidly abandoned and is now little known. The real energy behind the anti-ECT movement comes from individuals who have had ECT without benefit. Undoubtedly there were many, particularly when ECT was so overused up into the 1960s and 1970s. Depression can affect people in very different ways. For instance, some patients may be hostile or angry or impulsive for some time before their depressive symptoms eventually become clear. Such 'atypical presentations' sometimes responded well to ECT, so it is not completely illogical to try it as a 'diagnostic test'.

Psychiatrists have undoubtedly sometimes used ECT when at a loss to understand what is going on with someone, especially if they suspect an underlying depression. Obviously when we are wrong it does not work. Sometimes the difficult moods and experiences suspected to be an atypical depression are manifestations of personality struggles and ECT does not change personality despite its critics' claims to the contrary. People who are given ECT under these circumstances are often angry about it and, understandably, resent it.

ECT is the psychiatric treatment that demonstrates the power imbalance between doctor and patient most concretely. It can easily feel humiliating and abusive, all the more when resorted to out of desperation during a prolonged and angry hospital admission. Though it is vanishingly rare for ECT to be given against a patient's wishes in such circumstances, it undoubtedly did happen. Now ECT can only be given against a patient's wishes (in those countries where it can – not all permit it) in very special and controlled conditions. It requires a second independent psychiatric opinion and then usually only when survival is at risk, as was the case with my lady with the dog. So a good, if scary, treatment acquired a bad reputation and has gone from overuse probably to under-use. People who could really benefit from it may often now not get it.

High-profile critics of psychiatry (e.g. Richard Bentall, *Doctoring the Mind*) include insulin coma treatment in the roll-call of psychiatry's sins and failings, although this could be disputed. Considering it may focus our thinking on how we make such judgements, and why some treatments grab our attention more than others. Manfred Sakel developed insulin coma treatment in 1934 and it spread across Europe and the USA as outlined in Chapter 5. Insulin coma ('insulin shock' in the USA) is regularly cited as one more dangerous and ineffective psychiatric treatment based on spurious reasoning. It demonstrates, its critics claim, just how foolish and untrustworthy the profession is (as if they needed more examples).

But consider the facts. After its discovery in 1922 insulin, like any major discovery, was tested for potential therapeutic effects in just about every branch of medicine. Medical behaviour is no different today; once a powerful new drug or instrument is developed it will be tested across the full range of disorders, sometimes with surprising results. The anti-cancer drug methotrexate is effective in rheumatoid arthritis, aspirin reduces the risk of heart attacks. New uses establish themselves by clinical observation – doctors simply try it out and watch to see if the patient improves. We now know insulin coma treatment is ineffective, so how were we fooled? Again there is nothing unique to psychiatry about this. New remedies are generally tried on desperate cases when the usual treatments have failed, and a proportion of these will recover spontaneously. It is because we recognize the risk of confusing spontaneous improvement with the effect of our treatment that we have developed our rigorous trial methodology.

The gold standard for testing whether a treatment works is the randomized controlled trial (RCT), where half the patients receive the treatment and half do not. Insulin coma treatment was shown to be ineffective by a double-blind RCT published in 1957. It was rapidly abandoned despite the enormous investment in it. Ackner and Old-ham's 1957 RCT in *The Lancet* has the distinction of being the first ever RCT to disprove the effectiveness of a *medical treatment*. Not just the first psychiatric treatment, but the first *medical* treatment of any kind disproved in this way. Insulin coma treatment was tested using the highest scientific standards of the time, in the vanguard of evidence-based medicine. A mistake, yes. But one promptly investigated and abandoned as soon as the evidence was clear.

I have dwelt so long on ECT and insulin coma treatment because I believe they demonstrate the different standards we unfairly apply to psychiatry compared to the rest of medicine. Modern medicine has no shortage of effective treatments that arose from subsequently discredited theories. Nor is its history short of treatments which have eventually been recognized to be useless. Indeed there are many treatments in current use despite strong evidence that they are ineffective. The stories of insulin coma and ECT are not that different from those found in the rest of medicine, with its triumphs and failures.

ECT is regularly assailed because it 'only treats the symptoms' not the underlying cause, and because patients often relapse. True, but why 'only'? And what is so special about depression as a relapsing illness? Medicine is full of illnesses that keep recurring despite effective treatment. Every winter hospital wards fill up with patients suffering from severe bronchitis and pneumonia who are treated successfully with antibiotics. Many are back the next winter with another bout and, again, treated successfully with the same antibiotics. But we don't say that antibiotics 'only treat the symptoms' or that they should be abandoned because they don't abolish relapse. Yet we regularly apply these unrealistic standards to psychiatric treatments.

ECT is described as distressing and 'barbaric'. Is it really any more primitive than cutting out a cancer, evacuating a blood clot from the brain or passing a really massive voltage across an arrested heart? Of course not. Perhaps it is because we have greater difficulty in imagining ourselves suffering from a serious mental illness. Perhaps it is because we can't *see* mental illnesses or still harbour doubts that mental illnesses are 'real illnesses'. Whatever it is, these are striking double standards. We are much less prepared to accept the therapeutic limitations, the indignity or the pain involved in psychiatric treatments than those we accept without demure in physical illnesses. None of this is to say that there have not been real errors in psychiatry, only to encourage us to try to be disciplined in how we judge them. We should judge them with the same standards we apply to other medical treatments.

Similarly when we look back at old treatments we need, as historians keep reminding us, to be very wary of applying modern expectations. A hundred years ago pain, disability and sudden early death were commonplace. Medicine, all medicine, involved guesswork; treatments were often painful and risky with only a modest promise of success. That was the context in which all treatments were offered and the context in which they were accepted. People routinely tolerated discomforts and dangers that would seem inconceivable to us now. Psychiatric treatments should also be judged against the standards of their time.

WHEN PSYCHIATRISTS TAKE TO SURGERY

Leucotomy was developed by the truly remarkable psychiatrist/neurologist Egas Moniz, who received the Nobel Prize for it (Chapter 5). It was initially a radical intervention to be used only rarely in carefully chosen and severe, resistant cases and it continues today to be used in this way in several countries. In the UK four or five such operations are conducted each year, almost exclusively on patients with severe, crippling obsessive-compulsive disorder. And only then after several courses of medication and intensive behaviour therapy have failed, with each patient subject to the most stringent obligatory external review. The operation now is a highly precise stereotactic procedure destroying a very small, highly localized, pea-sized piece of brain tissue. The clinical effects are also correspondingly limited.

I have personally observed a dozen patients undergo these operations. I knew of their risks and was instinctively opposed to them. However, in truth, the worst effect I saw was disappointment when no improvement followed. In the most successful there was a dramatic lowering of anxiety and reduction in the rituals (usually washing or counting). I vividly remember a man in his thirties whose clothes were always sopping wet because he took them off and washed them several times a day. His hands and arms were raw and bleeding from his compulsive washing. The lives of his exhausted elderly Jewish parents were entirely devoted to caring for him. A week or two after the operation he was tolerating one change of clothes a day. Though he still washed frequently, his clothes were dry and his hands and arms were already healing. It was not a miracle, but it was wonderful to see.

Leucotomy's story, however, has not been good and I would not suggest otherwise. Its strongest advocates have been its worst enemies. Consider this outrageous quote from a prominent UK textbook still in use during my training (W. Sargant and E. Slater, *An Introduction to Physical Methods of Treatment in Psychiatry*, 5th edition, E. and S. Livingstone, 1972). It recommended considering a leucotomy for 'A depressed woman ... [who] ... owes her illness to a psychopathic husband. Separation might be the answer but ruled out by other ties such as children, by the patient's financial or emotional dependence, or by her religious views.'

Early leucotomies were fairly crude and destructive operations. They involved cutting the tracts (the communicating nerves) between the frontal lobes and the base of the brain with a sweeping motion of a fine scalpel. The frontal lobes are the part of the brain responsible for our finer judgements and would thereby be substantially disabled (hence the American term 'lobotomy'). Some patients did experience relief from distressing and disabling symptoms but for many it was at a terrible cost. They often became apathetic, and a pale shadow of their former selves. Some demonstrated a deterioration of personal habits and behaviour, often described as a 'coarsening'. Others developed epileptic fits and some patients died after bleeding or infection. It was not the finely focused intervention of later years. Despite this it was widely used in mental hospitals, predominantly for chronically disturbed psychotic patients.

In the USA it was taken up with enthusiasm and unlike in Europe most of the operations were conducted in mental hospitals themselves. Like the one in Pennsylvania where I spent time as a medical student these often had their own operating theatres. A neurologist called Walter Freeman (1895–1972) teamed up with a neurosurgeon, James Watts (1904–94), in 1936 to perform Moniz's operation. They modified it, making it somewhat more extensive, and called it a lobotomy. It came to be called the 'Freeman–Watts procedure'. Freeman became utterly carried away with his belief in its benefits and developed a simple and quick, but strikingly crude, technique. He inserted a specially designed probe which he called a 'leucotome' up through the eye socket and swept it round. This operation could be done under local anaesthetic and took only minutes.

Freeman, although not a trained surgeon, started to do the operations himself and was abandoned in disgust by Watts. Enthusiasm for the procedure mounted, however, and he toured the USA performing the operations in state hospitals. It is estimated that something like 18,000–20,000 lobotomies were carried out in the USA between 1939 and 1951. Over 3,400 were conducted by Freeman alone, one rumoured to be on the 23-year-old Rosemary Kennedy, sister of the future US president.

Lobotomies died out as more effective treatments developed, not, as we might now think, as a result of popular protest. In the UK only thirty have been carried out in the first ten years of this century. The level of improvement, or damage, caused by these early crude interventions is hard to determine. Most of the patients remained as neglected in their large mental hospitals after the surgery as they had been before, and few had any effective voice. The damage to the profession of psychiatry was immense. Although eventually barred from practice Freeman remained unrepentant and continued to advocate lobotomies up to his death in 1972.

A truly gothic episode in psychiatry's history concerns the New Jersey psychiatrist Henry Cotton (1876–1933). Cotton became convinced that bacterial infections and sepsis were responsible for psychosis. He embarked on a personal crusade to remove the assumed sources of infection, employing increasingly radical surgery. Initially he removed infected teeth, but if that did not work moved on to

tonsils and eventually colons. Cotton cannot be dismissed entirely as
an isolated crank. He was at the pinnacle of his profession having
studied in Europe with Kraepelin and Alzheimer and was also a
favoured student of the prestigious Adolph Meyer. He became the
medical director of the Trenton State Hospital in New Jersey in
1907 at the early age of thirty. Trenton was no backwater. It had been
founded by that driving force of USA mental health reform Dorothea
Dix herself, in 1848, and she always referred to it as her 'firstborn
child'. So this was an impressive appointment for a rising star, one of
the acknowledged pioneers of 'modern psychiatry'. In the beginning
Cotton fulfilled his promise, modernizing the institution, removing
restraints and opening many locked doors.

High fevers can produce strange mental states with vivid hallucinations ('delirium'); this has always been known. Cotton began to
wonder if the perceptual distortions of schizophrenia could be caused
by chronic low-grade infections and the 'intoxication' that arose from
such sepsis. He was not unique in his interest in this process. The Russian Metchnikoff, awarded the 1908 Nobel Prize in medicine for his
work on immunology, had earlier proposed that toxic bacteria in the
gut induced ageing by a similar process. The eminent British surgeon
Sir Arbuthnot Lane met Metchnikoff in 1904 and pioneered total
colectomies for constipation among the wealthy in the period leading
up to the First World War. These aimed to reduce 'auto-intoxication'.
Before rushing to judgement we should remember that persisting ill-
health from chronic infections was a commonplace of pre-antibiotic
life. It is also worth pausing to reflect how 'toxins' still have an enduring fascination for us. Think of the range of 'detox' products on sale
in every pharmacy and advertised in countless magazines. Health
farms worldwide still offer colonic irrigation treatments based on
essentially the same idea.

Chronic silent infections undoubtedly can give rise to unexpected
disorders. GPI had only recently and triumphantly been vanquished
by the malaria regime introduced in 1917 (Chapter 5). A similarly
outlandish theory of focal sepsis, initially derided by the profession,
led in 1982 to the virtual eradication of peptic ulcers and also earned
a Nobel Prize (Chapter 8). None of this should blind us, however, to

the extreme nature of Cotton's Messianic obsession, nor to the terrible havoc he wreaked.

Dental extractions became routine in Trenton and very soon high rates of more extensive surgery followed, encouraged by exaggerated reports of 'cure' rates as high as 85 per cent. Rumours, however, began to circulate about the death rates after these operations and the reality of their outcomes. Staff complained and left, particularly as they saw patients coerced into the operations. We should not imagine, however, that it was just the powerless who were subjected to these mutilations. Cotton, like Arbuthnot Lane in London, received a steady stream of wealthy patients seeking his cure, so much so that a private hospital had to be opened in Trenton to cope with them. He became a medical celebrity and publicized his work widely. He obviously believed he had made a vital breakthrough and operated on his own mentally unwell son. In 1922, even as concerns about his practice were beginning to be voiced, the *New York Times* wrote of his 'brilliant leadership ... the most searching, aggressive and profound scientific investigation ... of the whole field of mental and nervous disorders ...'

The hospital and Cotton's methods were investigated by one of Adolph Meyer's colleagues but the report was never finished or published. In 1925 the state initiated a formal investigation and Cotton received strong support from the hospital trustees and many senior professional colleagues. The *New York Times* reported from the investigation that Trenton was 'the most progressive institution in the world for the care of the insane ... by the removal of focal infection ...' However, the high infection rates from his operations became increasingly obvious and surgery was scaled down and eventually abandoned. Remarkably Cotton was not dismissed but remained Medical Director until 1930, and continued to work privately until his death in 1933. He was still hailed as a medical pioneer. A 1982 profile of Trenton Hospital in the *American Journal of Psychiatry* refers to Cotton bringing in 'a new era in the treatment of mental diseases' and praises his innovations. There is no mention of the focal sepsis scandal. The critical historian of psychiatry Andrew Scull's book of this sorry tale, *Madhouse* (2005), emphasizes perhaps its most disturbing aspect – how psychiatry closed ranks to cover it up, suppressing the independent report and effectively silencing its author.

PSYCHOTHERAPY OVERSTEPS THE LINE

It would be easy to think that only obsessive and arrogant medical-model psychiatrists go off the rails, but sadly it is not so. As we saw in the preceding chapter psychotherapists are also capable of holding fixed ideas against all the evidence and to everybody's cost. Of course, it is more difficult to be actively abusive in psychotherapy because the patient has to cooperate, but it is not impossible. The line between exploitation, an ever-present risk, and abuse is fine. Desperate people in awe of their therapists will tolerate an awful lot. In Chapter 12 we will explore controversial issues such as recovered memory syndrome and multiple personality disorder, which I believe fall into this grey area. These are imposed (so-called 'iatrogneic' or doctor-induced) disorders where the therapist convinces the patient of his or her (the therapist's) beliefs. These therapists are invariably very genuine in their motivation. But then so were Henry Cotton and Walter Freeman – few really suggest they were sadistic or evil; they were just blinkered and misguided.

Several psychotherapies have gone beyond what we would probably consider acceptable. Janov's 'primal scream' therapy attracted high-profile patients such as the late John Lennon in the early 1970s. It started with three weeks of intensive isolation with restricted sleep, no access to phone calls, tobacco or drugs. This was to break down resistance and allow the repressed primitive 'hurt' to escape and find its expression in 'the scream' (which was just that – a scream). Exhaustion and bullying were features of several 'encounter' group methods of the same period. 'Abusive' psychotherapies are generally quite short-term, often marketed as 'personal growth' experiences.

Of course, what is considered abusive is a very individual judgement. Janov's work was highly appreciated by most of his patients. Some of the extreme practices of the Church of Scientology or several 'human potential' groups might be considered abusive or bordering on it. However, their practitioners, and many who have experienced them, rate them highly and consider the suffering an essential part of the process. Patients usually know what they are letting themselves in for. They are often attracted by the extreme nature of what is on offer, perhaps desperate after more routine therapies have failed to help. Having submitted yourself to something that is gruelling and unpleasant there is a strong incentive to believe it works. Otherwise why did you put yourself through it?

'Psycholytic therapy' was a bizarre episode in a mental hospital in Worcester, in the UK, in the 1960s. It was not a classical psychotherapy, but shared psychotherapy's aim to uncover and work through unconscious conflicts. The Scottish psychiatrist and psychotherapist Ronald Sandison (1916–2010) came as medical superintendent in 1951 to the neglected and overcrowded backwater that was Powick Hospital. Finding out about LSD in Switzerland in 1952 when it was a perfectly legal drug, he began to use it with some of his patients. Like Timothy Leary, who encouraged a whole generation to 'turn on, tune in and drop out', he believed that LSD could free up frozen, inhibited minds. Sandison published his findings and in 1958 received funding for a specific unit, which continued until 1972. A total of 683 patients experienced 13,785 LSD sessions. Taking LSD was accompanied by various rather naïve and theatrical techniques to encourage self-exploration and expression and the dosages were often remarkably high. LSD is not without its risks and in 2002 forty-three of Sandison's patients received compensation from the NHS. Sandison, who had left the hospital in 1964, never attracted any personal criticism. He was a warm, clearly benign and religious Scot with his patients' best interests at heart.

Aversion therapy has flitted in and out of psychiatry for a century in one form or another. The theory underpinning it is variously referred to as conditioning, learning theory and behaviourism and arose from observations by the Russian physiologist Ivan Pavlov published in 1901. While researching gastric functioning in dogs Pavlov noted that they began salivating before their food arrived. They could quickly be trained to salivate at the sound of a bell rung just before food was delivered. This reflex salivation was 'conditioned' by the regular association of the bell and the food and soon worked just as well without the food. This 'classical conditioning' led the American psychologist John Watson to develop the theory of behaviourism.

This proposed that behaviour could be shaped by repeated experiences, hence 'learning theory'. In his notorious 1920 'little Albert' experiment Watson trained an eleven-month-old boy to be frightened of a tame rat by making a sudden loud noise whenever he touched it.

Watson proselytized for the value of behaviourism in child rearing but the approach only achieved international prominence with the work of the Harvard psychologist B. F. Skinner (1904–90). It was Skinner who described *operant conditioning*. This proposed that almost any behaviour can be shaped by rewarding it ('positive reinforcement') or punishing it ('negative reinforcement'). The crucial features of operant conditioning are that the reinforcement should be repeated often and provided as close as possible in time to the targeted behaviour. Treatment based on negative reinforcement is often referred to as 'aversion therapy'. In aversion therapy an unpleasant experience is linked to the behaviour to be reduced or removed ('extinguished' in the jargon).

Operant conditioning has a long history as behaviour modification in learning disability settings and is still used effectively, for instance, to treat bed-wetting. Aversion therapy has a more controversial place, particularly in the treatment of unwelcome habits including sexual practices and addictions. Some of the extreme treatments of shell shock used in the First World War (Chapter 6) such as the faradic, or electrical, approaches probably worked, if they worked at all, by aversion. They were certainly viewed as punishment rather than cure by the poor soldiers who suffered them and by the wider public.

A whole range of sexual behaviour has been subjected to aversion therapy. Usually painful but not dangerous electric shocks are administered simultaneously with images either in imagination or on screen, of the 'unacceptable' sexual practice. Initially therapists administered the shock but increasingly patients took on the responsibility themselves. This approach was once widely used to try and curb indecent exposure and paedophilic fantasies. Most notoriously it was used to try and 'convert' homosexual men to heterosexuality in the period up to 1973 when it was still classified as a psychiatric disorder.

Aversion therapy has faded mainly because it is not very successful, but also because it conveyed a corrosive impression of professional narrow-mindedness and bigotry. Electric shocks and drugs to induce vomiting were briefly in vogue for alcoholism. Their abandonment was hastened by the seedy air of brutality, almost sadism, in the writings of many of their advocates.

The line between abuse and punishment and a genuine attempt to help in otherwise desperate situations is a difficult one. Currently there are some institutions in the USA where autistic children wear special vests that can deliver small electric shocks when they misbehave or self-harm. Is this treatment or torture? Psychiatry's history has taught us that the patient's consent does not necessarily exonerate us. There are some treatments that, even if they are consensual and successful, go beyond what should be tolerated from health professionals in a civilized society. It would strike me that deliberately inflicting pain is one.

PSYCHIATRY'S HOLOCAUST

Psychiatry's cooperation with the Nazi extermination of mentally ill and mentally handicapped patients is undoubtedly its most shameful chapter. Between 1939 and 1941 an official programme effected the murder of a recorded 70,000 mentally ill and mentally handicapped individuals in Germany. The final figure was probably nearer 200,000 as the slaughter continued until 1945 and included the occupied territories. Indeed the first ever use of gas chambers by the Nazis was the 'clearing' of mental hospitals in Poland in July 1939 by SS commandos. Initially this systematic killing of those 'judged incurably sick, by critical medical examination' took place in isolated institutions to which they had been transferred from their local hospitals. Over time they became absorbed into the horror of the Holocaust along with Jews, gypsies, communists and homosexuals. The operation was overseen by a shadowy organization established in May 1939 officially called the Committee for the Scientific Treatment of Severe, Genetically Determined Illnesses. It was more generally referred to as 'Aktion T4' after the address of its head office in number 4, Tiergartenstrasse, Berlin.

How could such a terrible thing have happened and why was there no effective opposition from psychiatry? For there was none. Nor did this abomination just arise out of the blue, not simply some awful expedient of war. Terrible overcrowding and neglect were common in mental hospitals in the war throughout Europe and beyond as their patients were moved around to free wards for injured combatants. No, the systematic extermination of the mentally ill was a terrible consequence of more long-standing eugenic ideas which had been gaining strength in Europe, the UK and the USA for decades. 'Social Darwinism' and a moral panic that the unfit were 'breeding' faster than the educated and able had become a preoccupation at the turn of the twentieth century. It is never that far from the surface, even now.

Psychiatry was not immune to such Social Darwinism. The 'degeneracy' model of mental illness, prominent in the late nineteenth century, provided fertile ground for it to take hold. Some psychiatrists, such as the ever-gloomy Henry Maudsley, even wondered if all the good that psychiatry did might be more than outweighed by a 'tainted inheritance' from those (predominantly women in the thinking of the time) who recovered. Some of the more extreme writings of the late-nineteenth/early-twentieth-century psychiatrists are quite hair-raising on this subject and contributed to the unhealthy and distorted relationship with women explored below.

There has been an understandable desire to write off all this eugenic thinking as just one further, horrific, facet of the Nazi's 'racial purity' preoccupation. Nazi Germany certainly enacted the thinking with shocking brutality. Sterilization was the more common approach. The Nazis promulgated a specific law in 1933, 'Law for the prevention of hereditary diseased offspring', with compulsory sterilization for specific disorders such as schizophrenia, severe mental handicap, epilepsy and Huntington's disease. As a consequence over 350,000 individuals were sterilized. However, it is sobering to recognize how widespread the *thinking* was. Programmes took place in even forward-thinking countries such as Sweden, where over 60,000 were sterilized. The 1935 Swedish law, although long fallen into disuse, was only officially repealed in 1975. Eugenic ideas undoubtedly remained widespread. As a medical student I witnessed enormous pressure exerted on some women to accept sterilization because they 'obviously could not cope with further children'.

The step from enforced sterilization to active extermination is still a huge one. In Germany it was taken in August 1939, not first in psychiatry but with severely physically handicapped infants. Hitler passed his edict ostensibly responding to a plea from the father of a severely disabled child. Several thousand children died this way.

The terrible shame of the extermination of the mentally ill is compounded by several prominent psychiatrists leading it and none vigorously and publicly opposing it. Some, such as Professor Hans Creutzfeldt (who gave his name to 'Creutzfeldt–Jacob disease') did manage to protect his own patients, but there was no coordinated professional opposition. It was clearly not possible for this crime to have happened in ignorance. Opposition from family members, with some support from the church, became so strong that in 1941 the decree was rescinded and the Aktion T4 programme disbanded. German academic psychiatry, undoubtedly the world leader up to that time, was discredited and devastated. It is only now recovering.

It is neither possible nor appropriate to try and explain away psychiatry's terrible failing in this episode. Our critics hold it up as proof of the profession's fundamental misanthropy and cruelty, citing countless lurid and extreme utterances. It is simply not possible to know exactly what psychiatrists really thought in this period. The broad mass of the profession probably did not share the extreme views articulated, but they voiced no effective opposition. Psychiatry was no better than those around it and, arguably in this instance, worse. There is no excuse.

The Soviet Union developed its own diagnostic system for schizophrenia and between the end of the Stalin era and the mid-1980s appears to have exploited this lax category to lock up political dissidents. There had been a dramatic shake-up in psychiatry in the Soviet Academy of Medical Sciences in 1951 with a return to a strict Pavlovian orthodoxy. Andrei Snezhnevsky (1904–87), director of the Institute of Psychiatry, broadened the diagnosis, dividing it into a continuous form and a progressive form. He proposed that a mild progressive form consisted only of negative symptoms which he called 'sluggish schizophrenia'.

Sluggish schizophrenia exhibited no obvious symptoms and sufferers appeared otherwise to manage perfectly well in everyday life. However, the 'trained eye' could detect indications of self-reference, pathological thinking and anxiety. 'Sluggish schizophrenia' was used in the Soviet Union as a convenient label to detain politically awkward individuals and dissidents. A sustained campaign by the World Psychiatric Association had begun to break down barriers with the Soviet Academy of Medical Sciences but the collapse of the Soviet Union in 1989 saw an abrupt end to these practices.

Some cynical Soviet psychiatrists may have seen such abuse as the road to personal prestige and advancement but most simply didn't think enough (which is perhaps as bad). In a very regimented state, with little experience of the legitimacy of disagreement, dissent *may* seem 'unbalanced'. Probably some dissidents, by the law of averages, were unbalanced. That does not detract from the validity of their dissent but it does muddy the issue. The American poet Ezra Pound (1885–1972) was a serious embarrassment to his government. He had become a Fascist in the Second World War and regularly broadcast from Italy for Mussolini. His detention in St Elizabeth's Hospital, Washington, from 1945 to 1948 has been repeatedly criticized as political internment as he continued to produce world-class (albeit controversial) modernist poetry. The USA government was undoubtedly relieved to have him detained. He was a political dissident but he was also, in the opinions of even his best friends, quite severely deranged.

We can feel relatively hopeful that psychiatry is unlikely to be such an obviously unwitting tool of state oppression again. We have learnt our lesson and the profession is now more open and international. The strongest protection probably comes from the level of public scrutiny in this era of community care and social media. However, the current danger may be less the naked exercise of state power than insidious commercial and social pressures. These are anything but innocuous and will be considered in Chapters 11 and 12.

GENDER WARS

Before leaving behind these errors and transgressions we must acknowledge psychiatry's complex and troubled relationship with women. Like all professions psychiatry used to consist (though no longer) almost exclusively of men, usually successful middle-class men with their share of self-importance and establishment values. This is probably broadly correct, but is only part of the truth. Psychiatry has accommodated more than its fair share of eccentrics and original thinkers as these pages testify, and it is a more tolerant profession than most. In the second half of the twentieth century it has welcomed a high proportion of immigrants and has always been a refuge for Jewish doctors (often discriminated against elsewhere). Certainly in my time it was the one branch of medicine where it was perfectly safe to be openly gay or politically radical.

Psychiatry did, however, become established and formed its professional identity in nineteenth-century Europe, an intensely patriarchal culture. Women were excluded from higher education and denied independence or political influence. Male psychiatrists (just as 'male lawyers', 'male priests', 'male shopkeepers') viewed women as fundamentally different, often considering them as weaker or even inferior.

Feminist historians such as Elaine Showalter (*The Female Malady*, 1985) argue that women have always comprised the majority of psychiatric patients and endured the most 'aggressive' treatments. This is probably not true. In psychoses or asylum care, rates vary over time and place but men have generally outnumbered women. This male excess was exaggerated with the steep rise in male admissions towards the end of the nineteenth century as a consequence of general paralysis of the insane (Chapter 5) or the excess of unmarried men found in asylums in economically deprived areas such as the west of Ireland in the early twentieth century. Women, on the other hand, lived longer then, as they do now, and so have increasingly outnumbered male patients in dementia care. The picture is unclear but the details do not really matter. What matters is that mental illness in women was seen as different from that in men in many fundamental ways and they were treated differently.

Women were seen as more vulnerable emotionally and a variety of explanations were advanced. Some psychiatrists attributed it to hormonal changes, citing the menstrual cycle, childbirth and menopause as powerful precipitants of mental illness. Others noted the poverty and burden borne by women caring for many children with little or no support from exhausted husbands. Still others observed the tensions inherent in the lives of intelligent, privileged women with limited access to education and absolutely no outlet for their abilities and no control over their lives. The plight of these women struggling against society's constraints has, understandably, preoccupied feminist writers and it was undoubtedly instrumental in the rise and character of psychoanalysis.

The misogyny displayed in the writings of some Victorian psychiatrists is truly breathtaking. Elaine Showalter argues that the vindictiveness of much of this writing and practice arose from the threat that emerging female suffrage posed to men's position in a patriarchal world. It is hard to disagree. A common refrain was that women became ill when they directed energies into education or work because this conflicted with the 'natural' need for those energies in reproduction. Henry Maudsley was strongly opposed to women's education for this reason. Maudsley seems to have been a globally miserable individual. Despite his enormous success, his influence (editor of the *Journal of Mental Science*) and his wealth (his bequest established the hospital named after him in London) he became a bitter recluse consumed by regrets.

The plight of energetic and able women, and their clumsy treatment in the hands of psychiatrists, is richly documented. Many of them (Florence Nightingale, Alice James, Virginia Woolf) were highly productive and literate. A particularly clear-cut example was Edith Lanchester (1871–1966), the gifted daughter of a prominent London architect. Edith was active in the Social Democratic Foundation; she disapproved of marriage and insisted in 'living in sin' with an Irish railway clerk, James Sullivan. Her brother and father kidnapped her and had her compulsorily detained (albeit only for four days) in the Priory Hospital in south London. The cause of her insanity was recorded as 'over-education'. She subsequently had a long and successful life with James for a further fifty years bringing up their children.

Was there anything special about psychiatry that made it uniquely misogynistic? Lisa Appignanesi's history of women and psychiatry, *Mad, Bad and Sad*, suggests that diagnostic changes contributed to it. The distinction between sanity and insanity was softened by the French concept of 'monomania'. This proposed that madness could be limited in its scope and that individual patients could be mad but still 'appear normal'. The inherent dangers of this understanding are not restricted to gender politics as we have witnessed above in the Soviet Union. Both Showalter and Appignanesi describe the undoubted sexual abuse experienced by women in asylums. But is this a reflection of the nature of psychiatry or of prevailing social practice? It impresses us little today to argue that women were no worse treated by psychiatrists and in asylums than they were generally at that time. It might be accurate, but remains a shame that psychiatry did not aspire to better.

The very complex, and undoubtedly gendered, relationship in psychotherapy and non-asylum psychiatry does, rightly, raise several penetrating questions. These are addressed in several places in this book. I do not personally believe they are well understood from the narrow perspective of abuse. This obviously may be my limitation and others will draw different conclusions about childhood sexual abuse and eating disorders, recovered memory syndrome and so forth. I hope I have made it clear that I do accept that psychiatry has made grievous errors as a fellow traveller with indefensible social and political movements. As often as not this has been simply through naivety, although medicine's engagement in the eugenics movement was far from passive.

In the complex and shifting arena of gender politics (and some of the diagnostic developments picked up in Chapter 11) reducing the debate to a simple power-play may deprive us of the possibility of a richer understanding. Whether gender differences are predominantly biological or social in origin is constantly contested and some even deny there are any differences. However, if there are, and no matter how they arise, they are played out in technicolour in psychiatry. Women comprise over two thirds of those who *seek* psychiatric care, although men occupy an equal amount of that care. What they appear to want is different and what they get is different. Who is influencing whom can be debated and, without doubt, will change. Strong feelings are evoked and fixed adversarial positions readily adopted. It is a pity as a cool, dispassionate analysis of how men and women interact with psychiatry might provide a wonderful insight into our differing natures. Sadly, given psychiatry's history, such a neutral, reflective examination may be some time coming.

Few professions have not made mistakes. Indeed the only way to avoid any mistakes is to try nothing new and forgo progress. Psychiatry has made its mistakes but it has also certainly made progress. This chapter has outlined some of the more striking of its errors. Most of these were by well-meaning, if flawed, individuals. Some such as Ewen Cameron's depatterning experiments and the Nazi collaboration were clearly evil. Whether you consider the errors of those who were basically misguided as evil or not will depend on how you view psychiatry. On balance I find little evidence that it has been uniquely evil; not any worse than medicine generally.

For reasons that are easy to appreciate, but less easy to adequately explain, psychiatry labours under a unique double standard. Limitations in efficacy and unwanted consequences that we quite readily accept in general medicine and surgery become damning indictments in psychiatry. One of the main aims of this book is to provide enough background to put these things in perspective. Only with a sense of psychiatry in the round can one balance the sometimes excessive claims made for it and the excessive criticisms of it by those who see nothing of any value in it. The mistakes and false trails outlined here are surely regrettable, but an understanding of the impulses behind them and their context may aid a sense of proportion. Even if they remain unforgiven and unforgivable they should be weighed against the thousands of mentally ill people worldwide whose suffering is regularly relieved and whose lives are made livable by the practice of psychiatry.

10

Is bad behaviour any of our business? Psychiatry and the law

Psychiatrists become experienced in understanding people's desires and motives, what makes them tick and what makes them do what they do. It is little surprise then that they get drawn into courts of law, into assessments of 'intent', and into the question of evil. The law is not just concerned with establishing what people did; it has to come to some conclusion about *why* they did it to make judgments about guilt and innocence. Courts have to decide if defendants were able to make a real choice and consequently how severe the punishment should be. The distinction between mad and bad has been a refrain throughout most of psychiatry's history. One might have expected it to be getting easier, but it is not so. As psychiatry has become more sophisticated, and as society has become less punitive, so the questions asked of the profession have grown ever more difficult.

Madness from its very beginning implied that individuals were 'robbed of their reason', that they were not their 'normal selves'. Any moral judgements about what they had done were obliged to take some account of this. This is no new development. No society seems inclined to take seriously Thomas Szasz's repeated proposal (Chapter 8) to expose the mentally ill to the full rigours of the law and punishment. All make some allowance for their condition. In most instances the presence of a confirmed mental illness leads to a more lenient sentence. In more severe or violent offences, however, offenders who are sent to a secure hospital end up incarcerated on average twice as long as those sent to prison. The insane ('insanity' is a legal term broadly similar to 'madness') are, however, not *punished* for their offences. We intuitively understand this fundamental difference and there is surprisingly little dissent from it.

The severely mentally ill may avoid standing trial altogether, especially if they are very clearly disturbed. If they are too unwell to follow the legal processes or understand the issues involved, the court will usually adjourn the case while they are treated and if they remain unwell they can be declared 'unfit to plead'. This usually requires two psychiatrists to confirm that they suffer from a serious mental illness, usually a psychosis or severe intellectual impairment. You are judged unfit to plead if you cannot understand the charges, if you cannot grasp the difference between pleading guilty or not guilty or if you cannot follow the legal proceedings. The UK courts also often want to be sure that you can effectively instruct your counsel, give evidence in your own defence or challenge a juror. Being unfit to plead is usually very obvious and the courts are understandably reluctant to try such people. It would seem pointless and cruel and it undermines the dignity of the judicial process. Patients judged unfit to plead are invariably admitted directly to hospital. It makes no sense to consider someone unable to understand his or her criminal behaviour but fit to live independently. Being judged unfit to plead only happens in the most extreme cases. Most mentally ill people who have committed a serious crime are still tried, but the courts leave several options available. In lesser degrees of mental disorder deciding on *diminished responsibility* or *mitigating factors* may require psychiatric evidence.

How does the court deal with an individual charged with a crime who has been diagnosed with a severe illness, perhaps a psychosis? First it has the right to simply reject the psychiatric evidence and it sometimes does so. In this case it will convict and punish the individual in the normal manner. Often people may commit a crime while actively psychotic but will have substantially recovered by the time of the trial. The court will need good evidence that such defendants were mentally ill at the time of the crime. It then has to make a further decision about the severity of that mental illness. Was it sufficiently grave to deprive them of their understanding and their ability to assess the consequences of their act?

THE INSANITY DEFENCE

In England and most common-law jurisdictions such as the USA, Australia and New Zealand the original insanity defence is based on the so-called 'McNaughton rules'. These were named after Daniel McNaughton, who attempted to assassinate the British Prime Minister, Robert Peel, in 1843 but mistook him and killed his secretary. McNaughton had been deluded for some time that Peel was persecuting him. He was found not guilty on the grounds of insanity and hospitalized for life. Insanity was defined as:

> labouring under such a defect of reason, from disease of the mind, as not to know the nature and quality of the act he was doing; or, if he did know it, that he did not know he was doing what was wrong.

It is said that Queen Victoria was outraged by this decision, insisting that McNaughton must surely be guilty, as he fired the fatal shot. As a consequence the verdict was changed in English law to 'Guilty but insane' and indefinite hospital detention is still referred to as 'at his/her majesty's pleasure'. The classical insanity defence is now very rare. It is difficult to advance if the disorder consists only of delusions, particularly if patients normally keep them to themselves until they are exposed by the crime. This is usually referred to by psychiatrists as having 'guarded delusions' and is common with paranoid or suspicious patients. McNaughton's delusions about Peel, however, had been well known to the police for a year or so before the killing.

Mental illness does not excuse all crimes. Nor, despite a common belief, are all 'bizarre' or hideously cruel crimes evidence of mental illness. Far from it. There are individuals who commit vicious and cruel crimes with a crystal-clear understanding of the consequences for their victims. Some sadistic individuals are only too aware of these consequences and, indeed, perpetrate the crime for precisely that reason. Meeting such people is a particularly chilling experience, quite different from an encounter with a psychotic individual.

For an insanity defence there has to be some link between the illness and the crime. McNaughton tried to shoot Peel because he was deluded about him. Mentally ill people can, of course, be guilty of crimes committed out of simple greed or anger. I had a patient for many years whose clinical improvement was regularly heralded by his return to car theft. He suffered from long-standing schizophrenia, but he was also a thorough rogue and an unrepentant car thief. When he was off medicine and ill he was simply too disorganized to steal cars. When we got him back on treatment and it began to work, off he went and I invariably got a call from the police.

Overall psychiatry here fulfils a role that society appreciates. None of us want to punish people for things they have no control over, and none of us want to see severely mentally ill people in prison. There is a general sense of 'there but for the grace of God'. Prison is awful enough for anybody, even more so if locked in there with tormenting hallucinations and fears. Protecting the blatantly mentally ill from unfair punishment and imprisonment is an important contribution psychiatry makes to a humane and civilized society.

McNaughton was detained in hospital under the 1800 Criminal Lunatics Act. Prior to that Act the treatment of the insane who committed crimes was often very informal. Mary Lamb (1764–1847) is now remembered with her brother Charles as the author of *Tales From Shakespeare*, a bestseller which has remained constantly in print since 1807. Mary had a lifetime of recurrent mental illness. In 1796 she stabbed her mother to death and seriously wounded her father. She was profoundly deranged at the time and taken directly by her brother to a 'mad-house' to recover. She was never tried. What would seem inconceivable to us now is that she came back to live with her brother just a few weeks after the crime. Margaret Nicholson attempted to stab George III in 1786 as he stepped from his carriage and he called out that she should not be harmed as she was obviously deranged. She was simply admitted to the Bethlem Hospital without trial. With the increasing sophistication of psychiatric diagnoses, in particular the evolving concepts of monomania and automatism, things could not remain so casual and the treatment of those judged insane became much more formalized.

MONOMANIAS AND AUTOMATISMS

Until the early nineteenth century madness was an all-or-nothing state. You were either bereft of your reason or you were not. If you were mad it was obvious to all around you and did not take a doctor to determine it. Asylum doctors were initially only responsible for managing patients, not diagnosing and certifying them: that was the job of a lay magistrate. Things changed as psychiatrists improved their expertise and began to identify disorders that were not always so obvious. In the second half of the nineteenth century the idea gained ground that individuals could suffer from significant mental disorder and yet at the same time manage their daily lives. Psychiatrists started to appear as expert witnesses in courts. French forensic psychiatrists led the way in defined monomanias and automatism.

Monomanias sound more dramatic than they are. They are essentially just delusional disorders, but with the delusions (strange, powerful, unshiftable and generally false ideas) restricted in scope. This leaves the patient unaffected in other areas. Indeed the conviction generated by delusions can sometimes provide considerable energy and drive. Any conspiracy theory website on the internet testifies to the productivity and persistence of such individuals. Monomanias usually come to light when people act on their delusions, most often (as in McNaughton) if they attempt to defend themselves from their perceived persecutors. De Clérambault's syndrome is one of the classical monomanias, often coming to light in cases of stalking. De Clérambault worked in the Paris forensic ward and gave his name in 1921 to a form of 'erotomania' in which a patient becomes convinced that someone (usually someone famous or of higher social status) is in love with him or her. The delusion is utterly impervious to reason. Random behaviour is interpreted as coded signals of affection, and even blunt denials or returned gifts are construed as simply a social defence for a shared and forbidden love.

Stalking is a highly distressing consequence of the disorder and often the love object's wife (seen as blocking the consummation) can become the victim of harassment. De Clérambault initially described the condition in murder attempts on perceived rivals for the affection of the object of the delusion. Erotomania fascinates authors and several novels draw on it (e.g. Ian McEwan's *Enduring Love*, Sebastian Faulks's *Engleby*). Victims are often reluctant to prosecute because they fear it may attract more stalkers and also, perhaps, because they have learnt that it rarely dissuades the stalker. I have two family doctor friends who for decades have received love letters from patients they see regularly. Neither party ever alludes to it. The London Metropolitan Police have a special unit including a psychiatrist to scan unsolicited mail to protect the royal family and senior politicians from deluded individuals. It can be a very intractable problem with tragic consequences and in extreme cases patients need to be detained in hospital.

A number of protracted court cases of lurid murders (usually *crimes passionels*) fascinated the French public in the mid nineteenth century. The accused denied any recall of the crimes, and the defence was that they were committed during 'automatisms' – periods when the perpetrator was either asleep or in a sleep-like state. Automatism is still occasionally advanced as a defence, usually as 'somnambulistic homicide'. The individual is observed to commit an otherwise inexplicable murder, having risen immediately from sleep or appearing to be still asleep. The defence is that the individual (who may sometimes describe responding in self-defence in a dream) was not conscious and therefore cannot be held responsible for their crime.

This defence, for all its limitations, was a significant step in introducing the concept of the unconscious mind to the general public. Its success was highly variable and it is now generally treated with some scepticism. It is more likely to succeed if bolstered by additional diagnoses such as narcolepsy or epilepsy or conditions such as diabetes with the risk of confusion arising from hypoglycaemia.

Unfitness to plead and the insanity defence remove you from further decision making by the court; you are confined to hospital. However, psychiatric evidence is often used to help the court decide on just *how* culpable a defendant is. An individual may have undoubtedly committed a homicide understanding it to be wrong and illegal (and hence not covered by the McNaughton rules) but still have acted under the influence of a serious mental illness. If the psychiatrist believes, and can convince the court, that the person was unable to properly formulate the intention to murder then the verdict can be reduced to manslaughter on the grounds of diminished responsibility. Responsibility can be diminished if the individual is mentally ill, is of very low intelligence or suffers other profound limitations in their psychological development.

Asperger's syndrome presents the sort of dilemma that can now face the psychiatrist and the court. Asperger's individuals are eccentric and often shy, and they have marked difficulties in perceiving how others feel and think, particularly how others will respond to them. It is on a spectrum with classical autism but is less severe. Unable to understand the world from the point of view of other people, having no 'theory of mind' they may commit a serious offence with no real understanding of its human consequences.

Diminished responsibility is rarely straightforward. In learning disability or Asperger's syndrome we are dealing with qualities that lie on a continuum. All of us vary in our intellectual competence and in our sensitivity and understanding of others. A formal diagnosis may give some reassurance to the court but the judge will still have to make a decision about how much weight to give such expert evidence. Diminished responsibility is also sometimes claimed on the grounds of temporary or reversible conditions. Severe depression is one, particularly in a mother who has killed her child. Recently some abused and battered women have been defended on the grounds that their prolonged abuse had so distorted their judgement that it was equivalent to a mental illness. Such defences are often highly controversial.

PSYCHIATRY'S ROLE IN SENTENCING

When psychiatrists give evidence to the court about diminished responsibility they are operating as expert witnesses. The issues are seen as highly technical and judges often refer to them as 'issues of science' as opposed to 'issues of law'. The first question for the court is whether that opinion is right or not. Psychiatry's role is not, however, limited to technical advice influencing decisions of guilt and innocence. It has come to play an important part, both formal and informal, in sentencing. Courts take a number of issues into consideration when sentencing, referred to as aggravating and mitigating factors. Mitigating factors include previous good character, family obligations, provocation, stress and fear, expressed remorse and many more.

Careful psychiatric evidence can supply insights into puzzling aspects of a defendant's behaviour. Individuals who express no remorse for crimes are often treated very harshly by courts, and defendants who show little distress are often thought of as cold or 'psychopathic'. Some recent cases have involved apparently unemotional young women defendants whom juries found perplexing and unsympathetic. Yet they may simply be too emotionally paralysed by the horror of the crime or whole legal process to fully engage with it. Psychiatrists have also helped clarify the mechanisms which trap victimized women in abusive relationships and which can result in either collaboration with criminal behaviour or a final explosive attack on their abuser. Without such understanding courts feel obliged to deal with them in a manner that leaves everyone uncomfortable, convinced that the punishment is excessive and unfair.

We now have a better understanding of how prolonged fear and denigration can destroy self-esteem and lock people into pathological relationships. When victims express understanding, even affection, for their persecutor the court can easily withdraw sympathy. This 'identification with the aggressor', was first described by psychoanalysts in concentration camp survivors. We now usually call it the 'Stockholm syndrome' after some Swedish bank hostages who became friendly with their captors and pleaded in court for leniency. This seems puzzling but it has a logic and makes good biological sense. If you can get your captor to like you they are less likely to harm you, and finding a way to like them is the most effective way to get them to like you. It is a very primitive and successful survival strategy in an otherwise impossible situation. Of course the court does not always accept this explanation. Patty Hearst, a nineteen-year-old American newspaper heiress, was kidnapped in 1974 and held hostage for eighteen months by a radical urban terror group. During that time she was caught on film taking part in an armed bank raid with them and she distributed tapes supporting their cause. It was her decision not to escape when she could and her praise for her captors that probably led to her conviction and imprisonment despite strong psychiatric testimony that this mental process of identification lay behind her behaviour.

Mitigation often centres on factors that have limited an individual's ability to control and direct his or her behaviour. When the factors are extreme or sudden and unpredictable, the psychiatric defence is often successful, such as in shoplifting directly after bereavement. However, our behaviour is more powerfully moulded by persistent influences than by one-off events, and we all vary in our resilience. Those before the courts have generally had much grimmer early lives than most. Many have been brought up in care, in broken homes or in families blighted by violence, addiction or poverty. Magistrates and judges are well aware of this; does psychiatry have anything to contribute?

The psychiatrist and psychoanalyst John Bowlby (1907–90) studied 'affectionless' and delinquent boys. Commissioned by the World Health Organization to report on the mental health of homeless children in post-war Europe he produced a seminal work, *Maternal Care and Mental Health*, in 1951. The gist of this was that a secure, warm relationship in infancy is essential to develop a capacity for empathy, and to form trusting relationships in adult life. Bowlby called this process 'attachment'. Institutionalized or neglected children, particularly those who missed out on a mother's love, were likely to have persisting problems. This has come to be called 'maternal deprivation'. Bowlby's work had enormous influence, particularly on how children were treated in hospitals and other institutions. However, such thinking poses a challenge to the courts and to psychiatry.

If we accept that people's personalities are the result of neglect or early abuse, how fair is it to hold them responsible for their actions? Should a court consider these early experiences when sentencing; in short how much allowance can be made for an individual's personality? In the end the courts and all of us have to strike a balance. People have to be held accountable for their actions; otherwise civil society is simply unworkable. However, sometimes it is glaringly obvious that this person or that person is so very different that some allowance just has to be made. Psychiatry would be entering dangerous territory here if it suggested that human behaviour is entirely determined or predictable. Psychiatry does not insist that certain classes of individuals *must* be exempt from the legal process. It is not the case that psychiatry pushes itself forward to plead for these troubled individuals: most psychiatrists feel relatively unsure in this arena. It is more that the courts want all the help they can get. This is, after all, a fundamentally intractable human dilemma.

Giving evidence in court about personality is a fraught business for psychiatrists. Except in the most extreme cases it is a contested and uncertain area. Exactly the same is true for us outside the court. Psychiatry finds itself having to struggle to establish a sensible and consistent stance in dealing with personality problems, and particularly with so-called 'personality disorders'. In court the question of the individual's control and personal responsibility for their crime is often boiled down to a single yes/no decision. In clinical practice it fluctuates continuously over the succession of individual decisions that have to be made in ongoing care. Sometimes it can be ignored and sometimes it dominates entirely but it is never absent. Some personality disorders are associated with disturbing or criminal behaviour; hence the dialogue between the criminal justice system and psychiatry. When should these people be treated and when should they be punished?

Whether psychiatry ought to treat individuals with personality problems ('personality disorders') is a subject of dispute and is considered further in Chapter 11. Psychiatry uses about a dozen descriptive terms for the common, easily recognized personality disorders but there is no real theory behind the classification. They are often grouped together into three 'clusters' (imaginatively labelled A, B and C) and it is cluster B which attracts most attention. This contains the personality disorders that pose the greatest problems for those around them, so-called antisocial and borderline disorders. Antisocial personality disorder has been variously labelled sociopathic, psychopathic and dissocial personality disorder in a vain attempt to shake off its unsavoury reputation. Its features are a lack of empathy for others, a disregard for social conventions and the law, and it is most clearly manifest in selfish, even violent and criminal behaviour. It is mainly encountered in men, frequently in the criminal justice system, and often complicated by drug and alcohol abuse. Borderline personality disorder has an even more tortuous history as a diagnosis. It is more common in women and its features are an unstable emotional life, intense disruptive relationships, repeated episodes of self-harm (overdosing and self-cutting) and reckless behaviour. It also often leads to drug and alcohol abuse. Both disorders pose major challenges for the courts and prisons and also for mental health services.

Controversy has persisted for half a century over whether or not severe personality disorders are the business of psychiatry. The issue concerns the legitimate or sensible boundary for mental illnesses and runs throughout this book and is explored more in Chapter 11. While these intellectual discussions occupy philosophers and academics, the prisons and courts on the one side and psychiatry on the other are left with the very real problems associated with these turbulent individuals. And they do indeed create enormous problems for themselves and those around them. Both sides in the debate hope the other will solve it. Neither prison officers nor psychiatrists have any difficulty recognizing individuals with a severe psychopathic personality as a distinct and special group. They are qualitatively different from other prisoners: delinquency is simply not an adequate explanation. They do not appear to learn from the consequences of their actions nor to settle into prison routines and they appear to deliberately stir things up. They are as troublesome in prison or in hospital as they are outside and are an enormous headache to everyone who has to deal with them.

This came to a head in England at the start of the twenty-first century. The 1959 Mental Health Act had included psychopathy, permitting the compulsory treatment of such individuals. This original decision was the subject of fierce debate at the time and most of the profession was against it. Their argument was fairly straightforward. Psychopathy is not a mental illness, and we have no effective treatments. Nor, unlike mental illnesses, is there much prospect that it will spontaneously resolve if only the patient can be temporarily protected. Including psychopathy in the act was driven through by Maxwell Jones, an influential psychiatrist who was treating disturbed soldiers returned from the war in his new therapeutic community. Most had some form of personality disorder, lumped together under the then much wider concept of 'psychopathy'.

Maxwell Jones appeared to be achieving promising results with his treatment. If there was ever to be a hope of understanding and curing these men, he argued, we needed treatment and research and often that required compulsion. A compromise was reached. Psychopathic individuals, later relabelled 'personality disordered', could only be compulsorily detained if there was 'evidence that they responded to treatment'. No such strict condition was required for the detention of those with mental illness. So there was a higher threshold than for mental illness. Psychiatrists could, and did, refuse to detain them if they thought treatment was unlikely to achieve a real improvement. The use of this 'treatability' clause came to be seen by government as psychiatrists avoiding their responsibilities. It was repeatedly referred to as 'a loophole in the law' and pressure mounted to remove the distinction.

The lightning rod for change was a horrendous and random murder by a known psychopathic individual. Michael Stone was a chaotic and violent man, a drug addict who had spent time in both prisons and mental hospitals. Shortly before the murder he had sought hospital care, which was refused because his psychiatrist believed that previous admissions had not helped but caused enormous disruption in the ward. Irrespective of the rights and wrongs of this individual case the government, struggling with what to do with violent and unreformed prisoners approaching the end of their sentences, seized on it.

Both issues were dealt with in a review of the Mental Health Act which replaced mental illness and personality disorder (with its 'treat-ability' requirement) by the catch-all 'mental disorder'. Simultaneously a new administrative category of Dangerous Severe Personality Disorder (DSPD) was introduced. This decision raised legal and ethical concerns about pre-emptive incarceration and the spectre of 'medical treatment' being used as a smoke-screen for the detention of socially unacceptable individuals. Since then the introduction of indeterminate sentences has resolved this issue as most serious and violent offenders can be detained in prison for as long as they continue to pose a significant risk without involving psychiatry. This, in my opinion, is one example of the value of distinguishing 'mental illness' from the much looser category of mental disorder, of striving for a more limited psychiatry. Mental illness is an imperfect term but it carries a set of assumptions and consequences that have been argued out across several generations and lead to a more considered and restricted use. Mental disorder offers no such protection and carries an obvious potential for abuse.

No civilized country should have anything to do with either capital punishment or torture so the relationship of psychiatry and psychology to them should require no discussion. Unfortunately some developed countries do still engage in both. The World Psychiatric Association insists that psychiatrists should have no dealings whatsoever with either but some do. In countries that still use the death penalty, especially the USA and some Caribbean states, psychiatrists may be called upon to give evidence about the mental state of condemned individuals. No developed country admits to executing mentally incompetent individuals, either severely mentally ill or with profound intellectual impairments. Even those who defend capital punishment believe that the punishment, and the reason for its imposition, must be fully understood by those condemned. Few states would risk the obvious contempt that follows from executing an obviously mentally ill or incompetent individual.

What should a psychiatrist do if called upon to treat a prisoner who has, understandably, developed a psychotic illness while on death row? The psychiatrist may be asked to treat him so that he – or she – recovers sufficiently to be executed. Can a psychiatrist confronted with an acutely ill and suffering patient refuse treatment because of the inevitable consequences? In practice not all psychiatrists or psychologists share the World Psychiatric Association's stance and some work in prison services which carry out capital punishment. I once attended a psychiatric seminar in which the Louisiana prison service described their 'humane and Christian care regime' preparing prisoners for execution.

Assessment of the IQ of death row prisoners is a troubling issue in the USA. States may not execute murderers with a recorded IQ below 70: such an IQ should have mitigated their culpability and sentencing in the first place. IQ is widely considered an objective, highly stable and reliable measure. However, it is not. Assessing it in young, disturbed or poorly educated individuals is far from easy at the best of times. A strange feature of IQ is that it has shown a steady and substantial improvement over the last century, the so-called 'Flynn Effect' after the man who identified it. An IQ of 100 is by definition the average for the population measured. However, using exactly the same tests with exactly the same questions and exactly the same answers, the average has risen a staggering 30 points in the last century, about 10 points per generation. We know this because we have been able to compare stored completed test papers with exactly the same questions used in succeeding generations. It appears that we now, quite simply, think differently. Thus to measure someone's IQ, to place them on the current spectrum of ability accurately, the tests have to be regularly recalibrated. Prisons often use very old scales and consequently overestimate the IQ of individual prisoners. James Flynn is tireless in re-testing condemned prisoners against current ranges in the hope that their sentences will be commuted.

It would be wonderful if psychiatrists could take an Olympian stance above messy politics and human frailty. However, as we saw in Chapter 9, we broadly share the views of the society from which we are drawn. Indeed this is probably essential if we are to accurately anchor our judgements about the possible pathology of our patients' thoughts and feelings. So just as some prison psychiatrists may accept the legitimacy of capital punishment (presumably those who do not, do not seek work in those prisons), some military psychiatrists and psychologists accept the necessity of torture. Of course, they rarely call it torture. The official term used is 'unusual and degrading treatment' and the last decade has seen it regularly used in the wars in Afghanistan and Iraq and in the detention centre in Guantanamo Bay. Water-boarding is torture by any commonsense use of language, as were the hooding and exposure to 'white noise' of IRA prisoners in Northern Ireland. Euphemisms such as 'enhanced interrogation methods' are substituted to obscure the reality. It is clear from reports that psychiatrists and psychologists have been involved in these practices. Their role has usually been advising on the level of torture the victim can tolerate and even assisting in its design for maximal effect. The arguments used to defend torture and capital punishment are well known and well rehearsed. No doctors, least of all psychiatrists, should be taken in by them. Thank heavens such practices and their apologists are increasingly rejected.

The dilemmas that face psychiatrists in court are often very precisely defined but they mirror the same issues that the profession faces daily in its clinical practice. Some of these are explored further in Chapters 11 and 12. Where does normal human variation end and pathological processes begin? How much are individuals to be asked to take responsibility for their own behaviour and welfare and when is an expert, perhaps even a paternalistic, intervention justified? Psychiatry seems to be safer when it restricts itself to 'abnormalities' or differences that are obvious even to the layperson. Its expertise is often better limited to explaining these differences and explaining what may have given rise to them. We may often have expert knowledge about more subtle changes and influences but then it is up to the court to decide how much weight to give our testimony.

The relationship between the law and psychiatry is often uncomfortable. We certainly do have different ways of thinking. On the whole, however, the adversarial nature of courtroom interactions has sharpened thinking on both sides to mutual benefit. The presence of psychiatry in the courtroom has generally been welcomed and not just by defendants and defence attorneys. Judges, jurors and the prosecution are as keen as the rest of us to treat people fairly and with understanding. Granting mature and thoughtful attention to the mental state of those standing trial helps to produce a criminal justice system that we can all respect and trust. For all its limitations, psychiatry's contribution to legal decision making has probably been a significant force for good.

11

A diagnosis for everything and the medicalization of everyday life

'One in three women takes antidepressants at some time in their lives' reads the newspaper headline. Mental health is currently the major cause of sick leave and employment disability across the USA, UK and most of Europe. The World Health Organization (WHO) predicts depression will be the leading cause of medical disability worldwide by 2020, overtaking even malaria and cancer. One in four is regularly quoted as the annual risk for mental problems. What can all this mean? Is mental illness overwhelming us despite a century of psychiatric progress? Is there an epidemic of mental illnesses in the twenty-first century just as there are epidemics of obesity and diabetes? Could it be that the pace of modern life really is incompatible with mental health, as repeatedly claimed ever since Weir Mitchell introduced the diagnosis of neurasthenia? Or could it be, as Robert Whitaker writes in his books *Mad in America* and *Anatomy of an Epidemic*, that psychiatry itself is actually creating more mental illness? That it is the cause not the cure?

And what of all these improbable-sounding new diagnoses floating about? Do we really believe in 'sex addiction' in celebrities, or that stroppy teenagers suffer from 'oppositional defiant disorder' (ODD)? Is 'female sexual arousal disorder' (FSAD) a meaningful illness and do smoking and coffee drinking really deserve labelling as 'nicotine dependency' and 'caffeine intoxication'? All apart from sex addiction are already in the American Psychiatric Association's *DSM-IV* and for that the WHO's *ICD-10* has a diagnosis of 'excessive sexual drive'. Psychiatry does seem to have got into a muddle here; we need to pause and consider what is going on. Could psychiatry itself be making us sicker, is it medicalizing normal, everyday life? Or is it that we have just got better at recognizing and treating illnesses that have always been there?

There is clearly some truth in the accusation of the medicalization of everyday life and not just in psychiatry. Similar criticisms have been levelled against other branches of medicine, such as in the management of childbirth or the surgical management of obesity. However, it is most marked in psychiatry and is unlikely to reverse or disappear. Simply disapproving of it will not get us very far. Such medicalization poses real problems for all of us, but it is a much more serious problem for the profession of psychiatry itself. We need to try and understand it better.

The first thing to grasp is that this expansion of psychiatry is not so different from that in the rest of medicine. Most doctors believe what they do is helpful so it is not surprising that they try to spread the benefits. Add to this the acceleration in research findings and it is no surprise that medicine is expanding its reach. This expansion was not always self-evident. When the UK National Health Service was launched in 1948 the government confidently expected medical activity and costs to *shrink*, and to shrink rapidly. A healthier population would emerge from a backlog of long-overdue treatments and we would then need fewer doctors and fewer hospitals. How wrong. Demand for health care has simply grown and grown. It continues to expand inexorably wherever people can afford it, and there is no sign of its slowing down.

The threshold for diagnosis and treatment has been steadily lowering in all branches of medicine, accompanied by an ever lengthening list of diseases. The number of diagnoses has increased by about 20 per cent per decade in both psychiatry and in general medicine. Each revision of the two registers of psychiatric diagnoses, the WHO's *International Classification of Diseases* (ICD) and the American Psychiatric Association's *Diagnostic and Statistical Manual* (DSM), is thicker than its predecessor. *DSM-I* was published in 1952, was 130 pages long and listed 106 disorders, *DSM-II* in 1968 was 134 pages long with 182 disorders, and *DSM-III* in 1980 was 494 pages long with 265 disorders. The current *DSM-IV*, published in 1994, runs to a staggering 886 pages with 297 disorders. Of course, this does not mean that there really are hundreds more disorders; most psychiatrists still regularly use the same familiar ones.

Psychiatry does, though, have special problems. First, our diagnoses are more subjective, they cannot be confirmed or disproved with blood tests or X-rays. Nor is their presence as obvious as a swollen ankle or a skin rash. This makes them more elastic, highly sensitive to the assumptions and expectations of patients and of doctors. These assumptions and expectations about our emotional lives have expanded as psychotherapy and psychiatry have become more accepted, stretching our diagnoses even further. Psychiatry's very success has drawn it into an ever wider range of human problems, embracing alcohol and drug misuse, personality problems and relationship difficulties. This expansion comes at a time when traditional sources of support such as family, neighbourhood and churches are losing their power. Two internal issues have also powered the intrusion of psychiatry into our lives. The first is the adoption of 'criterion-based diagnosis', which we touched upon in considering post-traumatic stress disorder (PTSD) in Chapter 6. The second is the influence of the pharmaceutical industry, and this cannot be ignored. In its search for new drugs and for profit, the industry has undoubtedly stretched diagnostic practices. It has perhaps even 'invented' some diagnoses. Let us start with the changes in expectations.

If an Edwardian gentleman were to find himself set down in today's London, Madrid or New York he would obviously be amazed at our clothes, motor cars and our mobile phones. But he would probably be equally taken aback by our informality and by our preoccupation with our own feelings and experiences, which we share endlessly in conversation, and on Twitter, Facebook and blogs. He would be staggered by how open we are with each other and how much we question things. This continuous self-examination and emotional frankness is really very new, much more so than we often realize. It has a powerful impact on who comes to psychiatrists.

Many psychiatric disorders such as anxiety, phobias and depression are effectively 'self-declared'; only you know exactly how you feel. What you think about your feelings determines whether you consult your doctor, and what your doctor does about it. With our increased attention to our inner world it is not surprising that we seek help with it, nor that doctors feel they should intervene. Of course, psychiatric disorders are not entirely self-declared; there are some objective signs, particularly in more severe conditions. Someone with clinical depression, for example, will usually experience weight-loss, poor sleep and slowed thinking. But these would never establish the diagnosis on their own – half of those sitting in a family doctor's waiting room will complain of poor sleep or reduced appetite. So diagnosing depression still depends overwhelmingly on what the patient describes. It is almost as if it is the patient who makes the diagnosis and the doctor uses his or her knowledge and experience to confirm it. Our decision to consult a doctor depends on what we *expect* to feel, what we consider 'normal', and what we believe can be done about it. These have changed out of all recognition.

Psychoanalysis and psychotherapy have played their role in this increased preoccupation with our emotional lives. Freud may currently be out of favour, but few would deny his impact on how we understand ourselves and how we now manage our lives. We *want* to be aware of our emotions and to understand them. It colours all our thinking, from appreciating works of art, to electing politicians, to managing our family and romantic entanglements. We consider it the mark of a mature or sophisticated individual to understand emotions and relationships rather than simply being shaped by them. We believe that self-knowledge and the sharing of painful emotions can relieve suffering. They can even make us 'better people'. In Western societies stoicism and the stiff upper lip have been consigned to the bin of history.

Few of us would regret this change. The shallow, self-obsessed antics of a celebrity culture may grate, but are a small price for a more tolerant and compassionate society. We can be open about our sexual orientation or confide our fears and failings without expecting incomprehension and moral condemnation. It is surely better that people no longer suffer in silence. Undoubtedly too many antidepressants and tranquillizers are prescribed, but is this too high a price for ready access to effective treatments? In my first psychiatric post in rural Scotland I regularly met old farmers who had struggled with crippling depression for months and sometimes even years without a word of complaint. Yet easy and effective remedies had been available and they recovered rapidly often with just a simple course of antidepressants.

Psychiatry and psychotherapy have contributed to this openness, one of their real contributions to human wellbeing. It is ironic that psychoanalysis has played such a catalytic role in the 'wellbeing', 'personal growth' and 'happiness' movements. Freud himself had no time for such 'self-indulgence' and roundly dismissed a search for happiness as a goal in his psychotherapy.

Our more open and tolerant emotional lives are not solely a consequence of psychoanalysis. They are also a product of the unprecedented changes in our material circumstances. Industrialization and scientific progress have delivered undreamed-of prosperity, security and leisure. A hundred years ago untreatable painful conditions, high infant mortality and sudden death were facts of everyday life. People simply had to be more resilient. The 'self-indulgence' of psychotherapy was made possible by these improved conditions, but it in turn provided the language and mental framework for understanding and adapting to them.

The same period has witnessed a dramatic decline in the family. A hundred years ago most people lived all their lives within walking distance of where they were born. The family set the context of their lives and was their fundamental source of support and companionship during hardships. Such traditional families are very strong and predictable, but they are not always easy to live in. They are shaped by duty and obligation as much as affection and intimacy. Strong families are an amazing resource but they do exact a price with their rules about what can and cannot be said or done.

We still see such strong family structures in the developing world. On a working visit in India, I was struck by how families continued to support their psychotic member, never rejecting him or her no matter how difficult and disruptive. This was a genuinely humbling experience for a Western psychiatrist. These Indian families were unflinching in their commitment to patients, but they were also quite unsentimental. They had no doubts about what they should do; they regularly slipped medication into patients' food and often bossed them about. Individuals' needs came a clear second to the family's.

Psychiatry also made its contribution to the decline of the nuclear family with its sustained attack in the 1960s and 1970s (Chapter 8).

Greater flexibility in family structures has undoubtedly freed many from loveless and abusive relationships. For the mentally ill, however, it has generally been bad news. The evidence that secure traditional families improve health and wellbeing for all of us is extensive and consistent; we even live longer in them. For those with mental illnesses the benefits are even greater. It is almost only blood relatives (usually mothers) who stick with really ill patients through thick and thin and look after them.

In more fluid social networks we cannot always rely on our distress being noticed. We have to spell out our problems if we are to be helped. 'Help-seeking' behaviour and language have become part of our culture, as increasingly we turn to professionals. Psychiatrists and psychotherapists are rarely just 'paid friends' as they are sometimes caricatured. Those who come to us usually have serious problems, and then only after their family and friends have done their very best. It is often family members or friends who get them to come to us. Friendship and support are enormously protective and psychiatric help is sought when they are no longer enough. Psychoanalysts even make a point of *not* giving reassurance and support, but rather see their job as helping patients confront uncomfortable truths. There are exceptions. When I was training, psychiatrists spent much of their time in clinics providing 'supportive psychotherapy'. This involved offering acceptance and encouragement to isolated and troubled individuals who, because of their illness or personality, had no one else to turn to. This is much rarer now, viewed as 'paternalistic', and rather frowned upon.

Psychotherapy is explicitly not a substitute for family support, but general psychiatrists and their teams do get involved in it. Patients with severe mental illness are often alienated from their families or are struggling to emancipate themselves from them. They require social and personal supports not just medical treatments. These include many of the things that a family would normally do – making sure that they have clean clothes, getting them to hospital appointments, encouraging activity to fill the day. Psychiatric teams routinely provide such broad social input for patients with severe illnesses. The evidence is strong that psychotic individuals need both medical and social care to regain control of their lives. It is not enough to provide good treatment and expect psychotic patients to start organizing themselves. Neither is it sufficient, as some enthusiasts insist, to restrict ourselves to just social and personal support in the expect-ation that they will then manage their treatment. Simultaneous input of both kinds is usually needed for success. This is a tricky balance to get right. Are we providing enough support, without which treatment will fail, or are we being over-protective? Are we patronizing our patients or even stigmatizing them by linking everything to their illness?

People get very heated about these issues and there is no simple answer. The very directive family approach I witnessed in India is simply not possible in the industrialized West. By the time we become involved families are often exhausted and demoralized. Patients expect and demand their independence just like everyone else. We often have to go along with this even if it is not what we would really want for our patients; supporting autonomy may sometimes conflict with the patient's best interests. However, it would be a mistake to think that this trend will be easily reversed. Respect for individual choice, even foolish choices, is a hallmark of Western societies and psychiatry has to adapt its practice to the world it finds itself in. There is no return to a possibility of a 'golden age' of stable, mutually sup-portive nuclear families and 'doctor knows best' even if we wanted it.

A psychiatric diagnosis may be the only passport to the warmth, shelter, attention and affection previously available from families. For those with severe emotional problems professional services may be their only chance, and for this their problems have to be 'medicalized' in some form or other. Young self-harming patients will state this bluntly in the emergency room. 'Nobody listens to me otherwise,' they declare. Their actions are accepted as 'a cry for help', a communica-tion rather than a symptom. Pressure to expand psychiatry's diagnostic reach comes both from patients, who need help, and from staff, who perceive that need.

Psychiatry is in some measure a victim of its own success here. We were once a small, isolated and little-known profession, the object of considerable misgivings. In the twentieth century psychoanalysis raised our profile, attracting prestige and considerable mythology. In much of the artistic world and entertainment industry, 'being in therapy' and seeing a psychiatrist became almost a status symbol. No Woody Allen film was complete without jokes about his analyst. The *New Yorker* magazine prints so many jokes about psychotherapists and psychiatrists that it regularly publishes a separate anthology.

With psychotherapy's rising status and the drug treatments for depression and psychosis introduced in the late 1950s and 1960s, psychiatry staked its claim as a legitimate 'medical' specialty. Psychiatrists and psychotherapists were increasingly in demand, the gurus of the then modern age. They gave opinions on the whole range of human problems, very much as neuroscientists do now. This increased status was not unwelcome, and many of us have shared a rather inflated view of our abilities. Traditional diagnostic limits were stretched by these more effective and acceptable treatments. New territory, well beyond established mental illnesses, was colonized with the new-found therapeutic confidence.

Our current era has been labelled 'the age of depression', where this stretching of traditional diagnoses is most clearly seen. There is no simple, unequivocal cut-off between normal sadness and clinical depression; judgement is needed. Given that the early treatments (electroconvulsive therapy (ECT)) and the first antidepressants, Tofranil and amitriptyline) were so effective there was understandable enthusiasm to try them in milder clinical states. Attempts to construct a comprehensive classification of depression, to reliably predict treatment response, have repeatedly met with failure. The catch-all term of 'major depression' has been eventually adopted. The question now is how wide to cast the depression net. Prescribing rates for antidepressants leave us in no doubt that it is being cast increasingly wider. Whatever figures you choose, the growth is staggering. Antidepressant use rose by 240 per cent in the UK from 1992 to 2002. By 2002 11 per cent of adult women in the USA were taking them. The trend continues with the number of annual prescriptions in the UK up 95 per cent to a remarkable 39.1 million in the decade to 2009.

Because it is difficult to establish a clear boundary between depressed and not depressed, or between different forms of depression, it does not necessarily mean that depression is nothing other than one end of a spectrum of sadness. Experience suggests otherwise.

Drug treatments are effective in severe and moderate depression but less effective in mild forms. ECT seems to be only really needed for the most severe cases, particularly delusional depression. On the other hand psychotherapy for depression, which generally means cognitive behaviour therapy, has the opposite profile. It is more effective with mild depression, about equal to drugs in moderate depression, but not effective at all in severe depression. So if we do not differentiate between them, mildly depressed individuals will receive ineffective drugs and severely depressed individuals receive ineffective psychotherapy.

A fight-back against this expansion of depression is now gaining momentum. Books such as Gary Greenberg's *Manufacturing Depression* (2010) and Peter Breggin's *Talking Back to Prozac* (1994) see it as an entirely pernicious development. Both authors see the diagnostic over-simplification as diminishing our understanding of what it means to be truly human. They also detect the malign influence of the pharmaceutical industry in commercializing sadness for profit. In the last thirty years virtually everybody agrees that the threshold has become too low, generating what is referred to within evidence-based medicine circles as an excess of 'false positive diagnoses'. However, we continue to argue about exactly where that threshold should lie.

The introduction of the new Prozac-like antidepressants (called 'SSRIs') in the 1980s changed the rules. Older antidepressants had lots of unpleasant side effects and only helped if you really were quite significantly depressed. Getting the diagnosis right really did matter. If you were depressed they did eventually lift your mood but at the cost of some unpleasant side effects. However, if you were not clinically depressed all you got were the side effects and you felt even more wretched. The SSRIs have fewer side effects and can make you feel better even if you were not actually depressed to begin with. Books such as *Better Than Well: American Medicine Meets the American Dream* (Carl Elliott, 2003) highlighted how the effects and use of these drugs rapidly spread to those who were not mentally ill. Any of us might feel better with them, at least for a while. Maintaining the distinction between prescription and recreational drugs used to be fairly easy. Now several psychiatric prescription drugs (particularly those for depression and anxiety and for attention deficit hyperactivity disorder in children) are used by people without any pretentions to psychiatric disorder.

That some of our drugs work even on healthy people raises complex ethical concerns. If being on Prozac makes anyone feel better why do we not all take it, and take it all the time? Similar questions are asked about drugs called 'cognitive enhancers'. These were developed to treat disorders such as narcolepsy and sleep apnoea but they increase alertness and improve mental functioning generally. If there are drugs that make us 'smarter' is it fair if some students take them when preparing for exams? Should we not all take them, and if not why not? If cosmetic surgery and energy drinks are OK why not cognitive enhancers and Prozac? These questions will not be answered by psychiatry alone; they need a wider public debate.

Psychiatry has also moved into new areas and taken on new responsibilities. This branching out is not entirely unjustified. Working with mental illnesses exposes you to the full range of life's problems and all manner of human distress. The mentally ill have much more than their fair share of normal problems. Psychiatry gives privileged access to human frailty, to our hidden nature and our true motivations. We have to understand disappointment and fear and what people want from their varied relationships, family, marital and occupational. Psychiatrists learn to see the unvarnished truth – what people are and not what they want us to see.

Psychiatry has thus leaked out into areas of life far beyond its traditional professional territory. The psychiatric approach has even altered how we understand ourselves and our circumstances. We now think in terms of disorders and talk about 'work stress' and 'burn-out' rather than having chosen the wrong job. We say somebody is 'in denial' rather than they are just missing the point. Counselling is ubiquitous, routinely expected after traumatic events. Such traumas are no longer tests of our mettle but give rise to 'disorders' which may need 'treatment' or 'therapy'. We will consider the rash of new diagnoses later but these are minor in comparison to the two major areas of psychiatry's expansion – into addictions and into 'personality disorders'.

ARE ADDICTIONS MENTAL ILLNESSES?

Are addictions mental illnesses, and should they be treated by psychiatrists? The decision of the American Medical Association to call excessive and harmful drinking the disease of 'alcoholism' in 1956 did not arise from any new discovery. During the preceding generation alcohol abuse had changed in popular understanding from a moral issue (reprehensible behaviour stemming from self-indulgence or lack of willpower) to an essentially medical one (a biological disorder). Individuals who had been dismissively referred to as dipsomaniacs, drunkards or soaks, now became alcoholics. This was not an entirely new idea. It had been proposed on and off since the early nineteenth century and asylums had always housed many patients with alcohol-related disorders.

Alcoholics Anonymous, founded by Bill Wilson and Bob Smith ('Bill W. and Dr Bob') in Akron, Ohio, in 1935, was decisive. Their Twelve Steps approach to living with the 'incurable disease' of alcoholism was confirmed in Morton Jellinek's influential book *Alcohol Addiction and Chronic Alcoholism* (1942). There was no new information but the existing dots were joined up to make a different pattern; a less moralizing, less stigmatizing and more tolerant pattern. Drug addicts made the same journey from 'dope fiends' and 'junkies' via 'addicts' and 'drug dependency' to the current strikingly bland and unhelpful 'substance users'.

No one can deny the range of psychiatric, medical and social consequences of drug and alcohol abuse, nor the appalling human misery they entail. These include paranoid psychoses, dementia, depression, liver failure, HIV, crime, marital breakdown, trauma, child neglect and suicide. Psychiatrists and other doctors, psychologists, social workers and nurses obviously have a role in helping. But does that make it sensible or correct to consider them mental illnesses? On balance I do not believe it does, but should declare that in this opinion I am in a minority among psychiatrists.

The benefits of considering addictions as diseases are several. It provides access to non-stigmatizing and skilled professional help. Medications can remove the physical and psychological risks of delirium tremens or going 'cold turkey'. However, there are drawbacks. Considering addiction as a mental illness muddies our understanding of psychiatry and has already changed the language, replacing 'illness' and 'disease' with 'disorder'. Because mental illness is a difficult concept you have to continuously remind yourself about its meaning and this acts as a brake on the expansion of psychiatry. Illness also has implications for responsibility and control.

If we consider addictions as basically harmful habits then both the responsibility for them and the ability to change them lie primarily with the addict. This is not so with mental illnesses. Depressed or schizophrenic patients cannot simply change their mood or thinking, no matter how hard they try. Mental illnesses as we understand them are beyond conscious control: that is why they require treatment. The bewildering range of treatment procedures in addictions is a clue to the absence of established knowledge. Other than with the successful harm reduction strategies such as substituting oral methadone for heroin or providing needle exchanges there are very few constants. To suggest that the primary responsibility for changing addictive behaviour lies with addicts does not mean that we wash our hands of them. Nor does it imply that the change is easy, or that they don't need help. It does not mean that mental illnesses are serious and addictions are not. Far from it, addictions are very serious.

The current evidence for psychiatric treatments of addictions (including the whole range of 'rehab' practices) is really very disappointing. Helping people get off drink or drugs is relatively easy. What is difficult is helping them stay off. Despite half a century of research and development, our treatments are hardly effective at all. There is hardly a single randomized controlled trial in addiction treatments such as we generally require in medicine that shows a clear and sustained effect in keeping addicts 'clean' or alcoholics 'dry'. Treatments to remedy underlying psychological difficulties just do not seem to work. Some argue that this is understandable: addictions are very hard to treat. But could it be that we are just doing the wrong thing? During the last couple of decades while we have witnessed a steady, unbroken rise in alcoholism and all its consequences, we have successfully reduced smoking (in truth, a much more dangerous addiction) from 80 per cent of adult males to 20 per cent. Smoking cessation programmes do not use the language of illness or pathology. They emphasize the normality of smokers and the need for support and willpower to break a very dangerous habit. Much of the focus is on changing the context – non-smoking restaurants, raising costs, etc.

Would such an approach work for alcohol and drugs? Probably yes. We know that raising the price of alcohol reduces consumption, and overall consumption determines the number who 'become alcoholics' (this was an association that Dr Jellineck demonstrated half a century ago). 'Drunk for a penny, dead drunk for tuppence' in eighteenth-century London's Gin Lane meant just that. A steady imposition of taxes from 1736 onwards massively reduced public drunkenness. Restricting access, as with UK licensing hours or the state control of distribution in Scandinavia, demonstrably reduced rates of alcoholism.

We know all this but, perhaps understandably, don't really want to know it or do anything about it. We enjoy drinking or taking recreational drugs. There is comfort to be had in the belief that those who cannot control it are somehow different to us. We clutch at every new report of a genetic contribution or brain changes in the same way we search for a 'fat gene' (that hopefully we don't have). If the problem is *in them*, rather than with the alcohol or drug itself, then we are safe, we tell ourselves. Both Foucault and R. D. Laing argued that we construct identities for 'the mentally ill' to rid ourselves of aspects of ourselves we want to disown. Loss of control and addiction feel safer firmly located in someone else, with the responsibility for doing something about it handed over to the professionals. Psychiatry's role in the medicalization of addictions may not only be wasteful and ineffective for those afflicted. It may do us all a disservice by distracting us from the reality of the choices facing us. It obscures public health interventions that really would work.

Similar considerations apply in the care of individuals diagnosed with 'personality disorders'. We all have a personality. When we say someone has 'no personality' we mean they have a dull personality. Personality is how we distinguish and describe people. Although each individual personality is unique, with its one-off combination of traits, we easily recognize several distinct personality 'types' (shy, sensitive, outgoing, domineering). A small number of very specific personality types loom large in psychiatric practice. Some are associated with individual mental illnesses and have taken their names from them. Thus obsessive-compulsive disorders occur more often, but not exclusively, in someone with an 'obsessional personality', a paranoid psychosis is more likely in someone with a 'paranoid personality'. Psychiatrists call these personality types 'personality disorders' when they are very extreme and cause real problems for either the individual or the individual's family. They are recorded as diagnoses, albeit distinguished from mental illnesses as so called 'axis II' disorders in *DSM-IV*.

Personality disorders are important in psychiatry for several reasons. Some personality disorders make life very stressful and increase the risk of mental illnesses. Individuals with a paranoid personality disorder, for example, cannot trust those around them so are endlessly anxious and on the alert; obsessional individuals are often excessively self-critical, leading to depression. So they are important risk factors and need to be taken seriously. They also affect treatment outcomes. A paranoid patient who cannot trust his or her doctor will have difficulty complying with treatment. Those with a 'borderline personality disorder' struggle to sustain relationships and may easily become disappointed or angry with their therapist and break off contact.

It can also be very difficult to make an accurate diagnosis if someone has a very extreme personality. The persecutory ideas held by someone with a paranoid personality can be mistaken for psychotic delusions, the strange, eccentric behaviour in a schizotypal personality for the onset of schizophrenia. Mistakes occur in the opposite direction also. Mood disorders such as depression and anxiety can sometimes so exaggerate personality traits that the depression is missed altogether and the patients' distress put down to their personality disorder. The overlap of bipolar disorder and borderline personality is particularly troublesome. Bipolar disorder is a much wider diagnosis than the manic depression that it replaced and incorporates. Borderline personality disorder has also become an increasingly common diagnosis and both are characterized by extreme fluctuations of mood. Psychiatrists need to be able to distinguish them as their treatment implications are very different. We have to be aware of personality disorders to be good diagnosticians.

But are personality disorders the same as mental illnesses? Is it proper to *diagnose* them? Does treatment work, and is there ever justification for compulsory treatment? In practice these questions only arise with the disruptive personality disorders. These are antisocial or psychopathic personality in men, which is associated with violence, and borderline personality in women, which is associated with self-harm. Both are regularly complicated by alcohol and drug misuse or by depression and anxiety so regularly come to psychiatrists. Most psychiatrists are reluctant to treat people compulsorily whose *only* diagnosis is personality disorder. Despite the claims of some enthusiasts nobody really knows what to do for these very troubled and troublesome individuals, although governments and prisons are keen that we should do so (Chapter 10).

Psychiatrists are reluctant to treat people with personality disorders compulsorily for two reasons. First it seems illogical. We override personal autonomy in compulsory treatment on the grounds that someone is 'not their normal self', but a personality *is* the normal self, even if an unusual and distressed one. Second there is very little evidence that any of our treatments work, certainly no evidence that they work to change the personality itself. The therapeutic communities described in Chapter 6 and some more recent treatments for borderline personality disorder such as 'mentalization' and dialectical behaviour therapy (DBT) continue to be explored. They have produced some limited reduction in impulsiveness and in the 'neurotic' consequences of personality disorder (anxiety, depression, self-harm) but cannot claim to change the personality itself.

I believe psychiatrists should be well trained in identifying and working with personality disorders and that these categories are very important. For me it is more a practical decision than a theoretical one. Personalities have a massive impact on people's lives and set the context for their experiences and treatment. Psychiatrists who are blind to personality factors get into awful messes. Having no mental map for dealing with these manifestations they may shoe-horn such individuals into various medicalized diagnoses. The result is a persisting and futile attempt to treat disorders such as depression which are not present and therefore can't respond.

All this discussion of expansionism might suggest that psychiatry is imposing itself against the wishes of patients. This is only part of the picture. Because mental health services are seen to bring relief and help troubled individuals, we are more often drawn into these areas than we actively intrude. The sick role is an honourable one in our society. It confers protection and, in exchange for accepting the need to comply with treatment, offers care, sympathy and a variable exemption from social demands. A medical certificate can be a very powerful shield in our demanding, high-pressure society. For those with stressful or chaotic lives it can appear a welcome refuge.

Most of us have experienced the benefits of the sick role. It gives us the time to recoup our energies and it can also prompt welcome changes in the behaviour of those around us. It is not to be scoffed at. Psychiatrists, as all doctors, recognize that conferring the sick role by a diagnosis is one of the most powerful tools of our trade. Family doctors often sign someone 'off sick' without prescribing a specific treatment. They know that being 'off sick' can ensure someone will rest and recover when simply advising a holiday or rest would be futile. For individuals with long-term problems such as addictions or personality difficulties, however, it can carry real risks. It can distract from the need to confront and adapt behaviour. It has to be used with care and sensitivity; psychiatrists must ensure we are not colluding in avoidance and escapism.

A NEW WAY OF DIAGNOSING

Ironically it is probably psychiatry's attempt to strengthen its diagnostic boundaries, not relax them, that has led to its greatest expansion and the application of psychiatric diagnoses to individuals who almost certainly do not warrant them – 'false positives' in the jargon. We noted earlier the steady increase in number of diagnoses but the bigger change has been in how psychiatrists *make* those diagnoses. We are now in an era of 'criterion-based diagnosis' introduced in the USA and now used worldwide. Each diagnosis is carefully defined in a highly structured way. First there is a list of *essential* features, some of which must be present, followed by a list of *additional* features of which a minimum number is needed. These definitions are published in remarkable detail in the diagnostic manuals (*DSM-IV* and *ICD-10*) and they follow a similar format to that for PTSD (see p. 116).

To appreciate the radical nature of this innovation we have to understand how doctors learn to diagnose. Medical training was, and to a great extent still is, based on learning to recognize diseases by examining patients with them, not by reading about them in books. It emphasizes repetition – practising over and over again until things are second nature. Medical students and trainee doctors are shown patients with the diseases, usually very obvious, extreme cases to begin with. The disease is appreciated as a whole, doctors learn to recognize its shape, its gestalt. In this process individual signs and symptoms take their significance from the whole and then feed back into it. So having seen patients with depression psychiatrists note their sad faces, slowness of movement and preoccupation with unhappy past events. They see how these fit with the whole picture of depression. They don't start by recording an unhappy face and then morbid preoccupation and add them up until they have enough features to make a diagnosis. They *recognize* the disease from having met a multitude of people with depression and then look for confirmatory signs and symptoms, not vice versa. So you start with the whole person and then move back and forth between the whole and the parts. For several diseases I can clearly remember the first people I saw them in as a medical student forty years ago.

Earlier classifications mirrored this process by giving a *description* of a disease, not a *definition*. The traditional 'apprenticeship' of medical training involves this repeated exposure so that you learnt to recognize each disease's varying presentations. It is a long and expensive training and it emphasizes the skills (the 'art') of medicine more than its science. Criterion-based diagnosis takes a strikingly different approach.

A number of factors came together at a critical time to stimulate the shift to criterion-based diagnosis in psychiatry. In the early 1970s the USA was psychiatric research's superpower. It had as many academic psychiatrists as the rest of the world put together but in the

1970s was notorious for poor diagnostic practice. This was caused by over-reliance on psychoanalytical thinking and the high proportion of private psychiatrists working in isolation. These lacked the continuous professional feedback that sharpens practice which you get in a hospital setting. The new drugs then being developed could only be licensed after careful trials and these needed consistent and better diagnosis. The need to improve had also been brought home by international studies which showed that US psychiatrists grossly over-diagnosed schizophrenia. A joint UK–US diagnostic project found that US psychiatrists labelled most of their manic-depressive patients as schizophrenic. To rub salt into the wound another schizophrenia study conducted across nine countries by the WHO found the USA shared such poor practice only with its Cold War rival, Russia.

The chair of the *DSM-III* editorial committee, Robert Spitzer, had been involved in the UK–US diagnostic study. He wanted a simpler, more logical approach to diagnosis and was fiercely committed to basing diagnoses on observation, not theory, whether biological or psychoanalytical. Spitzer's drive for a simplified, 'atheoretical' approach was given momentum by the development of the PTSD concept (Chapter Six) and by the notorious Rosenhahn experiment.

As if things were not bad enough, in 1973 a psychology professor, David Rosenhahn, published his study entitled 'On being Sane in Insane Places'. Rosenhahn got twelve healthy individuals to go to different psychiatric units and say that they heard a voice saying such things as 'thud' and 'hollow'. Otherwise they were to behave absolutely normally. All were admitted to hospital, where they behaved impeccably, but virtually all were diagnosed as suffering from schizophrenia. They were discharged after stays averaging several weeks, all with the diagnosis 'schizophrenia, remitted'. No excuses would wash with such an embarrassment, something had to change. The result was the structured approach in *DSM-III* which has shaped diagnostic practice the last forty years.

There is much to recommend this criterion-based approach. It undoubtedly improved reliability; different psychiatrists can be more confident that they would diagnose the same disorder in patients and mean the same thing by it. However, this emphasis on reliability appears to have been at the cost of validity. *Validity* is a more elusive concept, but probably a more important one. It means that we are sure that what we are labelling 'really' is the disorder we mean it to be, whether it is diabetes or schizophrenia. A 'real' disorder here means that most patients with that diagnosis will have a relatively similar course of the disease and broadly similar responses to treatment. It also makes the assumption that there is some common process underlying it although it does not require a full understanding of that process. A valid diagnosis has a practical utility to the doctor for advising and treating the patient.

Reliability does not guarantee validity. That people can agree on something does not prove anything more than that, that they agree. It does not ensure by itself that there is anything coherent or enduring, anything 'real', about what they agree on. You could say that the identification of witches in the seventeenth century was highly reliable; inquisitors and witch-finders would confidently agree on all the criteria. When we see a picture now of an elderly woman dressed in black with a broomstick and a cat we know immediately it means a witch. But that does not mean that there ever were women who flew through the night and cast malign spells. There is no validity to this highly reliable construct.

Criterion-based diagnoses ended up being more inclusive than their predecessors rather than less. Previously psychiatrists formed the impression that patients were depressed from the totality of their presentation and then used the features of the disorder (depressed mood, anxiety, hallucinations) to confirm the diagnosis. They applied their experience of countless previous consultations, comparing what confronted them now with the myriad minor variations in the patterns of the disease. This is the art of medicine. Few experienced doctors (or indeed few patients) would discount the importance of such clinical intuition. Criterion-based diagnosis has shifted the balance towards a simpler process of counting the cardinal features of a disorder.

The diagnostic manuals caution against over-simplification, insisting that judgement is required and that the criteria are guides not rules. But the shift in practice is obvious. We increasingly rely on the criteria, following them unless there are overwhelming reasons not to.

There can be little doubt that this has led to a lowering of the threshold for diagnosis. Those diagnosed with depression in the past would almost certainly meet current criteria (though they may not have been recorded in that way). Others, while meeting the current criteria, would have failed to convey an adequate sense of desolation or emptiness, and earlier psychiatrists might have waited a while before deciding. The risk previously was that treatment was delayed or that mild disorders went untreated. The risk now is that people with a temporary dip in mood who might have soon recovered spontaneously end up with a diagnosis and possibly prolonged treatment.

It is probably too early to judge the effects of criterion-based diagnosis. I am confident that the quality of psychiatric diagnosis initially improved enormously. Combined with the rise of evidence-based medicine it has strengthened consistency of diagnosis and treatment with real benefits for patients. However, these two new developments have been 'grafted on' to traditional medical and psychiatric training. Most psychiatrists still make a diagnosis of schizophrenia by first recognizing the pervasive sense of diffused identity and impaired personal integration. They then confirm it by checking for the hallucinations and delusions that are listed in the manual. What we currently experience is a hybrid process of diagnosis. What will the pure form look like?

There are concerns that this approach can lead to an over-simplified 'cook-book' approach. Recently examining psychiatrists in a high-quality medical school in the Far East I was struck by how none of the patients presented to me in the viva-voce exams were described as 'suffering' from depression or anxiety or schizophrenia; they all 'met criteria for' depression or anxiety or schizophrenia. Patients complain that their assessment and treatment feels impersonal and superficial, that their unique individual history and circumstances are overlooked. These are not trivial issues; we all need to be heard and respected as individuals, never more so than when we are depressed or miserable. Dan Blazer, in *The Age of Melancholy* (2005), contrasts two psychiatric assessments of the same hypothetical depressed patient, one written in the style current in 1963 and the other as it would be recorded in 2003.

A Case in Point

If the same patient were to seek care from a psychiatrist in 1963 and in the year 2003, the diagnostic formulation would be quite different.

1963: A 46-year-old woman is experiencing many symptoms of anxiety and depression, including loss of sleep, subjective anxiety, and loss of appetite. The symptoms worsen when she has contact with her husband, who divorced her 3 years ago. Though she has custody of their 16-year-old daughter and 14-year-old son, when the husband visits with the children on weekends she becomes more depressed. The patient's father abused her physically as a child and later left the family when she was a teenager. When her husband divorced her, the feelings of abandonment she felt when her father left the family returned. Though she realized that the frequent verbal battles she and her husband engaged in were not good for the children and that overall she and the children were functioning better since the divorce, the anxiety returned when her daughter was with her former husband. She feared (she admitted unrealistically) that her husband would abuse her daughter as her father had abused her. One of the attractions to her husband, she admitted, was that he reminded her of some of the more favourable characteristics of her father. She also admitted that she ignored signs early in the relationship with her husband that he could become very angry and take that anger out on her verbally. She is experiencing a reactive depression secondary to the breakup of her marriage and the conflicts that breakup aroused regarding unresolved issues with her father.

2003: This 46-year-old woman, divorced, meets criteria for a major depressive episode, recurrent. She also has experienced a dysthymic disorder for the past 3 years. During the clinical examinations, she scored 20 on the *Hamilton Depression Rating Scale*. Symptoms include depressed mood, insomnia, loss of appetite, agitation, some memory problems, and loss of interest in many activities that interested her in the past. She is physically healthy. The divorce 3 years ago might contribute to some of her symptoms.

Axis I: Major depressive disorder, unipolar and recurrent

Axis II: No personality disorder

Axis III: No medical problems at present
Axis IV: Social problems (divorce from husband)
Axis V: 75 (obvious symptoms but continues to function)
(Dan G. Blazer, *The Age of Melancholy: 'Major Depression'
and Its Social Origins*, 2005)

In the former you get a vivid sense of the individual and her suffering and struggle, in the latter a succinct list of clearly described symptoms. I think most of us would want the 1963 assessment.

The second effect of criterion-based diagnosis has been to increase the number of new diagnoses. Psychiatry has included some strange and foolish diagnoses in the past (homosexuality was only eventually removed in 1973) but the recent addition of a whole range of questionable diagnoses, such as those mentioned at the start of this chapter, is truly dismal. It suggests a concrete mindset that dismisses experience and treats as important what can be measured rather than measuring what is important. Most of these diagnoses go unused – I have never come across a diagnosis of caffeine-induced insomnia in a patient's notes and hope never to do so. Some, however, have gained a foothold and become major components of modern practice. The dramatic expansion in the rate of diagnosis of manic-depressive disorder now that it has been reframed as bipolar disorder is one example. PTSD has moved from being a limited preoccupation of military psychiatry to a mainstream disorder. The epidemic of ADHD in children is now a source of international concern.

Public concern about the expansion of psychiatry is mainly about prescribing. It is the prescribing of antidepressants to more and more depressed patients that worries us, the prescribing of SSRIs to individuals with social phobia, the prescribing of stimulants to children with ADHD. Pills are the symbols of the medicalization of normal experience; purely medical treatments of human dilemmas appear to devalue them. It is as if psychotherapy confirms your struggle with life's challenges, whereas medication marks your failure to overcome them. Psychiatrists do not see it that way. We know that brave and decent people succumb to mental illnesses and that antidepressants are as effective with a depression following a cancer as following a divorce.

There is also a suspicion, not without some foundation, that psychiatry is being manipulated; that it is being hoodwinked by the pharmaceutical industry to diagnose more and more people in order to prescribe more and more pills. Only the most naïve could deny that all the millions of pounds spent on advertising do not affect prescribing. The sums involved, and the profits, are utterly staggering so it is no surprise the marketing is so fierce. In the last decade the cost to the US Federal budget of providing the new patented antipsychotic medications was more than the total salaries for public psychiatrists.

Pharmaceutical companies shoulder enormous research costs to develop new drugs. They argue they need to charge high prices when their drugs are in patent to fund this and reward their shareholders. However, marketing budgets are higher than research budgets, more is spent selling drugs than developing them. While this is true of much of commerce, whether selling motorcars or paint, it sits uneasily with health care.

It is really only in the last few decades that drug costs and marketing have become an issue in psychiatry. Prozac was probably the first new medication where cost and advertising mattered. It was soon to be followed by several SSRI antidepressants and then the newer 'atypical' antipsychotics such as olanzapine and risperidone. Before these, psychiatric drug costs were minimal. For most disorders there was just one 'class' of drugs to prescribe, with little to choose between the individual drugs. Psychiatrists were exposed for the first time to high-pressure advertising and marketing. We were undoubtedly flattered and easily manipulated; I remember it well. Changes in prescribing towards the new drugs were rapid and disproportionate. They did have some advantages but we now know these to be modest. These 'blockbuster' drugs hailed as vastly superior now simply play their part alongside the older ones. This onslaught of marketing by what has come to be referred to as 'Big Pharma' has waned somewhat in psychiatry, but is still a major concern as it is throughout medicine.

The relationship between professionals and the industry remains murky. Should I accept fees from them to lecture even if I scrupulously avoid endorsing their products? Should I let them fund me to attend conferences and training events knowing that their aim is really just to make me like and trust them and therefore become positively disposed to their products? Perhaps more importantly should we allow advertising at all? Surely I should be educating myself about different drugs from reputable scientific journals? Critics accuse Big Pharma of having 'hijacked' psychiatry and there has been some truth in this. Undoubtedly some prescribing practices are irrational and commercially rather than clinically driven. The multiple prescribing in the USA of newer patented anticonvulsant drugs in bipolar disorder instead of the equally (or perhaps more) effective lithium, which is unpatentable and unprofitable, is one example. Even more unsettling is the recent 'discovery' in the USA of bipolar disorder in children, with a fourfold increase in the rate of diagnosis in under a decade, and routine prescribing. This book is not the place to argue the scientific merits of each individual decision but the issues can be explored in one of the more disquieting examples.

ADHD has long been recognized as a rare but disruptive and distressing condition in some young children, usually boys. Unable to concentrate they are restless and disruptive at home and at school. In most cases careful management of the situation helped – smaller classes, shorter lessons and plenty of opportunity for exercise. Drugs were tried in severe cases and, surprisingly, children were found to respond better to stimulants than to sedatives. A theory developed that there may be some delay in brain development or function, hence the 'attention deficit', and that their concentration was helped by the stimulant. Amphetamines were initially used but these have problems both of addiction and of inhibiting growth so were tightly restricted. So far so good. In the 1990s, however, amphetamine derivatives were developed which did not stunt growth and were less obviously addictive.

An aggressive marketing campaign was mounted and stimulant prescribing appears to have moved from being the intervention of last resort to being almost the first line of treatment. The value of such stimulants is difficult to assess. An obvious problem is their lack of diagnostic specificity. They will, almost invariably, improve things for anyone in the short term – hence the thriving black market in them. We might all feel better for a few weeks on them. Similarly once you have adapted to taking them you will feel worse when you stop. You get a mild 'withdrawal' effect, a bit like stopping strong coffee if you are used to it. So the diagnosis and treatment appear to be confirmed: things improve immediately after starting treatment and deteriorate immediately after stopping it. The result is that their prescription has rocketed. The official explanation is of 'improved diagnosis', identifying previously untreated disease.

Rates rose first and most rapidly in the USA, although the rest of the world is fast catching up. The USA, unlike most of Europe, allows advertising of prescription drugs directly to the public ('tell your doctor to consider . . .') with obvious pressure on prescribers. The result is sobering. One in ten of ten-year-old boys in the USA, disproportionately those from disadvantaged families, is currently prescribed stimulants for ADHD. Now, wherever the threshold should lie (I am not a child psychiatrist so do not know) this level surely cannot make sense; it is much too high. There are several theories advanced to explain this increase in ADHD. Foremost is an observation of sedentary and over-stimulated lifestyles in these boys as addictive computer games have replaced rough and tumble in the park. Other theories include a concern about food additives and even the 'feminization' of society with few male role models and school routines adapted by predominantly female teachers which favour hard-working cooperative girls. There seems little tolerance for 'boys to be boys'. There is undoubtedly something in all these but the impact of marketing of these powerful drugs is indisputable. One in ten cannot make clinical sense.

There are other examples (overuse of antidepressants, polypharmacy in bipolar disorder and schizophrenia) which are increasingly serious and where a rebalancing is urgently needed. Whether it is true that drug companies consciously and actively foster 'pseudo-diagnoses' is a matter of debate. Many would argue that the origin, or at least prominence, of social phobia as a diagnosis is driven by its commercial potential for the sale of SSRIs. Similarly, female sexual arousal disorder may owe its existence to the drive to market anti-impotence drugs such as sildenafil (Viagra) and tadalafil (Cialis) to women.

Psychiatry has to wake up to Big Pharma and get its house in order. This is, however, part of a much larger issue. Pharma has been highly successful in discovering and developing drugs that have relieved misery in millions. We will continue to need them. The greater problem for psychiatry is to find a proper professional response to what society and our patients want from us. After all it is the parents and teachers of boys with ADHD who clamour for the stimulant drugs. Many psychiatrists are now facing the novel experience of patients coming already self-diagnosed ('I am sure I've got bipolar disorder. I've checked it out on the internet and I have all the symptoms') and with a clear treatment expectation. Family doctors have long experience of patients demanding antibiotics when they do not need them, and the signs are that they usually comply. Now it happens regularly with antidepressants. Psychiatry is a profession where historically most people resisted our diagnoses and often had to be convinced to take our treatments. Even if Big Pharma were not there to stoke the demand, multiple pressures exist within our society to stimulate perceived needs for more and more psychiatry.

So psychiatry and psychiatric diagnoses are everywhere, invading every aspect of our lives. The medical historian Roy Porter called the twentieth century the 'century of psychiatry'. Overall this is probably a good thing, that psychiatry has more to offer and is increasingly trusted. However, some of the forces driving this flowering and some features of its reach and direction are disquieting. They call for a mature debate within the profession and between the profession and society at large. Casually applied psychiatric diagnoses can be individually demeaning and socially impoverishing. None of us want to reduce the rich range of human experience to a collection of 'disorders'.

There is a widespread acknowledgement within the profession that since *DSM-III* and *DSM-IV* over-diagnosis has gone too far; there is now an epidemic of false positives. Concern is widely expressed that *DSM-V* due out in 2013 will make things even worse. This concern comes not only from those who fear the medicalization of normal life but also from psychiatrists and academics, including senior figures in the development of *DSM-III* and *DSM-IV*. They fear that flabby and over-inclusive diagnostic practice will undermine precisely the rigour in research trials for which the original criterion-based approach was developed. However, in our concern about these developments we should not overlook the fundamental motor in this expansion. The twentieth century has witnessed a step-change in psychiatry's ability to alleviate distress and to cure what were once awful illnesses. It should not surprise us that this success has led to some over-enthusiasm, some exaggerated claims and excesses. For all its failings the current situation is surely preferable to the alternative of stagnation and tolerating unnecessary suffering.

12

New treatments but old dilemmas

Like the rest of medicine, psychiatry has improved by leaps and bounds through the course of the twentieth century as treatments have become more effective, consistent and safer. It has improved the lives and wellbeing of countless patients. Psychiatry can now offer significant relief, and in some cases cure, in all the major groups of mental illnesses. In dementia anti-cholinesterase drugs can halt the course of the disease for a year or so and research in this area has really taken off. All our modern treatments are increasingly subjected to careful scientific examination and development. Both the volume and range of this scientific activity are now enormous.

'Neuroscience' is now probably the most vigorous and exciting area in the whole of bio-medical research, turbo-charged by an arsenal of powerful new tools. These include automated sequencing for genetic studies and laboratory techniques that can now operate down to the level of individual nerve-cell receptor sites. Several techniques of imaging brain activity are now available, a veritable alphabet soup of scans: MRI, fMRI, PET, SPECT and MEG.

Progress has not been confined to biological laboratories. Psychological investigation of brain processes has become increasingly sophisticated and rigorous, aided by high-precision computerized instruments to deliver stimuli and measure milliseconds of delay in responding. Experiences and behaviour can even be studied in simulated environments using virtual reality laboratories. Cognitive processing, memory functions, attribution, facial recognition and more are all now part of the language of psychology research. The boundaries between psychological and psychiatric research are dissolving.

It is not only the sciences basic to medicine, such as physiology, anatomy, pharmacology, psychology, that have been accelerating through the twentieth century but clinical science itself. The balance between the art and the science of medicine has been steadily shifting. 'Art' here means craft or skill, not some flamboyant creative performance. There is still a core set of skills to being a doctor but we increasingly expect practice to be dictated by the latest research findings. Medicine has become more consistent in its practice and gross variations have been steadily eliminated by an acceptance of published evidence-based guidelines.

Evidence-based medicine has become a branch of academic activity in its own right. It has developed sophisticated procedures for accessing, evaluating and combining research results and then feeding them into guidelines. In the UK, NICE (National Institute of Clinical Excellence) produces detailed guidance on the management of most groups of disorders, including psychiatric ones. The NICE schizophrenia guidelines include details of the drug treatments to be provided and the psychological treatments indicated. They even dictate the structure of teams and make recommendations about the 'tone' of the therapeutic relationship. These guidelines are not vague. At the time of writing NICE had published over thirty mental health guidelines with ten more on the way.

The result is that treatments are generally based on up-to-date evidence and what you can expect to receive is broadly similar within any given health care system. So brief problem-based therapy or cognitive behaviour therapy (CBT) would hopefully be provided for anxiety states and both antidepressants and CBT for depression. Psychiatrists have generally been good at taking up the message of evidence-based medicine. Provision of some of the psychotherapies, however, remains limited both by a shortage of trained therapists and the funding to employ them. They are also more difficult to standardize because psychotherapy evolves in the relationship and requires more personal commitment from both therapist and patient.

One might think from all this, therefore, that as psychiatry has become absorbed into the broad church of modern medicine it would no longer be controversial. Not so. Psychiatry remains as controversial in the era of evidence-based medicine as it ever was. Presumably it is destined to be controversial because of the areas in which it operates. The mind, personal choice and freedom, the vagaries of memory and the rich complexity of human relationships are all fraught with ambiguity and crowded with opinions and personal prejudices. These controversies are all too important to ignore and yet defy simple and permanent resolutions. The examination of these dilemmas in some of the previous chapters might be dismissed as examples of a limited understanding of mental illness and its treatment. They were 'of their time'. But this is not really so, these ambiguities are enduring. They arise from the complexity of our human nature, from our need for understanding and comfort as well as cure. To get a sense of these inherent tensions we will revisit three long-running disputes as they present themselves to our generation.

The first of these is the challenge presented by *dissociation*. The altered states of consciousness originally accessed in Mesmerism (Chapter 3) continue to perplex psychiatrists. We still struggle with what to do with the manifestations of what used to be called hysteria, and with multiple personality disorder and the highly charged issue of chronic fatigue syndrome (CFS). The second is the long-standing *nature–nurture* argument explored in Chapter 8, although the language has changed, from heredity versus upbringing to 'gene–environment interactions'. The contribution of early childhood experience is no longer expressed as blame ('the schizophrenogenic mother') but still has the power to ignite strong passions. It leads us back to how memory is formed in early life and how it is processed through adult suffering and therapy. Lastly we will return to *coercion*. Chains have been struck off, doors unlocked and forbidding institutions closed. Yet the mentally ill are still treated differently. They are regularly deprived of their right to refuse treatment and can still be admitted to hospitals against their clearly expressed wishes. Some of the most bitter arguments about psychiatry concern why free will and self-determination are uniquely compromised for this one group of our fellow citizens.

These issues remain controversial because there are no clear 'right' or 'wrong' answers. Increasing knowledge alters the language and shifts the balance of dispute but often just sharpens the contradictions. Unfortunately, as a profession, we cannot simply fold our arms and sit back until the evidence is in. Attractive as such a course might seem, the issues are just too pressing, the distress and suffering are too real and they demand a response. These questions test our moral integrity, not just our professional knowledge and skills. We have to be prepared to act in the face of sophisticated arguments which parade the all too human logical inconsistencies in our understanding. We have to operate in the face of uncertainty, relying on the best available evidence even if we know it is inadequate.

WHAT SENSE CAN WE MAKE OF DISSOCIATION?

Let me turn to the uncomfortable challenge of dissociation. Recognizing that we can have powerful, persistent and sophisticated mental processes of which we are totally unaware was one of the twin origins of modern psychiatry (Chapter 3). Mesmer demonstrated that behaviour could be influenced directly through altered states of consciousness and these were explored by early hypnotists such as de Puységur and James Baird. Psychoanalysts moved on from this to chart a complex mental structure yielding a rich understanding of the whole person (Chapter 4). Freud's understanding of hysterical disorders rested on the concepts of primary and secondary gain. It addressed a range of physical disorders such as blindness and paralyses with no obvious organic cause plus varied psychological disabilities such as disturbances of memory. These hysterical symptoms served a psychic purpose: they kept unacceptable, and painful, thoughts hidden (repressed). This 'dissociation' was the 'primary gain' for the patient. Freud also observed how the patients' symptoms affected those around them, eliciting caring and supportive responses which he called 'secondary gain'. Shell shock in the First World War, described in Chapter 6, demonstrates just how powerful these processes can be.

As psychoanalysis has lost influence within psychiatry, hysteria has become discredited and disused as a diagnosis. Undoubtedly early analysts exaggerated the specificity of the processes involved and generated a number of wild theories. Freud and his followers attributed far too much significance to the symbolism of individual symptoms.

A backlash against these excesses resulted in the term simply being abandoned, with hysterical disorders being shuffled into a range of broader, less emotive categories ('medically unexplained symptoms', 'psychosomatic disorders', 'somatoform disorder'). Dissociative disorders, however, won't go away – they keep surfacing in puzzling forms.

The 1970s and 1980s saw an apparent epidemic of multiple personality disorder (MPD), mainly in the USA but not exclusively so. It appeared as a formal diagnosis in 1980 in *DSM-III* which had very pointedly abandoned terms such as 'neurosis' and 'hysteria'. The diagnosis remains MPD in *ICD*, although now labelled Dissociative Identity Disorder in *DSM-IV*. Many patients were reported with several autonomous, parallel identities accessed in therapy. Why the upsurge occurred when it did is not clear, but it was undoubtedly helped along by *Sybil*. This bestseller by Flora Schreiber, like the equally successful film *The Three Faces of Eve* in 1957, tells the story of a patient uncovering her multiple personalities in psychotherapy. *Sybil* was published in 1973 and it sold half a million copies in its first year and was made into a highly successful film and then a TV series in 1976.

MPD became a highly controversial diagnosis and its critics, who included me, considered it essentially 'iatrogenic' (literally 'caused by doctors'). By this we mean that the 'discovered' personalities were not brought to therapy by the patient but were constructed in the therapy between the therapist and patient. Both partners were open to the possibility of multiple personalities and the therapist, unwittingly and indirectly, suggested the details or encouraged the patient to produce them. Neither was actively or deliberately making anything up; the whole process is testimony to the power of belief and suggestion.

The same mechanism has been proposed for 'recovered memory syndrome'. Like MPD there was an epidemic in the 1980s and 1990s, again mainly restricted to North America. Patients, usually in the course of intensive psychotherapy, recovered memories of childhood events of which they had been totally unaware throughout their early adult life and which they and their therapists considered were responsible for their current problems. The majority of the patients were young women referred for difficulties with relationships and impulse control, usually diagnosed with a 'borderline personality disorder'. The memories recovered were predominantly of sexual abuse, frequently by their fathers, echoing Freud's early thinking. These memories had very serious consequences; many families were destroyed and several men went to prison convicted of incest.

Recovered memory followed a similar, but more rapid, trajectory to MPD and is now generally considered a professional aberration. It was simply a terrible mistake in which therapists and patients were swept along in an infectious group-think. Its demise was hastened by its association with clearly outrageous witch-hunts by some psychotherapists and social workers. A particular problem in this process is that convinced practitioners believe that repeated denial of the trauma by the patient is itself confirmatory evidence of repression. In their intensified search for proof they unwittingly put ideas into their patients' heads. Several fictitious 'paedophile rings' were implicated by prolonged questioning of children during which false memories were induced. Despite the awful consequences of these mistakes there was never any doubt that the professionals involved were driven by the purest of intentions; many years later some still retain their belief that they acted entirely in the children's best interests.

It would be a mistake to dismiss these episodes as just an unfortunate meeting between naïve therapists and suggestible patients. All psychotherapies require a structure, a 'narrative' that both therapist and patient can share. This shared understanding serves as a map in their joint exploration in uncertain areas. Dissociative processes are tricky. Their presence is impossible to prove or disprove; it is based on a judgement, and one that inevitably conflicts with the patient's. Dissociation is, by its very nature, invisible to the patient. It exists, if you accept the psychodynamic understanding, for precisely that purpose. It protects the patient from emotional pain and he or she will rarely welcome its exposure. Freud rightly predicted strong resistance to uncovering dissociation because doing so destroys the primary gain and, as often as not, any associated secondary gain.

Dissociation and its varying and often strange manifestations remain a constant in the history of psychiatry. The epidemic of wandering *fugueurs* that challenged European philosophers in the 1870s (Chapter 3) clearly had some form of dissociatively generated multiple personality disorder. Dissociative disorders are common in the developing world and widely recognized by psychiatrists there. For the last half-century we have ignored them and downplayed dissociation as a mental mechanism. This is probably a reaction to the excesses of psychoanalysis but also because extreme examples really are less frequent now in our highly educated and psychologically sophisticated societies. Consequently we are much less confident or experienced in dealing with it when we are confronted by it.

Courts, and the psychiatrists they call as witnesses, cannot avoid coming to a decision about individuals when dissociation is advanced as a defence. This can be for one-off, out-of-character, offences attributed to an automatism; it can also be for more persistent abnormalities such as 'Munchausen's by proxy' where disturbed mothers repeatedly harm their children to obtain medical attention. The scope for controversy is clearly present in the need to make a judgement about something being 'out of character'. Courts have to make a decision about the presence or absence of conscious motivation; they must decide one way or the other. Did the mother know what she was doing at the time? Did she have an evil intent (*mens rea*, as lawyers call it) or did she not?

Inevitably one gets it wrong sometimes but the rewards for taking dissociation seriously can be great. I worked for some years as the psychiatrist in a neurology ward where classical hysterical disorders (partial paralyses, weakness, anaesthesia and even blindness) really were not that uncommon. The label of 'hysterical', even 'dissociative', was studiously avoided and patients were simply said to have 'a functional element' to their problem requiring a psychiatrist. My approach was to try and uncover their worries, combined with strong reassurance and non-confronting rehabilitation. I would tell them that the good news was that there was no life-threatening or irreversible disease. Their disorder was puzzling and serious, I would explain. However, it almost certainly would recover over time, despite some possible setbacks. We then planned a gradual series of exercises to work towards regaining full function. At the same time I would encourage them to discuss their worries, all their worries. I pointed out that recovery was made more difficult if they were preoccupied by stress and anxiety. I made absolutely no attempt to link these worries to their symptoms. One patient I recall vividly was a refuse worker admitted with a dense paralysis of his right arm after a minor accident at work. This had persisted, unchanged, for several weeks. It became clear in our discussions that he was terrified because he had to complete a supporting statement for his son's college admission. Over the years he had evolved complex tricks to avoid his total illiteracy becoming clear to his clever son of whom he was enormously proud. Engineering a supportive opportunity for this to be uncovered during a family visit produced a rapid recovery – and engendered a heart-warming show of admiration from his son. Many such patients made remarkably good recoveries, often after long periods of disability. Not all of course. For some, particularly after years of illness, there might be little left to get better for.

Dissociation remains a psychiatric process (disorder?) that really does not fit our current criterion-based approach. Its identification has to be based on the whole picture, in particular the non-specific 'feel' of the interview and on clinical experience. Sometimes it can only be satisfactorily confirmed by the response to treatment, and such retrospective diagnosis is out of step with our prevailing scientific aspirations. Tact and diplomacy are needed for work in this area, and sometimes it can simply be impossible to establish trust and cooperation.

No psychiatrist likes writing about CFS. Members of my profession have been threatened with violence for suggesting it is a psychiatric disorder, or even has a psychiatric or emotional component. A leading British expert has had to have his mail intercepted because of such threats. Chronic fatigue and lassitude occurring in previously high-performing individuals, often after a short physical illness and with no obvious psychiatric symptoms, has been treated by psychiatrists since the dawn of the profession. What we now call CFS would have been subsumed under hypochondriasis two centuries ago and neurasthenia a century ago. More recently it has been called myalgic encephalomyelitis (ME), post-viral syndrome and sometimes unhelpfully dismissed as 'yuppy flu'. For advocacy groups ME, with its explicit suggestion of a physical causation, is the preferred term.

CFS is no joke. It can ruin lives and be very disabling; it has even been fatal. There are many serious disorders with uncertain causation in medicine so in that there is nothing unusual about CFS in that. What is truly remarkable about it, however, is just how angry many of its sufferers, or more accurately their representative bodies, become with any suggestion that psychiatry could help. Psychiatrists are regularly accused of implying CFS is not a 'real' illness or of minimizing the distress. We are, of course, doing nothing of the sort. Of all people, we believe that mental illnesses are real illnesses. We are simply suggesting a different mechanism and treatment. Nobody denies the reality of the post-viral fatigue that so often precedes it.

It is this intense anger that, to me, suggests the dissociative mechanism. Normally patients with a grim and distressing disorder, whether physical or mental, welcome just about *any* help on offer; psychiatrists working on cancer wards don't find themselves sent packing. I have genuinely had a patient with CFS say to me, 'I would rather die than accept psychiatric treatment.' It simply doesn't make sense. Unless, that is, the offered psychiatric treatment threatens to destroy something that feels even more precious than relief from the fatigue. A fragile but vital defence mechanism such as dissociation with all its implications about personal character and identity could be that thing.

This stand-off is not trivial. There have been cases where children have died with a diagnosis of CFS, wasting away without ever being allowed a psychiatric examination by their parents. A recent 'mercy killing' tried in a UK court was by the mother of a young man diagnosed with CFS, which he and she believed to be incurable. Yet most CFS patients can, and do, recover. The balance of evidence is that CBT or a programme of carefully monitored, slowly increasing activity, so-called 'graded exercise', are the best treatments for CFS. The largest study to date that demonstrated successful outcomes was incredibly carefully designed to remove bias (it had to be). About 60 per cent of patients improved significantly over a year with either CBT or graded exercise. We learnt as long ago as the First World War that disuse of 'hysterically' paralysed limbs rapidly leads to their withering and the development of 'real' weakness. 'Living within the confines of CFS', as recommended by some patient groups, is likely to entrench the weakness and fatigue. Unfortunately this is not an issue that will be easily resolved by evidence. For psychiatrists to propose, as I essentially do here, that we may know your own mind on this matter better than you do yourself is not easy to swallow. It seems an affront. The specifics of the dissociation controversy may change as our treatments and theories develop, but this central stand-off is likely to persist.

NATURE–NURTURE IN THE TWENTY-FIRST CENTURY

Family 'causes' of mental illness remain a live issue. The relative contributions of childhood experience and constitution to mental illness received their most thorough testing in the schizophrenia nature–nurture controversy outlined in Chapter 8. But that was not the end of the story. We usually explain emotional problems or mental illnesses to ourselves in terms of crucial events in our personal history or as a consequence of our personality. Holocaust survivors who develop depression in later life will almost invariably assume it is a result of that experience (although, remarkably, there is little evidence for this). Conscientious and careful individuals will attribute their anxiety neurosis to their 'excessive super-ego'. Even when the onset of illness is abrupt and alien such as with mania or schizophrenia, patients and families search exhaustively for an explanation and understanding. Could it be earlier drug use, burning the candle at both ends, excessive shyness? For many patients understanding their illness, making some personal sense of their predicament, can be as important as relief from the symptoms. Virtually all psychotherapies emphasize understanding the causes and background of disorders.

A shared narrative has been a feature of all successful psychological treatments. A shared understanding of the causes of illnesses is necessary for all successful psychiatric treatments, even the most narrowly medical. If doctor and patient have conflicting opinions about what is wrong it is difficult to cooperate on a protracted treatment. Most psychiatrists are relatively sceptical that we know the specific 'cause' of any individual patient's illness. However, we are often confident that we know the various processes that can have contributed to it. There is a crucial difference in these two levels of explanation. Take

as an example an influential body of research into the social determin-
ants of depression in working-class women. This shows that the
risk of depression rises stepwise with each of four factors – having no
close female friend, having more than three young children at home,
being unemployed and having lost your mother early in life. While the
presence of any of these may help understand an individual woman's
depression it does not mean that early bereavement or unemployment
'caused' it. They simply increased the risk.

Risk factors in early life have recently been shown to interact with
individual genes to result in some mental illnesses. This 'gene–
environment interaction' has been identified for cannabis use and the
presence of some genes associated with schizophrenia. If you are
genetically predisposed for schizophrenia then heavy cannabis use in
adolescence significantly increases that risk. Yet schizophrenia can
occur without cannabis use, and you can be a heavy cannabis smoker
without developing schizophrenia. The Dunedin study which followed up 1,000 people from birth to adult life shows that there are
specific gene patterns which you need for the cannabis to have this
effect. The same study found that association of childhood adversity
with adult depression also demonstrates such a gene–environment
interaction. Adversity led to depression most often in individuals with
specific genes. So what is 'causing' the depression? Is it the genes or
the adversity?

Left at that point it seems just another nerdy question for psychiatric academics. However, 'early life events' are rarely perceived as
neutral. Childhood abuse, including sexual abuse, figures prominently
in this research and this is inevitably a highly charged issue. We have
struggled for forty years to remove blame from the parents of the
mentally ill. The re-emergence of data implicating families is highly
unwelcome for many. Usually the reports are from memory: adults
asked directly about specific unpleasant earlier events respond, 'Yes,
that happened.' Recall of such childhood abuse became very controversial in early psychoanalysis and is still treated with suspicion in
much therapy. However, current thinking on this issue does not draw
its evidence only from memories recovered in psychotherapy.

General population surveys find increased reports of early childhood abuse, including sexual abuse, in those with mental illnesses.

The strength of these surveys comes from their size, the numbers of people asked and thus their statistical power. Their weakness is that the definitions of abuse, and particularly sexual abuse, are very broad. Even what constitutes a family member is no longer that simple. So interpretation is not straightforward. There may also still be some over-reporting from those with mental illnesses. We know that depressed patients have what is called a 'negative recall bias' and a 'negative appraisal set'. Because of their mood they are more likely to describe neutral events as unpleasant, and to remember unpleasant rather than pleasant events. It is in the nature of the disorder. Similarly if you are unhappy or dissatisfied with your current lot, you are more likely to search the past for explanations. This may account for some of the difference, but not for all.

The clincher is to be found in birth cohort studies. Long-term memory is criticized as unreliable and subject to too much recall bias. So the answer is to follow a group of people from birth onwards and check their outcomes every few years. There are now several such studies. The 1946 Birth Cohort is one of the biggest and included all 13,000 children born in the UK in one week. Repeated follow-ups into adult life explored physical health and educational and psychological outcomes. Such cohort studies are difficult to conduct and enormously expensive. On the whole, they are best for examining the links between common behaviours and common outcomes. Several influential studies have also been conducted with selected groups. The British Doctors Study followed up 40,000 doctors in England from 1951 to 2001 and established the link between smoking and lung cancer. The Whitehall study of 18,000 civil servants showed the links not only between exercise, stress and heart disease but how your job status affected even how long you lived.

Birth cohort studies to examine psychiatric outcomes are more demanding because they need information from parents and teachers about childhood experiences and behaviour. This sort of information – shyness, poor school performance – also requires judgement, unlike simple measures such as weight or height. Despite the challenges several psychiatric birth cohort studies have been undertaken. Probably the most influential is based in Dunedin, New Zealand, and consists of all 1,037 babies born from April 1972 to March 1973 in this small university town. It has collected DNA and gene data, blood samples, developmental data and illness data, and has repeatedly conducted interviews and examinations over the years. The crucial difference is that information on childhood experiences was collected during childhood, not from memory. A whole series of childhood indicators have been identified for later mental illness and among these is the impact of abuse, physical, emotional and sexual. It is this study with its rich database, and staggeringly successful follow-up, that identified the interaction between specific genetic configurations and adverse events in depression mentioned above.

The evidence that difficult childhoods are much more common in those who go on to develop severe mental illnesses as adults is now overwhelming and unequivocal. What to make of this finding is less clear. The same studies show that those destined to become ill have difficulties very early on. Autistic and schizophrenic adults are often both identified by parents as less responsive already as infants. The direction of effect may go both ways. Parents with borderline psychotic disorders themselves may also have greater difficulty looking after their children so one cannot entirely rule out some genetic influence. However, it does seem the case that early abuse leads to mental illness. The link is very strong but not absolute. Early disturbances are very general. For instance, those destined to develop schizophrenia as adults show more disturbed behaviour – withdrawal in girls and disruptive behaviour in boys – even before they are eleven years old. But while only one in a hundred developed schizophrenia, ten to twenty had such problems during childhood in the Dunedin study. The association is strong and undeniable but its ability to predict is low; it hardly helps us pick out the person who will become ill later on. It is the same for reports of abuse. Yes, those who develop mental illnesses are more likely to be abused as children, but many more abused children *do not* develop mental illness than do.

Just as we do with genes we now tend to think of these experiences as *risk factors for*, rather than *causes of*, mental illness. I am personally very loath to get too moralistic about this. Few parents want to do anything other than the best for their children, but none of us is perfect. The number of loving and caring parents I have seen blaming themselves for their 'failings' when things go wrong for their child makes me very sceptical of this simple cause–effect thinking. Similarly most of us will know individuals who have weathered appalling misfortune to become rounded and successful adults. These findings remind me of an early ambition of social psychiatry, not only to help individual patients, but to influence society to give everyone the best possible chance. J. G. Querido, a Dutch social psychiatrist in the 1930s, declared a threefold ambition: to help patients adjust to society, to help society adjust to patients and lastly to act as a buffer between them.

So over a hundred years on from Freud's struggles with the reality or otherwise of early abuse, and half a century on from the antipsychiatrists and the 'schizophrenogenic' mother, we are still faced with what to make of these findings. Framed differently, it is true, but still unresolved. My conclusion, for what it is worth, is that human beings are obviously affected by how life treats them. Families are an important part of that experience, a very important one, but they are far from the only influence. Our peers and our wider experiences matter more than often acknowledged. Blaming families seems unhelpful and, frankly, unjustified; the links in any individual case are tenuous. What we do have, however, is strong evidential support for action at a population level. We should lend our voices to calls for maximum support for *every* child in their early years and, particularly for nonjudgemental support for parents who are struggling. Such investment can only be money well spent, in terms of both human suffering and the costs to society.

Some will consider my position complacent. They insist that psychiatry, by downplaying these findings, is still ducking its responsibilities exactly as Jeffrey Masson accused Freud. By denying the extent and impact of abuse we are clinging on to an exaggerated and unjustified medical model to explain human suffering. If the abuse is so widespread in those who become distressed an endless search for physiological mechanisms and genetic explanations serves only to increase the status and legitimacy of psychiatry and dismisses the authenticity of the individual experience. You have to decide for yourself.

WHY HAS COERCION PERSISTED?

A century ago only 3 or 4 per cent of the population would ever see a psychiatrist. Now about one in ten of us will be admitted to a psychiatric ward at some time in our lives and up to a quarter of us will seek psychiatric help. This is due to having more effective treatments, to raised expectations and to widening diagnostic practice. Progress has, however, been in fits and starts. 'Revolutionary' periods have generally been marked with iconic acts of liberalization. At psychiatry's birth Pinel strikes off the chains at the Bicêtre; during the 'first medical model' in the 1920s and 1930s voluntary inpatient care becomes widely available; the discovery of antipsychotic and antidepressive drugs in the 1950s opens locked doors, initiating the demise of the asylum. The slogan on Basaglia's Trieste asylum in the 1970s declared 'La libertà è terapeutica', yet liberty's antitheses, coercion and compulsory treatment, have not disappeared. We rarely lock people away for life now but, remarkably, *more* people are probably subjected to psychiatric compulsion now than ever before. Why should this be so?

The emphasis we place on personal independence may have something to do with it. For most of history, and still in much of the world, individuals were not considered free agents. From birth onwards, they were locked into a powerful network of obligations, duties and rights. These bound them primarily to their family and often to wider social groupings. In mental illness families took (in many parts of the world still take) responsibility for both the care and control of patients. Doctors would rely on family decisions when patients seemed unable to make them. When there was disagreement we would generally assume families had patients' best interests at heart and be guided by them. Earlier this took the form of caring for the patient and protecting him or her from harm until they recovered. The family's right to make decisions for its members when they were ill was considered self-evident. We saw with Mary Lamb (Chapter 10) how the exercise of such authority could result in a humane flexibility that would seem impossible today. Of course, it is not that simple; families also have their limitations.

With the rise of asylums more formalized processes were introduced to ensure legal oversight of admissions. Initially patients were 'certified' as insane by a magistrate. This restricted them to the hospital and put them under the authority of the doctor. It also removed all their normal civil rights such as control over their finances or voting until they were discharged. Between the wars certification was phased out and replaced by less-invalidating legislation, imposing only those restrictions needed to treat the illness and protect the individuals involved. Practice does not always keep pace with legislation, however. Patients were still denied their own clothes and free communication in many places and the level of personal freedom they enjoy still is very limited. Until recently compulsion was restricted to in-patient care. With improved community care many countries have now changed their laws to allow compulsory treatment outside the hospital.

Compulsory care seems an inevitable feature of psychiatry. No developed mental health service anywhere completely prohibits it but rates of its use vary wildly. A tenfold variation across Europe has no obvious explanation. Legislation is also equally variable, from countries with few safeguards for civil liberties to those with incredibly strict and detailed requirements. The number of inpatient beds and level of community support vary enormously, as does the quality of services. On the whole Northern Europe uses more coercion than Mediterranean countries but even here there are exceptions, and everywhere it is more common in cities. In my early years in rural Scotland I was able to get very ill patients to come to hospital simply by persuasion. Doctors still had a status and authority there that would mean absolutely nothing in inner London now. Local culture and professional custom exert an enduring effect.

How the decision is made also varies. The USA has always had a more libertarian tradition than Europe, prioritizing personal freedom and autonomy above all else, and its use of compulsion reflects this. In both the New and the Old World, concerns over autonomy and liberty dominate the discourse but in practice European mental health policy is much less libertarian. The USA was founded by waves of migrants escaping authoritarian European governments and monarchies, leaving an enduring mistrust of government and the state. In the USA only clear, immediate risk can justify deprivation of liberty.

Think of Patrick Henry's 1775 call to the Virginians to rise against the British:

> Is life so dear, or peace so sweet, as to be purchased at the price of chains and slavery? Forbid it, Almighty God! I know not what course others may take; but as for me, *Give me Liberty, or Give me Death!*

To compulsorily detain patients in the USA psychiatrists have to believe they pose an immediate risk of harm to themselves or to others. Compulsion tends to be short and patients discharged as soon as the danger is no longer clear and imminent. Europe has a more paternalistic culture. We use the same language of autonomy but our practice differs. Detention is permitted on the grounds of risk to patients' health, and that usually means mental health. So individuals with schizophrenia who are relapsing but pose no physical risk may still be detained on the grounds that they need treatment to prevent further serious deterioration in their mental health. They do not have to be actively suicidal or aggressive.

USA ethicists and lawyers despair at the intrusiveness and paternalism of European psychiatrists. European ethicists and psychiatrists in their turn despair at perceived clinical neglect justified as respect for autonomy – 'dying with your rights on'. The philosopher Isaiah Berlin in his famous essay 'Two Concepts of Liberty' distinguished between *freedom from* (oppression) and *freedom to* (self-fulfilment). The mentally ill may have to suffer some restriction of their 'freedom from' so that effective treatment can restore their 'freedom to'. To insist on freedom from interference for the mentally ill and the impoverished was, he wrote, to 'mock their condition'.

It would be misleading to present Europe or indeed the USA as entirely homogeneous. I observed some paternalistic and very high-quality practice in some small East Coast states such as New Hampshire and Vermont. There are endless variations and permutations of European legislation and practice, some emphasizing imminent harm more than others. Some even separate the grounds for detention from the grounds for treatment. For instance, in some Swiss cantons (each of the twenty-six has its own mental health laws) a patient can be detained on health grounds but only be compulsorily medicated on grounds of dangerousness. This can result in a stuttering regime with drug treatment varied every few days while the patient remains detained.

How you stand on this will reflect your views on justice and personhood, not so much your views on psychiatry's effectiveness. Protecting autonomy, or liberty, may seem self-evident and straightforward, but that simplicity is deceptive, as the US revolutionary Patrick Henry himself demonstrates. When he delivered his historical call for 'liberty or death' he was the owner of fifteen black slaves. How much did their liberty count? More poignantly, at the time of his historical address one of his female slaves was occupied in tending to his much-loved wife Sarah. She had been locked in the basement of his Virginia mansion for the preceding four years, often in a straitjacket, suffering from a psychosis. Nothing about people is simple.

We are accustomed to people being detained in hospital for necessary treatment when acutely ill. All countries do it, and most have some form of Mental Health Act to sanction and monitor it. We would all like to minimize it, and vocal civil rights groups in most countries press for this, but it is still broadly accepted as necessary. We can see that patients who are so unwell as to need round the clock nursing may be unable to decide for themselves. It is not so obvious, however, that the same can hold for individuals managing day to day outside hospital. If they are able to get by in the community why should they not be allowed to make a mess of things or behave oddly just like the rest of us?

Current community care practices mean we now have seriously unwell patients living among us. Few would want a return to the old asylums but there are undoubtedly problems with the current model. Violence committed by individuals with clear mental illness is rare but it has an enormous impact on public opinion. We are now a much more risk-averse culture. An act of violence by a patient is expected to be followed by a rapid and prolonged incarceration. A patient with a known mental illness who is allowed to remain at liberty suggests the professionals are reckless.

A number of countries have passed laws to provide compulsory treatment in the community. They have done so to address this concern with violence but also to try and reduce the burden of 'revolving-door' psychosis patients; to reduce the burden for the patient, the family and the taxpayer. Australia was the first in 1987 in Victoria state. Through the 1990s similar legislation was introduced throughout Australia and New Zealand and in over forty states in the USA. More recently it has been introduced in Canada and the UK and several continental European countries. These laws have sometimes been named after the victims of high-profile tragedies (Kendra's law in New York, Laura's law in California, Brian's law in Ontario, Canada). In England the initiative came from the random killing of a young Italian musician, Jonathan Zito, on a London underground station in 1992. That it took a further fifteen years to pass the bill shows the strength of feeling and opposition it aroused.

Compulsory community treatment goes by different names in different countries ('mandated outpatient care', 'community treatment orders', 'involuntary outpatient treatment') but the practice is similar the world over and patients are strikingly similar. They generally have long-standing psychosis (usually schizophrenia), they are middle-aged, more often are men, lack insight into their illness, and are isolated and prone to self-neglect. They are not usually considered dangerous and, most importantly, they are already known to respond well to antipsychotics but stop taking them soon after discharge. Legal safeguards and monitoring are invariably tight, as strict as for compulsory inpatient care. Most doctors and nurses use the orders simply to insist on regular supervision such as a weekly outpatient appointment or home visit and ongoing drug treatment. Regular injections of long-acting depot antipsychotic medication is the most common treatment.

The wording in this sort of legislation is convoluted and, frankly, rarely bears careful scrutiny. Read it carefully and you can see that it skirts over the inherent contradictions in mental illnesses that we have repeatedly encountered. Community Treatment Orders (CTOs) in Europe are likely to run for a year or two and may be prolonged even when a patient is as well as he or she ever gets. The justification is that it is in the individual's health interest because it will prevent a relapse. It is basically 'for the patient's own good' and the improvement shows that it is working so it should continue.

There is an obvious Catch-22 here. If you improve on a CTO it shows that it is working and should be prolonged; if you do not improve then you are very ill and need to continue on it until you do. How do you ever get off one? Lawyers call this the 'lobster pot' effect – easy to get into, impossible to get out of. There is no simple answer to this. UK psychiatrists in their original 1993 proposal suggested a limit of three years but it was rejected. In all jurisdictions the CTO duration is determined by a tension deliberately established between the clinicians who use them and the tribunals that monitor them. It is too early to know whether some patients may end up almost permanently on CTOs. It certainly looks possible.

In such complex territory how much of a role should evidence play? CTOs are subject to the same risks that we saw earlier with insulin coma treatment. They are not a magic bullet. Their effects, if any, will become manifest in the future, over several months, and then be only relative, a matter of degree. Nobody expects every patient to recover with the new treatment or every patient to do badly without it, so accumulating clinical experience of the fate of the handful of patients each individual psychiatrist treats cannot provide the answer. Hence the need for rigorous, hard-nosed scientific testing which controls for the influence of selection and wishful thinking. After twenty years of insulin coma treatment its lack of effect was only confirmed when it was subjected to a randomized controlled trial. With CTOs there have been two such RCTs, both in the USA, and neither found a clear benefit.

By the time this book is published my own RCT of CTOs will be published. We have randomized over 300 patients and followed them up for a year. There is absolutely no effect. The CTOs neither reduce relapse and readmission to hospital, nor appear to confer any real benefits in terms of symptoms or general wellbeing. So three studies have failed to find an advantage, despite substantial curtailment of patients' liberties. A salutary experience for me as I have been a strong advocate for twenty years. But I was clearly wrong. Will practice change dramatically in the light of these results? I think it should (otherwise why spend years doing the research?) but I doubt if it will. There are too many other factors involved. However, we cannot continue to insist that coercion in the community reduces relapse and readmission. Any argument for it must rely on other defences.

Most statutes permitting CTOs insist on the same threshold for applying them as for compulsory hospital admission. Patients have to urgently need treatment but, because of their illness, fail to understand that need. Both conditions, the need for treatment and the impaired understanding, are required for the duration of the order. However, this is simply not what happens. We persist with CTOs with patients who have made a substantial recovery and whom nobody would force back into hospital immediately if they stopped taking their treatment. This is obviously the intended purpose of the legislation (to keep patients well) and everyone involved knows it. The wording of the legislation fits very poorly with sensible practice, but luckily lawyers and clinicians seem to arrive at sensible working agreements in most countries.

Compulsory treatment in psychiatry presents a profound challenge to our view of ourselves as entirely autonomous individuals. The concept of the autonomous individual with clearly identified rights and potentially unfettered choices is essential for drafting legislation and running our sorts of societies. But it is not how we really are. It is not how we behave in the situations that matter to us. We may be equal before the law but we do not treat others equally; nor would we expect to be treated equally by our family and friends. Life would be simply impossible if we did not prioritize our close relationships. We devote massively more time, affection and consideration to those close to us and are bound by much stronger obligations. This is obvious in everything we do. Our identity and our agency as individuals are formed by the network of relationships we have had in our past and have now. These don't just enrich our lives, they are a fundamental necessity for it; we simply cannot exist without them.

The psychoanalyst D. W. Winnicott famously declared: 'There is no such thing as a baby.' What did he mean by such a strange statement? He meant that you have to have both a mother and a baby for a baby to exist. Without a mother to give birth to it and feed it there is no baby. It is not that the baby exists and forms a relationship; the relationship exists and slowly from it the baby emerges. The mother is not a desirable 'extra' for the baby but the necessary condition for its existence. And so it is for our wider relationships. Without relationships none of us can survive. This is not a 'touchy-feely' metaphorical statement but a statement of brute fact. Most of us recognize that without relationships we could not survive emotionally, but neither could we survive physically. We are utterly reliant on others for our food, our clothing, our shelter, as well as for our language and our emotional wellbeing and sense of self. We all depend on others from minute to minute, from day to day. Relationships always involve dependency and asymmetry; we are never entirely 'free' or 'equal' in a relationship. If there is no obligation somewhere in it, it is not a relationship, just a chance encounter or an acquaintance. The concept of a fully autonomous individual is a fantasy, an artificial, intellectual construct. Admittedly it is a useful fantasy, but still a fantasy. From day to day it serves us well but psychiatric practice continuously bumps up against it, exposing its limitations.

The overriding of another adult's will in compulsory psychiatric treatment starkly confronts us with this centrality of our relationships, one that we generally ignore. Psychiatry holds up a mirror to us, showing the primacy of our continuing interdependency rather than the fiction of our independence we assume day to day. No wonder it makes us uneasy. The same inherent contradiction confronts us over confidentiality. Psychiatrists are explicitly committed to patient confidentiality; all doctors are. Yet how sensible, fair or ethical is it to withhold information from the mother looking after her adult son because he says so? We know that she will continue to struggle to care for him no matter what; the freedom to walk away from her family duty is another legal fiction. We also know that without her help he could not survive outside hospital and we would otherwise be obliged to compulsorily admit him. Yet when he tells us that she must not be told of his delusions or intentions we are required to respect his autonomy.

Most of the psychiatrists and nurses I know struggle with this mismatch between the language and constraints of our profession and the human dilemmas we deal with. The poor fit between the crisp and logical language of autonomy and civil rights and the messy reality of intertwined human beings will not disappear. I do not believe this is because the language is faulty, or that we just need more carefully drafted legislation. No, it will not go away because this philosophical and ethical contradiction is real. The three 'modern' dilemmas addressed in this chapter all stem from it. Psychiatry is called upon to operate within a Western world view that assumes the interaction of fully conscious and rational, independent individuals. Our society builds its moral and legal systems on the patterns and the 'laws' it discerns in these interactions. Relationships, where they are thought important, such as with marriage or the family, are understood as products of the conscious actions of individuals. Yet the routine practice of psychiatry confirms the very opposite. It is relationships that make individuals possible. Obligations and involvements come first, they are not negotiable.

Dissociation, childhood adversity and coercion have occupied us in this chapter not because they form the bulk of a psychiatrist's working day. Far from it. They are important because they will not let us off the hook; they force us to confront what it is that continues to make psychiatry so puzzling. They also show how psychiatry may help us understand ourselves a bit better.

Solutions for these issues should not be anticipated any time soon and not from within psychiatry. We need acceptable solutions, and psychiatric practice keeps pushing the problems in front of us. But these are not new technical problems or simple matters of science; they are issues of what it is to be human, philosophical and ethical questions arising from our very nature. No research finding will solve them. They require us to balance important but conflicting principles such as autonomy, beneficence and fairness. In this psychiatry is dependent on the ethical stances of the society in which it operates, for good and ill. The luxury we do not have is to declare ourselves unsatisfied with current thinking and to tell our patients to go away and come back some years hence when we have the answers.

13

The rise of neuroscience and the future of psychiatry

Virtually every significant development in psychiatry has come completely out of the blue. Antidepressants were stumbled upon trying to cure tuberculosis, antipsychotics by a military anaesthetist. Who could have foreseen malaria treatment for GPI or the impact of psychoanalysis? There have been periods of steady, planned progress in refining treatments, but the big changes are just impossible to predict. Nothing strange about that really, it is the same in most of medicine and in life in general. Nobody predicted the internet or the HIV epidemic. So this chapter will be short and tentative.

There are a few things that seem fairly certain for the next half-century. We will get to know more, much more, about how the brain works; neuroscience is off the starting blocks and racing away. We will also have a vastly better understanding of genetics and how genes interact with experience in mental illnesses. My hunch is that the pay-off in mental illness may be as much in understanding the social as the biological contribution to this interaction. Third, the relationship between mind and brain (or mind and body, whichever you prefer) will be just as unclear a hundred years from now as it has been for the last four centuries. We will undoubtedly have a more scientific vocabulary for it, 'bio-babble' will have replaced 'psycho-babble'. But the fundamental question of who and what we are and the mystery of consciousness are unlikely to disappear. And lastly, on balance, I believe we will probably still have psychiatry and psychiatrists in some form that we can recognize.

Neuroscience is in the ascendant. It is the most intellectually exciting, and the most generously funded, area of bio-medicine research at the start of the twenty-first century. The rate of discovery is breathtaking and the volume of popular literature reflects this. Neuroscience and neuroscientists are everywhere – in our bookshops and newspapers, on radio and TV talk shows. Along with evolutionary biologists they are our new social pundits with advice on everything from the problem of evil to how to choose a mate. The range and confidence of their utterances are strikingly reminiscent of psychoanalysts in the 1950s and 1960s. It is not surprising. Two technologies have changed neuroscience out of all recognition. New neuro-imaging instruments visualize the structures of the brain in truly remarkable detail. Even more spectacularly, they can visualize its activity. They are light-years ahead of the older technologies such as EEG, air encephalography and CT scanners. Then there are the advances in genetics. We have moved on from the painstaking detective work of inferring the genes for specific disorders by tracking complex family trees. We are now able to replicate the genes themselves, manipulate them and locate their position on identified chromosomes. In the era of the human genome we can carry out cheaply and quickly in the laboratory deter-minations that used to take months or years – if they could be done at all.

Mental hospitals had always contained large numbers of patients with obvious damage to their brains (general paralysis of the insane, dementias, head injuries, post-encephalitic disorders, epilepsy). They were often collected together under an umbrella term of 'organic dis-orders', and their status as mental illnesses was ambiguous. Psychiatry is generally required to take responsibility for disturbances of behav-iour or experience if there is no obvious anatomical abnormality. This is why we use the term mental illnesses rather than brain illnesses, and why schizophrenia and manic depression used to be referred to as 'functional psychoses'. They were thought to be disorders of the func-tioning of the mind, not abnormalities of brain structure. For decades psychiatrists have examined post-mortem brains of these patients in a futile search for physical causes.

Changes are afoot. Until recently physical abnormalities in the brain had to be quite gross to be detected and so they almost in-variably also caused neurological symptoms. The first of the new imaging techniques was CT scanning, computed tomography. Intro-duced in the mid-1970s CT uses computer software to build a three-dimensional image from a series of cross-sectional (slice) X-rays. It improved the accuracy of identifying underlying physical problems in the brain such as small strokes but it failed to make any significant breakthroughs in mental illness.

Magnetic resonance imaging (MRI) produces much more accurate images, particularly in soft tissues such as the brain. It uses a powerful magnetic field rather than X-rays so it is safer than CT scanning and can be repeated to track changes over time. Because it gives such high-quality pictures it is possible to measure the size of individual brain structures with great accuracy. We now know that average brain sizes are slightly smaller in schizophrenia with some continued shrinkage in specific areas over time. These differences are not great and nor are they absolute; there are healthy individuals with small brain sizes and afflicted individuals with normal brain sizes. So while such findings illuminate possible disease processes they do not help with diagnosis. However, such investigations help bridge the cultural gap between psychiatry and medicine.

Functional MRI scanning (*f*MRI) measures activity in the brain by registering very localized changes in blood flow and oxygen uptake. This yields remarkable pictures where individual areas of the brain 'light up' when they are active. By asking people to do various things (talk, sing, look at faces, count) or simply think about them (scary thoughts, pleasant thoughts, mathematics) we can work out which parts of the brain are involved. One Dutch study even got people to make love in a scanner. We now know that the same parts of the brain are activated when psychotic patients hallucinate voices as when we hear real voices. The brain areas associated with empathy are less active in autistic patients and the frontal lobes less active in schizophrenia. These studies are a step-change in relating the pathological processes in mental illnesses to equivalent psychological processes in healthy individuals and promise ever greater understanding of what is going on in mental illnesses.

We can find out better how drugs such as antipsychotics or antidepressants work by measuring brain activity with and without them. We can identify the brain areas drugs act on, and even what doses are effective. By measuring the doses of antipsychotics needed to reduce neuro-transmitter over-activity in the frontal lobes, low doses of haloperidol were found to be as effective as the much larger doses commonly in use. We now use these lower doses to get the full anti-psychotic effect but with fewer side effects.

Mapping the human genome is one of the most outstanding achievements of modern biology. Since Watson and Crick described the double-helix structure of DNA in 1953 genetics has been revolutionized. We now investigate individual genes directly, rather than simply tracking their effects. Classical Mendelian inheritance, with either half or a quarter of all offspring affected, does not feature much in psychiatry. There is no schizophrenia gene, no alcoholism gene, but instead a range of relatively common genes with cumulative effects. Several so-called 'candidate' genes have been identified for each of the major mental illnesses. You can have the disease without the specific genes, and you can have the specific genes without the disease. However, the more of the implicated genes you have the higher your risk of developing the disease.

We can now identify relevant genes directly in individuals even if there is no sign of the disease. We now routinely test members of families with Huntington's disease (a single dominant gene disorder which means that half the offspring will develop it) and know if they are carrying the gene. This is important because the terrible dementia associated with this disease develops in middle age after victims have had their children. If they know their genetic status early on they can make better-informed decisions about whether to have a family. We will soon be able to map all the risky genes for an individual and in the longer term perhaps even replace them or deactivate them. Sequencing the first human genome took fifteen years from start to finish and cost over $3bn. By 2012 a single machine could sequence five individual human genomes in two weeks for just $5,000 each.

Already our genetic knowledge has improved diagnostics and prediction of response to drug treatments. We have already discussed progress in predicting psychiatric responses to different life experiences. Early childhood abuse is much more likely to result in depression in those individuals with specific, identified genes than those without them. But this is really just the start – the future possibilities seem limitless. These range from individually tailored treatments based on our genetic profile rather than our symptoms, right through to directly manipulating the genes themselves. Genes have already been introduced into mice to make them anxious, and we have been experimenting with finding ways to turn individual genes on and off.

The ethical challenges for psychiatry of the new genomics are obvious enough. We already screen embryos for a range of serious congenital disorders with the possibility of terminating the pregnancy. Will we start screening for risk genes for schizophrenia and depression or autism? Or might we go even further and screen for specific personality traits such as aggression? What would be an acceptable level of probability for considering a termination? Would it really make any difference? And what would the impact be on us if we did start to alter the behavioural profile of our species in this way? It is impossible to guess, but it is difficult to believe that such powerful technologies will not be fully exploited. The consequences will be far-reaching for every one of us.

'Mental Illnesses are Brain Illnesses' is no new slogan. Influential psychiatrists have been proclaiming brain diseases as their proper subject since the start of the nineteenth century. Modern neuroscientists insist with remarkable confidence that the distinction between mind and brain is now redundant, or it will be in the very near future. I often feel I must be missing something here. I am unaware of any fundamental philosophical breakthrough in our understanding of the mystery of consciousness and identity. Insisting that the mind is no more than the brain has a deceptively benign and contemporary ring to it. But it simply side-steps the question of human consciousness that has preoccupied our greatest philosophers for centuries; it is not a solution to it. When we think about it carefully we see, as generations of philosophers have seen, that it carries far-reaching implications. These include the existence of free will and the reality of moral choice. Not minor details.

Almost invariably the model put forward for the mind as brain is some form of analogy with computers. If we are no more than a computer that processes inputs according to a series of set algorithms, then where do choice and responsibility lie? How can we hold people morally accountable for their behaviour? Each new psychological experiment conducted within this paradigm confirms our predictability. Yet somehow this just does not fit with how we understand ourselves, nor with how we conduct our lives. As human beings we seem to *have* to believe in our own free will, otherwise everything, from self-awareness through to civilization itself, becomes impossible. Even faiths based on predetermination or fate hold their members personally accountable for their day-to-day behaviour. A striking irony is that in our rational and enlightened societies the more we accept scientific explanations of 'automatic' brain processes, the more we seem to value and defend individual choice and free will.

Even the most ardent proponents of the 'computer brain' behave as if they were themselves conscious agents. Our response to each new discovery about what is 'hard-wired' in our brains is to consider what its consequences are for us, how we *should* behave. Psychology may confirm what we are likely to do but it is not a guide to what we *should* do. We strive to accommodate such findings or, with some of the most important ones such as those on gender differences, to modify them through education and social pressure.

We know (or think we know) what we mean when we say 'I'. It involves a sense of continuity across time and, above all, choice, motivation, free will. Schizophrenia, that most iconic of mental illnesses, has at its core the terrifying experience of losing this sense of coherence and not being sure what 'I' means. Identity and consciousness as simple side effects of electrical activity in the brain convinces few of us.

Emphasizing the brain as the afflicted organ in mental illnesses in the 1990s 'Decade of the Brain' was primarily political; its aim was to reduce discrimination against the mentally ill. Stressing the equivalence between mental and physical illnesses was a step towards removing stigma and ensuring equal treatment. The message was that mental illnesses were not the result of weakness or self-indulgence; nor were they associated with violence and danger. They are just as much personal bad luck as diabetes or cancer. Anti-stigma campaigns stressed the 'normality' of mental illnesses and countered vague and primitive fears of psychic contagion. The fear that being around people with mental illness could affect our own sanity is never far below the surface. Psychiatrists have to live with it constantly in the endless jokes about how our job makes us become odd.

Anti-stigma campaigns have been relatively disappointing. We appear to be, if anything, more accepting of mental illness when we think of it as a personal struggle than as an impersonal medical process like diabetes or cancer. Overcoming adversity, despair and anxiety testify to the human spirit and courage. It is the very stuff of humanity and readily engages our sympathy. This is not, however, a plea to abandon anti-stigma campaigns or for some romantic vision of mental illness. We must find ways to reduce stigma and discrimination but it will require more than educational programmes stressing the brain. Public attitudes towards depression have become much more enlightened as celebrities and sportsmen talk openly about their experiences. What seems most successful is personal contact and engagement with individual sufferers. It is personal experience that really brings home how awful mental illnesses are. It shows us that the illness is only one aspect of the person who still retains much of his or her uniqueness. We also then can see that it is outside their control. In politics it is this direct personal experience that drives investment in mental health as President Kennedy exemplified.

Accepting that having a mental illness is as much pure bad luck as having arthritis or cancer does not mean we have to deny the very special nature of the suffering involved. Yes they are illnesses like others, but not *just* like others. The mind is not the brain and mental illnesses continue to be experienced as changing *us*, not a part of us. We are still a long way from mental illnesses being simply absorbed into general medicine.

The imminent demise of psychiatry has been predicted since its very inception. It has been in existence now for 200 years; will it survive another 200? There is plenty of doubt about it, even within the profession. Internally the commonest expectation is that we will split into two. Major mental illness, the psychoses, would remain broadly within medicine and the psychiatrists who diagnosed and treated them would move closer to neurology. The remaining disorders, and the treatments based on psychotherapy, would move to psychologists and psychotherapists. Another alternative being explored is a split more along the 'acute/chronic' divide. Acute care would remain with medicine, and long-term care of severe mental illnesses would move to social care. The more imaginative in the profession envisage us more as applied neuroscientists and physiologists rather than the sort of doctor we are used to now. Likewise psychotherapists will be a new breed of behavioural technicians, not the counsellors and careful, empathic listeners we are familiar with.

The call within the profession for such a split is not limited to a handful of eccentrics or visionaries. Many believe it is essential for progress, and that it is a real and imminent possibility. A change of name to 'behavioural neurologists' or 'clinical neuroscientists' is regularly proposed. The aim would be to make a break with what is considered a discredited past and a stigmatized present. On close examination this seems less a split, with the scope of psychiatry remaining basically unchanged, and more a retrenchment, with psychiatry shrinking to its more long-established, traditional responsibilities.

Even without such radical surgery many psychiatrists are already trying to alter the perception of our profession. They use newer, more scientific descriptions of treatments when consulting with patients. So instead of concluding, 'You have depression and I am going to prescribe antidepressants to help lift your mood', they offer the opportunity of medication to 'boost your lowered serotonin levels and reverse a negative appraisal set'. Many patients who reject psychiatric diagnoses on the grounds that they are of meagre validity and lack scientific credibility may accept these (in truth far more speculative) descriptions. Even if this is just window-dressing there is an important message in it, acknowledging an undeniable credibility gap still to be closed. This gap is not new in itself but the questions that fuel it change from generation to generation. Three likely developments will be considered, but who can predict what will drive change?

BETTER THAN WELL?

Has psychiatry a role in making us all feel happier? Should it be involved in helping us become 'better than well'? Freud certainly thought not; his goal was 'transforming [your] hysterical misery into common unhappiness'. But that was then and we now have a very different attitude towards our lot in life. The American declaration of independence guaranteed 'life, liberty and the *pursuit of happiness*' for its citizens and most of us now really do expect this. Happiness is seen as a legitimate individual aspiration that can, indeed *should*, be sought. It is not simply a consequence of living a good life. The goal of increasing human happiness and wellbeing consumes much scientific, social, economic and political energy.

Cognitive neuroscience provides a constant stream of insights into the sources and mechanisms of our wellbeing. It charts which parts of the brain are involved in it, what processes maintain it and how we can improve it. Ingenious experiments, one after another, demonstrate how our mood and thinking are directly influenced without us being aware of it so that we usually believe the changes are spontaneous. For instance, just a single dose of antidepressants causes people to view the world more positively. The changes are small but clearly measurable using reliable psychological measures. A neutral face shown on a computer screen is consistently more often described as friendly after just one antidepressant tablet. What is really remarkable is that the subjects describe absolutely no change in their mood at all.

Freud's 'fanciful theory' of the power of the unconscious is being richly confirmed by neuroscience research, although the accumulating evidence is that these unconscious processes underpin our healthy functioning, not just make us neurotic. All of us, not just those with psychiatric problems, are constantly at the mercy of our unconscious mental processes, and our unconscious processes are at the mercy of the events around us. These determine our wellbeing and our mood much more than we had ever previously recognized. A wonderful irony is that so many of these findings are made by the very scientists who would be the fiercest critics of Freudian psychotherapy.

The power of these processes is now so well established that even politicians and economists use them. Richard H. Thaler and Cass R. Sunstein outlined some of them in their celebrated 2008 book *Nudge: Improving Decisions about Health, Wealth and Happiness*. Using 'behavioural economics' they showed how our decisions are constantly being manipulated without us being aware, and are quoted by governments from across the political spectrum. Happiness indices are routinely used to compare subjective wellbeing across different nationalities and groups. One year the Finns are the happiest people in the world, the next it is the Brazilians or the Danes. Simple forms of psychotherapy have been made available nationwide, bypassing routine psychiatry entirely. What is radically different is not the treatments involved but that their aim is to improve wellbeing, not to treat illness. Few of those receiving them would be considered psychiatrically ill.

To achieve improved wellbeing just about anything and everything can be in the frame, from yoga to plastic surgery. Increasingly this includes prescription medicines, including psychiatric ones. We have traditionally taken a rather puritanical stand on this: 'We treat illnesses.' However, the public clearly think otherwise. Viagra was developed to treat impotence but already most of it is bought by healthy men to improve their sex lives. Several psychiatric medications are becoming lifestyle aids rather than treatments. Cognitive enhancers (so-called 'smart drugs') and the stimulants prescribed for ADHD are now commonplace on university campuses or used by jet-lagged executives. The indications on the packets are for narcolepsy or ADHD but that does not stop them being used to improve concentration and increase energy. What is defined as illness and as normality has always been fluid and psychiatry cannot always dictate on this; it has no immunity from such changes. Today's 'normal' may soon be considered unbearable suffering and psychiatrists will presumably be called upon to treat it. Just as anaesthetics changed our tolerance of pain irrevocably, so psychotropic drugs and effective psychotherapies are surely revolutionizing our tolerance of sadness and distress.

This could have an impact either way on psychiatry as a profession. The most likely in the short term is that it will continue the apparently inexorable widening of psychiatry's boundaries, extending the medicalization of everyday life. However, the opposite could happen. There might be a widespread disenchantment with psychiatry's ability to deliver on this front and a defection to alternative providers. Just as medical approaches have proved ineffective for obesity or excessive alcohol consumption, so antidepressants and psychotherapy may be abandoned as solutions for dissatisfaction or worry. Some psychological equivalent of the health club or gym could fill the gap. These may be less immediately effective but surely more accessible and sustainable, and ultimately more honest. Ironically the potential of the wellbeing movement to swamp psychiatry may be the profession's intellectual salvation. Simple economics may oblige a much needed review and retrenchment.

TREATING BEFORE SYMPTOMS START

Australians and Americans have already experimented with identifying individuals at 'ultra-high risk' for schizophrenia and treating them before the disease starts. The identification is based on family history and certain so-called 'prodromal symptoms' such as strange ideas or oddities of behaviour. A couple of trials with small groups of at-risk adolescents found that low-dose antipsychotics reduced the proportion of 'transitions' – those who go on to develop the full-blown disease. Some who received the drugs still went on to become ill and some who did not get them remained well but the drugs seemed to reduce the risk. These trials remain controversial, with small samples and inconsistent effects. It is not absolutely certain if the treatment prevents the start of the illness or simply treats its very earliest stages. However, it is the principle that matters, not the details. The dilemmas presented by such trials are fairly obvious. What happens if the prediction is wrong? If we started the medication we would never know that it was unnecessary; that the person receiving it failed to become ill would confirm the 'correctness' of the prediction. This would be quite a price for any of us to pay. How much greater a price, then, for an insecure teenager who has seen a brother or sister have a breakdown? Such an ultra-high-risk group has been proposed as a specific diagnosis in the new *DSM-V*.

These early trials are a timely warning of what lies ahead as inevitable consequences of current gene research. Medical geneticists call our genetic make-up the 'genotype' and our illnesses the 'phenotype'. They expect soon to be able to define many illnesses and target their treatments based on the genotype, rather than on the messy and variable clinical picture, the phenotype, as we do currently. They have good reason to be confident. The presence or absence of specific genes, the genotype, has already been used to identify differences in treatment outcome and susceptibility in patients with the same diagnosis, the same phenotype. We know from sequencing the genes of patients with some diseases that a specific treatment will work for one but not the other. In psychiatry we can already identify genetic pointers to level of response to treatment such as doses of antidepressants. So treatment strategies in patients with apparently identical illnesses may be very different, determined by the genes they have. We may sometimes know in advance that a treatment will not work. Explaining these clinical choices will not be easy but it is already a reality in many branches of medicine.

Knowing an individual's genetic make-up may also mean we can identify a need for treatment before there are any symptoms at all. This is why the research with ultra-high-risk schizophrenia patients is so important. Such knowledge is already stretching current medical ethics. The increasing precision and sophistication of genotyping will fundamentally alter medicine, and perhaps psychiatry most of all. We are already used to preventative measures in physical illnesses, such as healthy middle-aged men taking daily aspirin to reduce their risk of heart attacks. Individuals with strong family histories of some cancers may take even more drastic action, including pre-emptive surgery. What would a psychiatric equivalent be? If two of your family had suffered from depression should you take antidepressants 'just in case'? How feasible would it be to undertake preventative psychotherapy? We already have a potential model for this in mindfulness CBT. This is a successful form of psychotherapy for people who have suffered recurrent depression. They engage in the therapy when they are recovered rather than during the illness and it reduces the risk of falling ill again. But could you do it if you had never been depressed? Would it work? This will probably cease to be a purely academic question fairly soon. 'We only treat illnesses' is already a hollow slogan for psychiatry, even if it still gives some comfort.

NEW TECHNOLOGY OR SCIENCE FICTION?

I recently sat between two dinner guests with very contrasting views on psychiatry. One was an enthusiast for Jungian analysis who tried to convince me throughout the evening that all 'this medical stuff' was just a distraction from what really mattered and that we should get on and ditch it. From a neuroscientist across the table I got a similarly dusty assessment of present-day psychiatry. He told me to ignore our

Jungian; neuroscience was about to sweep psychiatry, psychotherapy and me into oblivion. Starting from the example of deep-brain stimulation he argued that within a generation we would be regularly using specific invasive treatments of the brain to treat psychiatric – or, as he insisted on calling them, brain – disorders directly. We would 'cut out the middle man'; there would be no need for all this history taking and discussion to identify the problem, or even to ask how it was going. Probes would locate the responsible brain dysfunction and confirm improvement and cure.

Deep brain stimulation is an example of such a direct brain treatment and is still very experimental. It involves placing electrodes into the brain and then using a machine like a heart pacemaker to deliver regular small bursts of electricity. There have been some promising results in Parkinson's disease and in depression. It would not stop there, I was told. Various procedures using laser surgery, light treatment and slow-release implants were just round the corner. I found it all a bit overwhelming but, in truth, is it that outlandish?

The practice of psychiatry in the future will surely involve vastly more technology. The use of computers and mobile phone technology is already being embraced. Self-administered computer programs for treating both anxiety and depression are widely available. Mobile phones and texting are increasingly used to monitor mood and to support adherence to long-term treatments. These are essentially just technical supports to established treatments and most depend on the patient using the technology rather than the psychiatrist. A cross-fertilization of current neuroscience discoveries with modern computer and software technologies is sure to give rise to radically new and creative approaches. Computerized speech pattern analysis, for instance, can already indicate potential depression, and mobility assessed by tracking mobile phones can be used to spot developing Parkinson's disease. So while I believe the profession will survive, it needs us to embrace the changes imposed upon it by new discoveries and technologies, but also to be much clearer about what we can and cannot do.

The main threat to psychiatry's survival may not be its critics or technological innovations. The last ten to fifteen years have seen a dramatic fall in the number of doctors choosing to go into it. In the

USA and the UK there is now an average of less than one applicant for every post. Posts remain unfilled, often for years in rural areas. In mainland Europe the fall is not so extreme nor yet so obvious thanks to a long-standing overproduction of doctors. In truth the shortage is much worse than the USA and UK figures indicate. Most doctors coming into psychiatry in these two countries are foreign graduates. While migrant doctors have always made a rich contribution to psychiatry (think of the Jewish diaspora in the 1930s) this cannot be a sustainable situation. Rich countries should not rely on luring away medical graduates needed in the homelands which trained them. Nor can it be good to staff psychiatry with large numbers of doctors who are often disappointed by not being able to get surgical or medical jobs. No matter how one dresses it up it sends a clear message about the current status of psychiatry within medicine. It is not high.

To maintain current psychiatric staffing we need about 4 per cent of all medical students to take it up, which is simply not happening. Even if it were it might not be adequate. After decades of underinvestment mental health services, long the 'Cinderella' specialty, are due some expansion. To reverse the trend needs agreement on its causes and currently there is no such agreement.

The strongest voice comes from academic psychiatry, where the recruitment crisis is even more acute. It is proving very difficult to attract talented doctors into research training and their place is being taken by psychologists and pre-clinical scientists (physiologists, pharmacologists, geneticists). The academics' diagnosis is that psychiatry's expertise has been diluted and devalued in the move to community care and multidisciplinary working with a drift more towards a more social sciences paradigm. They see an urgent need to 'remedicalize' it, and strategies to achieve it are urgently sought on both sides of the Atlantic. The proposal is a more explicitly medical training re-emphasizing physiology, pharmacology and scientific method and including extended periods in neurology or general medicine. A more medical training would result in a clearer definition of all the roles in the multidisciplinary team – doctors would do medical tasks, nurses nursing tasks, social workers social care etc. There is an immediately intuitive appeal in such a proposal. It would make a job in psychiatry much more hospital-based and much more like all the other specialties.

Lack of clarity about the psychiatrist's role in mental health services is something everyone complains about, not just the psychiatrists. I was personally very active in the early promotion of 'role blurring' in mental health teams but have to confess that it has gone much further than I had ever expected. I can now recognize it as a problem where once I saw it as a solution. I remain confident, however, that we can do something to strengthen the core skills of diagnosis, psychopharmacology and clinical management without a wholesale retreat from effective multidisciplinary working. The problems of status are, however, less tractable. Confusion over roles within these teams is intimately linked to conflict over hierarchy and the status of doctors, and there is no agreement here. Other professions in these teams reject a leadership role for medics. Doctors are fairly status-conscious individuals with a strong respect for expertise and authority and in all other branches of medicine they head the clinical team. It is difficult to see recruitment to psychiatry improving while their status remains reduced or ambiguous.

While this approach of remedicalizing psychiatry and making it more scientific has intuitive appeal it is not without its problems. I certainly have my doubts about it and there are a couple of observations which speak against it. First psychiatry's status, and its ability to attract good-quality people, was at its highest when psychotherapy and psychoanalysis held sway. We may be very sniffy now about the lack of science in this period but patients and families seemed to like it, and so did practitioners. I came into psychiatry when the anti-psychiatry controversies were raging and there was no shortage of recruits then. It may be that psychiatry appeals to psychologically and socially minded medical students, those more enamoured of ideas and human complexity than statistics and test-tubes. The academics who argue for a remedicalization often speak in terms of 'dumbing down', but one could just as easily argue that the abandonment of phenomenology and psychotherapy for a purely symptom-based profession is dumbing down.

There is a risk that in moving to a more medical approach we may lose those who in the past were attracted to psychiatry's holistic practice. Judged purely as a medical technology, psychiatry, with its limited range of drugs and few physical treatments, will struggle to compete with more developed and glamorous specialties. Perhaps most importantly highly medicalized psychiatry only gets you so far. It has been associated with a neglect of a whole-person perspective and attention to the social and psychological processes that most people want from modern care. This was essentially what the anti-psychiatrists such as Goffman and Laing wrote about. It has certainly been my experience. The white-coated medical-model psychiatrists are the ones who most often preside over limited, mechanical and one-sided treatment regimes with over-inclusive diagnoses. The medical approach is essential, and it is vital that it is done right, but in itself it is simply not enough.

Psychiatry does not operate in a vacuum and this recruitment crisis does not just affect us. Nurses, social workers and clinical psychologists all have something to say about it. In role-blurred teams they pick up the slack and make up for shortages. These teams may not be willing to wait while psychiatry sorts out its internal professional priorities. The future practice of psychiatry may not be determined by our academic working parties but by the impatience of our highly skilled colleagues forced to find alternative ways to meet patients' needs. It is they who may shape psychiatry's future.

Epilogue

Psychiatry is a child of the Enlightenment, a reflection of the rational impulse to explore our world and understand ourselves better. It arose from two quite improbable sources, the teeming madhouses of late-seventeenth-century France and England and from that travelling showman, Anton Mesmer, who used suggestion and hypnosis to relieve tormented individuals. In its 200 years it has both shaped the care and treatment of the mentally ill and also irrevocably changed how we understand ourselves. Psychoanalysis and psychotherapy have not just given us insights into the sufferings of the mentally ill but enabled us to look into our own souls. They have changed our language, our relationships and our institutions. It has not all been a steady triumphal march of progress. There have been some dead-ends, reversals and disputes along the way.

Psychiatry is not a tidy subject. It does not fit easily into a simple, logical framework. Science is, rightly, the dominant intellectual model of our age and we might want psychiatry to fit this mould – with its laws and predictions and deductions. Psychiatry certainly aspires to be scientific and increasingly brings such discipline and rigour to bear on its practice. But it is more than a science. It is a practical response to the reality of the mental illnesses which have determined its shape and character.

While it may not have the monolithic structure of a science it is far from being a random activity. There are a set of recognizable and consistent practices and enduring organizing principles. A psychiatrist has to first recognize a disorder, e.g. depression, as a whole in order to understand the significance of individual symptoms such as agitation or insomnia. So we need a broad grasp of what psychiatry is to understand each of the many individual controversies surrounding it. My belief is that it is difficult to form a coherent understanding of psychiatry today without some knowledge of its exotic origins and its eventful history, so the first part of the book has focused on that history before plunging into the challenges that this most human and personal branch of medicine confronts us with, and trying to understand what it is that makes many of us so uneasy about psychiatry.

This history has not glossed over psychiatry's errors; indeed it may have devoted too much space to them. They did, however, happen and they should be acknowledged. In psychiatry, as in much of life, confronting uncomfortable truths may have much to teach us. Psychiatrists have their failings and limitations like all human beings; whether we have more than average can be argued. As with any profession it has had its share of bad apples and people who really should never have been allowed to practise. Again it is impossible to say if this is more than in medicine generally. But even if that were the case it would not fully explain the persisting unease about psychiatry. I do not believe that it is the occasional error or disaster but psychiatry's very nature that makes us uneasy. It operates in uncharted, anxiety-laden and shifting territory. If the mind really were just the brain, and psychiatry simply the medical specialty concerned with that one organ, there would be no real fuss. Freeman's psycho-surgery crusade or Henry Cotton's misguided pursuit of sepsis were terrible aberrations but they are little known. They feed into the disquiet rather than cause it.

No, the real problem is that psychiatry cannot avoid intruding into those aspects of us that we find most frightening and threatening. These are precisely the things we try to ignore, to push away; what Jung called our shadow. Analysts have argued that madness and mental illness are so frightening because we recognize in them our own out-of-control impulses. We need to export these impulses and imprison them in some disturbed 'other'. Foucault argued that this is what psychiatry strives to do. Yet modern psychiatric practice unsettles this reassuring belief. By trying to make madness and mental illness more understandable we make it more personal and bring it closer. While it may be a shadow, it is a shadow that closely follows our outline and constantly reminds us about ourselves.

Psychiatry also meddles in our most intimate concerns, our hopes and expectations, self-understanding and self-image. It can itself become a player in the unfolding drama of our lives. It often *has* to intrude, both to make its diagnoses and then to effect its treatments. Nothing brings this home with more brutal clarity than its unique power of compulsory treatment, when it presumes to distinguish a person's 'real' self and wishes from his or her current 'ill' self and wishes. Whatever professional group takes on such meddling is sure to have its motives and authority questioned.

We object loudly to such compulsion and hedge it in with detailed rules and regulations, but is this meddling in others' lives really such an awful thing? How many of us would prefer a life where we were left entirely to our own devices? We value our freedom and independence but how lonely and empty would we feel if absolutely nobody cared strongly enough about us to interfere? Do we really want such respect for our autonomy that we are left to sink or swim? Few, I suspect, really would; I certainly would not.

We are social animals and cannot exist except in relationships with each other. Modern psychiatric research and our professional vocabulary treat the patient as a self-contained independent individual. In this we are no different to the society around us, emphasizing freedom and choice. We talk as if we can exist without relationships if we choose to do so, that we can decide which relationships to have and which to ignore. Psychiatric practice gives the lie to this construction; it is inextricably bound up in relationships.

Everything about psychiatry is rooted in social reality, definitions, diagnostics and treatment. Psychiatric symptoms only acquire significance when social meaning is given to them – being awake at four in the morning is only important if you don't want to be awake then or are usually not awake then. Diagnoses are constructed by a complex social process of comparison with those around the patient, a knowledge of the patient's usual self and a judgement of the 'value' of intervention. Lastly, all treatments take place in social relationships.

Whether understanding how our patients got into their current predicaments or working with them to deal with their dilemmas, we are never simply dispassionate observers of isolated self-contained phenomena. All our judgements and decisions, and all our actions, are determined within this relationship. It is no surprise there is a tension between this understanding and current scientific approaches based on investigating individuals. Nor should we be surprised that comprehensive and satisfactory ethical guidelines for managing autonomy and confidentiality remain tantalizingly just out of reach.

So will psychiatry soon be redundant, an exotic footnote in the triumphal march of medical history? I doubt it. It is currently struggling through one of its recurrent 'crises' but I believe it is likely to survive. That does not mean that I expect or want it to remain the same. On one level I fervently hope that I am wrong and that it does become redundant and disappear. A world without mental illness must be vastly better than one with it. Arguments that we would be deprived of art and creativity may bring some comfort, but they have a hollow ring. A world without mental illness would not be a world without suffering, but it would be a world spared suffering at its most cruel and unfair. Until that time when we are free of mental illness, mankind will seek comfort from psychiatry, its necessary shadow.

Glossary

Definitions are the author's

agitation An unpleasant sense of restlessness and over-activity.

agoraphobia An anxiety state in which people are anxious and panicky in public spaces such as shopping centres and crowded streets. Agoraphobic patients often become housebound to avoid such situations.

alcohol units One 'unit of alcohol' is equivalent to half a pint of beer or a small glass of wine. It is equivalent to 10 millilitres of pure alcohol. Health risks increase with the number of units consumed per week and there are guidelines for healthy consumption. Currently these are 14 units per week for women and 21 units per week for men in the UK. They are constantly under revision.

Alzheimer's dementia The most common form of *dementia* in old age. It is characterized by a gradual loss of short-term memory (although memory for distant events may be retained). In its severe forms it leads to disorientation so patients may not know where they are or what the date is, or even recognize family members.

anorexia nervosa A disorder marked by an individual's extreme avoidance of food, loss of weight, and persisting belief that he or she is fat. It is sometimes associated with vomiting and mainly affects teenage girls but can become chronic.

antisocial personality disorder See *psychopath*.

anxiety Unpleasant sense of fear and tension.

appraisal The manner in which experiences are judged. Depressed patients, for example, have a 'negative appraisal set' which emphasizes a pessimistic view of experiences.

Asperger's syndrome A developmental disorder similar to *autism* but less severe. Features are emotional rigidity, eccentricity and limited understanding of the emotional life of others.

attachment The shaping of adult relationships through the process of early bonding between child and mother. Introduced by the psychoanalyst John Bowlby.

attachment theory A theory emphasizing the need for an early secure relationship between infant and mother.

attention deficit hyperactivity disorder (ADHD) Over-activity and poor concentration usually diagnosed in pre-adolescents, mainly boys. Treatment is often by psychostimulants such as Ritalin.

attribution bias The tendency to explain events in terms of behaviour. We generally believe we have more influence over events than is the case.

autism A developmental disorder usually obvious in early childhood. In its most extreme form it interferes with all forms of communication. Features are preoccupation with routine and rigidity and the inability to understand the emotional responses of other people. More common in boys and increasingly diagnosed in recent decades.

automatism When an individual appears to be still sleeping or in a dream-like state, and does out-of-character things without being able to recall them later.

aversion therapy A treatment based on *learning theory* to reduce unwanted behaviour by associating it repeatedly with unpleasant stimuli such as small electric shocks.

behaviour therapy The rigorous application of *learning theory* to change behaviour by consistent reinforcement (rewarding desired behaviour, punishing unwanted behaviour).

belle indifférence Strange mood state in which there is a lack of appropriate concern. Often noted in patients with *hysterical* disorders who appear emotionally unaffected despite their disabling symptoms.

bipolar disorder A severe mental illness with periods of depression and sometimes elation. This includes but is wider than the older term *manic-depressive disorder*. Bipolar disorder is divided into bipolar I, which has at least a single period of elation, and bipolar II with no elated episodes but recurrent depressive episodes.

birth cohort study A *cohort study* in which individuals are followed up from birth and assessed at fixed intervals.

borderline personality disorder A personality disorder marked by extreme emotionality, intense relationships and self-harm. Most often diagnosed in women and often associated with histories of sexual abuse.

catharsis A sudden and dramatic release of emotion and tension. A prominent feature of early psychotherapies, particularly those involving hypnosis and suggestion.

certified An early form of compulsory detention for treatment. Certified patients lost not only their right to refuse treatment but most other civil and personal rights as well.

chronic fatigue syndrome (CFS) A highly controversial disorder consisting of lassitude and rapid fatigue. Often referred to as myalgic encephalomyelitis (ME). Controversy persists about whether its origins are predominantly physical or psychological.

cognitive behaviour therapy (CBT) A form of brief, focused psychotherapy which addresses dysfunctional thoughts more than emotions. Relies heavily on a 'Socratic dialogue' in which patients are challenged to question themselves to understand their behaviour and thoughts and utilizes psychological homework.

cognitive Various mental processes such as attention and memory in the handling of information in order to understand it and make decisions.

cohort study A study based on following up a stable group (cohort) of individuals and measuring their status at repeated intervals.

coma A state of persisting unconsciousness.

Community Mental Health Team (CMHT) A multidisciplinary group of professionals (e.g. doctors, psychiatrists, nurses, psychologists, social workers) who work together to care for a group of patients outside hospital.

Community Psychiatric Nurse (CPN) A qualified mental health nurse whose work is predominantly conducted outside hospital, visiting patients in their homes, monitoring and supporting them.

conditioning See *operant conditioning*.

conversion Physical symptoms without organic cause generated by the 'conversion' of unconscious psychological conflicts.

cortex The outer part of the brain containing the grey matter.

countertransference Strong emotions in a psychotherapist towards a patient and generated by transferred emotions from that patient. Frequently now used to indicate any emotion felt by a therapist during therapy.

cretinism Old term for a learning disability resulting from iodine deficiency, often associated with goitre. Now very rare but previously common in isolated and mountainous areas.

CT scan (computed tomography) Computer-assisted X-rays providing a 3D image by adding together 'slice' X-rays at small intervals through the body.

deinstitutionalization The process of moving long-term patients out of mental hospitals and settling them in the community.

delirium A period of clouded consciousness and confusion. Often caused by intoxication or physical illness. Patients are often unaware of who they are or where they are and may be very frightened and distressed.

delusional perception A powerful, utterly inexplicable new knowledge without any preceding explanatory chain of thought or stimulus. It has great significance for the patient and is a hallmark of *schizophrenia*.

delusions Unshakeable false beliefs with enormous power. They are not comprehensible in terms of the patient's culture or past experience. Are often persecutory and are common in psychotic illnesses.

dementia A gradual loss of memory and thinking power generally found in old age and associated with characteristic changes in the brain. The most common form is *Alzheimer's* disease.

dementia praecox Original term for *schizophrenia*.

denial Psychological mechanism in which uncomfortable thoughts are simply denied and driven into the subconcious.

Diagnostic and Statistical Manual (DSM) The manual for registering and classifying psychiatric disorders produced by the American Psychiatric Association. There have been several editions, e.g. *DSM-III, DMS-IV* and soon *DSM-V*. Very structured in its approach, relying on 'criterion-based' definitions.

dialectical behaviour therapy A comprehensive treatment approach for borderline personality disorder patients with impulsive behaviour. It includes *cognitive behaviour therapy* techniques and *mindfulness* approaches. A very close and intensive relationship is held with the therapist.

differential diagnosis A list of probable diagnoses under consideration when it is not possible to be immediately certain exactly which illness the patient suffers from.

dissociation A process by which separate mental processes can coexist without awareness. It often results in symptoms or behaviours obvious to those around but not to the patient.

double bind The theory proposing that confused communication with conflicting simultaneous statements can contribute to the development of *schizophrenia*. Now discredited but still influential.

double blind A form of *randomized controlled trial* in which neither the doctor nor the patient knows whether the patient has received the active treatment or the *placebo*.

EEG (electroencephalogram) A measurement of brain electrical activity obtained by attaching wires to different areas of the scalp.

ego The rational conscious part of the mind proposed by Freud.

electroconvulsive therapy (ECT) A treatment for severe depression. A small electric current is passed through the front part of the brain in an anaesthetized patient to produce a seizure. Its mechanism is not understood.

empathy The ability to understand and feel what another individual is experiencing.

evidence-based medicine (EBM) The increasingly common practice of limiting medical treatments where possible to those for which there is clear evidence of effect. It includes several techniques to improve the quality of that evidence.

*f*MRI (functional magnetic resonance imaging) An imaging process which measures brain activity by detecting local changes in blood flow and the level of oxygen in the blood.

focal sepsis A localized bacterial infection causing chronic low-grade malaise or intoxication.

folie à deux A rare condition in which somebody living an isolated life alongside a severely psychotic individual begins to take on that person's psychotic beliefs and behaviour.

forensic patient A patient with both a mental disorder and a significant criminal history associated with it. Includes patients with significant risk of violence.

formal thought disorder See *thought disorder*.

Freudian slip See *parapraxis*.

fugue An altered state of consciousness in which the individual, apparently fully alert, is not aware of his or her normal identity, and that cannot be recalled when the patient has recovered.

functional A term applied to psychoses for which no organic brain lesion can be found, mainly *schizophrenia* and *manic depression*. Also used in general medical practice to indicate a possible psychiatric origin of a complaint.

general paralysis of the insane (GPI) Syphilis of the brain, now eradicated but very common in the late nineteenth century. It developed up to twenty years after the first infection. Leads to a rapid dementia, often associated with fits, disorders of movement, and delusions of grandeur and early death.

Gramscian Theory developed by an Italian Marxist philosopher, Antonio Gramsci, which focused particularly on how different groups held power in society.

hallucination A perception reported by psychotic patients when there is no external stimulus to give rise to it, commonly hearing voices. Can also be of smell or touch and occasionally visual.

Hawthorne effect The improvement in general performance that occurs when people know they are being observed.

heritability The proportion of variation in a population which is due to genetic inheritance. It applies to groups or populations and not to individuals.

histology The microscopic examination of tissues and cells in the body.

hypnosis The inducing of an altered state of consciousness (a trance) by suggestion.

hypochondriasis Originally a broad term covering depression and irritability in the eighteenth and nineteenth centuries. It now denotes fixed ideas of physical illnesses despite clear evidence to the contrary.

hypomania Used interchangeably with *mania* to denote an elated, over-active and euphoric state.

hysteria/hysterical A term with several meanings. In common use it means over-emotional. In psychiatry and psychotherapy it denotes the presence of physical symptoms for which an organic cause cannot be demonstrated and for which psychological and emotional causes are presumed. These include paralyses, blindness, and disorders of movement. In psychoanalytical theory hysterical disorders were thought to be generated by the processes of *dissociation* and *conversion*. Patients often demonstrate a puzzling emotional detachment, *belle indifférence.*

id The unconscious primitive part of mental functioning proposed by Freud.

ideas of reference Excessive importance given to experiences, often casual remarks or events. Newspapers, radio or television reports are interpreted as directly relating to the patient.

legal highs Mind-altering drugs, usually obtained over the internet. They often have addictive qualities but are not classified as illegal.

illusion Misinterpretation of a genuine perception. Unlike *hallucination* there is stimulus but it is misinterpreted because of the patient's mood or preoccupation.

insight The ability to understand that one is ill and may need treatment.

institutionalization The erosion of identity and motivation arising from long-term residence in a *total institution* such as a monotonous, overwhelming hospital.

International Classification of Diseases (ICD) The WHO classification of diseases. Now on the tenth edition. Very similar to *DSM-IV.*

Kaufmann's cure A particularly brutal, short, sharp treatment for shell shock which consisted of a series of very painful electric shocks.

learning theory The psychological theory that knowledge and behaviour patterns are learnt entirely by repetition and association.

leucotomy A surgical operation to cut connections to the frontal lobes of the brain. Used widely in the 1940s and 1950s. Now very rare and restricted to severe obsessive-compulsive disorders. Referred to as lobotomy in the USA.

libido The instinctual life force. First used by Freud and generally interpreted in English with a very sexualized content. The original German meaning is more general.

lobotomy See *leucotomy.*

malingering Now often referred to as a factitious disorder. The deliberate pretence of symptoms and illness in order to avoid unwanted consequences.

mania A state of over-excitement, often euphoric and cheerful but sometimes irritable and out of control. Manic patients generally have very little insight into their condition. The term is often used interchangeably with *hypomania*.

manic depression A severe psychotic illness with periods of intense depression alternating with periods of *mania* when the patient is elated, over-active and excitable. Depressive phases are much more common. Now usually diagnosed as *bipolar disorder*.

ME (myalgic encephalomyelitis) Alternative term for *chronic fatigue syndrome*.

MEG (magnetoencephalography) A scanning and imaging technique which measures the magnetic fields at the surface of the brain.

mentalization A treatment focusing on helping individuals to focus on and understand their mental state when they are distressed rather than simply acting on it.

Mesmerism Old term for hypnosis, derived from Franz Anton Mesmer, its discoverer.

mindfulness A psychotherapy technique deriving broadly from Buddhist philosophy which aims to help individuals focus their full attention on the present moment. It is a component of several *cognitive behaviour* therapies currently in use, in particular for recurrent depression.

moral treatment A regime based on kindness, reason and routine. Moral here implies social rather than ethical.

myalgic encephalomyelitis (ME) Alternative term for *chronic fatigue syndrome*.

National Institute of Clinical Excellence (NICE) A UK organization which collates evidence on the effectiveness of medical treatments, gives approval for their funding and produces guidelines on their use.

neurasthaenia An emotional disorder with lack of energy and lassitude, often accompanied by headaches, dizziness, fainting.

neurotransmitters Chemicals which carry messages between one nerve cell and another.

NMRI (nuclear magnetic resonance imaging) A technique to visualize internal structures in the body using a strong magnetic field.

obsessive-compulsive disorder (OCD) A disorder with compulsions (acts) or obsessions (thoughts) which have to be repeated, often a set number of times. The patient experiences them as pointless but cannot resist them without overwhelming anxiety.

Oedipal The developmental stage when the child is seeking a strong intimate bond with the parent of the opposite sex. Causes rivalrous behaviour trying to drive the parents apart and exclude the same-sex parent. Named after the Greek myth of Oedipus, who killed his father and married his mother.

operant conditioning The shaping of behaviour by associating two stimuli together (e.g. ringing a bell and providing food to Pavlov's dogs).

panic An acute anxiety state usually lasting a few minutes in which patients have various bodily symptoms such as sweating and a racing pulse and are terrified that they are going to faint, die or lose control in some way.

parapraxis An error of speech or action which declares an unconscious motivation. Often called a *Freudian* slip.

personality The range of characteristics which we use to distinguish between people (e.g. warm, impulsive, emotional, generous). Usually well established by early adulthood and enduring.

personality disorder Widely recognized and extreme personality variations which interfere with personal functioning. Used as diagnoses within psychiatry but differ from mental illnesses in that they are enduring, not episodic.

PET scanning (positron emission tomography) A 3D imaging technique based on injecting a specific 'tracer' chemical whose concentration in different parts of the body is picked up by emitted gamma rays.

phobia An exaggerated fear such as of heights, spiders or social gatherings. Often divided into simple phobias (spiders, animals, thunder, etc.) and complex phobias (social phobia and agoraphobia).

placebo effect Has two quite different meanings. Commonly describes the improvement that patients immediately feel on starting treatment even when receiving inactive or ineffective compounds. It is also used in treatment trials to indicate the number of people who would get better as a consequence of the natural recovery rate in the untreated condition.

post-traumatic stress disorder (PTSD) An anxiety disorder with heightened arousal and flashbacks caused by a severe, often life-threatening event.

presenting complaint What doctors call the condition for which the patient consults them. This can be their main problem but also may simply be something associated with or even irrelevant to it.

primary gain The emotional or psychological relief afforded by *hysterical* symptoms as a consequence of unacceptable thoughts or impulses being kept *unconscious*. Now applied to any psychiatric condition.

psychopath A cold, callous and often manipulative individual. Usually male and often in conflict with the law. Alternatively referred to as antisocial personality disorder or sociopathic personality disorder. Not a mental illness although often confused with such.

psychopathology The experiences and mental processes described by individuals suffering from mental illnesses. 'Descriptive psychopathology' differs from simply listing symptoms in that it implies a fuller understanding of what the patient is going through.

psychosis A severe mental illness with strange experiences such as hearing voices, inexplicable mood changes and interference with thinking. Patients are often unable to distinguish their internal experiences from those in the world outside, 'losing contact with reality'. They may have limited understanding of how ill they are.

psychosomatic Used either to describe physical disorders with emotional causes, often stress induced, or to describe physical manifestations in emotional disorders, such as aches and pains.

railway spine Musculoskeletal symptoms following a train crash. The focus of continuing debate in the late nineteenth century about whether its origins were physical or psychological.

randomized controlled trial (RCT) A scientific method to test whether a treatment works. It involves randomly allocating patients to one or other treatment without the doctor or the patient being able to influence this. The outcome to be measured (and when it is to be measured) is decided before the trial.

reinforcement The shaping of behaviour by either rewarding it (positive reinforcement) or punishing it (negative reinforcement). See *operant conditioning*.

reliability The degree to which a measure consistently returns the same score. This can be inter-rater reliability, where different raters come to the same answer rating the same patient, or can be test/retest reliability, where the same score is obtained when the measurement is repeated after a short interval with the same patient.

repression Psychological mechanism in which unacceptable thoughts are forced out of conscious awareness.

schizophrenia A severe psychotic illness, often associated with a lifetime course and poor outcome. Most patients have several episodes of acute illness over their lives often interspersed with periods of increasing disability. Core features are loss of sense of self and integration with the world around. Patients often complain of hearing voices and being preoccupied with strange ideas and strange experiences in their bodies. Sufferers may have limited insight into how ill they are and need compulsory treatment.

schizophreniform psychosis A psychotic disorder which is similar to *schizophrenia* but whose diagnosis remains uncertain.

schizophrenogenic A now discredited concept that cold hostile parenting can cause *schizophrenia*.

Scientology An organization founded by L. Ron Hubbard in 1952 holding that people are immortal beings who have forgotten their true nature. Intensely antagonistic towards psychiatry and psychiatric treatments.

screen memory A false memory (e.g. of an event that never happened) which obscures early conflicts.

screening instrument A short questionnaire often used by researchers to identify people who are at a risk of having mental health problems and can then be examined more thoroughly.

secondary gain Emotional or psychological benefits from symptoms that arise from the changes in behaviour of those around the patient in response to their symptoms (e.g. sympathy, support).

sedative A drug to reduce anxiety and agitation but also to induce drowsiness.

social phobia An anxiety state developing in social situations where the individual may feel scrutinized and subject to criticism.

sociopathic personality disorder See *psychopath*.

SPECT (single-photon emission computed tomography) A refinement of *PET scanning* which gives more accurate 3D pictures based on cross-sectional slices.

stereotactic A procedure in which the point of a probe is accurately placed using X-rays. This avoids having to open the skull.

super-ego Broadly equivalent to conscience. Derived from both *ego* and *id*.

theory of mind Being able to understand a situation from another person's point of view. Impaired in conditions such as *autism* and *Asperger's syndrome*.

therapeutic community An institution (e.g. hospital, ward, prison, school) in which the daily routines are organized to be a treatment in themselves rather than just a structure within which to deliver treatments. Members are given the opportunity to reflect on and learn about their behaviour and how they respond to those around them.

thought disorder A disturbance of the logical flow of thinking as opposed to a disorder of its content. *Formal thought disorder* is a hallmark of *schizophrenia*.

total institution A term coined by the sociologist Erving Goffman to denote a monotonous, all-encompassing institution. It meets all the residents' needs and determines every detail of their day-to-day existence.

tranquillizer A drug to reduce anxiety and agitation but which causes minimal drowsiness, unlike a *sedative*.

transference Strong emotions generated in patients during psychotherapy which are derived from earlier, important relationships and 'transferred' on to the therapist.

transinstitutionalization The movement of individuals between institutions (e.g. from prison to mental hospital, from mental hospital to prison, from mental hospital to nursing home).

unconscious A part of the mind which is active and has effects on us but of which we are not aware.

validity The degree to which a structured measurement corresponds accurately to what it is supposed to measure. For example, a high score on a valid depression rating scale should identify a patient whom a psychiatrist would diagnose as depressed.

Sources and further reading

This list includes a mix of books and some classic papers that are referred to in this volume. The books range from textbooks, through popular science to novels centring on psychiatric experiences. Those in bold are the ones that I think most readers would find interesting and I have made a brief note of why they appeal to me. Most are fairly easy to get hold of.

Appignanesi, L., *Mad, Bad, and Sad: A History of Women and the Mind Doctors,* Virago Press, London (2008). A highly readable account of psychiatry's complex relationship with women.

Barker, P., *Regeneration*, Penguin Books, Harmondsworth (1992).

Barton, R., *Institutional Neurosis*, Wright and Sons, Bristol (1966).

Bateson, G., D. D. Jackson, J. Haley and J. Weakland, 'Toward a Theory of Schizophrenia', Behavioral Science 1 (1956), 251–64.

Bentall R. P., *Madness Explained: Psychosis and Human Nature*, Penguin Books, London (2003); —, ***Doctoring the Mind: Why Psychiatric Treatments Fail*,** Penguin Books, London (2009). Erudite and polemical books on psychiatry by a distinguished clinical psychologist. Somewhat one-sided in my opinion but both fascinating reads.

Berlin, I., *Two Concepts of Liberty*, Clarendon Press, Oxford (1958).

Blazer, D. G., *The Age of Melancholy: 'Major Depression' and Its Social Origins*, Brunner–Routledge, New York (2005).

Breggin, P., *Toxic Psychiatry: Why Empathy, Therapy and Love Must Replace the Drugs, Electroshock and Biochemical Theories of the 'New Psychiatry'*, St Martin's Press, New York (1991).

—, *Talking Back to Prozac: What Doctors aren't Telling You about Today's Most Controversial Drug*, St Martin's Press, New York (1994).

Ellenberger, H. F., *The Discovery of the Unconscious,* Basic Books, New York (1970). Unrivalled account of the genesis of psychological psychiatry and psychotherapy. Very long and detailed and only for the enthusiast.

Elliott, C., *Better Than Well: American Medicine Meets the American Dream*, W. W. Norton & Company, Inc., New York (2003).

Faulks, S., *Engleby*, Hutchinson, London (2007).

Foucault, M., *Madness and Civilization: A History of Insanity in the Age of Reason,* Pantheon Books, New York (1964). Early fundamental criticism of psychiatry from a philosopher. Basic message about diagnosis as a social tool has implications beyond psychiatry and he was central to the anti-psychiatry movement.

Freud, S., *The Interpretation of Dreams* (trans. A. A. Brill), Macmillan ([1900] 1913).

—, *Three Essays on Sexual Theory* (trans. J. Strachey), Basic Books, New York ([1905] 1962).

—, *The Ego and the Id.* (trans. Joan Riviere), W. W. Norton & Company ([1923] 1989).

Freud, S. and J. Breuer (1895), *Studies in Hysteria* (trans. N. Luckhurst), Penguin Books, London (2004).

Goffman, E. *The Presentation of Self in Everyday Life*, Anchor Books, New York (1959).

—,*Asylums: Essays on the Social Situation of Mental Patients and Other Inmates,* New York, Doubleday (1961). Classic anti-psychiatry text, profoundly influential for the deinstitutionalization movement. Well written and vivid.

Greenberg, G., *Manufacturing Depression*: *The Secret History of a Modern Disease*, Simon & Schuster, New York (2010).

Greenberg, J., *I Never Promised You a Rose Garden*, Holt Paperbacks, New York (1964).

Grinker, R. R., and J. P. Spiegel, *Men Under Stress*, McGraw-Hill, New York (1945).

Hacking, I. *Rewriting the Soul: Multiple Personality and the Sciences of Memory*, Princeton University Press, Princeton (1995).

—, *Mad Travelers: Reflections on the Reality of Transient Mental Illnesses.* University of Virginia Press, Charlottesville (1998). Fascinating account of the rise and fall of psychiatric diagnoses (and perhaps even disorders) by a philosopher. Very vivid clinical accounts and open-minded.

Horowitz, M. J., *Stress Response Syndromes*, Rowman & Littlefield Publishers Inc., Lanham (1976).

Jaspers, K., *General Psychopathology* (trans. J. Hoenig and Marian W. Hamilton), Manchester University Press, Manchester ([1913] 1963). Only for the committed and only the first chapter. A classic text describing mental experiences in psychosis.

Jung, C., *Psychological Types*, Princeton University Press, Princeton ([1921] 1971).

Kardiner, A., *The Traumatic Neuroses of War*, P. B. Hoeber, Inc., New York (1941).

Kesey, K., *One Flew Over the Cuckoo's Nest*, Viking Press & Signet Books, New York (1962).

Laing, R. D., *The Divided Self: An Existential Study in Sanity and Madness*, Tavistock Publications Ltd, London (1960). The best and most influential anti-psychiatry book. Very much worth reading.

—, *The Politics of Experience and the Bird of Paradise*, Harmondsworth, Penguin (1967).

Laing, R. D., and A. Esterson, *Sanity, Madness and the Family: Families of Schizophrenics*, Penguin Books, Harmondsworth (1964).

Marneros, A., 'Psychiatry's 200th birthday', *British Journal of Psychiatry* 193 (2008), 1–3.

Masson, J. M., *The Assault on Truth: Freud's Suppression of the Seduction Theory*, Faber and Faber, London (1984).

McEwan, I., *Enduring Love*, Jonathan Cape, London (1997).

Payne, C., *Asylum: Inside the Closed World of State Mental Hospitals*, MIT Press, Cambridge, Mass. (2009). A spectacular and evocative set of photographs of decaying US mental hospitals. A glimpse into a vanished world.

Pilgrim State Hospital, http://www.omh.ny.gov/omhweb/facilities/pgpc/facility.htm

Pilgrim State Hospital, http://www.opacity.us/site23_pilgrim_state_hospital.htm

Plath, S., *The Bell Jar*, William Heinemann Limited, London (1963).

Rothman, D., *The Discovery of the Asylum: Social Order and Disorder in the New Republic*, Little Brown, Boston (1971).

Schatzman, M., *Soul Murder: Persecution in the Family*, Penguin Books, Harmondsworth (1976).

Schreiber, F. R., *Sybil*, Regnery, Chicago (1973).

Scull, A. *Madhouse: A Tragic Tale of Megalomania and Modern Medicine*, Yale University Press, New Haven and London (2005). A gothic account of Henry Cotton's surgical crusade to cure schizophrenia. A highly readable book by one of psychiatry's heavyweight critics.

Sennett, R., *The Craftsman*, Penguin Books, London (2008).

Shephard, B., *A War of Nerves: Soldiers and Psychiatrists 1914–1994*, Jonathan Cape, London (2000). Wonderful account of psychiatry and war exploring a range of treatments and issues.

Showalter, E., *The Female Malady: Women, Madness and English Culture, 1830–1980*, Pantheon Books, New York (1985). Classic feminist critique of psychiatry from a distinguished literary critic.

Silva, P. A., and W. R. Stanton (eds.), *From Child to Adult: The Dunedin Multidisciplinary Health and Development Study*, Oxford University Press, Auckland (1996).

Szasz, T. S., *The Myths of Mental Illness: Foundations of a Theory of Personal Conduct,* Hoeber–Harper, New York (1960). Highly influential, much quoted attack on psychiatry. I find it deeply disappointing and unconvincing but you may want to decide for yourself.

Ward, M. J., *The Snake Pit*, Random House, New York (1946).

Whitaker, R., *Anatomy of an Epidemic,* Broadway Paperbacks, New York (2010). Journalistic and highly readable attack on the 'industry' of psychiatry and its possible contribution to increased mental disorders. A polemic rather than an investigation.

Index

Page references in *italic* indicate entries or information in the Glossary.